PAUL'S WAY

THE LIFE OF PAUL VINELLI

GIGI VINELLI VALERA

Lomas Press/Paul's Way
Printed in the United States of America

For more information please visit: lomaspress.com

Although every precaution has been taken to verify the accuracy of the information contained herein, the author and publisher assume no responsibility for any errors or omissions. No liability is assumed for damages that may result from the use of information contained within.

Paul's Way/ Gigi Vinelli Valera -- 1st ed.

Paperback ISBN: 979-8-9949803-0-9
ebook ISBN: 979-8-9949803-1-6
LCCN Number: 2026937207

For José, Claire and Alina

PAUL'S WAY

CONTENTS

WAY: [wā]

Noun

1 The course traveled from one place to another;

2 Manner or method of doing;

3 Habitual manner of being, behaving.

Merriam-Webster

INTRODUCTION

IN APRIL OF 2018, I was listening to NPR while driving to a bookstore. An author was being interviewed about her grandfather's immigration from India to the U.S.

I thought, "Dad's story is much more interesting than her grandfather's, and this woman's book has to be successful if she's being interviewed on NPR." When I arrived at the bookstore I went to the biography section. As I studied the shelves full of the lives of memorable women and men, I began to visualize writing Paul Vinelli's story.

That night I mentioned the idea to my husband José, who responded:

"You know, you already have plane tickets to the three places you'd need to go to research the book."

What José pointed out amazed me. In the next four months we had plans to travel to Naples, Italy; Portland, Maine; and Tegucigalpa, Honduras. The first two places were key to our family's history, yet in my 55 years I had never visited them.

Dad was born in Naples in 1922, later immigrating to the U.S. and finally Honduras. When I was in my twenties I wanted to visit Naples with him, and although we discussed it a few times, it didn't happen. He died in 1997 when I was 34, and my desire to go there disappeared. However, for our twenty-fifth wedding anniversary José and I had decided on a trip to the Amalfi Coast with a stop in Dad's birthplace.

Portland, Maine is where Dad's parents immigrated to from Italy, and where his older sisters were born. The family had moved to Naples by the time Dad was born, but they later decided to return to Portland because of unrest happening in Italy. Dad attended Portland High School. The only relatives we have on his side of the family live in Portland or nearby. For some reason I had never been to the city, and now I had an invitation to go to a wedding, unrelated to family. Seemed like I also needed to also see relatives while I was there!

Tegucigalpa, Honduras is where I was born, and where Dad lived for the last 47 years of his life. Most of his story happened there so going there would be key to learning about his life. That visit cemented the idea of writing a book, because there was so much material. Dad had kept thousands of letters, photographs and newspaper articles, which my brothers Bob and Rick had kept after he died in 1997. They generously shared everything they had with me. Much of what is in this book was taken from letters written by Dad or to him, so I have had the privilege of reading his story in his voice or that of his first wife Linda, often on the day something happened.

While in Honduras, and on subsequent trips, my sisters Liz and Pia helped me track down dozens of sources to interview. I had left Tegucigalpa when I was fourteen to attend school in the U.S., but they lived there much longer, so they were key to filling in the blanks of what I missed.

Back at home in Houston, I remembered that I had a large box that my oldest brother John had sent me after Dad died, with newspaper articles about his kidnapping. Having that material in my house allowed me to spend a lot of time studying the most intense moment in his life.

I am sure some of you will remember things differently than how I present them, and I understand, because I had forgotten or mis-remembered important parts of Dad's life. My pledge to you is that for everything written here I used either documented evidence like letters to/from him, newspaper articles, or interviews. Where the recollection of people I interviewed differed, I made every effort to double-check facts with multiple sources.

As I began to write, I enrolled in writing courses. The first issue I encountered was that my writing professors insisted I be in the book, rather than write a third-party biography as I had intended. Because I am the daughter of the protagonist, they said, I must also be a character in the book. I fought against this for a while but ultimately, they convinced me it didn't sound right for me to be distant from the main character. They guided me to write this book in first-person peripheral narrator style. Dad is the protagonist, and I tell the story as a supporting character.

Since I was not born until my father was forty years old, and I only lived with him for the first fourteen years of my life, most of his story took place when I wasn't around. I looked for a way to address him when I was not in a scene. I found my solution after reading how this was handled by Mary Soames in the biography of her father, Winston Churchill, *A Daughter's Tale*. She referred to her father as Winston, Mr. Churchill, Prime Minister, my father, and Papa, depending on the setting and her role in a scene. When I write about my father's life before I was born, or when I am not part of the story, I refer to him as others did: Paolo Vinella, Paul Vinella, Paul Vinelli, or Dr. Paul Vinelli. When I am in the scene, or the thoughts are mine, he's Dad.

For a time, I considered trying to get this book traditionally published in the United States. There were several reasons it didn't happen. The pandemic began just as I was ready to pitch the manuscript. That was a difficult time for an unknown writer to get the attention of a literary agent, because book tours were being cancelled and agents and publishers were prioritizing their commitments to established clients. Also, at that time it seemed that everyone in the world stayed home to write a book, and agents were inundated with proposals.

I worked with writing coaches. When I told them I might want to get the book traditionally published, their guidance was to narrow the scope of the story because publishing houses today won't buy the biography of someone who isn't famous. Their suggestions included eliminating entire areas of Dad's life, like his entrepreneurial success, his art collecting or his passion for food. I considered the advice but ultimately felt I wanted to show who he was in full, and he was a man of widely diverse interests.

I also was counseled by a book coach to make the book more emotional, because memoirs sell better than biographies. I understood the recommendation, but I felt wrong every time I attempted to write in that style. That is just not my voice, nor was it my father's.

Finally, I decided to publish this book as originally written for the Vinelli family and anyone else who is interested in Paul's story. Thank you for reading.

1

FAMILY AND CHILDHOOD IN ITALY
1922-1935

P aolo Vinella[1] came into the world on November 7, 1922, in Naples, Italy. He was born at home, as was the custom at the time. His parents, both born in near-by Castellaneta, had returned to their native country one year earlier after years of living in Portland, Maine.

Paolo's mother, Addolorata (Dora) Casavola, was so happy to be back in the land of good Italian food that she spent her pregnancy making up for the years in Portland, where ingredients from home were hard to find. By the time her pregnancy came to term, both she and the baby were overweight. Dora had difficult deliveries with all her children, but this one was the worst. When Paolo arrived that Tuesday at 7:00 p.m., weighing over ten pounds, his four-foot-ten mother came close to dying.

---

1. Paul's given name at birth was Paolo Vinella. His father was originally Angelo Vinelli, but a U.S. immigration clerk erroneously changed it to Vinella and Angelo never changed it back. His three children were born Vinellas. Paul changed his name back to Vinelli later in life.

1

Paolo's dramatic birth came at a calm time in his parents' lives. His father Angelo Vinella was semi-retired at age fifty. He and Dora ran a small grocery store and butcher shop around the corner from their apartment in the Vomero quarter of Naples. Their second-floor home was on a quiet, tree-lined street called Via Alessandro Scarlatti. The Vomero was high on the hill overlooking the city, facing the Bay of Naples and Mount Vesuvius. In those days it was where well-to-do Neapolitan families owned summer homes to escape the heat of the city below.[2]

Dora was bedridden for months after Paolo was born. She was too weak to breastfeed, so Paolo had several wet nurses. During this period Angelo worked longer hours at the two stores because he did not have Dora's help.

Their maid Elvira took Paolo and his two sisters out every day, allowing Dora to rest. Two blocks from the Vinella apartment stood the imposing, neoclassical Villa Floridiana. Elvira wheeled infant Paolo in his baby carriage to the villa's public gardens. Paolo's sisters, Pasqualina (Lina) age seven, and Elizabetta (Elizabeth) age four, walked next to the carriage. Paolo took naps in the shade of the huge oak, palm, cypress and pine trees. Lina and Elizabeth loved to run across the long stretches of soft, green grass and through the beautiful gardens surrounding the villa. They always stopped to look at the turtles sunbathing in the fountain at the base of a long set of marble stairs leading up to the entrance. These outings were a favorite childhood memory for the girls.

Paolo was not baptized for seven months, until his mother was well enough to attend. The baptism took place a few blocks from their

___

2. The Vinellas were not wealthy; their apartment was their primary residence. They lived in the Vomero to be close to their stores.

apartment, at the parish church of San Gennaro al Vomero. In 2018 I visited this small neoclassical church. To my surprise, the administrator opened a metal storage cabinet in his office, pulled out a large book, and showed me Paolo's original birth certificate. Almost one hundred years after the baptism took place, the records were still that accessible.

Lina, Elizabeth, and Paolo Vinella - Naples, Italy 1924

Paolo's parents did not start their lives in such a comfortable setting. Angelo and Dora were born in Castellaneta, a village in southern Italy, fourteen miles from the Mediterranean Sea. This mountainous town in the crook of the Italian boot, with white-washed houses and narrow streets paved with pale square stones, might have been charming and even prosperous at some point during its thousand-plus years of existence.

That would have been long before the end of the nineteenth century, when the town emptied out. From 1880 to 1920, many of its residents joined the millions of Italians who left for America.[i] Today Castellaneta's only claim to fame is that it was the birthplace of the famous silent movie actor Rudolph Valentino. Family legend is that he was a cousin of Angelo's – we do know that Angelo's mother's last name was Valentino.

Dora and her future husband were born in the same town, but they did not grow up together because Angelo was twenty-two years older.

In 1872 when Angelo was born, the southern region of Italy—known as *mezzogiorno*—was descending into chaos. In *La Storia*, the saga about the mass Italian migration to the U.S. between 1880 and 1924, authors Mangione and Morreale describe how dismal life was in the region during the second half of the 1800s. Over the 1,400 years between the fall of Rome and Italy's unification in 1861, Italy had been invaded by so many foreign cultures that there was no unifying language nor national identity. Southern Italy was so poor that families with modest means could only afford to eat meat twice a year. Drinking water was hard to find. By the late 1800s, cholera, malaria, crop disease and famine had devastated the *mezzogiorno.*

Angelo and his four siblings were born into this bleak world. Later in life, he spoke little of his childhood. All we know for sure is that the family of Angelo Vinelli was very poor.

His grandson Armando said to me, "I recall my grandfather telling me that in southern Italy one hundred years ago, many people were so poor and hungry they felt like eating their shoes." This extreme hunger was the reason for the Italian custom of *fare la scarpetta*, which is to sop up the remaining sauce on a plate with a piece of bread. *Scarpetta* is a little shoe and *fare la scarpetta* is to form a shoe shape out of a piece of bread and push it across a plate to sop up the remainder of the sauce. When you have experienced real hunger, you never again leave food on your plate. [ii]

The Vinellis and Casavolas were short people. Angelo was 5'4, Dora was only 4'10. Genetics were a factor, but malnutrition may also have been a cause.

Families in the region at the time worked to survive and could not prioritize educating children,[iii] so it is unlikely that Angelo received much education when growing up.

In 1892 Angelo turned twenty, the age at which the Italian government required that men serve in the military. He joined the cavalry, which had a four-year commitment of active duty.[iv] His timing was terrible (not that he had a choice of when he turned twenty). Three years after he joined the cavalry, Italy entered the First Italo-Ethiopian War, fought in Africa between Italy and Ethiopia from 1895-96 over a disputed treaty. The Italian army suffered severe losses due to insufficient food, weapons and maps. *La Storia* describes the bloodbath: on March 1, 1896, Italian forces advanced to Adwa "with 14,500 men against an Ethiopian army of some 100,000.... seventy percent of Italy's soldiers were killed or captured."[v]

Angelo survived and swore he would do anything to prevent a son of his from experiencing the horrors he witnessed in this war.

Angelo Vito Vinelli, Italian Cavalry, 1894

Dora was born in Castellaneta in 1895, while her future husband was fighting a war in Africa. She was one of eight children of the Casavola-Luisi family. Her father, Annunziato (Nunzio), was a cabinet maker, and her mother Antonietta was a dressmaker.

In 1901 Angelo made his way on a steamship to the United States. Like so many southern Italians, he was looking for a better life than could be found in the *mezzogiorno*. Angelo found work as a bricklayer, building the expansion of the United States Military Academy at West Point, New York. After two years of saving most of his dollar-a-day earnings, he had accumulated five hundred dollars.

That was enough to stop working as a day laborer and to go into business for himself.

He heard that an Italian community had formed in Portland, Maine. He moved there and opened a small grocery store that catered primarily to the immigrant population. Back in Castellaneta, a storekeeper was a respected profession, much more so than a bricklayer. Angelo was moving up in stature. He Americanized his name to John, to make it easier for his non-Italian customers to pronounce.

After a visit back to Italy in 1907, when he returned to the U.S. through Ellis Island, an immigration agent recorded his name as Angelo Vinella. Angelo never asked the U.S. government to change his name back, rather he kept the Vinella name until his death.

I found evidence of this when I visited Ellis Island and reviewed the passenger manifests of the various trips into the U.S. that Angelo made. On Angelo's first U.S. arrival on May 16, 1901, the *City of Washington* ship's passenger manifest lists him as Angelo Vinelli. His 1907 return after a visit home was on September 26 of that year, and the *Sannio* ship's manifest lists him as Angelo Vinella.

By 1913 Angelo's store at 49 Center Street in Portland was doing well, but he wasn't happy. He was a lonely forty-one-year-old bachelor with few dating opportunities. He claimed he didn't like the temperament of American women whom he found frivolous and spoiled. Surely American women found Angelo overbearing and too serious. Besides, an older 5'4 Italian immigrant wasn't what a young American girl was looking for.

Angelo concluded he needed to marry a woman from the old country, someone who had grown up with his same culture and values and who would take care of him. He wrote to his sisters in Castellaneta, asking that they find him a wife. Arranged marriages were common then, and attractive to poor families in Italy who wanted their children to get to "the land where streets were paved with gold," as America was imagined to be in those days.

Family lore says that Angelo's sisters sent him a photograph of the two youngest Casavola sisters, Dora and Lisa. According to the story, he commented how pretty Lisa was. But Lisa was too young for marriage. Dora was already eighteen years old, and the family needed her to be married before she was too old for anyone to be interested. Unfortunately, Angelo's observation about Lisa's beauty made its way back to Dora, and she never got over it. For the rest of her life, she was irritable whenever her younger sister was around.

Angelo agreed to marry Dora. He gained a bride, and most likely some money—in those days, it was mandatory for the family of a southern Italian bride to pay a dowry.[vi] For the Casavolas, this was a good opportunity. Everyone who could was leaving the *mezzogiorno.*

Dora's older brother Domenico offered to escort her to America where he also planned to stay. Like his father, he was a skilled woodworker, but there was not enough work for the two of them in Castellaneta. Domenico was newly married with a one-year-old baby girl. He saw Dora's marriage to Angelo as an opportunity to improve the life of his small family. The plan was for Domenico's wife Nicoletta to stay in Castellaneta with their daughter until he was settled in Portland, and then he would send for them.

Dora's arranged marriage was good fortune for her older sister Marietta also. She and her husband Felice Giampetruzzi had left Italy the year before. They were living in Montreal, where Felice worked at a hotel. They couldn't fulfill their dream of moving to America until Felice found someone to sponsor him with a job. Angelo hired him to work at his grocery store.

The three Casavola siblings—Marietta, Domenico and Dora—started making plans to move to America. Dora was the only one not happy with the arrangement. She did not want to be shipped across the ocean to marry a man she did not know, and who had initially chosen her sister over her. She was not told that he was twenty-two years her senior—that surprise was saved for their meeting. But in those days a woman didn't have much of a say in her own future. Dora's father informed her this is how it would be.

Six months after her eighteenth birthday, in August of 1913, Dora left her parents, five siblings, and her hometown. She was miserable, certain that the goodbye was permanent. Domenico kept close to her during the trip—to make sure she survived, and equally important, arrived a virgin. In those days it was common for a woman traveling alone to America to run into unscrupulous agents who demanded sex in return for safe passage.[vii]

The logical departure point for Dora and Domenico's trip would have been Naples, but for some reason—probably a lower fare—they booked passage on the *Rochambeau*, a steamship that departed from Le Havre, France. The 1,400-mile voyage by land would have most likely begun on a mule-drawn cart to the nearest town that had railroad access. There, the siblings took their first train ride all the way to the English Channel in northern France. Before boarding the ship, they were subjected to a medical inspection required by U.S. immigration authorities—to ensure they could meet the health requirements upon arrival in New York.[viii]

Following a week-long voyage across the Atlantic Ocean, the *Rochambeau* passed by the Statue of Liberty and arrived at Ellis Island. After the ship cleared quarantine, the passengers were made to stand in long lines for their medical examination.[ix] Once through the ordeal of immigration and customs, the siblings were met by Angelo. Dora was exhausted from the trip, overwhelmed by the crowds and unfamiliar surroundings. But overshadowing all that was the shock of discovering that her future husband was almost as old as her father.

Angelo escorted Dora and Domenico back to Portland by train. Dora couldn't believe what she found when they arrived in the harbor city. Angelo's family in Castellaneta had led her to believe she would lead a very comfortable life in America. Instead, she discovered that she and her new husband would be crowded with Domenico, Marietta and Felice into a small apartment occupying two floors above Angelo's grocery store. The building was dingy and in a gritty part of town. Angelo made it clear that she'd be working downstairs in the grocery store every day. She wanted to back out of the arrangement, but she couldn't figure out how.[x]

Dora and Angelo could not sleep under the same roof until they were married, so Angelo asked friends to house his bride-to-be and her brother while the marriage application was in process. When the license came in, Marietta and Felice still had not arrived from Montreal. Angelo did not want to impose on his friends any longer and decided to move forward with the marriage. Marietta would have to miss her sister's wedding. Three weeks after Dora arrived in America, a justice of the peace married her to Angelo. She was the mistress of 49 Center Street when Marietta and Felice arrived the following week.

Angelo Vinella and Dora Casavola
Wedding in Portland, Maine – September 1913

Portland for Dora was naturally a huge change from Castellaneta. One of her biggest hurdles was the language barrier. At first, Dora could only communicate with her family or the few other Italians who spoke her dialect. She had to rely on Angelo to understand their customers, whether they spoke English or Italian.

Dora became pregnant with their first child within a week of marriage. Angelo must have felt proud of his virility at age forty-one, especially since Felice and Marietta had been married for some time, were in their twenties, but Marietta had yet to become pregnant. Domenico lived with his sisters and their husbands until he found work as a cabinetmaker at Smith and Rumery building contractors.[3] Then he rented the home next door, at 45 Center Street. By Christmas, his wife Nicoletta and their one-year-old baby girl, Antoinette, joined him.

By the end of 1913, Angelo had formed a community made up of his wife's Casavola family on Center Street. He and Felice worked downstairs in the grocery store every day. They dressed in nice shirts whose American-sized sleeves were too long for their small stature. Since their work involved cleaning fish and butchering meat, they used sleeve garters placed tightly above their elbows to keep their shirt cuffs clean. Dora and Marietta helped them in the store in the mornings. After going upstairs to make lunch, the sisters spent the afternoon cleaning the apartment and making dinner.

Angelo and Dora were not blissful newlyweds, but they were united in their desire for children. Dora focused on the excitement of becoming a mother that first year of marriage. Unfortunately, her labor the following June was difficult and the baby girl they named Pasqualina died within hours. Burying this child must have been heartbreaking for Dora and Angelo. Dora's sister Marietta most likely had a difficult time supporting her younger sister as she grieved, because by that summer, she was twenty-seven years old and still had no children.

The news from their homeland was grim. Italy joined World War I in 1915, moving from an alliance with the empires of Germany, Austria and Hungary to join the Allied Powers of Great Britain,

---

3. Over his long career with Smith and Rumery, Domenico restored beautiful wood paneling and built stairways in churches, colleges around New England, and colonial homes as far away as Williamsburg, Virginia. During Prohibition Domenico became especially popular, because he was able to build secret doors needed to hide illicit gatherings where people consumed alcohol.

France and Russia. The country hoped to gain new territories, but instead Italy paid a brutal price: by the time the war ended in 1918, Italy had lost more than 500,000 soldiers, and their economy was in disastrous shape.[xi] Italians became dissatisfied with the alliances their government made during the war, and within four years turned their support to Benito Mussolini and his Fascist movement.

The news of their countrymen fighting made the Vinella - Casavola family in Portland grateful to have moved to America. In the same year Italy entered the war, fortune turned for the better for the immigrants: the family on Center Street began to grow both in size and happiness. In 1915 Dora and Angelo had a daughter who they named Pasqualina ("Lina")—the same name of the child they lost the prior year. Marietta and Nicoletta also had children that year. The three families on Center Street began to focus on the future of their children, rather than looking back on their lives in Castellaneta. Over the next six years, the three families on Center Street expanded to include nine children.

In May of 1921 Dora's younger sister Elisabetta (Lisa) left Castellaneta to join her three siblings in Portland. On the ship she met a young man named Francesco (Cici) Romano. By the time they arrived in America a week later, Cici was in love with Lisa and followed her to Portland. Lisa and Cici married two years later. According to the family, they were the happiest couple of all the Casavola siblings. Dora was not thrilled to have her little sister in town, much less with a young man who was madly in love with her. The comparison with her much-older grouchy husband only increased her jealousy of Lisa.

Angelo was now forty-nine years old and for some time had been speaking to Dora about returning to Italy. It may or may not have been a coincidence that once Lisa moved to Portland, Dora warmed to Angelo's idea. They decided to move to Naples where they would open a grocery store until they had saved enough to retire. Angelo sold the Center Street store to Felice.[4]

The following picture of the Vinella-Casavola-Giampetruzzi cousins was taken in 1921, just before the Vinellas' departure.

L to R: Elisabetta Vinella, Giovanni Giampetruzzi, Antoinette Giampetruzzi, Giovanni Casavola, Angelina Giampetruzzi, Nunzio Casavola, Pasqualina Vinella.

In September of that year, Angelo, Dora, and their two daughters—Lina, age five and Elizabeth, age three—traveled to Naples on the *Regina d'Italia* steamship. They set up their new life in an apartment

---

4. Felice ran the store until 1946 when his son Nino took it over and ran it for another twenty years.

building on a hill overlooking the city of Naples, the bay, and Mount Vesuvius. Angelo and Dora were so happy to be back at home that within months Dora was pregnant.

A year after they returned to Italy, two events occurred within weeks of each other. In November, their first son Paolo was born. Three weeks earlier, major political upheaval began to change the Italy that Angelo and Dora knew. In late October of 1922, Benito Mussolini organized a mass demonstration in Rome that resulted in his National Fascist Party taking over the government, when King Victor Emmanuel II named Mussolini prime minister. Over the next decade, as Mussolini expanded the Fascist's party's power through legal means and force, he anointed himself "*Il Duce*" (the leader). He dismantled democracy in Italy and replaced it with his totalitarian regime.[xii]

The balance of power in Angelo and Dora's marriage also began to shift at this same time. Angelo was mellowing with age, and Dora did not have a language barrier now that she was back in Italy. There are many family accounts of how jealous Angelo was of any man who approached Dora. Her relative youth probably made him insecure. By some accounts, she purposefully would strike up conversations with men while working at the store, to irritate her husband.

Angelo's jealousy was characteristic of men raised in southern Italy in the late 1800s. *La Storia* describes the culture:

"On … summer nights … [in] the *chiazza*, …men would stroll arm in arm, in groups of two or three, sometimes four or five…. As they walked, they nodded to one another…. A passing woman was greeted only if she were accompanied by her husband. A woman walking alone was ignored, for a man could be made cuckold by a glance".[xiii]

According to family lore, Angelo's peaceful days in Naples ended in 1927 when he killed a man. I have heard of two reasons for the incident, and both may be true. The first version was that the Camorra (a Mafia-type crime syndicate) sent a strongman to one of Angelo's stores, to extort money for "protection". This protection would have been from the Camorra themselves. Angelo knew that paying once meant he'd have to share the profits of his store for a lifetime. Instead of paying, he shot the man to show the Camorra he wasn't to be bullied. In the second version, Angelo carried a rifle into a bar and shot a man who had flirted with Dora at their store.

This is the version Dora told her children—whether because it was true, or because it flattered her, or because she was afraid of giving the true reason, we don't know. The reason she gave us for Angelo not going to jail was that it had been a killing of honor, and those were respected in southern Italy. But he had to leave Naples because the victim had relatives who would be looking for Angelo, and revenge for the murder of a family member was also respected in southern Italy.

Angelo did not want to move too far away, because he and Dora still owned the grocery store and butcher shop. He would be returning to Naples frequently to check on them. He hired managers to oversee the stores and moved the family to Salerno, thirty miles away. The town also faced the Mediterranean, but it was ten times smaller than Naples, with a population of only sixty thousand.

What he told his children about the move was that, at his advanced age of fifty-five years old he had concluded that what was missing in his life was education. He said he wanted a quiet environment in which to study, and Salerno was more peaceful than boisterous Naples. Paolo was four years old when the Vinellas moved.

When he was eight, Paolo began to study at the Scuola Elementare Garibaldi in Salerno. In Mussolini's Italy, school was held six days a week, and in their free time children were expected to stay off the street and pursue their studies.[xiv] He was required to study Latin in addition to Italian. From his first year of school, Paolo was an excellent student.

Discipline and strength were prized national virtues in those days, and Italian schoolteachers adopted rigid views. In many parts of the world, being left-handed was a negative trait: it meant you were less intelligent, less strong, or had bad luck. Italians were one of the cultures that practiced "conversion" of left-handed students. When Paolo's primary school teacher observed that he was left-handed, she tied that dominant hand to his classroom chair, forcing him to write with his right hand. Over time, he became ambidextrous in everything except the use of scissors, which he never learned to use with the right hand. Science has shown that forcing left-handed children to use their right hand may result in stuttering, speech impediments, dyslexia and learning disorders.[xv] This conversion is most likely what led to a slight speech impediment that stayed with Paolo his whole life.

By the 1930s the political climate in Europe had become unstable and violent. Both Mussolini in Italy and Adolf Hitler in Germany ran totalitarian governments that indoctrinated their citizens with extreme nationalism. There were ideological differences between Hitler's Nazism and Mussolini's Fascism, but the men increasingly collaborated after their first meeting in 1934. Both strongmen planned to spread their views beyond their country's borders.

Males of all ages in both countries were given military training. In Italy, Mussolini outlawed all political parties other than the Republican Fascist Party.[xvi] In order to transform the minds of Italy's youth he outlawed two popular Italian youth organizations: the Boy Scouts and the Roman Catholic Church youth group. These were replaced with a Fascist Youth Organization, known as the Opera Nazionale Balilla (members were known as Balillas). The movement was for boys eight to thirteen, and participation was mandatory. The organization aimed to instill national discipline by training Italian boys in Fascist ideology as well as religious, athletic and military instruction. Every weekend, there were public demonstrations of marching, athleticism and handling of weaponry.

Paolo was required to join the Balillas when he was eight.[5] Participation involved religious and para-military training. The millions of Balilla boys were forced to take an oath: "In the name of God and the Fatherland, I swear to follow the orders of the Duce and to serve with all my energy the cause of the Fascist revolution." The leaders of the Balillas—all military men— trained the boys in physical conditioning, the handling of rifles, and marching drills. Members wore black shirts and fez caps with a tassel.[xvii] The Catholic Church at this time supported the Fascist regime, so Paolo was allowed to be an altar boy at their local church.

Sundays were the only day of the week with no school nor Balilla training. The entire Vinella family usually spent the day at the beach across the street from their apartment building.

---

5. There was a parallel movement, Fascio Femminile, that educated girls about the management of home and family, but we do not know if Lina and Elizabeth were made to participate.

Beach in Salerno, Summer 1934. Paolo on man's shoulders, far right.

Angelo was alarmed at what was happening in Italy. Most Italians did not feel the Fascist fervor that Mussolini tried to establish. This became apparent later in World War II, when Italians did not fight hard against the Allies despite Mussolini's alliance with Hitler. But that war was far in the future. What Angelo saw was military training everywhere, reaching down to his school-aged son. Then Mussolini began to expand the influence of Italian Fascism into nearby countries. One he targeted was Italy's old foe, Ethiopia.

Angelo still had nightmares about fighting in the first Italo-Ethiopian war. He could not stand the thought of Paolo, now twelve, being drafted for a second war with Ethiopia when he came of age. By age fourteen, boys in the Balillas were moved up to training in the Avanguardisti, which prepared them for active duty in the military.

Members of the Avanguardisti joined specialized divisions. One was the Pre-Marinari (pre-sailors), which prepared boys for naval service. Paolo, like all Balilla boys, looked up to the Avanguardisti. He hoped to be a sailor one day. In every formal Vinella family portrait taken while living in Italy, Paolo is wearing a sailor suit.

Vinella family, Salerno 1934: Lina, Dora, Paolo, Angelo and Elizabeth

Angelo had enough warnings. For the second time in his life, he decided to move to America. This time, however, he had a wife and three children to consider. The attitude Americans had about immigration to their country was very different in 1934 than when Angelo came for the first time, thirty-three years earlier. The United States was overwhelmed by the number of Italians who had descended on its shores over the past fifty years. Now, following the Great

Depression, there were not enough jobs to go around. Angelo knew it would be very difficult to return.

Neither he nor Dora were U.S. citizens, but their two daughters were, having been born in Portland. Lina and Elizabeth were the Vinella family's ticket back—their citizenship allowed the family to obtain tourist visas to travel to the U.S. Both girls fought bitterly with their father about leaving Salerno. They were American citizens, but Italy had been their home since they were five and three years old. In 1934 when Angelo began talking about a move, his daughters were old enough to have plans and opinions of their own; Lina was eighteen, and Elizabeth was sixteen.

Lina was dating a doctor named Domenico (Mimi) Santoro. He was from Montecorvino Rovella, a neighboring town in the province of Salerno. The two met when Lina was studying at a music conservatory in Salerno. Mimi, six years older, was a graduate from the University of Naples with a degree in medicine and surgery. He planned to set up a medical practice in Naples. Naturally Lina wanted to stay where he was. A move seemed out of the question for Mimi, who didn't speak English and didn't have a medical degree to practice in the United States.

When Mimi asked for Lina's hand in marriage, Angelo informed him that the Vinella family was moving to the United States and was not leaving Lina behind. He told Mimi that if he wanted to marry his daughter, he would have to come to Portland. Given no option, the young couple began to plan their transatlantic move with Angelo's help. They both studied English, which was crucial for Mimi who didn't know how he would work as a doctor in a new country. Lina and Mimi were married in Italy in September of 1934 and traveled to the U.S. that December. Lina was pregnant by then and the boat ride made her nauseous. Their oldest daughter Anna was born soon after they arrived in Portland, Maine.

Mimi recognized that his English was still not strong enough to establish a private practice. He found a job working as the doctor for a paper mill in Millinocket, Maine and moved his family there. Their second daughter Hilda was born at home on the kitchen table. There was a law against a doctor delivering his own child, so Mimi had to call in another doctor.

Mimi surely resented the forced move. But it turned out well, because he was a brilliant man. Later in life he obtained his U.S. citizenship, became the Italian Consul in Maine, and then a senator for the state of Maine.

Lina's sister Elizabeth also fought passionately with her father over the move. She was in love with a boy named Antonio and hated to leave him. She spent the rest of her life lamenting the loss of that relationship. In her old age in Portland, she would reminisce to her children about swimming with Antonio in the Tyrrhenian Sea in the Gulf of Salerno.

A few months after Lina and Mimi moved, Angelo followed with Dora, Elizabeth and Paolo. It was a one-week voyage on the steamship *Conte di Savoia*, which departed Naples on May 1, 1935, and arrived in New York eight days later. Their arrival at Ellis Island was not a smooth one. The plan was to say that Elizabeth, a U.S. citizen, was bringing her parents and Paolo (who had tourist visas) to visit family in Portland. Once in the U.S., Angelo would start the process to obtain a work visa so they could stay.

An immigration officer asked Angelo if he wanted to stay in the United States. That question, designed to catch people on tourist visas who intended to stay in the country, tripped him up. He answered that of course he'd like to stay, and the response cost him: the Vinella family had to endure ten days of interrogation in an Ellis Island facility. They finally convinced the authorities that Paolo and his parents would not overstay the length of time their visas allowed.

Five months after they moved to America, in October of 1935, the second Italo-Ethiopian war broke out. Angelo's precautions were validated when they received news that Mimi's twin brother died in that war.

2

AN AMERICAN EDUCATION, PART 1
1935 – 1940

Angelo and Dora's second immigration to Maine was easier than their first. This time they had a large, established family in town. They already knew their way around Portland. Even though Lina and Elizabeth were frustrated about leaving Italy, their parents felt sure about having made a good decision, especially for Paolo.

For the first two months, Angelo, Dora, Elizabeth and Paolo stayed with Lina and Mimi while Angelo looked for a place to live. He immediately hired a lawyer to help them obtain work visas. Angelo had sold most of his property in Italy before leaving because he was now sixty-three years old and didn't expect to ever return. He bought two buildings in Portland with the money.

By the end of the summer of 1935, the Vinella family moved into a large, two-story, red-brick home at 188 Danforth Street. The house was elegant when it was built one hundred years earlier for Portland Shipmaster James Dockery. But it was now worn down, as was the neighborhood, which was predominantly populated with Irish, Italian, Polish and French-Canadian immigrants. Dora's sister Lisa and her husband Cici lived up the street, at 258 Danforth Street.

Their new neighborhood was on a hill overlooking the Portland harbor. There were always laborers looking to rent a room because the shipyards were within walking distance. Angelo converted most of the house into rental apartments. Dora, Angelo, Elizabeth and Paolo made their living quarters in a small corner of the house.

Angelo opened a new grocery store in a red brick building on York Street, a few blocks down the hill from their home. The store also overlooked the harbor and would attract dock workers. It was far enough away from the Center Street store that Felice still owned that there would be no competition. For the second time in his life, Angelo changed his name to John for his customers. The move to Portland had cost Angelo his hope of retiring soon. It was expensive to bring his family over from Italy. Costs were higher in the U.S. than in Italy. Late in life, he was forced to work, both in the store and as a landlord, to make ends meet.

Every day he woke up early and, after eating the breakfast Dora prepared for him, walked down the hill to the store. He was a stern man with his family, but his customers found "John" to be a kind man. His store catered to longshoremen, dock people who did not have much money. Someone would often come in hungry, and Angelo would sell them a couple of slices of bologna on credit. They returned to settle their bill on pay day. Dora worked at the store every morning, stocking shelves and shoveling coal into the potbellied stove. At 1:00 p.m. she walked up the hill to their home. After making lunch for Angelo and Elizabeth, Dora did housework before starting dinner.

A big joke in the Vinella-Casavola family was the obsession the women had with cleanliness. Dora's cleaning day was Saturday, when all the house smelled like ammonia. After she finished, the only way anyone was allowed onto the gleaming kitchen floor was by putting a cloth under each shoe and scooting across, polishing it even more for Grandma. This is why, when the weather was warm enough, family gatherings did not take place indoors.

Every weekend, the entire Vinella-Casavola family got together. Sometimes they met in Dora and Angelo's backyard. Sometimes they walked three miles to the house Dora's brother Domenico had built on Tremaine Street. In the summer, they organized picnics accompanied by blueberry picking. Many Fall weekends they went into the woods around Portland to hunt for mushrooms. These excursions were reminiscent of their weekend drives up to the mountains around Salerno to harvest chestnuts from the trees that looked over the Mediterranean.

When the weather was cold or rainy, the adults held poker games on the second floor of Dora and Angelo's house. Dora and her two sisters Marietta and Lisa, together with their husbands, stayed up late playing cards, bickering at each other and telling stories.

Paolo started eighth grade at age twelve in September of 1935. On his first day at The North School his teacher changed his name to Paul. This was a common practice of American teachers who didn't want to battle with the pronunciation of foreign names. Immigrants rarely protested because they wanted to fit in. Paul didn't speak English when he first arrived in the United States, but he worked hard to learn so he could communicate at school and at his parents' grocery store. Angelo put him to work as soon as the grocery store was set up.

Paul woke up at 5:00 a.m. every day. After he ate a quick breakfast made by Dora, he walked down the hill to the store to set things up before going to middle school. He returned right after school to work until late in the evening. He did his homework behind the counter, in between customers.

The language barrier made school difficult academically and socially. The students at the North School were the children of the low-income immigrants in the neighborhood: Italians, Irish, Poles and French-Canadians. Even though being immigrants might have given them something in common, their language barrier made them all feel out of place. Middle school is a difficult time in anyone's adolescence, but even more challenging when one doesn't share language or culture with one's peers.

An unusual thing happened in 2018 while I was writing this book. I was visiting Portland for the first time in my life to interview family members who still live in the area. My brother Rick spontaneously decided to fly up from Honduras to see the family as well. One afternoon he stopped at a bookstore near our hotel, where he picked up a book on the history of Portland. He took it back to his room and started leafing through it. He couldn't believe it when he turned a page to a photo of the 1936 eighth-grade class at The North School. Thirteen-year-old Paul stood in the top left corner, looking confident in a black blazer. Eighty-two years after the photo was taken, it was waiting in a Portland bookstore for his son to come from Honduras and find it.

Paul entered ninth grade at Portland High School in the Fall of 1936. His days were busy between schoolwork and working for his father at the store. But he loved athletics, ingrained in him during his Balilla days. He joined the swim team, swimming breaststroke. Angelo allowed Paul time for swimming practices, but as his son's

English improved, he increased his responsibilities at the store. Paul was being trained to take it over after high school.

He was now fourteen and Angelo taught him to drive, even though he was too young to get a driver's license. Every morning Paul drove a truck to buy fresh meat, fish, bread and produce from suppliers. Before the days of much refrigeration, it was necessary to pick up perishable items daily. Later in life he told me that he particularly remembered buying bunches of bananas. At that time, he had no idea that he would end up living in the country where those bananas most likely were grown. Once Paul finished unloading the truck at the store, he went to school. After class he was back at the store, alternating between waiting on customers, stocking shelves and writing papers for school.

Almost two years had passed since they immigrated from Italy, when in February of 1937 their lawyer brought them good news: the family had been approved for legal residency. The process required having their passports stamped with their visa at the U.S. Consulate in a foreign country. They took a train to Montreal, Canada where friends of Marietta and Felice invited them to stay at their home so they would not have to pay for a hotel.

The move to Portland had been hardest for Paul's sister Elizabeth. She still longed for her Italian boyfriend, and there weren't many people she could communicate with because of the language barrier. Her older sister Lina was married and had moved to another town. When Paul was not studying or swimming, he was working at the store.[6] Her parents were busy with their routine of running their store and home and being landlords.

---

6. In Paul's letters he recalled that his father made him work at the store 365 days a year, with the only night off being Christmas Eve.

Elizabeth's resentment about being forced to move built up. She met a handsome barber from Calabria, Adam Romano. She was ambitious and would have preferred a more successful suitor like the doctor Lina had married. But Adam was charming, she was beautiful, and a relationship began. In February of 1938, she became pregnant.

This caused a great commotion within the family. When the yelling subsided, the Vinella-Casavola family did what was expected: they planned a wedding. Elizabeth and Adam were married, and in November of 1938, when Paul was a junior in high school, his first nephew, Armando Romano, was born.

By that year, Paul was feeling confident in his English language skills. He joined the yearbook staff, writing for the editorial page. He continued to pour himself into his schoolwork and his swimming. His cousin Antoinette, who I interviewed during my trip to Portland in 2018 when she was in her mid-nineties, remembered that Paul often missed the weekend family gatherings because he was studying or attending swim meets. She said, "All the cousins could tell Paul had a goal and he knew where he was going."

Paul had been swimming breaststroke for the Portland High School swim team since he was a freshman. In the Spring of his junior year, he was elected team captain by his teammates. The Portland Herald wrote:

> "One of the hardest workers on the team and also one of the most popular, Vinella won his way to a varsity position by constant practice and hard plugging, and this year, his third on the squad, found him rewarded by becoming a letterman. He is big and rugged and next year should find him one of the best natators in his event in the state.[xviii]

Portland High School swim team, Paul seated in front row, third from left
Portland Press Herald

When senior year started Paul changed his last name to Vinelli. My brother Rick has his high school workbooks, and we saw that Dad signed them Paul Vinella until the end of junior year, and then he changed to Paul Vinelli for his last year of high school. Later in life he told us that he was teased about the name Vinella, because it sounded like vanilla. In some newspaper articles about his swimming, he was referred to as "Paul Vinilla". However, his parents never changed their names, and his sisters took their husbands' names. The Vinella name died with Angelo, and today Paul's entire family uses Vinelli.

Paul's English and his grades were now excellent. He won a state swim tournament in breaststroke. His Portland High School teachers encouraged him to go to college. They told Angelo and Dora they saw great potential in their son.

Angelo was angry. He had left Italy to protect Paul. He had extended his working years and opened a new store at age sixty-three for his son. By Italian tradition, the oldest son inherits the family business, and Paul was his only son. Angelo expected him to take over the grocery store, which would provide him a good livelihood. Angelo said to his son, "If everybody goes to college, who's going to clean the fish?"

But Paul was certain he could have a more interesting future than working in the store. His teachers continued to appeal to Angelo. Finally, Angelo said to Paul, "Well if you think you are man enough, go on. But you will not receive a penny from me."

After that confrontation Angelo lost a lot of his bluster. He was sixty-eight and tired. Dora, only forty-five years old, began to have more control over the family finances. One day, she hired a workman to install a brick wall to block off a bedroom and bathroom in their house that had a separate exterior entrance. That night after dinner, Angelo walked past the room and encountered the new wall instead of a door. When he turned to confront his wife, Dora said, "We got one son, and he ain't gonna be stupid". She rented the room to a boarder and saved the money, sixteen dollars a month, to help Paul with college expenses.

The two universities Paul was happiest about being accepted to were Harvard University and University of Michigan. At that time, the tuition at Harvard was six hundred dollars per year, and at Michigan the non-resident tuition was two hundred dollars per year. Paul chose Michigan.

3

AN AMERICAN EDUCATION, PART 2
1940 – 1944

Paul said goodbye to his family in September of 1940. He hitchhiked nine hundred miles from Portland, Maine to Ann Arbor, Michigan, carrying a leather suitcase containing clothes, pencils, and sandwiches prepared by Dora. When he arrived on the University of Michigan campus, he asked other students where he could find inexpensive lodging. He was directed to a landlord some distance from the campus, where he rented a room for $2.50/week. Once he had a place to live, he bought a bicycle so he could get to campus.

Paul intended to major in aeronautical engineering and enrolled in the prerequisite classes for that major. When he went to the bookstore to purchase the textbooks for his first semester, he was shocked: each one cost four dollars. He worried about being able to pay for his tuition, housing, and food. Immediately he looked for work. The FRAM Corporation, less than two miles from campus on Main Street, was hiring. They made automobile oil filters for Ford Motor Company. Paul was hired to assemble filters thirty-five hours a week, from 6:00 p.m. to 1:00 a.m, Monday through Friday.

With college courses, housing, transportation and work resolved, Paul looked for a way to socialize, which was a necessity for the gregarious young man. He did not know anyone in Ann Arbor. It occurred to him that he could make friends through sports, so he tried out for two teams at the university, swimming and tennis. He made both. But within weeks he acknowledged that he could not keep up with work, school, and team practices. Because he was at FRAM every weeknight, he needed the days for homework, which meant he had to miss practices. He dropped both sports.

There were twelve thousand students enrolled at University of Michigan, but Paul felt alone walking to class in a sea of students. Fortunately, the university had founded its International Center two years before. This gathering place, created to support a growing number of international students, was in a wing next to the Michigan Union where most American students congregated. Paul went to the International Center when his schedule allowed. Over time he made friends, mostly from Latin America. Many people can relate to the lonely feeling of being a freshman on a college campus, but international students have the added barrier that their fellow students cannot imagine the worlds they come from. Paul's twelve years of living in Italy gave him an instant bond with the international students. Soon he had formed what he called a "gang". His two closest friends, Flavio and Carvalho, were Brazilian. They liked to get together for poker games on weekends.

Paul's greatest challenge his freshman year of college was juggling the time he spent studying with his need to earn money. When she could, Dora added a few dollars to the money she sent monthly from the boarder, but Paul had to pay for most of his school and living expenses. He took on extra work shoveling snow that winter, when temperatures in Ann Arbor reached ten below zero. The room Paul rented had insufficient heating. His nightly bicycle trips home after his shift at FRAM ended at one in the morning were often on snowy roads. His health was suffering from lack of sleep and exposure to cold weather. Because of all this, his grades were not as good as they had been in high school.

When the long Michigan winter ended, Paul traded shoveling snow for the more pleasant job of mowing grass. By the time the school year ended, he started thinking about changing jobs. He knew his sophomore year classes were going to be more demanding and he didn't want to go through another winter of working until 1:00am at FRAM. In the fall of 1941, as his sophomore year began, he was hired as an assistant for a university research program. He quit working at FRAM and kept occasional jobs mowing grass and shoveling snow to supplement his income. His schedule became more reasonable, and he started focusing on getting good grades in the math and science courses necessary for his aerospace engineering major.

A few months into that school year, on December 7, 1941, Japanese planes attacked Pearl Harbor. The U.S. suddenly entered World War II, joining its allies in battling the Axis powers of Japan, Germany and Italy. Four days after the attack on Pearl Harbor, Italy declared war on the United States. Paul, like fellow students from Italy, Germany and Japan were suddenly enemy aliens.

President Franklin D. Roosevelt issued proclamations authorizing the U.S. to detain potentially dangerous enemy aliens. [xix] Within days, the FBI came onto Michigan's campus, picked up Paul and others, and drove them to Detroit for interrogation. Paul sat in an interrogation room, facing two FBI agents. He declared that his sisters were U.S citizens by birth, and that his father had petitioned for naturalization in 1937. The only reason Paul had not started the process was that he was not yet twenty-one years old. The agents informed him that now things had changed. He could not become a U.S. citizen for as long as the war continued.

An agent asked him if he had ever been a member of a Fascist organization. Paul answered truthfully. He told them that when he lived in Italy, between age eight and twelve he was a member of the youth Fascist organization called the Balillas. He emphasized that his parents had not made a political statement by signing him up. All boys were required to join this organization in the years that Benito Mussolini was in power.

What mattered to the FBI was that Paul had received Fascist indoctrination. Now both Paul and his father were "suspicious individuals". This interview was the cause of both having trouble obtaining U.S. citizenship for years.

Americans were paranoid about enemy aliens in those early days of the war. The anger towards the Japanese bombing of Pearl Harbor led to the confinement of approximately one hundred twenty thousand Japanese Americans in U.S. internment camps.[xx] In the case of Italians, the prejudice was only partly because Mussolini was aligning with Hitler. As a result of millions immigrating to the U.S. in the previous fifty years, Italians were the largest group of immigrants in America. Anti-Italian sentiment was already high before World War II began. Italians were often thought of as undesirable. The derogatory terms of "wop" and "dago" were commonly aimed at dark-skinned Europeans presumed to be Italian. Employers refused to hire them simply because of their ethnicity.

When the U.S. entered the war in Europe, this attitude led to persecution of Italians who were in many cases already naturalized citizens. Many were also sent to internment camps. Some had nighttime curfews from 8:00 p.m. to 6:00 a.m. Some Italians had to surrender weapons, radios and cameras. Others were banned from sensitive areas such as the San Francisco waterfront or areas near military bases.[xxi]

Paul left the meeting in Detroit feeling fortunate. The only restriction the FBI placed on him was one that all Italians and Italian Americans were subjected to: he was issued a Certification of Identification, also known as an Alien Registration ID. He had to carry this red, passport-looking document at all times. His movements were confined to within five miles of the university, but he could move about day and night within that radius. He must, however, apply to the FBI for permission to visit his family in Portland on holidays.

When he returned to campus, he was told to report to his counselor. That's when he learned of another restriction: he would have to change his major. Aeronautical engineering was not allowed because it was a subject related to the nation's defense. Paul was frustrated that he would not be allowed to study what interested him. More painful was that changing degrees meant new course requirements. He had paid hard-earned money and spent time taking courses that would not apply towards whatever he studied next.

Paul had already been studying Italian, Spanish, French and Portuguese towards a minor in Romance Languages, so he decided to make that subject his new major. And because he loved math, he chose to simultaneously pursue a master's degree in economics. In those days, students were allowed to work towards undergraduate and master's degrees at the same time.

As 1942 began, the University of Michigan changed the school year schedule. They turned a two-semester school year into a three-trimester year by making each semester shorter and shortening the breaks between terms. Summer school was eliminated – the third trimester was from May to September. This would allow boys to finish college before being drafted. Four-year programs could now be completed in three. The change was daunting for students because they were given less time to finish the semester's coursework and prepare for exams.

College, most would agree, is not only about education. Paul was handsome, intelligent and athletic but had little time to date during his first year and a half at Michigan. Things changed in February of 1942 when he walked into the International Center. Across the room was a beautiful girl, blonde and innocent looking. He started up a conversation.

Her name was Linda Laine Reisman, and she was also a sophomore. Linda was born in Tallinn, Estonia and had immigrated to Michigan with her family when she was four years old. Linda told Paul she had been a good student at her high school in Grand Rapids and was attending University of Michigan on a scholarship. The university's decision to shorten the semester was upsetting to her because she was struggling with the math coursework required for her economics major. Paul offered to help her study.

The two immigrants felt an immediate attraction, and they were soon spending as much time together as his work and their class schedules would allow. Most of their dates were to study as they pushed to prepare for early exams. By April, the cold winter began to retreat and the weather in Ann Arbor turned pleasant. Paul and Linda's feelings for each other blossomed along with the yellow forsythia blooms that filled the bushes on campus. While they studied, Paul wrote notes to himself about how wonderful Linda was. She was fascinated by the exotic man who pursued her, but she worried about the reaction her parents would have to her going out with an Italian.

Linda had been writing detailed letters to her family at least twice a week since she entered college in 1940.[7] After she met Paul, her letters home continued, but with no mention of her new love interest.

She was a devoted daughter to her Estonian parents Ella Kiilas and Otto Reisman. She adored her only brother, also named Otto, who was seven years younger. In her letters Linda asked about every detail of her family's life. Her mother Ella, who she called Momma, Mommie or Mama, dedicated her time to maintaining their home, as well as a second house that they rented out. She wrote to Linda in depth about her cleaning routine, which included washing walls and windows, and varnishing floors. Ella wrote to her daughter in Estonian so Linda would keep up the language. Ella often sent Linda homemade cakes and biscuits. These fostered a sweet tooth and a love of baking that lasted Linda's entire life.

Linda's father Otto, who she called Poppa or Daddy, worked at General Motors. Linda liked to worry over him, for example asking that he not drive too fast. She helped him do his taxes. Linda was frugal, as were most people, post-Depression. She fretted about her parents spending too much money on gifts they sent her.

---

7. Linda's parents kept all her letters, and they later were given to our family. They are the reason I have so much detail about their lives.

Linda was very maternal about her "little" brother Otto, who thanks to his Estonian genes eventually grew to be over six feet tall and weighed two hundred pounds. Linda monitored his grades in school, and encouraged him to take up stamp-collecting, which had been her hobby since high school. She soon passed this interest onto Paul.

The subject of war closed in on the students at Michigan by the end of the Spring trimester. Linda's history professor was sent to Turkey as an Army officer. Professors lectured on what World War II meant for the United States. One was accused of being a fear monger for recommending that the United States government have one hundred thousand planes at the ready to support England. The Army converted a dorm across the street from Linda's dorm into ROTC barracks. They removed the beds and replaced them with bunk beds—they even removed the bedroom doors. When Linda studied in her room, she could hear the cadets practicing drills.

Paul stayed on campus to continue studying over the summer term of 1942. There was barely a break between the spring and summer session which started in May. He took a tremendous course load—twenty-one hours—to recover from the setback of changing his major. His courses were: Economics, Accounting, Geography of Latin America, History, Spanish Drama, Five Famous Spanish Novelists of the 19th Century, and Advanced English Composition.

When Paul stayed in Michigan that summer, Angelo finally acknowledged that his son would never come home to run the York Street store. Angelo was now seventy years old and ready to fully retire. He turned the management of the store over to his son-in-law, Adam Romano, Elizabeth's husband. Adam was happy being a barber, but Elizabeth urged him to take the job because she hoped the store would make Adam as well off as it had her father.[8]

Linda did go home for the summer. Even though she dreaded the four-month separation from Paul, the rigor of the spring trimester had worn her down. She had thyroid problems and a history of anemia, and for several years had taken iron pills. Her mother often worried about her frail constitution, accusing her of not eating enough. Linda said to Paul, "Silly! They can't understand that I eat to live, rather than live to eat."

Once home, Linda wrote to Paul several times a week. She begged him to write to her only occasionally, and to pretend he was her housemate, Betty. She said her mother would be suspicious of her receiving too many letters from anyone, female or male. Ella was hyper-vigilant because Linda's grades had dropped during the Spring trimester, and she lost the scholarship that had helped pay for her first two years of college. Linda's father Otto was understanding, but her mother was not. Ella's pride was hurt. For two years she had bragged to friends about Linda's scholarship. Ella believed that Linda's college friendships were distracting her (she envisioned only relationships with girls, she had no idea about Paul). She wanted Linda to change friends, residence, and even talked about her changing schools. She said to Linda, "One goes to school to study, not to fool around!"

The letters between Linda and Paul were light and playful at first, then became more intense as the summer progressed. Mail took only one day to travel between Ann Arbor and Grand Rapids, so their

---

8. Adam ran the store for only a few years before going back to working as a barber. Angelo ended up selling the store to Marietta and Felice's children. Their son Nino Giampetruzzi later also owned the original Center Street store, which he inherited from Felice when he retired in 1946.

correspondence felt like a conversation. At first Paul was careful to write letters from the perspective of "Betty". Soon, Linda figured out how to get to the mailbox before her mother did and the pretense was dropped. Linda had appeared casual during the first months they knew each other but missing him led to her being more open about her feelings for Paul. In response, he started writing of love.

Linda's concerns about their cultural differences slipped into her letters. She told him she was not sure she fit in with Paul's gang. From Paul's letters I know that his friends were like him: loud with dark skin and heavy accents, and they enjoyed women, drinking and gambling. They were "wilder" than Linda was comfortable with. They took risks: on a dare one day, Paul and two of his friends jumped out of a lecture hall window mid-class. The professor, who was writing on the blackboard with his back to them, did not notice. But the story made Linda nervous. Paul was charming and gentle when alone with Linda, but the dynamic of his friend group when they were all together intimidated her. Paul assured Linda he would give anyone up for her.

He asked if he might visit her in Grand Rapids. She reminded him of his travel restrictions as an enemy alien. The couple had a code for the FBI, "Franciscan Brothers", and Linda often mentioned in her letters that Paul would get in trouble with them if he traveled.

More of an issue was that Linda had not told her parents about their relationship because she worried about their reaction. She told Paul that she expected that her father Otto would accept any man that made her happy, even if he didn't like the choice. But she added,

"Mother will try her hardest to prevent me leaving home. She's always had ambitions for me but her plans never included men. She has the queer notion that I will be happiest if I'm outstanding in some community serving humanity and being a devoted daughter. I love my family and I love you too. It seems impossible to make everyone happy. Oh Paul, why must some people think they can decide another's future and know what another person wants?"

His response was,

"I do think that if I had a daughter, I should give her a certain amount of freedom so as to make her conscious of the part that she is going to take in this world."

As his daughter I can confirm that he meant that and remained true to his word.

They also wrote about Paul's intense course load. He confessed that he slept very little. Linda warned him that his "cast-iron constitution" would not last if he kept neglecting his health. It's as if she could see into the future. By the end of July, he complained of chest tightness, but he continued studying late into the night. It was mid-session—exams were piling up. He told Linda the one consolation was that his workload helped him take his mind off their separation.

One morning Linda's thirteen-year-old brother Otto walked into her room unannounced and caught her reading a stack of Paul's letters. She admitted to him that she had a suitor but claimed she was not going steady. He kept her secret and began to help her get to the mailbox early every morning.

One letter worried her. Paul informed her he was going to attend a formal dance with a friend named Helen, who had broken up with her boyfriend. The two had bonded over their sadness of being separated from the one they loved. Paul said, "She cries at times, and I can't stand crying women, so I occasionally take her out and show her some fun." Paul again spoke of visiting Linda in Grand Rapids. He even suggested he could arrive at her house disguised as a cooking pot salesman. For an alternative, he asked that Linda call him. Linda realized Paul was lonely. Many of his friends had either been drafted or gone on to graduate school at other universities. She agreed to call. Hearing each other's voices after so long intensified their feelings.

In early September Paul participated in a five-day poker marathon hosted by his Brazilian friend Carvalho. The players took four-hour sleeping breaks, and shorter breaks to eat. They drank so much alcohol that Paul told Linda it took him a full day to "recover his senses". He won forty-three dollars. He assured Linda that for the final three weeks of classes he would focus on studying.

Linda woke up later than usual one mid-September morning. As she walked through the living room towards the front door to check the mail, she froze when she saw her mother going through correspondence on the sofa. Fortunately, there were no letters from Paul that day. The event scared Linda, and she wrote Paul asking that he send her only one more letter, and to once again pretend he was Betty. She reminded him she would soon be returning to campus, and they would be able to catch up in person.

Paul did not receive that letter because he had been admitted to the University of Michigan Health Service with a fever of one hundred and four degrees. The late nights studying, combined with the recent poker and drinking binge with his friends, had pushed his body beyond its limits. Paul's doctors thought he had tuberculosis at first. They eventually determined that he had both pericarditis and pleurisy, inflammations of the linings of the heart and lungs caused by a virus. As a result of the inflammation his heart was larger than normal at this time, which led to the story later in his life that his heart was permanently enlarged. This was not true—his heart returned to a normal size after the illness, although he did have recurrences of pleurisy over the years.

He was frantic about being in the hospital because semester exams were about to start. He begged his doctor to let him out for his exams the following day if his temperature dropped below one hundred. Paul's fever was one hundred two point six the next morning. He snuck out of his hospital room by mixing with visitors who were leaving an adjacent room. After taking his exam, he returned to the hospital with a fever of one hundred three point four. The nurses were furious. His mother called from Maine to suggest he forget about exams and come home for a month of rest. Three days later, doctors assigned a nurse to guard Paul's door because his fever was still high, and they knew he had an exam that afternoon. He dressed and crawled out the window, followed the ledge to enter the open window of an empty room, and went to his exam anyway.

When Linda returned to Ann Arbor in late September, Paul was still in the Health Service. She loathed hospitals and did not want to go see him there. From friends she learned that their friend Helen visited Paul's bedside often. Hurt, Linda refused to go see him.

Paul was pale and gaunt when he was released from the Health Service. He called Linda, asking to visit her in her dorm room. Linda agreed and anticipated a passionate reunion after their long separation. Instead, Paul asked if she minded if he took Helen to an upcoming football game because they had made the date already. It was a slap in the face.

After that conversation, Linda began to analyze whether he was the right man for her. She knew he had a history of drinking, and she suspected womanizing as well. She wondered if he could give those up. She reconciled the "cooling" of his attitude towards her with the fact that he was very sick and struggling to keep up with schoolwork. Her sympathy for his situation and the feelings that had grown over the summer stopped her from refusing to see him again. But her pride made it difficult to even look at him.

Ten days later Paul was re-admitted to the Health Service. While there, in October of 1942, the U.S. Attorney's office of the state of Michigan wrote to inform him that all enemy alien restrictions had been lifted from Italian citizens and that he was now free to travel as he wished.

During this second hospitalization, he again began to pursue Linda. He called her and asked her to visit him. He had friends appeal to her and even enlisted his doctor to call her. They told Linda Paul missed her and that her presence would help his healing. She felt insecure when she first went to see him. Sick as he was, he convinced her that he was in love with her.

Dora, Lina, and Mimi visited Paul at the university's health service in late November. They were shocked to find a thin, pale, bearded young man. Paul's doctors discussed his medical situation with

Mimi and suggested that Paul withdraw from the university and go home to Portland to recover. He left Ann Arbor knowing he would not be back for the following trimester. This was a huge setback for him, personally, financially and academically. It was the second time in his college career that he fell behind in his educational goals.

For Christmas Paul sent Linda a music box to her home in Grand Rapids. Ella was suspicious about the sender, so Linda made up a story that a friend had sent it. She intended to keep Paul a secret from her parents until she had made up her mind about him. She warned him that if he did not give up his "odd way of life", they were done.

While Paul was at home, Dora made sure he rested. He slept ten to thirteen hours a day. At this time Paul's sisters and their families were all living with Angelo and Dora. In the case of Elizabeth and Adam, it was for financial reasons. When Angelo turned the store over to Adam, he also gave Elizabeth and him an apartment within his house. Lina and her husband Mimi were living with them because of a wartime real estate shortage. They had spent a few years in the small mill town of Millinocket, three hours south of Portland, where Mimi was the doctor for the Great Northern Paper Mill. When the small town's economy began to suffer due to the war, they moved to Portland, which had doubled in size, and where doctors were in short supply. However, because of this boom, real estate was hard to come by, and they had trouble finding a place to buy. Angelo evicted a tenant from one of the apartments within his house to give Lina, Mimi and their two daughters a place to live until they could find a home to buy.

As Paul became stronger, he looked for ways to keep busy. Occasionally he helped Adam at the store. He tutored his sisters' children. Lina's daughters were Anna, age eight, and Hilda, age five. Elizabeth's son Armando was four. Paul also became a prolific letter writer. His letters strengthened his relationship with Linda, and he also wrote to friends who had left University of Michigan, either to fight in the war or to continue their studies elsewhere. Letter writing took up so much of his day that he bought a typewriter and taught himself to type.

All anyone could talk about was the war, and the longer Paul was away from campus the more he considered enlisting in the Army. He blamed his not yet being a U.S. citizen on the two setbacks to his college trajectory, as well as the forced change in major and his subsequent health problems trying to overcome that change in major. He read that the fastest way for a former enemy alien to obtain citizenship was to serve in the U.S. Armed Forces. Paul went to the draft board in Portland for a physical exam and was strong enough to pass. However, because of his recent hospitalization he was classified as 4F: not acceptable for service due to medical or other reasons. He had no choice: he would return to college when he was able.

In early March Paul visited Linda at the University of Michigan. He returned to Portland with a photograph of her, which he proudly showed to his family. Linda turned twenty-one years old on March 19 and wrote to Paul that she was ready to tell her family that they would not be getting her back after college. The night Paul read that letter he went to a Portland bar with his brother-in-law Adam. They returned home full of liquor and Paul impulsively called Linda and proposed that they marry within a few months. She answered that she did want to marry him but always thought it would happen after they both got their degrees.

Paul had a clearer head the next morning and wrote to Linda assuring her that he wanted to be on firm financial footing before they married, and that he was in favor of her having a career after she graduated. He did not believe in a woman studying for years only to ignore that education and becoming a housewife. She felt a bit differently: she agreed that Paul should finish his education before they married, but she did not care that he be well off. She believed some struggle in a young couple's life bonded them. She also stated she was willing to work if necessary but had no desire to be a career woman. Keeping a home and raising a family appealed to her.

In May of 1943 Paul returned to the University of Michigan campus. In total, his illness and recovery had lasted nine months. The Health Service tested him thoroughly before the university decided he was well enough to enroll in summer classes. Linda didn't want to be separated from Paul now that they were finally together again, so she decided to also stay for the summer trimester. She went home to see her parents for the short break in between terms, and Paul rode with her on the train to Grand Rapids. During the ride they discussed how Linda still had not told her family about him, fifteen months after they started dating. Paul gave her the courage to finally speak to them. He watched out the window as she disembarked and greeted her mother. He stayed on the train and returned to Ann Arbor.

The first thing Linda did when she arrived home was talk to her parents about Paul. They could see her struggle to tell the story and encouraged her to be honest with them. Ella told her daughter that she had sensed there was a man in her life because she had asked to return to university for the summer term. They were very kind, told her that she was old enough to make this decision, and asked her to consider that they were once young also. Linda cried with relief.

The next day Ella and Otto asked more questions. Linda showed them Paul's picture and explained that he was Italian but no longer an enemy alien. The Reismans expressed their concern that Paul might be forced to return to Europe and that Linda might not be accepted there. However, they asked her to bring Paul home one weekend so they could meet him. Linda realized she had misinterpreted her mother's curiosity. It seemed that Ella didn't object to her dating, only to her daughter hiding it from her. When Linda returned to campus, she and Paul celebrated that their relationship was finally out in the open.

Life was also looking up for Paul in other ways. On June 14 he learned that he was assigned a quota number, which meant he would be eligible to become a naturalized citizen within a year. As the summer trimester began, he threw himself into his studies fully. He also went back to playing tennis, the sport that would become his lifelong passion.

In September of 1943, the university recruited Paul for an unusual task. At this point in World War II, there were several divisions of the Royal Italian Army, the co-belligerents, that were fighting on the side of the Allies. This happened after Benito Mussolini was removed as Prime Minister by King Victor Emmanuel III. Ten of these soldiers, who had previously been held as prisoners of war in the U.S., were moved to Michigan's campus to perform menial tasks such as kitchen duty at the University Law Club. These were young men, ages twenty-one to twenty-five, from the Italian countryside.[xxii] Paul was asked by the university to teach the soldiers English. He worked with them for a year, from late 1943 to late 1944, and even started a soccer team to boost their morale.

When the term ended in October, Paul went to see his family in Portland. The day after he arrived, his extended family came to see him. In total there were almost forty relatives. In the thirty years since Angelo had sent to Castellaneta for a wife, Dora's family, the Casavolas and Giampetruzzis, had grown into a large community. During that visit Paul bought an engagement ring. His parents sent him back to Michigan with two hundred dollars for the couple to start a joint savings account. When Paul arrived on Michigan's campus, he proposed to Linda. She said yes.

Linda wrote to her parents about accepting Paul's proposal, saying in her letter that she had waited until after her father's birthday because she was worried the news might spoil his celebration. She described the engagement ring Paul gave her, which had a diamond in the center set higher than two side diamonds. She also told them about the money Paul's parents had given them. She begged her family not to be too startled.

The Reismans invited Paul to spend the Christmas break with them in Grand Rapids. It was to be the first time they met the man Linda had been dating for almost two years. Linda asked Paul to bring his friend Flavio, to reduce the scrutiny on the newly engaged couple.

I don't know what happened during that visit, but it must not have gone well. From later correspondence I have concluded that the Reismans did not have a good first impression of Paul, and vice versa. December 1943 is the only time that Paul, Linda and her parents were ever in a room together.

Paul and Linda were married on February 26, 1944 in Detroit. Six college friends attended, but no family. Even though Linda's parents lived an hour away, they only sent a card. Paul's family also did not come.

For the first time since Linda started college four years earlier, her communication with her parents slowed down to almost nothing. Whereas before she wrote them once or twice a week, after her wedding she wrote only three letters for the remainder of 1944: in April, October, and December. The Reismans sent gifts for various occasions, but they didn't visit.

Paul Vinelli and Linda Reisman, 1944

In March of 1944, Paul and Linda both graduated from University of Michigan – Paul with a degree in Romance Languages and Linda with a degree in economics. Linda found a job at the university while Paul finished his graduate work in economics. They moved into a small apartment one mile from campus. It was near the railroad tracks, which meant it got very dirty. Linda wrote to her mother about constant cleaning. She and Paul cohabited with a pair of pet turtles and unfortunately also a rat that they couldn't seem to catch.

Paul had become close to one of his economics professors by the name of Watkins, who wrote Paul a flattering letter of recommendation. In September, with that letter in hand, Paul traveled to New York to look for a job. He walked all over the city in rainy weather to dozens of job interviews at banks. He hoped to work in an international field but found nothing. There were two reasons that jobs were not easy to find. Many former bank employees were away fighting in the war, and employers were holding their jobs for their expected return. For the same reason, banks preferred to hire women. The thinking was that, post-war, the women would get married, and their jobs would be available for returning veterans. Paul was offered only clerical jobs and one as an accountant. He decided to hold out for something more interesting.

Paul then went to Washington, D.C. for more interviews. He liked Washington more than New York but found nothing there as well. Most of his interviews were at federal institutions, and his being an Italian citizen was too big a strike against him during wartime. More than a year had passed since he received his quota number, but his progress towards U.S. citizenship had not advanced.

In November he finished his year of work with the Italian prisoners of war on Michigan's campus. A commandant in the war department sent him a letter thanking him for his service and recognizing how much Paul helped with the Italian soldiers by teaching them English and in translating administrative and disciplinary matters. The letter mentioned that the men appreciated his advice on personal matters, indicating Paul had become close to them.

That month, November of 1944, Paul received his Master of Economics degree. Two months of job searches had yielded nothing, and he was starting to panic. Linda had already told the university she was leaving her job, and they had found her replacement. Paul and she intended to leave Ann Arbor right after his graduation. But with no job, they had no idea where they would go. Paul went back to Washington, D.C. after graduation for more interviews. He was hoping for an international research job with some government entity. On his first night he stayed up until 2:00 a.m. typing out federal employment applications on a typewriter borrowed from his hotel. Over the next week he met with dozens of departments in many government offices, including at the State Department, the Federal Reserve Board, Department of Agriculture and the Department of Commerce. At every interview, the obstacle was that he was an Italian citizen—he was told several times that if he were a U.S. citizen, the job would be his.

Security was tight in Washington, especially for foreigners. Paul had to obtain a special visitor badge issued by the person who was going to interview him just to enter the Department of Commerce building. He also had to pass inspection by two government officials. At the Office of Strategic Services (this was the wartime intelligence agency of the United States during World War II, which preceded the Central Intelligence Agency), he first had to fill out a long form in the lobby. When an armed guard walked him to the office where he was to be interviewed, Paul was dismayed at how many guards were around them. He was interviewed by a Navy officer who told him they wanted to hire him as a political attaché and would send him to Italy on behalf of the State Department to interview Italian government officials.

He was tempted. They needed his language skills so the pay was higher than any local position was offering, and he would get to travel to his homeland. But he knew that Linda did not want him to work in Italy, nor would she want to move there with him. Paul told the officer that he was interested in economics, not political science, and that he also wished to work in Latin America, not Europe. His response was ignored. The officer repeated his offer to Paul and asked that he let him know when his citizenship papers came through. Then they sent him to the OSS Latin American Section, located in a converted movie theater four blocks away. He was escorted by an armed guard the entire way. There he met with two representatives who asked for a writing sample and sent him away with application forms.

On Sunday, November 26 Paul had a free day to tour Washington D.C. He walked over ten miles, covering both sides of the Potomac River. His favorite monument was the Washington Monument, because it was "beautiful but also useful – from there you could orient yourself all around the city". He was disappointed to find temporary barracks erected in front of the Lincoln Memorial, but observed, "War is war".

He was discouraged at not finding a job, but he still believed Washington D.C. was the best place for them to live because of the international work done there. He decided he and Linda would find an inexpensive apartment and he would work at a department store until his citizenship could be worked out. He began to look at apartments in between job interviews and found nothing in his price range. At nights he walked miles looking for places for rent and soon understood that anything they could afford would have to be far from the center of the city.

Finally, at the end of November Paul was approved for an entry-level position with the Federal Reserve System, doing research on Latin American foreign trade. The position had to be approved by the Civil Service Commission because of his citizenship status, but he was hopeful. He wrote to Linda that they would be moving in two weeks. He had rented an unfurnished house, which he described to her: "It is smaller than our apartment. It is a thirty-minute ride from the heart of the city. It is dirty. It is ugly. But on the whole, it is cute, and I am sure you will like it. I have been told that I'm terribly lucky to get anything in this overcrowded madhouse."

4

ECONOMIST IN WASHINGTON, D.C.
1944 – 1949

Paul and Linda moved to Washington D.C. on December 11, 1944. Their one-story house, rented for thirty-seven dollars a month, was on Ridge Road, which ran alongside Fort Dupont Park near the Maryland border. The house was tiny, but because it faced the park and had a large front and backyard, they felt like they lived out in the country. They were excited about their plans to have a vegetable garden in their backyard when spring came.

The front of the house was a parquet-floored living room and kitchen. The bedroom, bathroom and furnace room were in the back. The day they moved in Paul and Linda bought a sofa bed for the living room so they would have a place to sleep that night. They ordered furniture and a cardboard closet for the bedroom. Their landlords, who lived next door, welcomed them with a gift of curtains, a swing for their front porch, and a card table for their kitchen.

As soon as they unpacked their belongings, they went to Maine to spend Christmas with Paul's family. This was the first time Linda met the Vinella-Casavolas. It was so cold during their visit that they didn't spend much time touring the city of Portland. Their days were mostly in Dora and Angelo's home, eating and visiting with Paul's large and boisterous family. When they returned to Washington, Paul and Linda received their Christmas gifts. Dora shipped a set of used chairs to go with the card table their landlord had given them, and Paul's uncle Domenico sent two of his hand carved bookcases.

As 1945 began, Paul started his job at the Federal Reserve, and Linda explored the city. She was pleasantly surprised to learn that shopping in D.C. was much better than in Ann Arbor—prices were lower and supply greater. What most surprised her was the availability of metal objects. During World War II, metal products for civilian use—everything from bobby pins and zippers to bread boxes and kitchen appliances—were hard to find. Most metal was directed towards manufacturing planes, ships, jeeps, guns and soldiers' helmets. However, in Washington Linda found many items she did not expect to see until the war ended.

They were careful to spend as little money as possible. Linda sewed many of their clothes, as well as slipcovers for the furniture. Since they could not afford even a used sewing machine, she cut out all the patterns first and then rented a machine for one month to finish everything in a short time. When their roof leaked, Paul climbed up and repaired it with roofing cement.

Because Paul's parents owned a store, they were allotted more wartime ration points than their family needed. Dora sent Paul and Linda so many that they were also able to share some with the Reismans in Michigan. Dora's points allowed Linda to buy butter, which had not been available at all their last year in Ann Arbor. Linda was thrilled she could bake her favorite sweets again.

Washington had much milder winters than Michigan. January temperatures rarely dropped below freezing. Their neighborhood was idyllic. Every morning, they woke up to the chirping of birds. In March, spring burst into action and the flowers in the park made the air smell delicious. Blossoms appeared in cherry and magnolia trees all over the city. Washington looked just like the postcards they had seen before they moved. By the end of the month, the temperature crept into the eighties on some days. Paul and Linda screened in the front porch in preparation for summer, planning to eat and even sleep out there if the house became too warm.

They worked over several weekends to level the land and plant grass in front of their house. Then in April they started planting a garden in a fifty by seventy-foot space in their backyard. When their college friend Flavio and his wife Jean visited from New York that May, Flavio helped Paul finish digging the garden. The men were so hungry when they came into the house – wearing what seemed like half the dirt they dug up—that they ate five pounds of French fries.

Immediately after that visit, Paul's family arrived: Dora, Elizabeth and Lina with her two daughters, Anna and Hilda. They toured Washington's memorials and art galleries and spent Memorial Day at the fantastic Washington Zoo. Linda enjoyed having visitors, but she fretted over feeding them. Meat was scarce in May of 1945, so she and Paul usually ate fish, purchased at a market along the Potomac River. Linda had befriended a local butcher who occasionally found her a leg of lamb or some beef. Pork was very scarce, and they could not find ham at all. Linda's parents had better luck finding ham in Michigan and sent one every few months. One of these hams arrived just before Paul's family visited, which was a huge relief for Linda.

Paul had been working at the Federal Reserve for six months when his boss walked into his office and sheepishly informed him that the report of the Civil Service Commission, who performed background checks on prospective employees, arrived half a year late. The Fed had just been notified that Paul was an enemy alien, which meant he could not work for an agency of the United States government. The six-month delay was a gift for Paul, because by that time his work had impressed his employers. They helped him find a job as a trust investment advisor with American Security & Trust Company.

On Tuesday night, August 14, 1945, the surrender of Japan was announced, ending World War II.[9] That night, Paul and Linda went to a park across from the White House where they could see President Harry Truman making the announcement, his wife Bess smiling beside him. The crowd around them was exuberant. By 9:00pm the scene became quite rowdy, so they went home. The next day most offices in Washington, including Paul's, were closed.

Their garden was very successful, and in September Linda canned seventy quarts of tomatoes. Paul suggested they include more exotic and decorative vegetables, such as a variety of Italian squash.

Linda continued to suffer from anemia and frequent colds. When she was sick Paul doted on her, bringing her breakfast in bed and insisting she rest throughout the day. On Friday October 5, Linda was resting when she heard the thunderous sound of more than a thousand planes flying in formation over their house. She got out of bed and went outside to see navy aircraft, returning from the parade

---

9. The surrender actually occurred in Japan on Wednesday, August 15, but because of the time difference it was announced in the U.S. on Tuesday. The formal surrender documents were not signed until Sept. 2, 1945.

honoring Fleet Admiral Chester Nimitz for his part in the Navy's victory in the Pacific, which ended World War II.

One Saturday before Christmas Paul and Linda walked across the street into the park and collected fallen evergreen branches to decorate the house. Snow began to fall hard, and by the time they had filled the house with the smell of pine, the hill next to their house was loud with the squeals of children sliding down on sleds and trays. Linda was very happy, because for her it didn't seem like Christmas without snow. She and Paul wished they were young enough to go sliding. She wrote to her parents asking that they send her ice skates, with the hope that the ice on neighboring ponds would become thick enough in January.

Unfortunately, the cold didn't last, and by late January of 1946, afternoon temperatures were over seventy degrees. Linda felt sad when she looked out the window and saw rain instead of snow. Paul decided to cheer her up by bringing home a German Shepherd puppy. They named him Zulu. Linda and Paul doted on the new member of the family.

The Reismans wrote, inviting Linda and Paul to visit them in Grand Rapids for Easter. Linda declined, saying that Paul had just started a new job and that they could not take vacation until he achieved more seniority. Whether this was true or not, it appeared that she and Paul were as hesitant about visiting the Reismans as her parents were about visiting them in Washington.

Paul was interested in learning more about the functions of a commercial bank. He had developed a good relationship with Daniel W. Bell, the president of American Security & Trust, so he approached him with an idea. Bell approved Paul's proposal that he spend his summer vacation time rotating through every department of the bank. Paul likened the concept to the captain of a ship needing to know all tasks performed on board. Unfortunately, this plan was thwarted shortly after being conceived.

Paul not having U.S. citizenship was a problem for the Federal Reserve, but not for the U.S. Army. In April 1946 he was drafted. Even though the war was formally over, and there was a major demobilization movement bringing soldiers back home, the military was still drafting soldiers to keep a presence in Europe and the Pacific. He was ordered to report for duty in Maine the following month.

Linda was devastated that she and Paul would be separated. Daniel Bell tried to help. Bell had previously been Director of the Bureau of the Budget and later served as Undersecretary of the Treasury. From his recent time in government, he was a friend of the Undersecretary of War. Bell hoped he might be able to get Paul a position in the War Department in Washington. This didn't end up being possible for the same reason as always: Paul was not a U.S. citizen.

Paul was desperate to obtain American citizenship, so he began to look at his upcoming Army service positively. He had heard that many foreign citizens automatically received U.S. citizenship for serving in the armed forces. But when he started asking around, he was frustrated to learn that this privilege did not apply to aliens from countries at war with the United States, including Italy. Paul would not be eligible for American citizenship unless a peace treaty was signed between Italy and the U.S.

Paul and Linda visited Maine before he reported for duty. They spent part of the time with his family in Portland and toured much of the Maine coast. Paul introduced Linda to amazing seafood—things she had never tasted. She laughed when she tasted the cold water from the Atlantic Ocean – it really was salty! Along the seashore they climbed all over large rocks worn soft by the water, while Paul pointed out the various types of seaweed. They found clams and mussels. Linda loved watching the tide come in and out. They took a ferry to Peaks Island on Casco Bay, where they boiled lobsters on the beach. They saw a large school of seals. They even tried to fish but caught nothing.

Linda was exhausted when they returned to Portland. Paul had been excited to show her everything and as usual had much more energy than she did. He asked his brother-in-law Mimi to perform a checkup on her. Other than low blood pressure she seemed fine. Linda remarked that she had never been able to stand late hours and excitement. "Nothing wrong with me, just a sissy, needing a very regular life".

Paul reported for service in Maine and Linda returned to Washington alone. She was heartbroken. She didn't fear for Paul's life, because the fighting was over. She just hated being separated from her husband. Five-month-old Zulu missed Paul too. The dog went from room to room, looking for him in every corner of the house. Both Linda and Zulu lost their appetites. Linda was grateful to have the German Shepherd with her, both for company and as a watchdog. Living alone scared her. She and Paul wrote to each other almost daily.

After Paul reported for duty in Maine, he was sent to Fort Dix, near Trenton, New Jersey. Fort Dix was enormous, covering forty square miles. At the height of the war, it held one hundred thousand men, but with the war winding down, there were now fifteen thousand U.S. soldiers and five thousand prisoners of war performing maintenance duties. The fort had hundreds of post exchanges (stores), sixteen chapels, two airports, three bus lines, seven theaters, and several thousand tanks. The fort was used for processing servicemen, which included issuance of uniforms, clothing and toiletries, instruction in the Articles of War, a course on sexually transmitted diseases and another on religious matters, tetanus and typhoid vaccines, insurance, bonds, savings, dependency allotments, and an interview with Army personnel. Paul's dog tag was stamped with his blood type (O), and his religious preference (N) for None.

He was made to take an IQ test. Paul's score was 132. Less than two percent of the U.S. population scores over 130.[xxiii] Based on his results Paul was placed in Class I, the highest of six classes. This qualified him for top jobs in the military. He requested a finance job, but the Army wanted to make him an interpreter because of his language skills. The decision would not be made until after basic training.

While waiting to know where he would be sent for basic training, Paul was assigned warehouse duty. He observed to Linda that in just one of fifty warehouses at Fort Dix, there were twenty thousand bags containing fifty white sheets each. He wrote, "That is one million reasons why sheets are hard to find on the market."

On June 30, Paul left Fort Dix on a two-day train ride to Fort McClellan in Alabama. Exhaust poured into the train car he was in so the men, their belongings, and the food they ate were all black. Basic training at Fort McClellan meant a lot of marching, military maneuvers, learning military rank, and learning how to take apart a rifle as well as fire it. The men were also issued helmets, footlockers, puptents, camping equipment and canteens. Paul was made a squad leader, which he said didn't mean much except that he led a line of soldiers, was exempt from KP (Kitchen Police) duty, and was rarely inspected during the weekly Saturday morning inspections.

July in Alabama was hotter than anything Paul had ever experienced. The training exercises made the soldiers sweat so much that they were given two salt tablets with every meal to replenish their sodium levels. On days where the temperatures were in the nineties and as high as one hundred ten degrees, the men stripped to their waist for morning exercises. After an hour, at least twenty-five collapsed from heatstroke, and often one or two were taken off in an ambulance. Paul told Linda that the heat barely bothered him. He said the grueling workouts had improved his stamina and physical appearance, "more muscle, less pouch". One of the more unpleasant parts of training was in mustard gas and tear gas, which the soldiers had to experience both with a gas mask on and off.

Linda was in an uproar about Paul being in the Army. In her daily letters she confessed their separation was unbearable for her, worse than she anticipated. She begged Paul to find a way to avoid being shipped overseas. She asked him to tell the Army about his health problems in college and even offered to ask his doctor at the Michigan Health Service to write a letter, in hopes that he would be kept in the United States. Paul responded that he would not consider shirking his duties, which the Army called goldbricking. He wrote,

"You see baby, I'm no hero, but there are a number of standards to which I must stick to maintain my self-respect. Society, with which I have willed to share my lot, has picked me to do an unpleasant job. If I am to continue living among the same fellow-men, I cannot let down on that job. It matters little whether the purpose is a just one; if I live in this community, I must adhere to all the laws. You see darling, I am not dealing with a particular individual that I can outwit. I am dealing with an organization that is powerful enough to do me great harm. This is my way of explanation that the Army is not going to use me for what I am best fitted for, but for what it thinks there is a temporary need at the time."

Desperate for company, Linda took Zulu by train to see her family. They arrived in Grand Rapids more than a day after they left Washington D.C. Not long after Linda walked into her parents' house, Ella peppered her with questions about the friends she and Paul associated with in Washington. She wanted to know everyone's nationality, color, race, religion, manner of thinking. She seemed more narrow-minded and prejudiced than Linda remembered. Or maybe it was Linda who had changed.

Ella avoided bringing up Paul. Linda believed her mother had managed to convince herself that he didn't exist. Ella did, however, gossip about the successful marriages Linda's high school friends had, making sure to point out that their husbands were blond and financially successful. As Linda was being questioned, she looked around the living room and realized her parents had never put up the framed pictures of Paul and her she had sent. All that was displayed were high school pictures of Linda. Zulu was kept in the backyard on a short leash. Linda's father Otto went outside to play with him, but Ella told her she was crazy to own a large dog.

Linda wrote a furious letter to Paul about the treatment she and Zulu were receiving in Grand Rapids. He acknowledged there were irreconcilable differences between her parents and him, and by extension her. But Paul suggested she be patient with her parents.

"Their dislike of me is hardly intended. It is merely that I'm the scapegoat for their unhappiness. I can only feel pity for them, certainly not hate. I would try anything that might help our relations along. If you think that a letter might help, I will correspond with them. My best cure for their hate is of course you. If I can care for you properly, and try to smooth out your relations with them, I cannot think of a better way out of this mess. I have erred in front of them in many ways – do not try and consider me infallible. Do not lose your parents' affection. There may still be times when you'll find your family's affection a necessary link in your life span. We are of a new generation. We think and act differently. Our children will face a good many of the problems now facing us. Let understanding, forgiveness and love be the guiding elements."

For the few days before Linda's departure, Ella and Otto made an effort to be pleasant. Linda also did her best to get along with them and gave her mother the gift Ella would most appreciate—she cleaned their house thoroughly, scrubbing ceilings, walls, and floors, and washing curtains.

On Linda's last day home, Ella pulled Linda over to the living room sofa. She looked angry. She started the conversation by asking Linda how she would feel about giving Zulu to someone who hated her. Ella then began to attack Paul. When Linda retorted that Paul was her husband, and if they were happy, she should be happy for them, Ella went wild with anger. The tirade lasted for two hours. Unaware that their daughter would never visit again, the Reismans sent her back to Washington with new dresses, ham, soap and butter.

Linda's perspective changed after that visit. She still ached for Paul to return, but she no longer hated being alone in the Washington,

D.C. house. It now was a refuge where she and Zulu could be themselves. That summer Linda's brother Otto came to stay with her for two weeks, to help her with the gardening work. With his help she canned thirty quarts of tomatoes. Seventeen-year-old Otto enjoyed being away from the restrictions of their parents' home. He did things Ella and Otto forbade: he smoked and learned to make a variety of cocktails. He also enjoyed going through the small library of books Paul and she had collected and often read until after midnight.

A First Sergeant called Paul to his office and informed him that he was being recommended for Officer Candidate School (O.C.S.). Paul revealed his citizenship issues, but the sergeant thought he could obtain the U.S. citizenship for Paul in advance of entering officer's training. Although Paul was not interested in a military career, he found the idea of O.C.S. interesting because it would keep him in the U.S. during the nine months of training. The downside was the requirement that he serve in the Army for another year and a half after training finished. Linda was in favor of the idea, because the Army permitted married men to live with their wives during Officer Candidate School.

By mid-August, Paul was promoted to Platoon Guide. The days with his company included digging foxholes, many miles of marching, strenuous drills carrying very heavy equipment, and assembling machine guns.

Paul and Linda had known each other for more than four years, yet their letters exhibited the passion of a couple who had just met. Paul wrote that his love for Linda was his sole reason for happiness, and that he imagined life without her a terrestrial hell. Linda showed unwavering adoration for her husband, who she wanted by her side every minute that circumstances would allow.

Paul completed basic training in August. As he had anticipated, the Army could not propose him for Officer Candidate School because of his Italian citizenship. He was told his next move would be to Camp Stoneman in California, where the Army prepared soldiers for deployment to the Pacific and Asia. [xxiv] The only good thing about that development was that he might be given two weeks leave before going to California.

Linda continued to write daily letters, but now Paul didn't receive many of them. With basic training over and no new orders issued, he was no longer part of a "formal" company. Mail was sporadic, many letters were returned or simply lost. Paul started calling every few days. Linda stopped eating. Paul ate enough for three men, quickly regaining some of the weight he had lost in his eight weeks of basic training.

Then Linda decided to take matters into her own hands. She insisted Paul try to get an emergency furlough, citing her "mental collapse". To appease her, he followed the procedure, which involved sending an application to the Red Cross office in Washington D.C. for verification of her mental state. She must have convinced the Red Cross in her interview that she was close to an emotional breakdown, because on Sept. 21, Paul's emergency furlough was approved. He went home for the month of October. Their reunion was like a honeymoon.

Private Paul Vinelli, October 1946, Washington, D.C.
Photo by Linda Reisman Vinelli

When his furlough ended, Paul flew on a military transport plane from Washington to California. The flight on a Douglas C-54 Skymaster was one of the first nonstop transcontinental flights in the United States and was such a novelty that the Naval Air Transport Service handed out brochures about the journey to the soldiers. Paul was amazed that they covered 2,800 miles in "only" fourteen hours.[xxv]

Dora invited Linda and Zulu to spend some time with their family in Portland. Linda went to Maine the day after Paul left. There were less than fifty dollars in their joint bank account, so Dora helped pay her travel expenses. Linda vowed to look for a job as soon as she returned to Washington.

This was Linda's first visit to Paul's family without him. She studied her father-in-law, Angelo. It was hard to reconcile the stories

Paul had told her about what a brute Angelo was when Paul was little, with the man she was now visiting. Of course, he was a different man at seventy-four years old. When Linda reported to Paul how beautifully Angelo played with Zulu, he gave Zulu the credit: "I have always believed that animals can bring out the finer things in human beings."

Elizabeth and Adam lived in an apartment inside Angelo and Dora's house, now with two children, Armando and Diana. Lina, Mimi and their daughters lived nearby. Dora was busy all day, cooking for the family and helping Elizabeth take care of her children. Linda became very fond of her mother-in-law. Zulu loved Dora also, for she spoiled him with leftovers from the family's meals.

Linda felt at home with Paul's family but also overfed and sleep deprived. She wrote to her husband,

"How in the world do they do it? Do Italians ever spend a quiet evening alone reading? I'd like nothing more than to go to sleep at 9:00 p.m. tonight. Everyone has been simply wonderful to me. But I don't fit very well with the role of being a social butterfly. Peace and quiet are completely unheard of in this house. Sometimes I wonder if you were happy with the quiet of our home."

On November 7, 1946, Paul received a present for his twenty-fourth birthday. He was placed in the new Separation Detachment at Camp Stoneman. The unit was created to process the large number of troops returning from overseas now that the fighting was over. This assignment meant Paul would not be shipped overseas at least until the end of the year. He did not expect to come home for Christmas. Dora and Angelo pleaded with Linda to stay in Portland. But Linda was exhausted by the pace the Vinella-Casavola family kept. She wanted to go back to Washington D.C., even if it meant spending Christmas with nobody but Zulu for company. On November 20, Dora gave Linda two hundred dollars to replenish their dwindling savings. Linda and Zulu took the train back to Washington, D.C.

A week after being home, Linda started craving salt. She ate several cans of anchovies a day and then drank cup after cup of tea to combat the thirst caused by the salt in the anchovies. At first, she could not understand what had come over her. But then she tied her cravings to the exhaustion she felt in Portland, and she made an appointment to see a doctor.

Paul started work in the Separation Detachment at the end of November. The goal was to process the most soldiers as possible for discharge. These men, who had seen battle, were to be brought home for Christmas. However, there was still a need for soldiers overseas because the Army kept a presence there. So even as it was rushing to bring men back from overseas duty, the Army felt an urgency to get as many soldiers as possible to the Pacific before Congress reconvened in January. There was a sense that the new Republican-dominated Congress would not reinstate the draft. Camp Stoneman began processing new soldiers twenty-four hours a day, seven days a week. New soldiers that arrived at Camp Stoneman from basic training were shipped overseas in less than two days. The need for more soldiers caught up with Paul, and he was informed that he would be re-evaluated for overseas duty.

On December 9, Linda went to Walter Reed General Hospital, the U.S. Army medical center. The doctor confirmed her suspicions: she was pregnant. She wrote to Paul with the news.

He was beyond thrilled.

"My precious darling,
To say that I am happy at this turn of events is a gross minimization. I'm so glad that it has happened that I want to shout to the world with pride about it. You are going to have a full-time job keeping me from spoiling our child. Since I can remember I have been attracted to little tots. I could not have made a better choice for the mother of my children. My hat is off and my heart is at the feet of my better half.
A very happy and proud papá, Paul"

A few days later Paul called Linda to inform her that her pregnancy had an unexpected and happy consequence. Only two weeks before Linda learned she was pregnant the Army issued a new discharge order: soldiers whose wives were expecting a child could immediately apply for discharge. Paul asked Linda to obtain a Statement of Pregnancy for him to present to his superiors. Linda went to Walter Reed early the next morning. The secretary at the desk had not heard of the order and called General Headquarters for confirmation. She informed Linda that she was the first woman at Walter Reed to receive a statement for the new order. When Linda sent the statement to Paul at Camp Stoneman, his colleagues in the Separation Detachment got to work immediately processing his discharge.

Linda was so excited about Paul coming home that she cleaned every corner of their home, washing curtains and slipcovers, and airing out Paul's civilian clothes which she had stored with mothballs. She and Zulu went into the woods next to the house to find evergreen branches so the house would smell like a holiday.

Paul was discharged from the Army on December 23, six months after he entered the military. It took five days and several trains to cross the country from California to Washington, and on December

28 he was back in Linda's arms, with Zulu leaping up to get his attention. On New Year's Eve, heading into 1947, they celebrated their upcoming child, the end of Paul's time in the Army, and as Linda worded it, "the return of our good luck." They made plans for the arrival of their baby and talked about the possibility of finding a larger house to rent. Linda wanted Paul to stay home through the end of January, but Paul was anxious to return to work. On January 13 he was back at American Security & Trust Company.

One month later, in February of 1947, the peace treaty between the U.S. and Italy was signed. This meant Paul could finally aspire to U.S. citizenship.

Pregnancy agreed with Linda. She felt wonderful even during her first trimester. She kept busy with her new sewing machine, making pregnancy and baby clothes. Paul walked by stores on his way from work to the bus and often stopped to buy fabric for her. The Reismans were excited about the arrival of the baby, and packages started arriving containing handsewn diapers, blankets and clothes.

The house on Ridge Road was going to be very small for a family of three and a dog. Paul and Linda investigated renting a larger home but could find nothing to rent in Washington at that time. Paul began to study the possibility of buying a home under the GI loan program. They found that new houses often cost less than old ones because they were built under the provision that they be sold to veterans.

Paul was bored by his work at the bank's trust department. He learned that several of his former Federal Reserve colleagues were working for the World Bank and the International Monetary Fund (IMF). These entities had been created two years earlier at about the same time as the United Nations. Their work was complementary:

the IMF focused on macroeconomic and financial stability issues, and the World Bank concentrated on long-term economic development and poverty reduction.[xxvi]

Paul found out that The International Monetary Fund needed economists. His nationality was not an obstacle since the IMF was an international organization, so he applied for a job. He was hired immediately. As soon as he started work at the IMF, Paul began to travel to Latin America. The IMF had a policy stating that a representative could not go on missions to the area they came from. No staffer from Latin America was assigned to work with Latin American member countries. These representatives were sent to Europe or the Far East. Only North Americans, Europeans or Asians could travel to IMF missions in Latin America. Not many team members from these regions spoke any Spanish. Paul did speak the language, thanks to his studies at Michigan. He was immediately sent on missions to Central and South America. Some of the first projects he worked on were the devaluation of the Mexican peso and the exchange systems in Costa Rica and Ecuador.

In March Paul and Linda found the house they were looking for. It was still under construction, three months from completion, and was a great price, nine thousand five hundred dollars. It was in a suburb of Washington called Falls Church, Virginia, about seven miles from the center of Washington. Linda said, "Now we will be southerners!" It had two bedrooms and a finished basement. The lot was sixty-five feet by one hundred sixty feet, which would provide both the baby and Zulu plenty of room to play outside. An apple tree stood in the backyard, a reminder that the land had once been part of an apple orchard.

John Vinelli[10] was born on July 1, 1947, at Walter Reed General Hospital. He had a thick crop of light brown hair and blue eyes. Paul and Linda nicknamed their firstborn Johnny. The construction of their new home was delayed so they brought Johnny home to the rented house on Ridge Road. In September, Linda's brother Otto came to meet his nephew and to help the family move to their new house.

As they settled into their life as a family of three, Linda focused on Johnny and their new home while Paul learned about the economies of the Latin American countries where the IMF sent him. He loved the analytical and research aspects of being an economist and especially valued that the work he did helped the developing countries. By 1948 he traveled regularly to Central and South America.

In May of 1948, Linda learned that she was pregnant again. She was happy because she wanted two children close together. Their second son, Craig Vinelli, was born on November 22, 1948. Dora flew from Portland to Washington to help care for Johnny while Linda was in the hospital.

Paul purchased their first car that December: a ten-year-old Plymouth. It had a good heater, important for winters in Washington. The night he brought it home, the whole family—baby Craig included—went for a drive. On Christmas Eve, Paul and Linda put up the Christmas tree and set a rocking horse and sled that the Reismans had sent for Johnny under it. When he saw the tree with its lights and presents the next morning, Johnny's eyes were big as saucers.

As 1949 began Paul was on a plane every month. Linda was very busy with the two boys, especially because John was active and

---

10. I have never been formally told this, but I imagine John is named after Paul's father Angelo, who used the nickname John the whole time he lived in the United States.

curious. She was careful to keep the doors locked because he had learned to open them and dash out of the house. Paul and she made plans to fence in their yard so Johnny could go outside safely and play. He was very resourceful: before he was two years old, he could push a chair to the sink and get his own water, but he also got into frequent mischief and broke many things. He wanted to test everything mechanical: when Linda wrote letters, Johnny pulled the pen out of her hand to study how it worked.[11] He also suffered from frequent colds due to his tonsils.

Craig was much calmer baby than his older brother. He was growing rapidly and was a relatively big child: fifteen pounds at two months old. Johnny was sweet with his baby brother. He would peer at Craig closely, pat him on the head and say, "Nice, nice."

One evening in May of 1949, Paul came home from work and informed Linda that the IMF had assigned him to a major economic mission. The government of Honduras had requested help structuring its finance and economic sectors, including possibly forming a central bank. Paul was going to the small nation with two other economists to see what was needed. While they were headed to Central America, the IMF wanted the three to also stop in Mexico City, Guatemala City and San Salvador to meet with government officials about ongoing projects. Paul expected to be gone a long time, probably months.

---

11. John grew up to be a scientist with a career in technology.

5

WELCOME TO HONDURAS
1949-1950

Paul left Washington in July. Two IMF colleagues traveled with him: Javier Márquez and Alexander (Alex) McLeod. Their first stop was Mexico City, where the three economists were picked up at the airport by limousines sent by Don Rodriguez Gómez, President of the Bank of Mexico (the country's central bank). Paul was strongly affected by the economic inequality he observed as they drove through the city. He wrote to Linda, "Just the trip between the airport and the center of town revealed the paradox of this city: squalor and poverty aside pompousness and luxury."

The men were shown to their suites at the luxurious and spacious Hotel Cortes, after which they were driven to breakfast. Paul tasted an exotic fruit—mango—for the first time. After touring the Palacio Nacional and several sites around it, they were taken to lunch where Paul had a filet mignon and tortillas filled with *gusanos de maguey* (cactus worms), which he declared "one of the most delicious delicacies I have ever eaten."

The group toured more of the city that afternoon, driving through elegant neighborhoods. When they returned to their hotel for a rest, the hotel owner invited them to sit in the courtyard and have some tequila cocktails. Paul never knew tequila tasted so good. A duo of mariachis sang for them. Paul was dazzled by the luxurious atmosphere, which he described to Linda as "out of this world". It was in sharp contrast to his and Linda's reality, given their savings rarely exceeded fifty dollars.

After meetings at the Mexican Central Bank the next day, the group flew to Guatemala City. Paul thought the clean, white city was beautiful, sprinkled across a Shangri-La of a valley within tall mountains. They were only in Guatemala City for one night, meeting with government officials, then they flew to San Salvador. This city left Paul cold, because in his opinion it did not have the natural beauty of Mexico and Guatemala.

After a couple of nights in San Salvador the three men flew on to Tegucigalpa, Honduras, which Paul described as "entirely surrounded by mountains, very lovely from the air. The red tiled roofs stand out among the abundant vegetation". The word Honduras means "depths" in Spanish. According to legend, the country is so named because in 1502 Cristopher Columbus declared, as his ship arrived at the Bay of Trujillo: "*Gracias a Dios que hemos salido de esas honduras*" ("Thank God we have come out of those [ocean] depths").[xxvii]

Paul's landing at the Toncontín Airport was memorable. Tegucigalpa sits in a valley at 3,200 feet elevation, surrounded by mountains that are 4,700 feet high. To reach the airport, the plane had to circle ever lower within the bowl of mountains, and then quickly descend to the runway built on a hill in the center of the city. Upon touching down, the pilot had to slam on the brakes to stop the plane before reaching the end of a very short landing strip, which is considered one of the most dangerous in the world.

The IMF team was met on the airport's tarmac by a seven-man presidential welcoming committee. It included the President of Congress, various congressmen, and two close associates of President Juan Manuel Gálvez. These seven men comprised a commission formed by the president to draft new banking and tax legislation with the help of Paul and the IMF team.

Paul, Márquez and McLeod were whisked through immigration and customs without their passports being checked, thanks to their government escorts. They were driven to the Hotel Lincoln in downtown Tegucigalpa to check in and wash up while the commission waited in the lobby. They were then taken to meet Minister of Finance Marco Batres, who formally welcomed the mission. After an hour of discussion on the scope of the work ahead, the commission gave them a tour of a park in the mountains overlooking the city, where the government was building a replica of the Mayan ruins in Copán.

The next morning the team awoke to Tegucigalpa's pleasant climate: seventy-five degrees and low humidity. They would soon learn that it rained most days at this time of year, but only in the afternoon and only for an hour or two.

At 11:00 a.m. they went to meet President Gálvez. He was a tall, heavy man, mild mannered and pleasant. The Honduran president had several reasons for asking the IMF to send the mission to Honduras. When he took office earlier that year, he realized that the two American fruit companies that operated in the country, Standard Fruit Company and United Fruit Company, exerted an exceptionally large influence on the Honduran economy. There was no national financial system, no central bank, and no private bank that lent to ordinary businesses. At that time there were only three banks in the tiny country, total population 1.2 million. The second largest bank, Banco Atlántida, had been formed in the northern city of La Ceiba by the Standard Fruit Company and was used for the purposes of their enormous banana export business. The other two banks were El Ahorro Hondureño (the only savings bank in the country), and Banco de Honduras. All currency was issued by Banco Atlántida and Banco de Honduras—there was no national currency issued by the government. Gálvez spoke at length to Paul, Márquez and McLeod of his desires for the agricultural and industrial development of Honduras and he concluded by asking the team to help his government create banking and monetary legislation.[xxviii]

In his book, *Los Oligarcas: ¿De Donde Salieron los Ricos?*, Honduran author César Indiano described President Gálvez's vision for Honduras:

Gálvez thought it was time for the country to pass from a country of wood to a country of cement. By 1950, Honduras's income was supported by five pillars besides bananas, and they were sugar, wood, mining, cattle and beer production. Everything else, including the second largest private bank in the country, Banco Atlántida, belonged to the Standard Fruit Company empire. Notwithstanding, the ancillary businesses of the United Fruit Company—beer, sugar mills, sugar cane, milk, leather, flour, coffee and wood—began to appear much more promising in the *new times* announced by JM Gálvez. Gálvez wished to demonstrate that the country was more than a giant, technologically advanced farm colonized by foreigners. For Gálvez it was urgent that the native professional class have a leading role, it was important to review labor conditions in the farms, it was necessary to diversify production and crucial to build at least three main highways throughout the country, considering that the country's rail system was one that Honduras had hardly any sovereignty over (the majority belonged to the fruit companies). Gálvez believed that his government should pass from one of a single agricultural product (bananas) to one of diversity, from manufacturing to industrialization.[xxix]

The IMF team promised the president that they would do their best to help the country create institutions that would facilitate his development programs. They left President Gálvez's office to the salutes and clicking of heels of his personal military guard.

The IMF team went to Congress to discuss the scope of work. They were pleasantly surprised when they were handed a completed draft for the legislation to establish the Central Bank. At first Paul hoped this would shorten their mission. However, after reading the draft, the team realized that most of it would have to be re-written.

On Saturday, July 9, the three went to the office of the Secretary of Agriculture, Benjamin Membreño. They had a three-hour meeting with him where they discussed Honduras's agricultural prospects and farmers' need for credit. Then they went to the Banco de Honduras to meet with the Chairman of the Board, Adolfo Midence, and the president of the bank. Congressman Tomás Cálix Moncada accompanied them. Everyone was embarrassed when the bank executives accused the president's commission, of which Congressman Cálix Moncada was a member, of failing to consult with them when drafting the legislation for the formation of the Central Bank. The IMF team had to adjourn the meeting before things got too agitated, and they promised the bankers to return in a few days without Cálix Moncada.

When they returned to their hotel, the three men still had hours of work left. They divided their duties, because while they were in Honduras, Márquez and McLeod were still working on projects in other countries. Since Paul was the lead economist on the Honduras mission, he was responsible for writing up the reports of every meeting they attended to his IMF superiors in Washington. It had not seemed appropriate to take notes during the meetings with Membreño and Midence, so the reports that night tested his memorization skills.

The next day being Sunday, there were no scheduled meetings. At lunch, hotel management informed them the government had arranged for them to have an honorary membership to the exclusive Country Club of Tegucigalpa. The men were happy to have a change of pace and went. It became apparent that everyone in Tegucigalpa was following their movements when, after they bowled three rounds and played some billiard, they were surprised by a visit from Adolfo Midence of the Bank of Honduras. He engaged them in "unofficial discussions" until 9:00 p.m.

The next day a letter arrived from Linda. She wrote to Paul, "Johnny is very interested in planes and seems to understand that you left in one. I can't tell you how much I've missed you. I hope you never have to go on a long trip again-two weeks is the limit. Last week I was almost ready to have you quit your job and come home."

One of Linda's biggest frustrations was that she did not know how to drive, so it was difficult to get groceries and take the children on outings. Before the trip Paul had arranged for some of the ladies in the neighborhood to borrow their car in return for giving Linda rides on occasion. The plan worked fairly well, but Linda spent a lot of time negotiating whose turn it was to use the car. She wrote to Paul, "When you come home, I'm going to learn to drive if it kills me!"

That week the IMF team met with the entire board of directors of the Banco de Honduras, discussing the participation of that institution in the creation of the Central Bank. The board expressed a great deal of opposition to the IMF mission plans. They remained frustrated about not being consulted by the Honduran government when it first started planning a central bank.

After the meeting, Adolfo Midence took them to his house for lunch. Midence and his wife Doña Maruca belonged to two of the oldest and wealthiest families in Honduras. Paul was surprised by the grandeur of their home: modeled after a French mansion, with enormous rooms, gilt antique furniture, tapestries on the walls, huge staircases, ornate silver, and marble statues. Their staff numbered more than twenty including four chauffeurs. On the ground floor was an enormous ballroom.

In the afternoon the IMF team met with Julio Lozano Díaz, the Vice President of Honduras, who Paul found to be very knowledgeable about the fiscal and financial matters of the country.

Once the scope of work was outlined, Paul knew he would remain in Honduras for some months. He wrote to Linda asking that she send him several cartons of cigarettes through the IMF, because they were expensive in Tegucigalpa. Communication with Linda was difficult, as there were no phone lines between Honduras and Washington. There was a radiophone, but it cost fourteen dollars for three minutes. They sent letters instead.

The Ministry of Finance provided an office for the IMF mission in their building downtown. Paul and Márquez worked on monetary and banking legislation, and McLeod worked on a fiscal and tax study. They worked long hours, often until midnight, and half days on Saturdays, as was the custom for businesses in Tegucigalpa.

Paul had a master's degree in economics. In Honduras at that time, few people had a master's degree, because the university didn't offer advanced degrees, and not many could afford to study abroad. Those with a four-year undergraduate degree were referred to as *Licenciado*. It didn't seem enough to address someone with a master's degree that way, so Hondurans addressed professionals with a master's degree as "Doctor". In the U.S. that meant one had achieved PhD or medical degree, but not in Honduras. Soon after his arrival, Paul became Dr. Vinelli. The title stuck for the rest of his life.

At the end of July, the IMF mission traveled to the north coast of Honduras, where most of the economic activity of the country took place. The major industry in Honduras was the production of bananas, hence the country being referred to as a "banana republic". Two American companies ran this business: United Fruit Company (who operated under the name Tela Railroad Company) and the Standard Fruit Company. President Galvez's worries about the country were well illustrated by the reality that in 1949, the capital of Honduras was somewhat cut off from business on the north coast because there were no paved roads nor railroads connecting it to Tegucigalpa. The banana companies had only built the transportation infrastructure they needed to move along the north coast, where their banana plantations and ports were. Airplane travel was new and expensive yet adopted quickly for travel between Tegucigalpa and the major cities in the north because the dirt roads were so bad.

Congressman Cálix Moncada traveled with the IMF team. The government had assigned him to escort them to their visits with fruit company executives, north coast bankers and merchants. Their flight departed from Tegucigalpa to San Pedro Sula. They had planned to drive twenty miles from there to the tiny town of La Lima, where the United Fruit Company had its headquarters. To their surprise, their commercial airline flight landed an hour later at the private airport of United Fruit in La Lima. They later learned that the company could request the flight stop there on the way to San Pedro if there were VIPs on board who needed to visit headquarters.

It was during this flight over the interior of Honduras that Paul learned how mountainous the country was. The only plains were found as they neared the north coast, and all this land was owned by the banana companies. It was beautiful: thousands of acres of lush, green cultivation, primarily bananas but also pineapple and African palm. From the plane they could see twenty-foot-high sprinkler systems spraying water over the plants. In 1949 the country was suffering from the worst drought since 1923, so the sprinklers were in use much more often than normal.

The moment the airplane doors opened, they really understood they were in the tropics. The north coast climate had nothing in common with temperate, mountainous Tegucigalpa. They were now at sea level, assaulted by heat and humidity. Despite immediately taking off their suit jackets, the men began to sweat profusely.

Three United Fruit Company executives met them and escorted them to the La Lima Hotel, where they had drinks and a filet mignon lunch. They then toured the company's operations and residential areas, where the company had built a swimming pool for the employees and a zoo of animals trapped on their grounds including *tigrillos*, a spotted leopard-like cat native to Central America. The executives' homes were very luxurious, each sitting on five to ten acres, surrounded by lush vegetation. The driveways leading to these houses were lined with seventy-foot-tall royal palm trees. Paul was fascinated with the breadfruit trees: tall, with shiny green leaves, and covered with fruit the size of large melons. Royal poinciana trees were everywhere, their umbrella-like canopies laden with red and orange blooms. The gardens were full of blooming plants, which Paul described as "a feast of color".

In the afternoon they were driven the short way to San Pedro Sula, the second-largest city in Honduras, where they met with prominent merchants and bankers. They toured the Coca Cola bottling operation which had air-conditioned offices, the first they had encountered in Honduras. After that visit, two United Fruit executives picked them up at the train station in a private rail car, to take them to the coastal town of Puerto Cortés. On this trip they passed palm and banana plantations, interspersed with miles of virgin forest. All along the railroad tracks they saw workers walking home from work, each carrying a machete. They learned that people followed the railroad tracks because there were no roads connecting major cities like San Pedro Sula and Puerto Cortés.

At a railroad intersection their train was stopped to let a banana train pass through. Paul was fascinated as the United Fruit men described the meticulous care taken in the packing of the bananas, which were destined to travel to New Orleans. Banana plants were split in half at the stem, and carefully wrapped clusters of fruit were cushioned within the halves for protection. Two hundred bunches were packed in each rail car. The train also stopped at a tiny village of five houses so the men could buy pineapple. The fruit company executives claimed these were the best pineapples in the world, and Paul agreed he had never tasted one more delicious. They were extremely juicy and sweet with no fiber whatsoever. They ate them with a spoon.

After dinner in Puerto Cortés, they went to the docks to watch the loading of bananas onto the ships headed north. Dock workers unloaded the banana clusters from the trains and carried them over their shoulders to an enormous elevator which carried the bananas to the ships' holds. Just before each cluster dropped into the elevator, a second man cut off the base of the stem with a machete. The process happened seamlessly, with the worker carrying the bananas not slowing down as the machete came down on his load.

By this time, it was 10:00 p.m. and the fruit company executives took them to a dilapidated honky-tonk called Mamacitas. Women-for-hire loitered at some tables, but the businessmen chose drinking over the bedraggled prostitutes. Mamacita, the owner, stood nearby ensuring their drinks were re-filled as soon as they were empty.

The next morning, after a breakfast of *huevos rancheros*, they went back to the wharf to observe what happened inside the ships' holds. The refrigerated ships each carried seventy-five thousand bunches of bananas. There were also luxurious staterooms which were available for passenger travel. Paul was surprised to learn that depending on the season and demand, it could be less expensive to fly to Honduras than to travel by United Fruit ship.

To end their tour, each visitor was invited to lug a seventy-pound cluster of bananas to the ship. Paul felt more than a bit uncomfortable when he walked past the man with the machete, and felt it fly past his head to remove the stem.

The afternoon was spent driving through plantations of exotic varieties of fruit trees that United Fruit was experimenting with, most of which Paul had never seen nor heard of before. When Paul asked about the strong scent of lemon in the air, he learned that they were surrounded by fields of citronella grasses, harvested for oil to be used in soaps. Overhead, monkeys languished in tree branches, doing their best not to move in the oppressive mid-day heat.

That evening they were hosted for drinks and dinner by J.F. Aycock, the General Manager of United Fruit. His enormous home was staffed with about twenty people running the house plus twenty gardeners managing the lush grounds. Paul described cocktail hour to Linda as "a heated discussion cooled off by half a dozen highballs. It is my impression that both men and women drink like fishes in the tropics". Dinner was a seven-course meal accompanied by several wines, followed by coffee and French cognac. At 11:00 p.m. everyone went to the country club for the last part of a formal dance which was held every Saturday night. More drinks followed, and at 1:00 a.m. they were told it was time for a swim. Paul and his team went back to the house where they were staying under the pretext of changing into bathing suits and headed to bed rather than to the pool.

It was a relief to return south to Tegucigalpa, where the mountains cooled the city and where everyone went to bed at 9:00 p.m. Paul was an exception: he stayed up past midnight the first several nights, dictating the details of the north coast trip for Edward Bernstein, his boss at the IMF Research Department.

On July 28 the team was driven to the Zamorano Pan-American Agricultural School. The distance from Tegucigalpa was only twenty miles, but the narrow unpaved road wound hairpin turns through tall pine tree covered mountains, so the drive took two hours. Paul was delighted to encounter surprises the whole way. There were goats grazing along the side of the road and wild orchids growing at the top of the mountains that sloped upwards at seventy-degree angles. At every turn there were breath-taking panoramic views of the purple-blue mountains. Suddenly the Zamorano Valley opened beneath them with a beautiful checkerboard of crops.

The agricultural school was founded by Samuel Zemurray, president of the United Fruit Company, to foster the vocation of agriculture for students that came primarily from Central and South America. Zamorano was not created to train United Fruit employees, but rather to share the company's knowledge for the purpose of furthering agricultural development Latin America. The caliber of education was very high: among the one hundred seventy-five students at the time Paul visited were the son of the president of Colombia, a member of the Dupont family and a member of the Rockefeller family.

The school was distinguished by the know-how to grow every kind of crop (sugar cane, rice, beans, coffee, grapefruit, oranges, bananas, wheat, potatoes, among others) in very poor soil. Students learned to fight for a crop in unfertile land. They also bred pigs, cows and goats.

Paul and his colleagues spent the day discussing the agricultural prospects for Honduras with the Founding Director of the Zamorano School,

Dr. Wilson Popenoe. He had been the chief agronomist for United Fruit until 1941 when Zemurray asked him to establish the school.[xxx]

When the IMF team returned to Tegucigalpa and their research, they ran into difficulties. Even though President Gálvez and the commission assigned to work with them were very supportive, Paul, Marquez and McLeod had to struggle to obtain statistical information from other Honduran entities such as the banks. It became difficult to complete their reports and draft legislation. Because Márquez and McLeod also worked in other Latin American countries during this time, they could compare the treatment they received. Both men observed that other governments were much more helpful.

On August 15, newspaper headlines stated that the IMF team was sabotaging the creation of an agricultural bank. The accusation was that they had been corrupted by the United Fruit Company because the company did not want Honduras to make the changes President Gálvez proposed. The members of the mission were labeled traitors to Honduras, serving American interests. [xxxi] The international representatives could not speak with the press as a matter of policy. Minister of Finance Batres assured the team that they were performing a great service for Honduras, and President Gálvez directed the commission they worked with to respond to the accusations. The next day the executive and congressional commissions published a rebuttal to the accusations: they defended the team's work and assured the country of their good will and excellent progress. Soon afterwards the newspaper printed a sheepish apology, claiming they had only repeated commentary they had overheard.

Paul asked the Honduran commission to organize a trip to the northern city of La Ceiba, where the Standard Fruit Company was headquartered. He wanted to meet with executives of the fruit company's bank, Banco Atlántida, which was also based there. When the authorization for the trip came, Paul went to meet Fernando Sempé who managed the bank's Tegucigalpa office. In Sempé's office he met John Miceli, an Italian American who was Vice-President of both the Standard Fruit Company and of Banco Atlántida. Miceli planned to return to La Ceiba the following week and offered to receive Paul at Banco Atlántida's headquarters.

On August 19 Paul, McLeod and Tomás Cálix Moncada traveled to La Ceiba. McLeod was to call on the Standard Fruit Company and Paul on Banco Atlántida. They were met at the airport by a delegation from both the Standard Fruit and the bank. After dropping off Paul's suitcase at the Hotel Paris, the delegation took him on a tour of a grapefruit packing operation. Then he went to Banco Atlántida's headquarters. The art deco building was built in 1913, one block from the original banana company dock on the Atlantic Ocean. Angled facing the corner of First Street and Avenida San Isidro, the building was elegant, with teller booths of brass and marble. Paul met with Felix Lloveras, the bank's CEO. Their meeting was soon interrupted because work stopped for lunch at 11:00 a.m. in La Ceiba. After the meal came siesta time. Paul returned in the afternoon and spent several hours learning about the bank's systems. At dinner that night he tried something new: fried *mazapán*, or breadfruit. This experience initiated his lifelong love for the tropical savory appetizer.

The next morning, Paul and McLeod went to the wharf to see bananas loaded onto a Standard Fruit ship, *The Cefalú*. This company had a ship arrive every week, empty of the bananas that were offloaded in the U.S. and carrying tourists. For these guests a dance was held in the company mess hall on Saturday nights. Paul, McLeod and Cálix Moncada were invited to the dance. After enough drinks, Paul convinced the band to let him play the drums. As far as I can tell he had never played a musical instrument before, nor since.

On Sunday Felix Lloveras hosted them for lunch at his apartment on the second floor of the Banco Atlántida building. He and his gracious wife Robbie, both originally from New Orleans, lived over the bank's offices in a home with views of the Atlantic Ocean. The apartment was decorated with elegant antiques purchased in New Orleans and shipped to La Ceiba on a Standard Fruit Company banana boat.

Lloveras also invited John Miceli and his wife, a much-younger Honduran woman named Iris Ulargui. During their conversation Paul learned that Miceli was the brother-in-law of one of the founders of Standard Fruit, Salvador D'Antoni, who at that time was the chair of Banco Atlántida. La Ceiba was a small place: Miceli's wife Iris was previously married to Felix Vaccaro, one of the three brothers who co-founded Standard Fruit with D'Antoni. As the luncheon lasted late into the day, Paul reflected on the wonderful time he was having in this exotic country, where the work was challenging and rewarding and where his hosts treated him as if he were royalty.

Linda was having the opposite experience. Washington, D.C. was experiencing a heat wave and both boys had heat rashes. Water was rationed and often cut off by 4:00 p.m., so she had to fill their bathtub early in the day to have water for three evening baths. She was still nursing nine-month-old Craig. Both he and his two-year-old brother Johnny were very active and into constant mischief. One day, Johnny fed Craig a lima bean. Linda turned away from the stove in time to see that Craig was blue. She held him upside-down by his feet and slapped his back until the bean came out of his mouth. Later that same day, Craig was crawling near the stairs where Linda had set an open can of paint (she was painting the living room as a surprise for Paul's return). She had run to the kitchen to get Craig's highchair and when she turned towards the stairs, she saw that her baby had learned to crawl up a step. He pulled the can of paint all over himself before she could get to him. Linda spent the rest of the day cleaning paint from both Craig and the stairs and comforting two crying boys.

The IMF visit to Honduras lasted two months. The Washington economists crafted a plan and legislation for the creation of a Central Bank which would handle the business of the Honduran government, a National Development Bank which would make loans for the development of local industry, as well as banking and tax regulatory policies.

For the tax legislation Paul had worked with Gabriel Mejía, who was the tax revenue administrator for President Tiburcio Carías Andino from 1940-1949. (Later, when the new tax legislation was passed, Mejía was named Director for the newly created General Bureau of Income Revenues and remained in that position until 1956.)[xxxii] Paul and Mejía forged a professional relationship that turned into a close friendship over time.

The Honduran Congress quickly approved the income tax law that the two men and the government commission drafted. They had recommended a maximum rate for individuals of twenty-five percent, but the congress reduced the amount to between two and fifteen percent, depending on income level. Most Hondurans would pay no income tax, because they did not meet the minimum income threshold. Corporate income taxes were set at between four and fifteen percent.

In mid-September, Paul returned to Washington carrying gifts for Linda and his sons. He had bought Linda an elegant alligator handbag and matching shoes, and a blouse. He was excited to show Linda a machete that had been used to kill wild animals as well as used for a weapon, which he thought would make a great butcher knife for their home. Linda was not happy about having it in the house with two little boys.

When Paul returned to the IMF office there was a mountain of work waiting for him. The representatives were busy working on monetary devaluations, because the IMF had to approve all devaluations before a member country could announce it. Paul stayed at the office until late many nights and on weekends.

News from Honduras was that the congress was preparing to vote on the laws for the creation of a Central Bank and National Development Bank. Paul's boss at the IMF told him that if the laws were approved, Paul would most likely be asked to move to Honduras for six months, or as long as it took to get the new banks created and operating successfully. When Paul discussed the possibility with Linda, she was a bit nervous about moving to a third world country. He pointed out that he would travel much less if he was stationed in Honduras. And that the move was for a short while. Linda was strongly in favor of Paul being at home more and started adjusting to the possibility of a move.

That Fall, Paul and Linda's social life in Washington picked up significantly. Paul wanted to broaden his professional contacts and took every opportunity to connect with people. It was likely that his time in Honduras had reminded him how much he enjoyed socializing. The couple began to attend embassy cocktail parties, and Paul often invited new friends to drop by their house, giving Linda little notice. She saw the Vinella-Casavola social side emerge in her husband.

Paul and a colleague were sent to Quito, Ecuador on a mission in December. Paul's first impression was that Quito was very similar to Tegucigalpa, with red-tiled-roof homes surrounded by mountains. The major difference was that Quito's altitude was much higher. One cold, rainy afternoon the two economists were being driven from their hotel in the suburbs towards the Ecuadorian Central Bank in the center of Quito. As they neared the main plaza, the men were amazed to see a large crowd of indigenous women, bundled in colorful woven wool dresses, carrying their "red-cheeked papooses" on their backs. Women not carrying babies had lambs, chicken, ducks or pigs on their backs. Some carried very heavy loads: hundred-pound bags of cement or pieces of furniture.

At the Central Bank, the IMF team first met with Guillermo Perez Chiriboga, General Manager, and then with Mr. Ormaza, president of the Monetary Board. After spending the afternoon gathering statistics for their reports, they met the Minister of Economy, Clemente Yerovi. After dinner at a downtown restaurant, Perez Chiriboga and Ormaza took them to meet the president of the country, Galo Plaza Lasso de la Vega. They spent a pleasant hour together. Paul wrote to Linda that the Ecuadorian president spoke better English than he did. The Minister of Economy was present at the meeting but left out of the conversation because he did not speak English. This worked to the advantage of the IMF team, because the minister disagreed with their proposed solutions to Ecuador's monetary and exchange difficulties. Galo Plaza Lasso seemed amenable to adopting the suggestions of the IMF, so the group left his office encouraged. Paul returned home from Ecuador just in time for Christmas, and he gave Linda a painting he bought in Quito. My brother Bob still has it. That trip launched Paul's lifetime appreciation for Latin American art.

Paul's trip to Ecuador created another setback for his efforts to obtain U.S. citizenship, something he had been attempting since he moved from Italy fourteen years earlier. He had been scheduled to appear in Federal Court on December 20, and he had to postpone his hearing for January. That same month he started the process of obtaining passports for Linda, Johnny, and Craig so that they would be ready to travel if the move to Honduras became a reality.

In mid-February Paul and Linda were told they would be moving to Tegucigalpa in two weeks. The IMF and the Honduran government had reached an agreement where Paul would remain an IMF employee with his salary paid by them, while moving expenses and his apartment in Tegucigalpa would be paid by the Hondurans. Paul and Linda sold their car but kept their house in Washington. They were encouraged to take their furniture to furnish their temporary apartment in Tegucigalpa. They were relieved when a friend agreed to adopt their dog Zulu.

In March of 1950, Paul, Linda, Johnny (age 2 ½), and Craig (age 1 ½) traveled from New York City to Puerto Cortes, Honduras on a United Fruit ship, a two-week trip. The voyage was a wonderful vacation for all of them and especially restful for Linda. She loved having Paul's help caring for their two active boys. After a first day of choppy seas, the seas became calm for the remainder of the voyage. Every day they sailed into a warmer climate. Their banana boat could accommodate twelve passengers. It was returning to Honduras with its cargo holds empty of bananas. The staterooms were also empty, except for the Vinelli family. They had two luxurious staterooms and the passenger lounge all to themselves. Linda was dazzled by the attentive service from the ship's stewards.

They arrived in Puerto Cortés, Honduras on March 17. When they disembarked from the ship the humid, hot air hit them with force. Coconut trees popped randomly out of the pale grey sand on the beaches, waving their fronds flirtatiously over clear, turquoise-blue ocean water. Their drive inland towards the San Pedro Sula airport took them past enormous banana plantations that stretched for miles. Linda had never seen, felt or smelled a tropical world like this one.

They boarded a plane in San Pedro Sula to fly south to the capital, Tegucigalpa. The occasional valley broke up what looked like a sea of mountains, covered densely with trees. Some were as high as ten thousand feet. When they landed in Tegucigalpa less than an hour later, it felt like they were in a different country. The capital was cool and dry, surrounded by a bowl of green-purple mountains.

The family spent the first five days at the Gran Hotel Lincoln. Since the hotel had no connecting rooms, they all stayed in one room. Johnny and Craig were restless and unhappy in such confined quarters, so Paul immediately hired a maid to help Linda take the children to the park every morning. He got straight to work.

The government of Honduras, through Finance Minister Marco Batres, appointed a Committee for the Organization of National

Banks.[xxxiii] This committee was headed by Congressman Tomás Cálix Moncada and included: Roberto Ramirez (an attorney who became the first chairman of the Central Bank), Adolfo Midence (President of Banco de Honduras), and Congressman Guillermo Lopez Rodezno (who became president of the National Development Bank).[xxxiv] Other advisors included Arturo Medrano (an attorney who became the first CEO of the Central Bank), Oscar Bueso Arias, René Cruz, and Samuel Dacosta.

Paul, representing the IMF, was an external advisor to the committee. The group met for the first time on March 21, 1950. Their ambitious goal was to establish a Central Bank (Banco Central) and a National Development Bank (Banco de Fomento), and for both banks to begin operations on July 1, only three months later. Honduran newspapers reported with excitement the hope of these banks encouraging the national economy in three sectors: agriculture, industry and commerce. [xxxv]

There were almost no economists in the country because the national university did not teach the subject. For these banks to succeed, Honduran economists needed to be trained. To accomplish this, the committee set the groundwork for a School of Economics at the national university of Honduras (Universidad Autónoma de Honduras, or UNAH).

The Honduran government had rented a very nice apartment for Paul and Linda downtown. They moved in less than a week after arriving. Linda, who was fastidious, declared it filthy and worked hard to clean it to her standards. She loved the apartment, though, which had two living rooms, dining room, kitchen, two huge bedrooms and a bath all wrapped around a center patio, plus a maid's room and bath.

Linda was glad they had shipped all their furniture. There was almost no industry in Honduras so everything from household furnishings to canned food was imported, and therefore three times more expensive than in the U.S. The only things that were cheap were food products produced locally. The weather was her favorite part about Tegucigalpa. She wrote to her parents, "It is plain marvelous. I've never seen anything like it. It's never really hot here, nor ever really cool, the temperature variation during the day is slight and the humidity is always low—perfect weather for Johnny's tonsils." Linda loved having a maid to help her with cleaning and with Johnny and Craig, despite the challenge that Linda spoke limited Spanish, and the maid spoke no English.

Soon after the March 21 committee meeting, Paul began to travel. He first traveled around Honduras to ascertain the credit situation in the country. On April 4 he met with the executive team of Banco Atlántida in La Ceiba. In April he flew to Guatemala City with Max Jiménez Pinto, the General Manager of the Bank of Guatemala. Jiménez Pinto had already traveled to Tegucigalpa to see what was needed, and he and Paul flew back to Guatemala to get more help. They added to the team Joaquín Prieto Barrios, Superintendent of Bank of Guatemala and Ramiro Aragón Castañeda, Auditor of Bank of Guatemala [xxxvi]

On April 13 Paul flew to San Salvador, where he met with Jorge Sol Castellanos, the Minister of Economy, and Rafael Meza Ayau, the president of the Mortgage Bank of El Salvador. Paul asked these men to assign some of their bankers specialized in agricultural lending to help the Honduran government. The bankers agreed immediately to send a Salvadoran team.[xxxvii] Who they selected were

Benjamín Vides Segui, an accountant with the Mortgage Bank of El Salvador, and Carlos Perez Figueroa, an economist with Ministry of Finance of El Salvador.[xxxviii] Another expert from El Salvador had joined the National Development Bank team: Efraín Calderón, who had worked on the organization of the Banco Territorial in the Dominican Republic.[xxxix]

On April 25 Vittorio Marrama arrived from the International Bank for Reconstruction and Development (IBRD), an arm of the World Bank based in Washington, D.C. He was tasked specifically to work on the National Development Bank. Marrama was expected to stay for a long time, so he brought his wife and two young daughters. They moved into a hotel.

A Salvadoran banking expert named Alfonso Rochac arrived from New York to help him.[xl] Dr. Rochac was sent by the United Nations Economic Commission for Latin America. His primary task was to travel throughout Honduras to select locations where credit work would begin. He met with coffee producers, local authorities, and parties interested in increasing agribusiness. Paul and other members of the committee usually traveled with him to make these evaluations. The populations of the many small towns they visited were very excited about the visits, given that the purpose was to improve the business conditions of those towns.[xli]

Honduras was poor and underdeveloped even by Central American/Caribbean standards. Only eleven percent of the population lived in a town with a population greater than five thousand people. Railroads mostly serviced the northern part where the two large American banana companies, United Fruit and Standard Fruit, operated. There were very few roads connecting the rest of the country and no paved roads except inside the major cities. There were many rivers, but none large enough to travel by ship.[xlii]

By the end of April, the government decided where the organizing committee would work. In front of the Presidential Palace in downtown Tegucigalpa was a building called La Urbana that the Honduran government had purchased from a casino during a previous administration. Next to it was another building called the Presidential Palace annex. These two buildings were where the enormous changes to Honduras's economy were drafted, and where the Central and National Development Banks would be located until they could build their own buildings.

Given Paul's central role in organizing the international teams, he and Linda did a great deal of business entertaining. Linda enjoyed having people drop in now that she had a maid. She and Paul also frequently went out for a couple of hours in the evening. This was a welcome change from her solitary days in D.C. while Paul traveled on IMF mission trips. She spent a lot of time sewing because she did not have the clothes for their new social lifestyle. Women in Tegucigalpa dressed beautifully, nobody wore cotton house dresses like she had in Washington.

Linda's quality of life had improved, but she was terribly bothered by the poverty all around her. People lived in shacks with no running water and electricity. Barefoot women carrying tremendous baskets on their heads came to her door every day selling vegetables. She was thankful that the weather in Honduras was mild, so they did not suffer from the cold.

There was no pasteurized milk in Tegucigalpa, so for the boys Linda bought milk that was flown in from San Pedro Sula. The milk she used for cooking was brought in by a boy on a donkey from the mountains every day. This boy also brought her eggs, and he killed and dressed several chickens a week for her. Butcher shops only carried red meat because people bought live chickens at market and killed them at home. Beef was cheap except for the tenderloin cut. Most people and most stores did not have refrigerators. Linda bought canned goods sparingly at an American store because they were very expensive.

Linda had not yet ventured into a Honduran store because she heard they were very dirty. Her maid bought fruits and vegetables for her at the market. Linda boiled all their water and washed the produce with a strong soap and water solution. Despite the differences from her life in Washington, she was happy. Paul was around more, she had help with the cleaning and the children, and she was starting to make friends.

On May 10, the joint banking missions hosted an elegant dinner in honor of the newly appointed:

Chairman of the Central Bank: Roberto Ramirez
Vice-chairman of the Central Bank: Tomás Cálix Moncada
CEO of the Central Bank: Arturo Medrano
Chairman of the National Development Bank: Guillermo López Rodezno

Paul was the main organizer of the evening. His attention to detail and good appetite were evident. The menu was: lobster cocktail, cream of vegetable soup, steamed snapper, salad, paella of seafood, sausage and chicken, fruit chiffon cake, coffee, Alsacian white wine,

Bordeaux red wine, and Veuve Cliquot champagne. A live orchestra accompanied the festivities.[xliii]

Since his first visit to Honduras a year before, Paul had collaborated with Javier Márquez, Alexander McLeod, and a third economist named Julio Gonzalez del Solar on a comprehensive economic analysis of Honduras. Their work, *Estudio Sobre la Economía de Honduras*, was published June of 1950. Before this, no one had ever analyzed the country's economy so thoroughly.

Americans in Honduras received worrisome news from home during this time. The U.S. entered the Korean War on June 25, 1950. Linda worried about her brother Otto being drafted. Paul worried about being able to buy a car when they returned to Washington, if auto manufacturers converted to war production like they had during World War II.

Paul, Vittorio Marrama and the Honduran committee accomplished their work right on time. On July 1, 1950, both banks opened. The date coincided with Johnny's third birthday.

The effect of new banking and tax legislation, and a new Central Bank and National Development Bank, was transformational for the economy of Honduras. The monetary reform these men designed completely changed the Honduran government's relationship to the country's currency, called the lempira. This currency had been introduced twenty years before in 1931 by both Banco Atlántida and Banco de Honduras. Lempira was a Honduran national hero, a native war chieftain who had been killed by the Spanish *conquistadores* as he fought to prevent the enslavement of his people.[xliv] When the Honduran Central Bank opened it became the only issuer of currency—the other two banks stopped printing money. The Central

Bank kept the name of the currency, lempira.[xlv] With this change the Honduran government achieved seigniorage, the profit made from issuing money. This profit allowed the Central Bank to finance government operations.

The Honduran government asked the IMF and IBRD representatives to head a Department of Economic Studies that was created at the Central Bank. Paul oversaw economic and monetary policy, and Emmanuel Tosco ran the statistics area. The department had sixteen employees, most of whom had only a basic background in accounting. To train them, Paul and the other foreign advisors created a School of Economics at the Universidad Autónoma de Honduras (UNAH). Classes started the same month the two banks were formed. Paul and Tosco taught at the university, so their employees were also their students.

The School of Economics was designed for students that worked full time, so the curriculum was spread out over four years and students were given a choice of one-hour class times outside of working hours: 7:00 – 8:00 a.m., 1:00 – 2:00 p.m., 6:00 – 7:00 p.m., and 7:00 – 8:00 p.m. Paul alternated his teaching schedule: one semester he taught a 7:00 a.m. class, the next semester a 6:00 p.m. class.

The first year Paul taught Money and Credit. The class covered the function of money and money creation (the process by which the money supply of a country is increased). The course also explained the functions of a central bank and the operations of commercial banks. The second year his course was Money and Banking, which built on what students learned the first year. The third year he taught International Commerce in two parts, theory and policy. His series culminated in the fourth year with Public Finance, where students analyzed taxes, public spending, public debt and fiscal policy.

I was interested to learn that half of the employees in the Department of Economic Studies were women, which was surprising for Latin America in the early 1950's. According to former colleagues, Paul always championed women getting an education and building careers. One of his students, Maria Isabel Martel, described what it was like to have Dr. Vinelli as both a boss and professor. In the book *Doctor Paul Vinelli, Biografías Ilustradas*, she wrote,

"His knowledge of the subjects he taught was deep. He was excellent at explaining complex points in a clear manner. He knew how to mix economic theory and policy, by citing examples of what was happening in Honduras at the time. This clear manner extended to his written work. He prepared for us a pamphlet on Money and Credit that was so understandable that it was a great tool for understanding the function of money.

He was a strict grader. It was very difficult to get a good grade in his class. To correctly answer his exam questions required not only a lot of studying, but the ability to analyze well.

He believed that the profession of economics required perpetual study. He recommended that we buy and read books if we wanted to increase and update our knowledge on the subject. Since most of the books about economics were written in English, he felt it was essential that we learn that language.

His teaching continued at work. If he was strict as a professor, he was even more so as a boss. He required that we be efficient and analytical when he asked us a question about the economy." [xlvi]

Dr. Vinelli teaching his economics students, who were older than typical college students because most were his employees at the Central Bank of Honduras.

It surprised me to learn that Paul taught university level economics in Spanish so soon after arriving in Honduras. He had only studied Spanish for only a few years in college. The Latin he learned in grammar school in Italy must have helped him learn Spanish quickly. Also, the first year spent analyzing the Honduran economy must have given him a crash course in economic terminology. Colleagues who knew him during his early days in Honduras told me that his spoken Spanish was excellent compared to that of many foreign advisors sent to Honduras. He did need help with grammar for the Central Bank reports and books he wrote, and for that he turned to his staff.

Nobody in Honduras spoke Italian so Paul rarely used his native language. He had a heavy accent when speaking English or Spanish, and the speech mannerism he developed during childhood was noticeable. When he gave a speech or taught class, he often had to pause to retrieve a word. Every time this happened, he filled the pause with a term that sounded like "la-hay". We think it stood for "Let's say". Carlos Flores, a former president of Honduras, told me that he believed Paul had hired a speech therapist, who suggested he find some word to use as a place holder when the pauses came. The phrase should signal to him "Go ahead".[xlvii]

The employees of the Department of Economic Studies of the Central Bank spent so much time together at work and school that they became close to each other and to their professors. Paul liked to organize weekend picnics in the countryside where Linda, Johnny and Craig joined him and the class for recreation. As they became good friends, Paul's playful side became evident. During his early morning classes, if he saw a student falling asleep, he'd take a piece of chalk from the blackboard and throw it at them to wake them up.

He cared about each student's progress and made a greater effort than is normally expected of a professor. One of his employees and students was Macky Salinas. Bright and feisty, she shrugged off the pronounced limp caused by a childhood bout with polio and could be found at a party most nights. She delayed completing the thesis that he required of his students before they could take the final exam. When Paul urged Macky to finish the thesis she resisted, laughing as she informed her professor and boss that she was more interested in going out with friends than studying. He finally called her into his office and told her, "I won't be able to give you a raise unless you have the credentials of an economist. Finish your thesis and I'll help you study for the exam." He did, and she passed.[xlviii]

After students finished the four-year curriculum, Paul encouraged them to travel to the United States, both to obtain a master's degree and to improve their English. He arranged for the Central Bank to provide scholarships to postgraduate programs at Yale, Harvard, NYU, and University of Michigan, among others. This practice was continued by the Central Bank for years and formed some of the best economists in Honduras.[xlix] When employees returned from studying abroad, Paul emphasized their moral obligation to share what they had learned by teaching at the university. These initiatives are why Paul is credited with educating so many of the top Honduran economists.

Guillermo Bueso, who chaired the Central Bank of Honduras and was later chairman and CEO of Banco Atlántida,[12] was one of Paul's most accomplished students. He said that Paul taught, "It is better to be criticized for acting, creating and building when one has the chance; than to later be criticized for having had an opportunity and not doing anything towards the development of Honduras."[l]

---

12. This was Guillermo Bueso Sr. who succeeded Paul as CEO and later chairman of Banco Atlántida. In 2026 his son Guillermo Bueso Anduray is the CEO of Banco Atlántida.

6

TEGUCIGALPA BECOMES HOME
1950 – 1955

While Paul was learning to be a professor, Linda was learning the ways of Hondurans. Three months after they arrived in Tegucigalpa, their maid became ill with malaria. Linda took her to a doctor who gave her medicine and sent her home to recover. When the lady returned to work, she confessed to one of Linda's friends that she had not taken the medicine because her family was suspicious about taking pills. The friend warned Linda that her family could be at risk for malaria if a mosquito bit their maid and then one of them. Linda fired her, in disbelief that she now had maid trouble, when a few months earlier she wouldn't have dreamt of ever having a maid.

Her brother Otto, intrigued about Honduras, asked if he could come work in Tegucigalpa for a few months. Linda warned him that he wouldn't earn much. The average laborer in Honduras made fifty cents a day in 1950. Her observation was that Hondurans produced one tenth of what people in the United States could, because Honduran methods and tools were so primitive. She described to Otto the remodeling of the post office near their apartment. Large blocks of blue granite were being installed around the front entrance. One by one the blocks were brought down the mountain into town, carried on the backs of both donkeys and men. The blocks were polished by hand and cut with a little saw, like a meat slicer one used at home. Then they were chipped with a small chisel and polished. She watched a man work on a single block for over two weeks. Linda told Otto that office salaries were better, between forty and one hundred dollars a month. She and Paul had concluded that the money to be made in Honduras was not in working for others, but in starting new ventures. The country was in many ways like the U.S. had been one hundred years prior, there was much industry to be developed.

Paul wanted Linda to learn about the rest of Honduras during their six months in the country. When possible, he took her and the boys with him on business trips. In mid-July the family went to the north coast of Honduras. They started in La Ceiba, where Paul needed to do research at Banco Atlántida's headquarters. This oceanfront town, built by the banana industry, was mostly populated by Spanish-speaking *mestizos* of combined indigenous and European heritage. It was a tropical paradise, where salty breezes battled air so humid you could chew it. When Paul finished his workday, the family went to the beach which was only a few blocks from the bank. He and Linda took Johnny and Craig for their first "swim" in the turquoise Caribbean Sea, which felt like warm bath water compared to the ocean in Maine or the lakes in Michigan.

A few days later they flew the short distance to Roatán on a tiny propeller plane. This beautiful Honduran island was discovered by Christopher Columbus in the 1500's and was settled by English-speaking people of both European and British-Afro-Caribbean heritage. It felt incredible to Linda that she was in Honduras but surrounded by English speakers. The family spent a few days exploring the mountainous island surrounded by transparent blue-green waters. Here the Caribbean was populated with brightly colored coral reefs filled with exotic tropical fish. [li]

In August Paul took the opportunity of a business trip to San Salvador and Guatemala City to show Linda and the boys two new countries. Paul had friends in both places who showed the family around. San Salvador was a hot, busy and thriving capital. Guatemala City was cooler and immaculately maintained. Linda was delighted by the colorful dresses the indigenous women and children wore.

Paul had an agreement with the Honduran government to stay for six months which ended in October. The IMF urged Paul to return to Washington at that time because they were short-staffed. In September, the Hondurans asked that Paul be permitted to stay in Tegucigalpa longer because the newly formed Central Bank was going through one crisis after another. The IMF agreed to an extension, but only until December.

At the end of November, Linda began packing their apartment in anticipation of moving the family back to Washington by Christmas. Two weeks before their moving day, President Gálvez called Paul to his office and asked if he would stay in Honduras for another year. The government had obtained the funds to pay him directly. Paul informed President Gálvez that he did not want to resign from his job with the International Monetary Fund but would consider staying another year if the IMF granted him a leave of absence. He promised to ask his boss about it when in Washington.

In early December Paul and Linda shipped their belongings, and a week later they traveled with their little boys on a United Fruit steamship from Puerto Cortes to New York. After a train ride to Washington, Linda unpacked their belongings in their Falls Church home which their tenants had vacated. While she prepared for Christmas, Paul took a train to Portland, Maine. On December 19, 1950, Paul finally received his Certificate of Naturalization, becoming a U.S. citizen more than fifteen years after arriving to the country. As part of this process, he was required to renounce his Italian citizenship.

The week before Christmas Paul returned to the offices of the IMF and reconnected with his former colleagues. He told his boss about the offer President Gálvez had made for Paul to return to Honduras for one more year. The management team at the IMF agreed to the idea, because they saw the importance of ensuring the success of the newly formed Central Bank. The IMF granted Paul a leave of absence to return to Honduras and continue his work, this time as an employee of the Honduran government. When Paul called to book passage on a banana boat out of New York, he learned that the earliest reservation was for March. He secured passage for the family.

He began 1951 doing small projects for the IMF while he and Linda prepared their house to rent for the next year. This time they were not going to take all their furniture to Tegucigalpa, it was too much work. The government of Honduras assured Paul that they would find him a furnished apartment. On weekends Paul re-plastered windows and Linda painted rooms. The hardest job was keeping Johnny and Craig, who were cooped up in the house because of the cold weather outside, from getting into the paint. At the end of January, they found a tenant who committed to lease the furnished house for a year.

Paul was surprised by a call from the Honduran government in early February, informing him that United Fruit was sending an unplanned ship from New York to Honduras to pick up an extra load of bananas. They could travel on the ship if they could get to New York in a day and a half. Paul and Linda packed in a hurry and made it to New York in time for the voyage south. Once the family was settled on board Linda remembered something she had left in their backyard: the sled Johnny had been given by the Reismans for Christmas. She thought, "He won't need it in Tegucigalpa!"

They again lived at the Lincoln Hotel until their rental house was ready. It was a great house: near Paul's office downtown, with two large patios where Johnny and Craig could play and get some fresh air. Five blocks away there was a park where the boys could run. Most houses in Honduras still had wood stoves, so Linda was delighted that the landlord had installed a butane gas stove (the concept was new to Honduras) and a water heater.

One of Paul's new roles was advisor to the Central Bank's board of directors. The board included the heads of the few existing Honduran banks. These men were not very familiar with central banking and economic policy. One of them was Jorge Bueso Arias, who had just founded Banco de Occidente that year. I interviewed Bueso Arias in 2018, the day before his ninety-ninth birthday. He told me how much Paul taught him when Bueso Arias was on that first Central Bank board. Back then, Bueso Arias commuted to Tegucigalpa from his home in the mountain town of Santa Rosa de Copán. After board meetings, he left Tegucigalpa and drove back to Santa Rosa, where he studied the economics and banking policy theories Paul taught him. Because Santa Rosa did not have electricity, he hurried to finish studying by the time the sun set at 6:30, since it was more difficult to read by candlelight. He told me he did this in preparation for his debates with "Paolo", as he called him, at the next board meeting. Through these exchanges the two men gained mutual respect and friendship, and as banking leaders they continued to debate the economic and financial policy of Honduras for decades.[lii]

That summer, on July 5, 1951, Paul was decorated by President Gálvez for his role in the creation of the Central Bank.[13]

Paul cared about developing the Central Bank in more ways than in banking structure and policy. He valued sports and socialization and believed they fostered a healthy and collaborative working environment. In the summer of 1951, at his suggestion, the Central Bank inaugurated the Social Club for Central Bank Staff and Employees. [liii]

During the first years Paul was in Honduras he befriended Luis (Chito) Kafie. Chito was a man of Palestinian descent who was born in El Salvador and moved to Honduras in the 1930s. He married Elena (Nena), a Honduran woman also of Palestinian descent. They owned a successful textile business in downtown Tegucigalpa. Chito and Paul were both young and enterprising. Despite their modest beginnings, their intellect and drive destined both for great success. Over the years they became like brothers, and as their families grew, they grew together.

That July Paul learned that a Navy Commander who was their neighbor back in Falls Church, Virginia was anxious to sell his

---

13. See Appendix for a list of all of Paul's decorations from various governments.

house. Paul knew the white stucco house—it was much larger and nicer than Paul and Linda's. It had four bedrooms, two baths, living room with fireplace, dining room, and a kitchen with all the latest electric appliances including a dishwasher and garbage disposal. It also boasted a full basement. Paul and Linda had dreamed of buying a larger home when they returned to Washington because they both wanted more children. Paul now had the money to afford it. He flew to Washington and bought the house for $21,500. Paul gave the Commander plenty of time to move out since he intended to leave it empty until their return the following March. He planned to sell their old house at that time, when their renters' lease expired.

As if the house purchase had been a cue, in August Linda wrote to Paul while he was on a business trip to Panama, informing him that he was going to be a father again. He was extremely happy and urged her to take afternoon naps and drink two quarts of milk daily.

When word got around the Central Bank that Paul had bought the house, his employers faced the reality that their advisor would be leaving the following March. Roberto Ramirez, chairman of the Central Bank, called Paul's colleague and friend Macky to his office and asked her what she thought would keep Paul in Honduras. Macky told him that Linda was tiring of their temporary status in Tegucigalpa. They were getting only short-term commitments from the Hondurans, which meant moving back and forth from Washington on short notice to live in a different rental house every year. Linda and Paul wanted to live in their own home and have a more stable base with which to raise their growing family. Paul had told Macky, "My family comes before anything."[liv]

Dr. Ramirez wanted Paul to continue advising him and immediately worked to remedy the situation. He asked Paul to agree to stay in Tegucigalpa for two additional years. To entice him, he offered several things. First, a promotion: in addition to continuing as advisor to the board of the Central Bank, he would also be named advisor to Minister of Finance Batres. Second, a raise: his combined salary for the two positions would be $18,000 per year. Third, the government offered to build him a house. Paul said he and Linda would consider the offer.

He went home to discuss it with Linda. Their current plan was to return to the States in March because Paul was to report to the IMF at the end of his leave of absence. Their third child was due to be born in May, and Paul and Linda wanted the baby to be born in Washington. They had a new house waiting for them that Linda wanted to see. They decided they would return to Washington in early 1952 as planned. If Paul decided to accept the offer to return to Tegucigalpa for two more years, they would do so after their baby was born.

On November 7, 1951, Paul celebrated his twenty-ninth birthday at their rental home in Tegucigalpa. The Central Bank threw the party for seventy guests, sending over the food, whiskey, sodas and an enormous birthday cake. Clearly, he was being courted.

Linda began December as she did every year, baking fruitcakes. She quickly became frustrated by the lack of variety in Honduran grocery stores—she had to go all over town to find the ingredients she needed. While she baked with the boys' "help", she thought about the offer the Central Bank had made to Paul. There were things about living in Honduras that Linda very much enjoyed. But she missed the United States, especially at Christmastime. Even though they had bought a fresh pine tree to decorate the house, it felt strange to be getting ready for Christmas in warm weather and with flowers in bloom. Linda missed the cold weather and possibility of snow.

December was a very social time in Honduras, and Paul enjoyed having many parties to attend. On the nights they didn't have plans, he and Linda talked about their options. Paul loved the work he did with the Central Bank, and he loved teaching at the university. The offer the government had made was very generous. Most importantly, their quality of life was better in Tegucigalpa. Paul traveled less. The household help they could afford made life easier for Linda, who was now expecting their third child. Having live-in help allowed Paul and Linda to have a social life in the evenings. This social interaction was becoming increasingly important to Paul, for professional and social reasons. All these things outweighed the benefits of the contacts he made because he was a representative of the International Monetary Fund. Paul decided to resign from the IMF.

He told Dr. Ramirez that he needed to return to Washington in March. He wanted to wrap things up with the IMF, sell his old Falls Church house, rent out his new house, and wait for his child to be born. After that he would return to Honduras and work for the Central Bank for two more years. There was one part of the offer that Paul did not feel comfortable about: the bank building him a house. Dr. Ramirez offered instead to extend him a fifty-thousand-dollar line of credit, interest-free.

He also had a suggestion for where Paul might want to build. By 1951 many people were moving away from downtown Tegucigalpa, because it had become a business center. The city had been founded in 1578 with streets designed for horses and carriages, not cars. The congestion caused by automobile traffic was miserable, and the narrow sidewalks were no place for the boys to run and play. Dr. Ramirez's secretary was a woman named Trinita Lara, whose family owned land in an area that was considered outside of the city. Trinita told Paul that her family had just divided their land into lots for sale. He and Linda visited the area and fell in love with the wide-open spaces. They decided to begin construction on a new house as soon as possible, so that the work would have progressed by the time they returned. Theirs would be one of the first houses to be built in Colonia Lara.

Linda and Paul traveled with Johnny and Craig to Washington in March of 1952. Linda and the boys were excited to explore their beautiful new Falls Church house even though they knew they would only be there a short time. Paul immediately went to the IMF and resigned. He assured his colleagues that he would see them at the IMF/World Bank meetings every September. Then he got to work on selling the old Falls Church house and finding a renter for the new one, which they planned to keep. Linda and he traveled to New York City to buy furniture and fixtures for the house they were building in Tegucigalpa, which they shipped by banana boat to Honduras.

Linda went into labor after midnight on Saturday, April 26. Paul ran next door and woke up a neighbor to ask that she stay at his house where the boys were sleeping while he took Linda in a cab to George Washington University Hospital. He left his wife to continue her labor alone and raced back home to be with Johnny and Craig when they woke up.

Their brother Robert Vinelli was born at 6:13 a.m.

The family of five moved back to Tegucigalpa in June. They repeated the now-familiar pattern of first living at the Gran Hotel Lincoln and then moving to a rental house. Their home in Colonia Lara would not be ready for another year. Linda felt very tired. The previous two years had been a blur of packing and moving. Fortunately, baby Bobby had a wonderful, calm disposition. He slept from 7:00 p.m. to 5:00 a.m. at two months of age. It also helped that Johnny started kindergarten that year.

Over the next year Paul, Linda and their boys settled into life in Honduras. Paul was established in his work and as a professor. Linda was busy with three young sons. The couple started to have close friendships. In early 1953 Linda learned she was expecting another child. They moved into the Lara house while she was pregnant. The house was built in the shape of a V — V for Vinelli. The property covered a full block, which gave the home a very large backyard. Paul installed a sandbox for the boys. That same year, a Swiss Honduran couple named Enrique and Eva Bahr built on the lot directly across the street. They had three children, Lico, Anny and Henry. The Bahr and Vinelli families instantly became close friends. The group of six children—five boys and one girl—played together every day, riding their bikes all over the neighborhood which was mostly empty lots full of brush. Johnny and Anny were the same age and classmates at the American School, and Craig was only a year younger. Henry and Bobby were the same age, two years younger than Craig. Lico Bahr, the oldest by four years, often tried to disrupt the games the younger kids played, which led to strong words from Linda.

Paul frequently had business and social engagements in the evenings, but with three sons to care for, Linda did not often attend with him. She was a doting mother to her boys. Friends suggested she leave them with the maid, but Linda was not comfortable with her ability to handle all three.

Macky said to her, "This is not normal, Linda. [Paul's colleague] Tosco takes his wife Rossina everywhere, and they have two daughters. You need to go out with your husband, or someone is going to take him from you! I'll stay with the boys."

At first Paul objected to Macky's offer, worried she was limiting her own social life. She assured Paul she had plenty of social opportunities and wasn't interested in attending the boring bank functions he went to. She promised to find them a full-time nanny as soon as she could. In the meantime, she often babysat for the Vinelli boys and in this way, besides being Paul's employee at the bank and student at the university, Macky became an important part of Paul's family life.

Macky eventually found a nanny for the boys, a woman named Jesus who she had known and trusted for many years. Jesus moved in full time and became invaluable to Linda in the care of the boys. Another maid oversaw housekeeping.[lv] From then on, Macky only babysat when Paul took Linda away for a weekend in Miami or to a friend's beach house. On those occasions, she stayed at their house. Linda left lists for Macky with all the details she needed to know about the boys' routine and care.[lvi]

Paul and Linda's three boys were born in Washington, D.C., but now that they were settled in Tegucigalpa, they planned for their fourth child to be delivered at the Hospital Viera. Richard Vinelli was born at 1:00 a.m. on October 21. Paul was on a business trip, and it was Macky who was with Linda. The nurse put Ricky in Macky's arms first.[lvii] Linda told her friend she was thrilled with a fourth boy. She felt it would have been tough for a girl to grow up around three older brothers. Soon after Ricky was born Paul returned from a trip to Washington with a suitcase full of gifts that the Reismans had sent for the children. By this time Johnny and Craig knew of Linda's parents because of their generous gifts and equated the Reismans with Santa Claus.

Paul still traveled to many of the same international meetings he attended before, but now it was as an employee of the Honduran government rather than an IMF advisor. In February of 1954 he was part of the Honduran Treaty Delegation that was hosted in Washington by Henry Holland, the Assistant Secretary of State.

He was essential to Finance Minister Marco Batres and accompanied him to meetings around Latin America. In March, Paul attended the tenth annual conference of Inter-American bankers in Caracas with Minister Batres, who was the Honduran delegate. Paul wrote the speech Batres gave on Honduran economic policy. Eventually Batres offered to send Paul as the formal Honduran delegate to banking conferences in the region, but Paul declined because he worried it would put his U.S. citizenship at risk. He preferred to attend as an advisor.

April 1st was the start of the school year in Tegucigalpa. Johnny was in the second grade and Craig in the first grade. Craig was only five years old and the youngest in his grade, yet the teacher said he was the brightest student in the class.

Bobby, Paul, Johnny, Craig, Ricky and Linda, April 1954

In addition to their two maids, Linda and Paul now employed a gardener named Cesar. He helped Johnny, Craig and Anny Bahr build an elaborate tree fort in their backyard where they spent hours playing. Bobby and Ricky spent most of their days outside also. Once he learned to walk, Ricky wandered all over the property with only a t-shirt on, bare-bottomed. He was quite the handful. Linda wrote to her parents, "He's a little devil that causes all of us a lot of trouble. He's by far the naughtiest of all the boys and in many ways the cutest".

Paul stayed in frequent contact with his parents in Portland, Maine through letters. Angelo and Dora still lived in a small part of their large brick house and closed off the rest for rental apartments.

Their home consisted of one bedroom and bath, a living room and a very small kitchen. Downstairs in the basement Dora had a second kitchen where she did most of her cooking. That room had a stove, sink and a washing machine. In one corner was a toilet with a pull string to flush, covered by a curtain for privacy. In the other corner was a huge furnace where Angelo burned trash.

Because they lived in such cramped quarters, when the weather allowed Angelo spent hours sitting in the shade of the trees lining the side yard of his house. This suited both Dora and him—after forty-two years of marriage they still did not enjoy each other's company. Their daughter Elizabeth and her family lived just across the alley. Elizabeth's twelve-year-old daughter Diana visited her grandparents daily for lunch. Often after the meal Angelo sent Diana down Brackett Street to buy vanilla ice cream. They ate next to each other on the bench in the side yard, not saying a word. When Angelo was done, he would reach out his hand for Diana to pull up his feeble eighty-two-year-old body.

By the time Paul completed his two-year commitment to the Honduran government in June of 1954, President Gálvez and Minister Batres had made sure he would remain in the country as their advisor. They made him a permanent employee at the Central Bank. This is when Paul urged bank management to institute the employee benefits he had seen offered at American financial institutions. He structured the creation of an employee retirement fund and ensured that there was excellent health insurance for everyone who worked for the bank. The bank's insurance policy even covered health care in the United States.

In November of 1954, Paul went on a trip through Latin America, expanding the Honduran government's relationships with finance ministers and central bank officials. The trip lasted one month, and took him through Panama City, Lima, Sao Paulo, Rio, Montevideo, Buenos Aires and Santiago. In most cities he was given a tour by the Honduran ambassador to that country. Paul loved to discover new places, people, culture and food. In every city he took advantage of the time he was not in meetings to call on former IMF colleagues, tour, try out the local foods, and shop for gifts for the family. The trip ended in Petrópolis, Brazil, near Rio de Janeiro, where Paul accompanied Minister of Finance Batres to the Inter-American Economic Conference, focused on strengthening relationships between the U.S and Latin America. Paul prepared the speech given by Minister Batres on behalf of the Honduran government. The Sunday after the conference, he spent the day with his college friend Flavio and his wife Jean.

1954 had been a tumultuous year in Honduras. President Gálvez dealt with national strikes by workers in the mining, brewing, textile and beverage industries, as well as more than one hundred thousand workers from the Standard Fruit and United Fruit companies.[lviii] He asked U.S. President Eisenhower to send warships into the Gulf of Honduras in case military support was needed.[lix] In September Tropical Storm Gilda left thousands of Hondurans homeless and destroyed banana plantations which led to more layoffs. In November, President Gálvez left Honduras to be treated for a heart condition brought on by the stress of the troublesome year. Within weeks, on December 5, 1954, his government was seized by Vice-President Julio Lozano Díaz.[lx][lx]

Soon after Paul and Batres returned to Honduras at the beginning of December, they learned they now worked for a new administration.

Despite the political problems in the country that Paul saw up close because he worked for the government, in 1955 Paul was probably the happiest he had been in his life. When he turned thirty-three that November, I imagine he must have reflected on how far he had come in life. He had a wife he adored, four marvelous sons, a large house and staff, and a job that was interesting, important and that gave him the opportunity to travel and see the world.

In December Linda told him he she was sick.

She explained that she had gone to her gynecologist because she didn't feel well. The doctor suspected she had cancer. [14]

Paul must have felt kicked in the stomach, but he acted immediately. The following week, he and Linda flew to Miami for an appointment with an oncologist at Mount Sinai Hospital. Tests confirmed a malignancy, and doctors operated immediately to remove a tumor. Linda was allowed to return to Tegucigalpa to spend Christmas with the boys, but she was told to return in January for what she called "x-ray treatments" (radiation).

---

14. It is not clear what cancer she had: it was either cervical, uterine or ovarian.

7

LOSING HIS WAY
1956

Linda's letters to her family in Michigan contained only good news. She wrote that she enjoyed living in Tegucigalpa because the weather was so much milder than Washington's and the boys had fewer colds. She told them Paul found his work with the Central Bank interesting, and that she was grateful to have maids to help with the boys, cooking and cleaning. She described their large house in "the country" as dreamy, with an enormous backyard for the boys to run around in. She told of the boys finding a rabbit's nest with two baby bunnies and how they spent most of the day feeding and watching the bunnies. She never mentioned her illness nor the trips to Miami for radiation treatment. Paul, however, did call Linda's father to inform him she was sick.

With Linda back and forth to Miami, Paul had to dedicate more time to the boys' care. He and his neighbor Enrique Bahr took turns taking their older children to the American School downtown. Bobby and Ricky, ages four and two, stayed home with the maids. [lxi] Eva Bahr and Macky helped take care of them. At nights when Linda was gone, Paul cooked dinner for the boys. To cheer up his sons, Paul bought a German Shepherd puppy who he named Rox. He had a v-shaped doghouse that was a miniature of their main house built close to the sandbox in the backyard.

Those were the days when schools and businesses in Honduras still took a break in the middle of their day. Children and their parents came home from school and work for lunch—a *siesta* often followed. Paul never napped. He stayed at the office through lunch to get his work done because he needed to get home as early in the evening as possible to help Linda and the boys.

Years later Paul was a pioneer in establishing *jornada única*, a work schedule that included only an hour for lunch, requiring that people have a quick lunch closer to the office. He viewed the schedule change as family friendly. Prior to *jornada única*, an employee, usually the father in a household, stayed at work until 8:00 p.m. to complete a full workday because of the time taken mid-day. *Jornada única* permitted families to be home together for dinner and before the children's bedtime.

Linda traveled regularly to Miami for her radiation treatments from January through June of 1956. Paul often flew with her there but then returned home to be with the boys. When both Linda and Paul were gone, Johnny and Craig stayed with the Bahrs who took them to school. Paul did not want to impose all four boys on their friends, so in March he took Bobby and Ricky to Miami with them.

Linda's parents wrote to her, concerned about her illness and asking that she visit them in Michigan. She claimed her radiation schedule was too busy to allow for the trip. Probably she didn't want to spend any more time away from Paul and her sons.

In June, Paul flew Linda to Miami for a month of treatments, scheduled for five days a week. He settled her into an oceanfront room with a kitchenette at the South Seas Hotel. She worried about the expense, but he wanted her to be comfortable. Linda admitted the view of the ships on the sparkling water was a treat.

Paul hated to leave Linda alone for a month, but she knew that he needed to be in Honduras. He had taken all the permitted vacation time from his job. In the evenings, it was best if he was at home with the boys. He arranged for Linda to have someone with her for the first two weeks: first his sister Lina and then other friends. Paul had planned to come to Miami immediately after they left, but Linda asked him not to. She was suffering from nausea and stomach pain. Dr. Read prescribed pain pills that helped but left her with no energy. She said to Paul, "I can't even go to the beach."

The boys wrote several times. In mid-June Linda responded,

"June 15, 1956
Dearest Johnny and Craig,
Today Mama received two letters from you. You can't imagine how happy that made me. I'm glad that you're being good and that you're having such a good time. You asked Mama when I'll be coming home. If all goes well, I'll be home two weeks from today. Every day Mama goes to the doctor and she hopes everything goes well.
P.S. Wish Mama could be with Daddy on Father's Day."

Paul flew up on June 23 to stay with Linda for the last week of treatment. His friend Marta Cruz stayed with the boys that week, which meant having others care for her own four children. When Paul brought Linda home, they focused on their family time. For the rest of summer Linda enjoyed being home with her boys, even though she did not feel well. In the beginning of September, Paul took Linda back to Miami for a scan. The doctors spoke to him as he waited outside of her treatment room. They said there was no point in prolonging treatment. The cancer was everywhere.

Sept. 19, 1956

Dear papa and mamma,

It is with a heavy heart that I write you these few lines.

As Otto has already informed you Linda is critically ill. The five doctors who have seen her in Miami the past year seem to think that there is nothing more that can be done. At least that is what they have informed me after Linda's return at the beginning of September. It appears that this trouble has been with her from childhood, revealing itself at first only in the form of anemia. Later in college she had a cyst removed which was apparently another evidence of her illness. It appears almost fantastic that at such time the doctors that took care of her did not discover her real trouble. After the tumor was removed last December there was still hope that through X-Rays the malignancy could be eliminated. However fate was otherwise as the tumor spread to the lung. This was complicated by an attack of pneumonia from which she has not recovered yet. Linda has not been told her true status. The doctors have felt that she would need all the willpower necessary to carry on the fight as long as possible. Linda thinks that she had a non-malignant tumor removed and that her present difficulties are due to the burning of the X-Rays and to the pneumonia. Until today when I brought her home she had been in a local hospital. The doctors have thought that it was better to take her home where she would be happier with the children and she might eat better. Of course I have a nurse taking care of her and the doctors will drop in daily. Through the use of narcotics we are keeping her as comfortable as possible. Her spirits are very high which give promise that she will keep on fighting. The children fortunately are all well and are giving her a lot of comfort. As time passes I shall try to keep you informed of developments. In the meantime there is little else that can be done. By phone the doctors in the States have told me that the best place for her is at home and that there is no sense taking her back to the States, even if she could survive the trip, because they could not do anything for her.

If there is anything else you like to know or you should want me to do, you could write me through Otto.

With love I am jointly with the children

affectionately yours,

Paul

Linda declined rapidly. Paul hired a nurse to be with her during the weekdays. He hurried home from work every afternoon to sit by her bedside. When the nurse was not there, he had to give Linda morphine shots for her pain. They left lumps under Linda's translucent skin because he was not experienced in giving them.

Linda wrote her last letter to her parents in mid-October. She still didn't know her prognosis. "I am feeling a bit better but still have to take it very easy. I can't believe how long it is taking to recover from pneumonia. The boys are all being very good. Even Ricky knows that when I am taking a nap he should stay outside with Bobby."

October 21 was Ricky's third birthday. Linda got out of bed with great difficulty, and still wearing her pajamas, baked and iced a birthday cake for her youngest son.[lxii]

Across town that same day, a military *junta* composed of three military leaders, General Roque Rodriguez, Coronel Hector Caraccioli, and Major Roberto Gálvez Barnes (the son of President Juan Manuel Gálvez), joined forces to overthrow the government of President Julio Lozano.[lxiii] Once again, Paul had a new employer.

Five days later, on the evening of October 26, Paul called an ambulance to take Linda to the Hospital Viera. He went across the street to arrange for the four boys to spend the night at the Bahr's home. He then drove up the hill to accompany his wife in her last hours. Just before midnight, Linda passed away while Paul held her. The nurse who monitored Linda's vital signs looked down at the young couple sadly.

Paul's grief was almost unbearable, but he couldn't succumb to it. He had to deal with the reality that his four young sons had lost their mother, and the government he worked for had just been overthrown.

When one doesn't know what to say, it's best to say little. How was he to word news no parent can stomach receiving, about a daughter only thirty-four years old, who left behind four heartbroken little boys ages nine, seven, four and three?

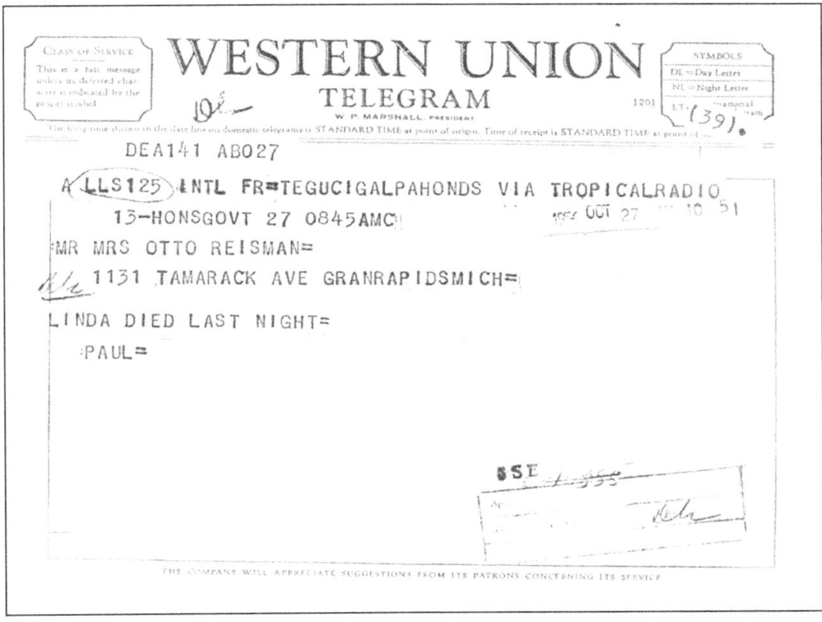

It was not until her final days that Linda had realized she was sick enough to die. That is when she told Paul she would like to be buried in Grand Rapids, Michigan where her family lived. Always frugal, she had requested cremation to reduce the cost of transporting a body and casket that far. Cremation was not performed in the Catholic country of Honduras in the 1950s. Paul left the boys with the Bahr family and on October 30 he flew with Linda's body to Miami. Most travelers to the city come for the fun, the warmth, the vacation atmosphere. Paul sat alone in a crematorium waiting room for several hours while his love was reduced to ashes.

Macky Salinas told me what happened over the next few days. After the cremation, Paul called her in New York, where she was studying English at his recommendation. When she learned that he planned to take Linda's ashes to the Reismans in Michigan, Macky offered to go with him. Paul was fulfilling his wife's final request, and Macky knew it was a very difficult one. He had to come face to face with Linda's parents, who had only met him once and who had refused to visit them ever since he married her thirteen years earlier.

Macky flew to Miami the next day and checked into the Fontainbleu Hotel where Paul was staying. He asked her to meet him in the lobby to go to the hotel restaurant for dinner. She informed him she would be bringing a friend, a doctor she knew who lived in Miami. They found Paul in the lobby, unshaven, angry and totally inebriated. He was holding a square bronze box about the size of a tissue box. Macky realized he was holding Linda's ashes and began to cry. Paul pushed the box towards her and gruffly said, "There's your Linda".

Paul could barely speak by the time their dinner came, but he kept drinking. Macky asked her doctor friend, "Can't we give him a pill to calm him down?" He responded, "We can't put any medicine in him with the amount of alcohol he has already consumed. The only option we have is to pour him more champagne until he's sleepy enough to let us take him to his room."

Macky walked with a cane, so her friend had the task of standing Paul up from the table and guiding him, staggering, to his hotel room where they deposited him on his bed.

The next morning Paul and Macky met in the lobby for their journey to Michigan. Paul said nothing the entire trip: not in the cab on the way to the Miami airport, not on the flight north, and not in the cab to the Reisman's home. When they drove up to the house that Paul had visited only once thirteen years before, Macky stayed in the car. She watched out the window as Paul got out in the freezing November air and walked to the front door. Linda's father Otto opened it. Behind him was Ella carrying a handkerchief she had obviously been crying into. Paul handed them the box holding their daughter's ashes.[lxiv]

What must have Otto and Ella felt in that moment? For years their only daughter, who they adored, had begged them to visit her. They sent letters and gifts for Linda, the children, and even for Paul, but never came to see them. All because she married this man who they thought was wrong for her. Now he was on their doorstep bringing them what was left of their daughter in a small box. The image of him carrying her remains must have been seared into their memories.

Paul stood there for only moments, although it probably felt much longer. He gave Otto the box, turned around, and returned to the cab. He did not ask to stay for Linda's interment, nor did the Reismans offer that he do so. He and Macky did not discuss what happened on their way back to the airport—nor ever. She offered to go with him to Honduras to help with the boys, but Paul insisted she return to New York and finish her studies.[lxv]

Paul learned from the Reismans that there is nothing a parent can do to change the mind of a child in love. His in-laws lost the relationship with their daughter because of their prejudice. They must have stopped hoping she would leave Paul at some point in the many years of their marriage, but their pride kept them at a distance. Their son Otto never had children, so they also missed out on the joy of enjoying grandchildren while their child was living.

Paul had learned this lesson first from his own family. His mother was forced to marry his father and never grew to love him. His sister Elizabeth spent the rest of her life resenting that she was separated from her first boyfriend. The effect of these lessons was that Paul never offered an opinion about the person his children chose to marry, even when he thought the choice was wrong.

Paul returned to Honduras on November 7, his thirty-fourth birthday. His sister Lina flew to Tegucigalpa to help Paul with the boys. This was a temporary fix as Lina had her own family to care for.

Lina with Ricky and Bobby, November 1956

Paul didn't know how he was going to properly care for four sons and do his job well. A week after returning to Tegucigalpa, he received a letter from the Reismans that surprised him tremendously. Otto and Ella offered that Johnny and Craig live with them in Michigan for a while. Paul knew this would help and agreed to the idea. He was still going to have to leave Bobby and Ricky in the care of his maids all day long. He asked Lina to take Johnny and Craig to the Reismans in the U.S. The boys, who were still crying over the loss of their mother, did not want to leave their father. Paul promised them he would visit at Christmastime. On November 20 Paul said goodbye to Johnny and Craig at the Toncontín airport. Lina flew with the boys to New York, where she met Linda's brother Otto. He then took the boys to Grand Rapids. Johnny and Craig had only once met their uncle and had never met their grandparents. Three weeks after losing their mother, they were separated from their father and younger brothers, sent to live with strangers, in a freezing cold climate far from the tropics they were used to. Their grandparents enrolled them in the Stocking Elementary School where they started classes right away, even though the semester was about to end for the winter holiday.

This had been what Paul instructed in a letter he sent to the Reismans about the care of Johnny and Craig. He asked that the boys enter school immediately and that a tutor be found if needed. His instructions were that they are not given more than one soda pop a day. If they did something wrong, they should be sent to their room as punishment. Paul had been in the habit of giving them fifty cents each for pocket money every Saturday. He suggested they might go to a movie once a week. Because Johnny was high strung and emotional, he told them that Linda and he had always tried to avoid excitement in his surroundings. Craig should not be allowed to eat too much.

Paul attempted to turn his attention to his work, which had been neglected over the past months. One of Paul's roles at the Central Bank was to create the country's budget and oversee its distribution. He now had new bosses: the military junta that had removed President Lozano from office. On December 18, representatives of the new regime walked into Paul's office and asked him to adjust the budget so that they could purchase artillery and military vehicles. Paul refused—he told them their spending plan would bankrupt Honduras. Their response was to give Paul twenty-four hours to leave the country.

Paul had one day to pack Bobby, Ricky and himself to leave Tegucigalpa. On Wednesday, December 19, he flew with his younger sons to Portland, Maine. The boys did not own long pants since they lived in a tropical country. They arrived at Dora and Angelo's home in the freezing Maine weather wearing shorts. Family members who were there have told me that Paul looked terrible, his grief and stress evident. His family took over the care and entertainment of Bobby and Ricky.

At this time Paul's father Angelo was dying in a nursing home. The family went to see him once a week. Bobby and Ricky played on the floor next to the bed where the old man was lying. By all accounts Dora had little time for, nor patience with, Angelo's failing health. She was more concerned with the troubles of her son and grandsons.

Paul spent much of that time in Portland alone in his room. He never went to see Johnny and Craig in Grand Rapids. My guess is he was processing how much had unraveled in one year. He no longer had a wife, job nor home. His sons were separated from each other, living with grandparents they did not know in cold cities where customs were different. They missed their mother, their dog, their friends and their home. Johnny and Craig were in a new school. And Paul had to find work to support all of them. Linda's treatment, and the travel back and forth for that, had emptied his savings account.

He called the IMF in Washington.

8

REBOUND

1957-1958

Paul set up a meeting with his former employers at the IMF for January of 1957. His mother offered to keep Bobby and Ricky while Paul sorted out his next steps. Before leaving Portland, Paul went to see his father at the retirement home. He knew his father was dying and he did not expect they would see each other again. Angelo and he had little to say to each other, but Angelo did ask Paul to sell some land he still owned near Salerno after he died.

Paul left his younger sons with Dora and went to Washington, D.C. The International Monetary Fund team told him they were willing to hire Paul if he was certain he wanted to leave Honduras, but they preferred he return. Both the IMF and the World Bank were furious that the military junta had exiled Paul. The international organizations expected the autonomy of the Central Bank to be respected by the Honduran government. As far as they were concerned, if Honduras's new government wanted their help in the future, they would have to give Paul his job back.

Paul wasn't sure what he wanted. He was not enthusiastic about working under a regime that had kicked him out of the country. He stayed in Washington for a few weeks, meeting with former associates and considering various job opportunities.

On February 18, Angelo died at age eighty-four. Paul flew to Portland for his father's burial. Angelo was placed in the family plot that he had bought forty years earlier when little Antoinette Casavola died. Antoinette's parents and sister were also buried there. Angelo was the only Vinella among the Casavolas in the funeral plot.

Paul then went to Salerno to sell the land Angelo told him about before dying. While he was finding a buyer and completing the transaction, he had time to think. It was restorative to be back in the country of his birth, far away from the traumatic events in Honduras. While Paul was in Italy, the IMF expressed its displeasure to the military junta in Tegucigalpa in such terms that the government asked Paul to return to work. When he returned by ship to the U.S. in March, Paul had been in exile for almost three months.

He gave the decision a great deal of thought. He was certain that he did not want to work for the current Honduran government. But there was a very important reason to choose life in Honduras: the ability to keep his family together. In Tegucigalpa he could afford household help to care for the boys. He also felt responsible for continuing President Gálvez's vision for Honduras. Paul was proud of the economic and financial changes that he had helped set in motion in 1950. He didn't want to leave the country when there was more to be done. [lxvi] He also knew there was opportunity in every sector of the Honduran economy, and was sure he could have more of an impact there than in the U.S.

By 1957 he had been an advisor to three Honduran governments in almost eight years. Working for a military junta was not a good long-term prospect, so he decided to look for another job. In the meantime, he returned to work at the Central Bank in Tegucigalpa. He explained to his four sons that they must stay with their grandparents in Portland and Grand Rapids until he could arrange a stable situation for them to return to.

In Portland, the close-knit Vinella-Casavola family helped Dora care for Bobby and Ricky. When the weather turned warm enough, Elizabeth's husband Adam took Bobby and Ricky to Deering Oaks Park on weekends. The boys played on the swings and fed the ducks in the pond. Afterwards Adam took them out for a hamburger.

Bobby was so quiet that some days it was hard to know he was there. Ricky was the opposite, and particularly difficult for sixty-two-year-old Dora to manage. His teenage cousin Diana, who attended an all-girls Catholic school, remembers being shocked when more than once three-year-old Ricky cursed in Spanish, "*Puta, puta, puta*!" Everyone would exclaim, "No, no Ricky, bad boy - bad boy!" Diana affectionately called him "the bad boy of the family" for the rest of his life. It was during this time that Ricky became Dora's favorite grandson. He tested her patience, but she couldn't be angry with him for long. He made her feel necessary when she no longer had children nor a husband to care for. Dora sent Paul letters that included reports about Ricky acting up. In response, he arranged for an adorable cocker spaniel to be delivered to Dora's front door. Bobby and Ricky named him Dusty. The idea did not work for Dora, who wrote to Paul, "I have enough with these two boys, I don't need a dog to take care of!" Dusty didn't last three weeks at her house. Dora gave him to a barber who worked with her son-in-law Adam.

Portland, Spring 1957
Back row, L to R: Anna Santoro, Lina Vinella Santoro, Adam Romano,
Dora Casavola Vinella, Elizabeth Vinella Romano (holding Dusty the cocker spaniel)
Front row, L to R: Hilda Santoro w Bobby, Mimi Santoro w Ricky

Paul was miserable back in Tegucigalpa. His days at the office were tense, given that he had caused his superiors to be reprimanded by the IMF and because they knew he wanted to leave the bank. At night and on weekends his house was deathly silent. He walked from room to room with his dog Rox, seeking and not finding the sounds of family life that Linda and the four boys once made. The loneliness drove him out of the house.

He often visited Chito Kafie's house after work. Chito and Nena lived above their textile store and their house was full of activity, with four children and daily visitors. Chito attracted a vibrant group of the country's top thinkers: merchants, bankers, business executives and politicians. On any given evening one might run into former president Juan Manuel Gálvez (who had originally brought Paul to

Honduras and who was the godfather of Chito's oldest son Schucry), prominent Jewish businessman Boris Goldstein, and many of the top merchants and businessmen in the community of Palestinian descent of which Chito was quickly becoming the figurehead. In these meetings Paul discussed the potential he saw in Honduras and encouraged the business leaders to start manufacturing basic goods such as paper, cardboard boxes, candy, sugar, leather, soap, cosmetics, and cement. He explained to all who would listen the theory of import substitution industrialization, through which developing countries could reduce their dependence on more developed countries by forming domestic industries. Paul told the men that now that Honduras had a National Development Bank, these new enterprises could obtain financing. And the government could further support these initiatives by placing tariffs on imports that competed with local goods. [lxvii]

Chito wasn't convinced about Paul's idea of industrializing Honduras. He was a merchant at heart, interested in buying and selling product, not manufacturing. He also wasn't convinced that the country needed both a central bank and a national development bank because he worried about excess government involvement in business. Paul replied that a country needed a modern financial and monetary structure. He told Chito that a best practice economic model could not be launched without industry having access to lending. He believed that the primary interest of any government, no matter how poor, was to incentivize industry and the primary sector of its economy, which includes farming, fishing, logging, hunting, and mining. Over time, Chito relented and agreed to invest a modest amount in new ventures so others would follow suit. Boris Goldstein was a major collaborator with Paul in developing ideas for new businesses, and he invested heavily in Honduran industry. Boris lived in San Pedro Sula, which became the industrial center of the country in part due to his initiatives.[lxviii]

Paul didn't want to bother the Kafie family with nightly visits, so he also went to see Macky some evenings after work. By this time, she had finished her studies in New York and was again working for Paul at the Central Bank. When her doorbell rang after she returned from work, she would find Paul on the front step.

"What do you want, Doctor?"

"That you sit with me."

She made drinks for both, and they sat for a while, saying nothing. Then he got up and left.[lxix]

On weekends he sought out his neighbors in Colonia Lara for company. It was commonplace for Paul to walk into someone's house at cocktail hour, a drink already in his hand. The Bahr family saw him the most. That summer he asked Eva and Enrique Bahr to invite a woman named Iris Ulargui to a cocktail party they were having. Paul had met Iris and her then-husband John Miceli of Standard Fruit Company in La Ceiba during his first trip to Honduras eight years before. Miceli had died in 1953, and Iris now lived in Tegucigalpa.

Iris was the daughter of a seamstress, Doña Augusta (Gusta), from the port town of Amapala. Gusta's mother was a Honduran woman who had a brief relationship with a German merchant named Schönborn. He abandoned his wife and his daughter Gusta and returned to Germany. The story repeated itself in the next generation. Gusta had a relationship with a man named Ulargui that produced

Iris and her brother Oscar. Ulargui left Honduras and Gusta, like her mother before her, became a single parent.

Gusta vowed not to have the pattern repeat a third time with her only daughter Iris. She moved with her children to Tegucigalpa where she established herself as an excellent seamstress. They did not have much money, but Gusta always dressed Iris beautifully and in the latest styles. Iris was not beautiful, but her mother made sure she was elegant. Gusta was determined that her daughter marry well.

Iris did just that. She first married Felix Vaccaro, a member of the powerful and wealthy Vaccaro/D'Antoni family from New Orleans. This family had created an empire in Honduras that included the Standard Fruit Company, Cervecería Hondureña (the country's largest beer operation), a sugar company, as well as a majority interest in Banco Atlántida. Iris and Vaccaro lived in La Ceiba, the headquarters of Standard Fruit and Banco Atlántida. He was twenty-one years older than her. Not long into the marriage, the couple began to fight. Vaccaro started to spend most of his time in New Orleans, leaving Iris in La Ceiba. He eventually divorced Iris, making her a millionaire.[lxx]

Soon after the divorce, Iris married John Miceli, the Vice-President of Standard Fruit Company. Miceli had worked for the Vaccaro brothers in Honduras for fifty years.[lxxi] He was much older than Iris like Vaccaro was, and he had been ill for several years. When he died less than five years after they married, Iris was his sole heir. She became an even wealthier woman. Among the assets Miceli left her were more than two thousand shares of Banco Atlántida stock.

After Miceli's death, Iris moved to Tegucigalpa. She lived at the home of Dr. José Mendoza. Dr. Mendoza was a Honduran physician, trained in England, who was the director of the D'Antoni hospital in La Ceiba for many years. He was also a director of Banco Atlántida. [lxxii] Iris had become close with Mendoza and his wife during her years in La Ceiba, and they welcomed her into their home.[lxxiii]

The night of that summer cocktail party at the Bahr's home, and on many other nights, Paul and Iris danced late into the night.[lxxiv] They married not long after, in August of 1957.

Paul and Iris Ulargui, 1957

The wedding was in Guatemala, probably because Paul wanted to avoid the attention of the Honduran press. He and Iris honeymooned in Miami. Many were shocked by the news. Paul's family in Portland could not understand. Macky, when told the news, said, "What? He's married WHO?" She later told me that she would have been less surprised if he had married a street sweeper. [lxxv]

There were problems from the beginning, starting with that their personalities clashed. Iris's age and wealth gave her an arrogance that was hard for Paul to swallow. She was completely different than Linda, who was gentle-natured and had always allowed Paul to be the decision maker in their marriage.[lxxvi]

For Paul it was clearly a rebound relationship. He had not healed from losing his great love only eight months earlier. Iris moved into Paul's house and immediately got rid of all the furniture Paul and Linda had lovingly and painstakingly purchased over their twelve years of marriage. Iris had the money to completely re-do the house, and she erased any memory of Linda.[lxxvii]

For Iris, this third marriage was the first where the motivator was not money. Her first two husbands were old when she married them. Paul was nine years younger than her, and she was very attracted to him. Ironically, Iris couldn't shake the concern that Paul had married her for her money.[lxxviii] It was probably a factor given the financial setbacks Paul had experienced in the previous year.

Paul hoped that his new wife would help him raise his sons. Although Iris had no children of her own, during their brief courtship she told Paul she was attracted to the idea of having an instant family. Paul brought Bobby and Ricky back from Portland right after the honeymoon. He had John and Craig remain with their Reisman grandparents in Grand Rapids. They were about to start their first full year at Stocking Elementary, and he thought Iris should get to know two boys before being asked to raise four. He promised his older sons he would bring them home for Christmas.

But Iris didn't understand what she was getting into. At first, she treated Ricky and Bobby like dolls, dressing them in elegant clothes.

But little boys can't look nor behave like dolls for long. Especially not Ricky. One day, he decided to light matches under his bed. The resulting scene was not something Iris handled well.[lxxix] It didn't take long for her to decide she did not want to raise little boys. She placed one of her maids in charge of their care. Apparently, this lady was good to them.[lxxx] To relieve some of the stress Iris felt from the children romping through her pristine house all day, Paul enrolled the boys in preschool, even though Ricky was a year too young.

That same month, in addition to a new wife, Paul got a new job. By 1957 Banco Atlántida had moved its headquarters from La Ceiba to downtown Tegucigalpa. The chairman of the board was the bank's co-founder Salvador D'Antoni, brother-in-law of the Vaccaro brothers. D'Antoni had been chairman of the bank since its founding by the Vaccaros and D'Antoni in 1913. The bank's CEO was Felix Lloveras, who Paul had known since his first trip to Honduras in 1949. Upon the retirement of the bank's Assistant CEO Dr. Emile Stouse, Lloveras hired Paul for the position. Paul was relieved to wrap up his work with the volatile Honduran government and move to the private sector. Coincidentally, the Banco Atlántida building in Tegucigalpa was next door to Chito Kafie's business and home. Paul and Chito's relationship was cemented even further because Chito was a client of the bank and both men could visit each other frequently by walking next door.

Paul continued to teach economics at the university, and now he donated his salary back to the School of Economics. Occasionally there was a strike at the university. At those times, Paul taught his students at his house.

Paul brought Johnny and Craig back to Tegucigalpa for a visit at Christmastime. It was the first time they had seen their father and two younger brothers in a year. They were much happier with the warm Tegucigalpa weather than the Michigan winter. But the climate inside their house was frigid. Months into their marriage Iris and Paul were drinking often and arguing all the time.

Their problems stemmed from their different backgrounds and from their expectations for the marriage. Iris had been raised to be a princess and later married two wealthy men. By the time she married Paul she was forty-five years old and financially independent. She felt no need to cater to her third husband.

When the yelling became too loud, Paul sent Bobby and Ricky across the street to the Bahr's house. At first, he had a maid pack an overnight bag for them. Later, the boys just grabbed a dresser drawer full of clothes and went. Bobby referred to 1958 as the "year of the drawers". The fights were not only at home. At the Bahr's Christmas party that year, Paul and Iris got into a loud argument in the dining room. The Vinelli and Bahr children, playing in another room, could hear the crash of crystal goblets being thrown.[lxxxi]

When Johnny and Craig came home again in the summer of 1958, they told Paul they wanted to leave Michigan. Craig was the least happy about living with his maternal grandparents. Ella and Otto did not treat him as nicely as they did Johnny, maybe because Craig had a dark complexion like his father and reminded them of him. Paul acknowledged that a year and a half was enough time for the Reismans to keep the boys. He thanked the Reismans for their care of the boys and informed them that Johnny and Craig would not be returning. Then he considered the options. Bringing the two boys back to Tegucigalpa was not a good idea, as Iris was already on the verge of a breakdown during the few months the four boys were home together.

That September Paul flew to Miami with Johnny and Craig to enroll them in Miami Military Academy. This boarding school, for three hundred boys in grades one through twelve, attracted students from Florida and Latin America. Its motto was "Boys Today-Men Tomorrow". By the time the boys went there, the academy was a National Defense Cadet Corps facility, meaning cadets drilled with Army-issued M1 rifles.[lxxxii]

Johnny and Craig hated the place. They were told when to eat, sleep, study. There were hours of marching and drills and no privacy. The students from Florida often were allowed to go home on weekends, but Johnny and Craig had to live on campus seven days a week.

In October, Paul took Iris, Bobby and Ricky to Miami to visit his older sons.

John (11), Rick (4), Craig (9) and Bob (6) – Miami Military Academy, Fall 1958

Soon after they returned to Tegucigalpa, Iris and Ricky were in a serious car accident on Avenida La Paz. Iris broke a leg and Ricky broke an arm. Since Iris was bedridden and not in the frame of mind to host anyone for the holidays, Paul sent Johnny and Craig to their Reisman grandparents in Grand Rapids that Christmas.

9

THREE YEARS, THREE WIVES
1959-1961

Paul and Iris' marriage lasted less than two years. There were too many differences in how each wanted to live. What made things worse was that Iris's mother Doña Gusta wanted them to separate. She did not like for Paul to be in Iris' life because he oversaw her finances. Gusta wanted to retain some control over her daughter's money.

Paul and Iris divorced in July of 1959. There were only two things to negotiate. The first was that Iris wanted to adopt Ricky, with whom she had developed a connection. Paul refused to split up his sons. The second was the house in Colonia Lara they were living in, which Paul and Linda had built together. Iris wanted to buy the house. Paul agreed because he needed the money. Iris paid for the house in cash, counting out a large stack of bills. She remained in that house for the rest of her life. When Iris died many decades later, she left the house to the Catholic Church, which was ironic considering it had been built with so much care by Linda and Paul, who were both non-believers.

Paul and Iris remained friendly because both had a relationship with Banco Atlántida, he as an executive of the bank and she as a major stockholder. After the divorce Paul continued to help Iris with her investments. Many who knew them credit Paul with multiplying Iris's wealth several times over. After the divorce, Doña Gusta moved in with Iris. She never stopped worrying that Paul was a threat to her power over her daughter. Occasionally Paul would have a letter delivered to Iris's house regarding a business matter. Doña Gusta instructed Cesar, Paul's former gardener who had stayed with the house, to intercept anything from Paul and bring it to her. Years later Iris would discover Paul's letters hidden in books around the house.[lxxxiii]

Paul rented a house one block away from the home he sold to Iris. It was much smaller, but it still had a large backyard for the boys to play in. In June of 1959 Paul brought Johnny and Craig home from Miami Military Academy. They would attend the American School in Tegucigalpa that September. July 1 was Johnny's twelfth birthday. Paul had a big party, with horses for the children to ride around the backyard. The four boys had much to celebrate; after almost three years of separation, they and their father were back together. Paul enjoyed the reunion as much as the boys did. He took them to ball games and cooked for them. He was coming out of the cloud of grief for Linda (the marriage to Iris was not much more than a distraction). He focused on his sons that summer.

His mother had good news too: that summer sixty-three-year-old Dora re-married. Her second husband, Angelo Bufano, was from her hometown of Castellaneta, Italy. He was two years older, and they had known each other as children. Bufano's first wife, who had died four years earlier, was Dora's first cousin Marietta. The Casavola family in Italy re-connected Bufano and Dora through letters and when he proposed, she agreed to move to Rochester, New York and marry him.

This Angelo made Dora very happy. Many people remarked that it was a coincidence she married two men named Angelo. She liked to respond that this husband was her *"Angelo angelo"* (angel angel), and the first had been an *"Angelo diavolo"* (devil angel). The couple was a delight to watch. They danced, laughed, and behaved like young newlyweds despite both being over sixty years old.

At age thirty-seven Paul felt too young to be single, especially considering his mother's marriage. Never one to enjoy an evening alone, he sought social opportunities everywhere he went. In the last week of September, Paul attended the annual World Bank Board of Governors meeting in Washington, D.C. His friend Gabriel Mejía, with whom he had written the Honduran tax code in 1950, was at that time working for the IMF in Washington.[15] One night, Paul invited Gabriel and his wife Angelina to dinner. They invited Gabriel's sister Maria Esther to join them. Paul knew Maria Esther not only because she was Gabriel's sister, but because she was also the sister of Valentina Mejía, his former student and Central Bank colleague.

Maria Esther was a former schoolteacher who had studied English at the Instituto Hondureño de Cultura Interamericana (IHCI). She had been living in New York City since 1956, working as a secretary in the Freight and Accounting Bureau at the Standard Fruit Company. When Gabriel called to invite her to dinner, she took the train from New York to Washington.

---

15. Mejía was General Director of the Honduran Tax Revenue Agency from 1950-1956 and then became Secretary of Treasury and Commerce from 1956-57. He was also a director of the Banco de Fomento (National Development Bank).

Paul and Maria Esther enjoyed each other's company and ended up taking a trip around New England. The relationship was a casual one to both, neither was thinking long-term.

Paul and Maria Esther Mejía, 1959

Maria Esther became pregnant on that trip. When she called Paul in Tegucigalpa to inform him, they agreed that neither wanted to live together, and they discussed the support of their future child. Their plan was to marry when the child was born so the baby would be recognized as Paul's. They would remain married while they worked out a child support arrangement, brokered by her brother Gabriel, and then they would divorce. Paul suggested they marry and divorce by proxy in Mexico to keep their situation as private as possible. She agreed. Maria Esther did not want to stay in New York pregnant and unmarried, so accepted an offer from close friends in Los Angeles to stay with them until the delivery. The baby was due in July of 1960.

One April day in 1960, Paul walked next door to the house of Jim Cunningham who was a Political Officer for the U.S. Embassy. When he walked in the back door, beer in hand, he saw an attractive woman with auburn hair sitting on the living room sofa. Frances Smith was a secretary for the Economics Officer of the U.S. Embassy. She was there to speak with Jim's son, who wanted her help typing up a neighborhood newsletter he planned to write.

Paul had met Fran the previous summer, during a coup attempt. Fran was then living at the Hotel Prado with other U.S. Embassy secretaries. On Sunday, July 12, 1959, forces led by Colonel Armando Velásquez attempted to overthrow the government of President Ramón Villeda.[lxxxiv]

Being a Sunday, Fran and some friends were sunbathing on the roof of the hotel when they saw Honduran military personnel run up to the roof. The men at first were started to see American ladies in bikinis up there. They quickly recovered and ran to the edge of the rooftop, looking down over the city where a commotion was developing at the city jail, five blocks from the hotel. She thought it was funny that every time a soldier ran up or down the stairs to the roof, they would pause and says *Permiso* ("Excuse me") to the sunbathers.

Eventually rioting at the city jail became violent. Prisoners set fire to the building. The embassy contacted their staff at the Prado, instructing them to stay inside. Fran went to her room and looked out the window to see the Honduran army marching prisoners down the street in front of the hotel. They marched three abreast, with their hands on their heads.

The U.S. embassy notified the secretaries to get ready because the American Marines were coming to pick them up. When they arrived, Fran and the others were instructed to lay down on the back seats of their vehicles as the caravan of cars headed to the U.S. Embassy, located on Avenida La Paz. When they approached the Guanacaste bridge, they were stopped by Honduran police who told them to turn around because there was fighting ahead. The Marines brought the women back to the hotel and told them to stay in their rooms with the doors locked. Several hours later, the Marines came back and drove the women to the U.S. Embassy. Most of the Americans in Tegucigalpa had been assembled there for their safety. This was the most fortified building in Tegucigalpa.

Paul was at the embassy, part of a group of American citizens who had been asked to help with logistics. He and Fran met as discussions were held about where the secretaries should stay that night. It was decided that the secretaries would be safer in the homes of officers than in the downtown hotel because of its proximity to the jail. Paul's neighbor, Jim Cunningham, offered for Fran to stay at his house and had his driver take Fran and him there. He let her in the house and showed her where the guest room was, then returned to the embassy. She was alone, because his family was staying with friends.

Paul returned from the Embassy to the house he had just rented in Colonia Lara next door to Cunningham's home. A few weeks earlier his divorce with Iris was final. His mother Dora and her second husband Angelo were visiting him on their honeymoon. Paul asked their permission to invite Fran over since she was alone. She spent a few hours with Paul, his parents and his sons before returning next door.

Paul ran into Fran a few times at cocktail parties over the next nine months. She thought of him as "that loud man". One Saturday night he walked into the Club Reforma, where Fran was singing with the orchestra. She was tall and thin with green eyes. Her red satin halter dress had a bow tied behind her neck under her short hair, the ends of the bow hanging down her back. After Fran finished singing, Paul walked up to her and flirtatiously pulled on the satin ribbons at her back. She ignored him.

On the April day that Paul went to Jim's house, Fran told Jim and Paul that she had decided to leave Honduras. She had lived in Tegucigalpa for a year and concluded it was not a place for a single woman. The men suggested she join them on a trip that a group of Americans was planning for Easter week, which was coming up. The country of Honduras took off work and school for the entire week leading up to Easter Sunday. Their group was going to rent a boat to go from La Ceiba to Cayos Cochinos, a beautiful cluster of tiny islands and cays off the north coast of Honduras. Fran said she would think about it. A few days later, Jim approached Fran at the embassy and asked if she'd decided to go on the trip. She told him she could not.

Her reason for declining was financial. Several months earlier, she had traveled to the Mosquitia Jungle of Honduras with two American geologists who were searching for the storied "White City".[16] Fran was along for the adventure and to look for exotic orchids. While on this trip, she met an indigenous family who had many children. Their six-year-old son captured her heart, and his family asked Fran

---

16. They did not find the city in the dense jungle. It was discovered fifty-five years later, in 2015.

if she would adopt him. She was saving her money in hopes of proceeding with the adoption before moving back to the United States.

When Jim told Paul what Fran had said, Paul replied, "Tell her all she needs to bring is her bathing suit." That night at the Hotel Prado, Fran told her close friend Angelina about the trip offer. Angelina was an Italian American secretary who worked for the CIA office of the U.S. Embassy. The women analyzed where Fran's life was at age thirty-five.

She was born in 1924 on a farm in Boonville, Missouri. Her childhood had been loving but very poor, as one can expect of a farming family with seven children during the Great Depression. When she was eighteen, she left home to work at North American Aviation in Kansas City, building the nacelles of B-25 Mitchell bombers for the World War II effort. She was one of the later-famous "Rosie the Riveters". After two years of this work she moved to California, hoping to become a singer. She lived in both San Francisco and Los Angeles for a total of fifteen years. The closest she came to her dream of singing was to work as the secretary of a small record label.

By her mid-thirties she was considered an "old maid". She had given up on the idea of marrying. On an impulse, she applied to the U.S. State Department for a job as a secretary in an embassy anywhere in the world. She thought it would be a way to travel, since she didn't have the money to do so. When the recruiter came to Los Angeles to interview her, he said there was a secretarial position open at the U.S. Embassy in Tegucigalpa Honduras.

Fran replied, "Oh!"

Recruiter: "You've heard of it?"

Fran: "Yes, the Andrews Sisters had a single called "Tegucigalpa, Honduras".

Knowing only that about the tiny Central American country, she moved.

As Fran and Angelina talked, Fran concluded that discovering new places was why she was in Honduras. Before she left, she might as well accept a free trip to the beautiful Caribbean beaches of the north coast—it would be her only chance to see them. She decided she would go on this trip, move forward with the adoption, and then return to the States.

When Easter week arrived, Fran packed her bathing suit and joined Paul, Jim and the embassy group as they explored the warm Caribbean waters of Cayos Cochinos. In that beautiful setting, a spark ignited between Paul and her. Her thoughts of leaving Honduras evaporated. She and Paul began to date, but not in public. Nobody outside of Maria Esther's family knew about the pregnancy, including Fran. She thought the secrecy about their relationship was because Paul had divorced Iris less than a year before.

On July 3, 1960, Maria Esther gave birth to Paul's fifth child, Elizabeth, in Los Angeles, California. On July 11, Paul flew to Mexico City to arrange for their marriage by proxy at a lawyer's office, as he and Maria Esther had agreed. Paul invited Fran to join him on this trip, which she thought was about bank business.

Soon after Paul and Fran returned from Mexico, they were surprised by the announcement of Elizabeth's birth in the Tegucigalpa newspaper. It had been placed by Maria Esther's sister Marta Luz. Paul was revealed as the father. In this way Fran and the rest of Tegucigalpa learned about Paul's relationship with Maria Esther, and of their baby daughter. Paul explained the situation to Fran. She was understanding and agreed that they needed to keep their relationship quiet until Paul and Maria Esther worked out the child support arrangement and then obtained a divorce.

John and Craig had lived at home for only one year when Paul decided they should again study in the United States. Possibly his experience with Iris had taught him the difficulty a new wife could have with four boys, and he didn't want to run the risk of ruining the relationship with Fran. He sent John back to Grand Rapids where the Reismans happily received him and enrolled him in ninth grade. Craig was sent to The Choate School, an all-boys boarding school in Connecticut, for seventh grade.

Ricky started kindergarten at the American School in Tegucigalpa this year. He hated school from the first day he entered. Later it would be understood that he probably had dyslexia, but in Honduras in 1960 that was not evaluated. Ricky hated the structure of school. He once told me, "I thought that if I didn't study, Dad would get me out of school. Only much later did I understand that it's hard to flunk kindergarten".

Some evenings, Fran visited Paul, Bobby and Ricky after she finished work at the Embassy. One night, Paul and she walked into the living room where Bobby was playing on the floor in front of the sofa. Bobby, who was a quiet, serious child, dutifully stood up to greet Fran in the manner customary in Honduras, a kiss on the cheek. He then sat back down on the floor, and saying nothing, continued with what he was doing. Paul walked into the kitchen to make drinks. Bobby surprised Fran by suddenly jumping up off the floor and climbing in her lap. He put his arms around her neck and held her tightly, without saying a word. Fran was thrilled and didn't move a muscle, hoping the moment wouldn't end. Paul walked into the room and said, "Well, what is this, love?" Fran replied, "I do hope so, because I love him."

In April of 1961, Fran's two-year assignment with the embassy was complete. She resigned from the Foreign Service and moved in with Paul and the boys. She and Paul still did not go out in public, because he continued to be married to Maria Esther who had moved back to New York with baby Liz. In July their financial arrangements were complete and on July 29, 1961, Paul flew back to Mexico City and arranged for their divorce. Maria Esther again gave her consent by proxy.

Paul and Frances Smith, 1961

The next week, Paul took Fran to Washington, D.C. and they married on August 7. The judge who officiated remarked, "Frances Smith from Boonville, Missouri and Paul Vinelli from Naples, Italy: how did you two get together?" They answered, "Tegucigalpa,

Honduras"! Fran asked for a gold wedding band, like her mother's wedding ring. From Washington they went to New York and stayed at the Waldorf Astoria Hotel for a business trip that also counted as a honeymoon.

Fran was Paul's fourth wife, and the third wife in a three-year period. He clearly preferred to be married than to be single, but at this point he wasn't excited about the act of getting married. During their New York "honeymoon", Paul sent Fran out alone to buy herself a wedding gift from him—a mink stole—while he attended a bank meeting.

10

FAMILY AND FRIENDS: A TANGLED WEB
1961-1975

Fran had been on unsure footing since she and Paul started dating. He had kept their relationship a secret for the first sixteen months because of Maria Esther's pregnancy. Now that they were married, Fran expected she would finally be treated like Paul's partner. But some of his closest friends like Eva Bahr and Macky Salinas behaved coolly towards her. They had been Linda's friends and had seen Paul marry and divorce twice in the short time since Linda died. They probably didn't give the marriage with Fran much hope. They also felt proprietary about the Vinelli boys because they had cared for them during Linda's illness and after her death. Adding to the tension: Iris, who lived in Paul's former house, had become close to Eva Bahr who lived across the street. Fran was finding it very difficult to live in Colonia Lara next door to these women and the memories of Paul's history with Linda.

Soon after Paul and she married, Fran learned she was pregnant. She was thrilled, for she had always wanted a child and had begun to think she was too old for that to happen. Paul, who already had five children, was less enthusiastic. Not long after, Fran miscarried.

Fran had fallen in love with Paul despite her initial resistance to him. She had been in serious relationships before, and even been engaged twice, but Paul was the first man she had married and committed to. She imagined developing a lifelong love affair with her husband. Paul only wanted companionship and help raising his sons. He had no desire to fall in love. In fact, throughout their marriage he never told Fran he loved her. He did not talk to her about his feelings, nor share his past, nor did he even talk about his workday. Their relationship was very superficial: they spoke about current events, the boys' needs, and they socialized.

Another challenge to their relationship was that Ricky, now eight years old, did not get along with Fran. He had bonded with Eva and Iris. Ricky resisted Fran's attempts to befriend him. When Paul traveled for business, Ricky begged his father not to make him stay with his stepmother. On many occasions Paul let Ricky and Bobby stay at the Bahr's house.[lxxxv] This further strained the relationship between Fran and the Bahr family.

Paul had developed relationships with people in all sectors of Tegucigalpa. Over time, he became involved in many community and charitable organizations. In early 1961 he was serving as the chairman of the board of the American School of Tegucigalpa. All his sons had attended the school, although by this time only Bobby and Ricky were enrolled; John and Craig studied in the United States.

Years earlier, the school board had decided the American School needed larger facilities, and that it should move away from downtown, which had become very congested with traffic. Paul's boss at Banco Atlántida, Felix Lloveras, lived in a hilltop neighborhood called Las Lomas del Guijarro and owned land near his house. He had agreed to sell a large plot of land to the school at a good price.

The groundbreaking ceremony for the new American School on March 6, 1961, was attended by the president of Honduras Ramón Villeda Morales, U.S. Ambassador Charles Burrows, and other representatives from the Honduran government and the U.S. Embassy. In their speeches they praised the collaboration between the Honduran and American governments in making the building of the school possible. Paul spoke of the importance of a strong, bilingual education for Honduran children.[lxxxvi] The American School of Tegucigalpa became the best school in the city, and its location on top of the Las Lomas hill is enviable.

In early 1962 Fran learned she was pregnant again, at age thirty-seven. She convinced Paul to move out of the Lara neighborhood. Paul rented a two-story house in Colonia Palmira. The house had a large backyard full of eucalyptus trees. Fran started preparing a nursery for their child, who was due in November.

Next to their Palmira home lived an Italian family, the Faldos. Pasquale, the father, quickly became close to Paul because they were both from Naples. The Italian community in Tegucigalpa gathered at Pasquale's for great parties.[lxxxvii] Pasquale and his brother-in-law Salvatore De Rosa owned the Restaurante Roma downtown. In the 1960s it was one of very few restaurants in Tegucigalpa. Soon Paul, Fran and the boys went to eat there almost every weekend. When the family walked in, they were treated as if they were in their home. When the children got bored, the Faldo/De Rosa family invited them to sit on a stool in the kitchen and place pepperonis on the pizzas so that Paul and Fran could linger over their meal.

In April of 1962, nine months after her divorce from Paul, Maria Esther moved from New York to Tegucigalpa with her two-year-old daughter Liz. She came to help care for her sister Valentina who was very ill. Maria Esther took a job as a commercial secretary at Banco de Honduras, and she and Liz moved in with Valentina and Marta Luz, a third sister.

Maria Esther's return to Tegucigalpa had nothing to do with Paul, but her arrival made Fran nervous. The possibility of running into Iris at parties already had Fran on edge, and now a second ex-wife of Paul's was in Tegucigalpa, where society was a small circle. Since Paul was close with Maria Esther's siblings Gabriel and Valentina, Fran knew he would now be seeing Maria Esther and would meet his daughter. Maybe it was pregnancy hormones, but Fran became almost paranoid about what might happen.

That summer when John and Craig came home from school, Fran got to know them. John had the inquisitive mind of a scientist, often distracted by daydreams of building a rocket. One day Fran sent him to the store to buy eggs. In those days, eggs were sold in a brown paper bag. When he returned and she opened the door, she said, "Oh John!" He had been holding the bag too closely and there was egg dripping from his shirt all the way down his jeans. He hadn't noticed. "Oh John!" became a common thing. His mind moved faster than his body could react. When he put a glass on a table, everybody lunged to catch the glass, because he let go before the glass reached the table.

Craig was the charmer. He had a funny, larger-than-life personality. Fran mentioned this to Paul once, and he responded, "But you know who the most insecure one is?" Later when Craig grew up and was so often compared with his father, she realized that the two shared that trait of insecurity. It's what drove Paul so intensely to succeed.

On Sundays Paul and Fran put the four boys in the back seat of their Chevrolet Caprice and drove up the mountain to the weekend home of their friends Chito and Nena Kafie. The house was in a neighborhood called El Hatillo, high in the mountains overlooking Tegucigalpa. To get there required a thirty-minute drive up a winding mountain road that had no shoulders and a steep cliff on one side. The large Kafie property was dotted with pine trees. One heard and smelled the ever-present breeze blowing through the branches. The temperature was much cooler than down in the city. Guests congregated at tables on the patio and in the garden and stayed from lunchtime until late into the night, when a panoramic view of the twinkling lights of Tegucigalpa opened below them.

The four Vinelli boys and four Kafie children played all over the grounds. There was a basketball court and some caged *tigrillos* which fascinated the boys. One Saturday Ricky, the youngest of all the boys in the group, became upset and threw a tantrum. Paul calmly picked Ricky up, walked over to their car, and locked him inside. Ricky was screaming, red-faced, and the women at the luncheon pleaded with Paul to let him out. He didn't, until Ricky calmed down.[lxxxviii] This was Paul's parenting style, firm and calm. A stern look from him was usually enough to stop any bad behavior. A few times there was a lecture, which Ricky called sermons.

I was born on November 28, 1962. Fran wanted to name me Angelina, after her embassy friend who had by then died of cancer. Dad didn't want people to think I was named after his father and stepfather, who were both named Angelo. He told Mom my middle name could be Angelina and chose Gigi for my first name.

Soon after I was born, Dad planned a trip to Italy with his friend Bishara Kawas. He planned to show Mom, Bishara and his wife Mary both Naples and Salerno where he had grown up. The highlight of the trip would be an eight-day cruise returning from Naples to New York on the new *Leonardo da Vinci* Ocean liner. In those days it could take days to get a message from Honduras to a ship in the Atlantic. Mom's stomach started hurting the day Dad brought up the trip. She did not want to leave me in Honduras with their maids. To relieve her concerns, he asked his sister Elizabeth in Portland, Maine to watch me while they were in Europe. When I was three months old, Dad and Mom flew me to Portland before going on to Italy. Aunt Elizabeth was an enthusiastic babysitter. She was a skilled seamstress and had even made an elaborate bassinet for my short time with her.

When we returned to Honduras, Mom was focused on me. I was a small baby, her first child, and she had missed me tremendously during the trip. Ricky felt ignored and, to get attention, picked fights with Mom. Dad had little tolerance for the complaints both brought to him when he came home from work.

Since Ricky had bonded with his grandmother Dora after Linda's death, Paul decided to send him to live with Dora and Angelo in Rochester, New York. Bobby and I would be the only two children at home that year. In September of 1963 Paul sent ten-year-old Ricky to the much-colder climate of Rochester. Dora and Angelo enrolled him in the fifth grade at Nazareth Hall Cadet School. The school was taught by Roman Catholic nuns who wore full habits—students wore military uniforms. Every Wednesday, a sergeant presided over military drills: marching and standing in formation. Nazareth Hall required students to attend Sunday mass. Ricky had never been to any church. Dora didn't attend mass (she declared she had to cook the big Sunday meal) so she asked Angelo to take Ricky to church. The old man and boy sat in a back pew where Angelo spent the entire time telling stories. Later when the nuns asked Ricky if he had attended mass, he said yes. When they asked what the priest spoke of, he admitted, "I don't know!"

Ricky, Nazareth Hall Cadet School, Rochester NY

In Tegucigalpa, Hondurans were gearing up for the presidential election scheduled for October 13, 1963. One morning ten days before, Paul and Fran woke up to the sound of gunfire. The Honduran army had attacked the *Guardia Civil* while the guards slept. This special unit had been created by President Ramón Villeda Morales to protect him after the 1959 coup attempt. The surprise attack was successful: that very day the army succeeded in replacing the president with their choice, Colonel Oswaldo López Arellano. This takeover initiated almost two decades of military rule in Honduras. [lxxxix]

Paul no longer worked for the Honduran government, but government officials still asked him for advice. In April of 1964, he attended the meeting of Central Bank presidents in Antigua, Guatemala as advisor to the president of the Central Bank of Honduras. The same month he represented the government at the inaugural meeting of the Central American Monetary Council, held in San Salvador. Soon after, the Honduran Ministry of Finance named him to a council that was to review the country's tax laws which he had helped draft fifteen years earlier.

Paul had fallen in love with Honduras and its potential. He saw opportunity everywhere in the country and continued to incentivize new industry. He became the principal project developer for the private sector in Honduras. [xc] His approach to development later became the motto he created for Banco Atlántida: "Deeds and not words". [xci]

He also had an ambitious vision for Banco Atlántida, who until the 1950s existed only for the business of the Standard Fruit Company. Paul knew the entire country needed access to banking services for the Honduran economy to grow. He launched a great period of expansion for the bank, opening branches all over Honduras.

He also made significant changes within the bank. He improved both the health and retirement plans. On September 25,1964 Paul created the *Union de Inversionistas*. This was a fund that gave bank employees with tenure some ownership in the bank.[xcii]

By the Fall of 1966, John, Craig and Bob all studied in the United States. John was at the University of Michigan, Craig was at the University of Pennsylvania, Bob was at Choate in Connecticut. Paul brought them home to Tegucigalpa for summers and at Christmastime. Ricky had returned that summer from living with his grandmother in New York. His grades at Nazareth Hall were poor so it was recommended that he repeat sixth grade. Paul asked him if he wanted to return to the American School and Ricky did not, because he knew his former classmates would be moving on to seventh grade. Paul enrolled him in an English language school run by American Mennonites called Academia Los Pinares, located high in the mountains above Tegucigalpa.

Maria Esther's sister Valentina had recovered from her health problems. The three Mejía sisters and six-year-old Liz enjoyed living together and Maria Esther had decided to stay in Tegucigalpa. She was about to be named Director of an English language institute called IHCI (Instituto Hondureño de Cultura Interamericana). Before accepting the position, she traveled to New York for a routine medical checkup. Liz stayed in Tegucigalpa with her aunts. During her checkup, Maria Esther's doctor recommended a minor surgical procedure, which took place on October 26, 1966. Nobody could have anticipated that she would die that day from a pulmonary embolism. She was forty-six years old.

Maria Esther Mejia and Liz Vinelli, 1966

Paul now had five children who had lost their mother. Liz's aunts insisted she remain living with them.[17] Paul agreed because Liz was so well cared for and it would make things less complicated with Fran. However, he began to visit Liz with more frequency, often taking the four boys. Neither Liz nor I were told the other existed, although we were only two years apart in age.

In 1966 plans were approved for a hotel to be built in Tegucigalpa that was more luxurious than any in the city. It would be called

---

17. This was the second generation of Mejía women who lived through the same story. When Maria Esther was seven, her mother also died during surgery. Maria Esther, Valentina, Marta Luz and their four brothers were raised by two aunts just as Liz later was.

the Hotel Honduras Maya. The property selected was directly across from our home in Colonia Palmira. Paul knew the construction noise would be terrible. Years before, at around the time of the American School relocation, he had purchased a property from Felix Lloveras in the Las Lomas del Guijarro neighborhood. Paul decided this was the moment to build his dream house.

Paul had a very specific vision of what he wanted, as if he had been building the house in his mind for years. He hired Mario Valenzuela, the same architect who had designed the Hotel Honduras Maya. Paul was involved in every detail, and not once did he ask Fran for her input. He had always been attracted to clean, modern architecture. The new house would be a stunning example of this style, more dramatic than any home ever built in Honduras. The property was on a steep hillside. Before construction could begin, massive amounts of fill dirt were required to create five different levels. Thirteen-year-old Ricky was given an assignment to ensure Paul was billed correctly. He sat on the side of the hill, wearing a hard hat and holding a clipboard, counting the number of trucks that came in to deliver fill dirt. There were more than three hundred truckloads of dirt.

In 1967 Mom began to talk to Dad about having a second child. He resisted. Six children were enough of a financial responsibility, especially since the oldest three studied at expensive schools in the United States and needed a plane ticket to visit home twice a year. Mom pleaded with him, arguing that Ricky was nine years older than me, so I didn't have a sibling for company. (She still refused for me to know I had a sister). Dad relented. In June of that year, Mom and I went to Missouri to visit her family. It was there that she learned she was pregnant. She was very excited and hoped for another girl.

That summer Dad and Mom were sitting at the bar in their Palmira house when their Neapolitan friend Salvatore de la Rosa came over. They told him they were thinking of names for the baby. For a girl, they were thinking of Mia. In 1967 the actress Mia Farrow was in the news for her affair and marriage with the much-older Frank Sinatra. Don Salvatore did not approve of a child being associated with the controversial actress's name. He said to Mom, "Oh no, *signora*, name her Maria Pia, like the Neapolitan princess." My parents liked the name Pia.

The Las Lomas house was ready for move-in by December of 1967. It clung to a five-level property on the side of a hill in the middle of the bowl of mountains that surrounded Tegucigalpa, which gave it an extraordinary view. The center of the house was an ultra-modern living room in the shape of a football. The room was eighty feet long and thirty-five feet wide, with a forty-six-foot length of windows plus two more six-foot-wide windows on each end of the room to take full advantage of the view. The living room had white tile floors and a tall beige marble fireplace. On the level below the living room was a game room almost as large. This had wood paneled walls, red and white Spanish tiled floors, and a black slate fireplace.

Running off the ends of the living room were two wings. One was for the bedrooms, the other for dining room, kitchen, maids' quarters and laundry patio. These two wings ended in the hill, creating a large central patio. Paul's stepfather Angelo Bufano was skilled at stonework and came down from Rochester, New York to build a huge stone wall along the hillside part of the patio. In the center of that wall was a waterfall. In one corner of the patio was a greenhouse for Fran's orchid collection.

Just after moving in, Paul and Fran hosted a memorable Christmas party. Five hundred guests came, a mix of Paul's contacts from business, banking, and diplomatic circles. Car after car drove through two tall iron gates and down the long driveway to the large house. Soon there were so many drivers waiting by their owner's cars that it looked like there was a second party in the parking lot. Guests got out at the base of a long stone stairway and walked up to the double front doors where Paul and Fran, eight months pregnant and wearing a colorful caftan, greeted them. Inside, the Toño Medina orchestra played dance music at one end of the living room. The other end was anchored by a twenty-foot bar manned by a team of bartenders. The dining room table was loaded with hors d'oeuvres. Tuxedoed waiters circulated all night, passing trays of drinks and food. The living room furniture was pushed against the walls of the room to open space for gathering. Hondurans love to dance, and the white tile floor made a perfect dance floor. Late in the night, Fran took the microphone and sang "I Left My Heart in San Francisco". The party lasted until dawn.

Rick, Craig, Paul, John and Bob Vinelli at Christmas party

Pia Vinelli, Paul's seventh child, was born one month later, on January 23, 1968. Paul was forty-five, Fran was forty-three. Fran had a difficult delivery that resulted in a hysterectomy. For Paul, this was a relief. No more children sounded like a good plan.

When Pia was born, our sister Liz was seven years old and in second grade at the American School. On the bus to school one morning, her Spanish teacher Mrs. Erazo sat down on the seat next to her and said, "Congratulations on your new little sister, you and Gigi must be so happy!" It was the first Liz knew that she had sisters.

That September I started first grade. Mom and Dad sent me to Academia Los Pinares, the Mennonite school in the mountains where Ricky attended middle school. Ricky had his reasons for choosing Los Pinares after returning from New York, but our friends thought it was strange that my parents sent me to such an out of the way place when the American School was five minutes from our new house. It was so close that Mom could hear the children playing in the school yard, and she often thought of Liz playing there.

Dad had been so involved with the board at the American School and almost everyone we knew sent their kids there. When asked, my parents told everyone that I wanted to go to the school where my older brother went. The real reason I was sent to Los Pinares was that Mom did not want me to run into Liz at the American School. We were the only Vinellis in Honduras so it wouldn't have taken long for someone to point her out to me. It's amazing how successful this separation was. I was twelve before I learned I had an older sister.

Rick and I coincided at Los Pinares for only two years before he had to transfer because the Mennonite school only went through grade nine. When Rick entered high school at the American School,

I asked my parents if I might go also. I was tired of the forty-five-minute bus ride on winding cliff-hanging roads, especially in the afternoon sun—I got motion sickness every day. The answer was no, with no explanation given.

Paul didn't only have to worry about paying for his children's education. His sons were American citizens, and the Vietnam War was in progress. In February of 1970, Craig, age twenty-one, was drafted by the U.S. Army after completing college. He went through basic training and twelve weeks of Officer Candidate School, after which he was commissioned as a Second Lieutenant. Craig visited us in Tegucigalpa before leaving for Vietnam. When his visit ended, the whole family went to the Toncontín airport to see him off for his long trip to Chu Lai, Vietnam. That farewell was the first time I ever saw Dad cry. It was such a relief when Craig's first letter arrived weeks later. He was not assigned to combat but rather was a Quartermaster. His responsibility was management and distribution of supplies for soldiers in the field. The job aligned perfectly with Craig's gregarious personality. My brother served in Vietnam for three years.

Paul's open-door policy and concern for the wellbeing of Honduras led to some unusual friendships. Despite his having no religious beliefs, he became close to many members of the clergy because he cared about the work they did with the poor in Honduras. Since the great majority of Hondurans were Catholics in those days, priests and nuns are who he met. It was not unusual for a priest to visit him at his office or come to the house on a weekend for lunch. Paul donated personally and through the bank to many of their causes, even supporting the education of seminarians studying to become Catholic priests.

Paul was closest to Father James McShane, an Irish Jesuit priest who was stationed in a Honduran village called Progreso. Father McShane was a Harvard Law School graduate who stayed at our house several times a year when he visited Tegucigalpa. He had a beautiful voice and loved musicals. Every time he saw me, he broke into the song "Gigi", from the 1962 musical by the same name. My conversations with Father McShane about God were a major reason that I later wanted to be baptized. I don't recall discussing with him why my parents did not go to church nor why Dad didn't want to baptize us, but I would think he and Dad talked about the subject. I do know that Dad's beliefs didn't hurt their decades-long relationship.

Dad told me that he would not impose religious beliefs on anyone, the way Catholicism was forced on him when he was little. For this reason, he was opposed to the Catholic practice of baptizing babies right after birth, which was the norm in Honduras. He assured me that he had no problem with his children having a religious faith, but it needed to be our decision.

Another friend of his was a nun named Sor Maria Rosa. They met when she wanted to form a non-profit organization to care for orphans. This would not be a traditional orphanage but would be modeled after an Austrian organization where orphaned children lived in home-like settings. She planned to name the project Aldeas SOS. The idea was to take in orphans as well as children whose parents could not care for them temporarily. She made an appointment to meet Paul at the recommendation of a friend. She told him that to receive guidance and funds from the original Austrian charity, she needed to create a non-profit in the U.S. For that, she needed to open a U.S. bank account. This required five thousand dollars – a major sum in 1963, especially for a nun. The funds would be returned to the charity after a period. He listened carefully to her request and immediately agreed to lend her the money.

When the money was returned to Sor Maria Rosa months later, she went to the bank to repay the loan. Paul told her that he would like for her charity to keep the money. She insisted on honoring the terms of the loan, and suggested he help her in other ways down the road. Paul did so, supporting the organization for many years. Aldeas SOS helped almost one hundred thousand children and there were eventually "aldea" children in all levels of business in Honduras. Sor Maria Rosa later said to me about Paul, "There are people who do great things in the world without anyone, not even their family, knowing."[xciii]

In 1970 Rick, Pia and I were the three Vinelli siblings living at home. During the week everyone in the house lived separate lives. Rick had a social life because he was seventeen. Pia and I stayed home and had dinner in the kitchen with our cook Ursula. Dad and Mom went to cocktail parties almost every night, because Dad accepted all invitations—business, personal, and diplomatic. We would see him only briefly when he came home from work. Every evening, his driver dropped him off at the foot of the front staircase. By the time Dad reached the front door at the top, a maid had opened it. Dad walked back to their bedroom where Mom was getting herself ready to go out. A maid always set out a tray with his drink—Johnny Walker Black and water—and salami and cheese. Soon after, Dad and Mom emerged from the bedroom dressed for the evening and stopped by our rooms to say goodnight.

Dad did not like to be alone with his thoughts. If he and Mom didn't have a party to go to, he invited friends over. His days were full of serious business discussions so by nighttime and weekends he preferred to surround himself with lively groups of people where the conversation was on a lighter level. Our family's favorite time of the year was in December, when my brothers came home for Christmas. The house was fun, loud and even chaotic at times. Dad had a ping pong table set up in the downstairs game room, with black curtains hung at either end to catch wayward balls. He loved to compete against my brothers' friends, usually winning. A few feet away Mom presided over the octagonal poker table covered in green felt, playing with more of my brothers' friends. There were small cocktail tables by each chair holding drinks and food. Ursula, our cook, sent down platter after platter of homemade pizza and fried breadfruit. The bar was always open, and the fun lasted until late into the night. Pia and I were too young to participate, but we were entertained by watching from the edge of the room.

When we got bored, we went outside to the grounds surrounding our house. There were trees to climb, blackberry and prickly pear bushes up by our water well, a large vegetable garden, a grove of citrus trees, and a tetherball court. Matilda, our macaw with brilliant orange, blue and yellow feathers, waddled all over the property because her wings were clipped to keep her from flying away.

Dad loved animals. Just as he had bought dogs to entertain my brothers when they were little, he bought pets to entertain Pia and me. When I was very little, he brought home a kinkajou, which looked like a cross between a monkey and a little bear. Cute as he was, he wasn't a great pet because he was nocturnal and slept all day.

Then Dad gave me a baby deer. Eventually that pet didn't make sense and Dad brought home two black cats he named Zuzu and Zito.

He maintained his habit of corresponding with family, friends and colleagues regularly even as his career, teaching and family placed many demands on his time. If nothing else, he made sure everyone he knew heard from him at Christmastime. His secretary mailed more than one thousand Christmas cards signed Paul and Fran. He instructed bank staff to prepare gift baskets for important clients. He sent presents—usually a case of liquor—to his closest friends. Fran oversaw the assembly of gift boxes for the household staff in our downstairs game room. Inside there was food, necessities like t-shirts and socks, and toys and candy for their children.

The Christmas parties Paul and Fran hosted grew larger in the 1970s as Paul developed more business and social contacts. After they had one party where more than 1,000 guests came—some of whom were not invited—security had to be increased. Paul and Fran were forced to close the front gates and require that guards check guest names off a list before they were allowed to enter.

These parties opened Rick's eyes to a potential career. Paul, noticing Rick's organizational skills and social bent, put Rick in charge of arranging food on the dining room table and of provisioning the bar. Rick had no interest in the science and math his three older brothers studied in college, but he really enjoyed organizing events. That's when he first thought of learning about the food and beverage industry. After high school, Rick went to Florida to study hotel administration.

In August of 1974, Dora's second husband Angelo Bufano passed away. Paul sent Bob to Rochester, New York to pack up Grandma and bring her to Tegucigalpa. Before she arrived, Paul bought Dora a house two blocks from ours. When his mother was about to land in Tegucigalpa, Paul warned Fran, "She does not like women, and she especially doesn't like any woman who is married to me".[18]

Paul had his driver take him to Dora's house every morning on his way to the office. He sat and spoke with his mother for ten minutes, always asking how she was feeling. He often went into the kitchen to inspect her pantry, making sure it was well stocked. Together they planned gatherings for the following weekend. Our Sundays were reserved for Grandma, who got up at dawn to start making an enormous Italian meal for the family. We arrived at her home at noon. She ordered us to sit at the table while she brought out course after course of food. In the center of the table there was antipasto, usually marinated zucchini and eggplant. The first course was pasta with both red and ricotta sauces, followed by a meat course. Sponge cake for dessert. She was offended if we didn't have a good portion or even seconds of everything. Rick was known to put eggplant parmigiana in his pocket to avoid angering her. The meal lasted for hours.

What I didn't know until I started writing this book was that Grandma also frequently hosted a luncheon on Saturday—one that Mom, Pia and I were not invited to. As Dad had predicted, Grandma and Mom did not get along. For her Saturday meals, Dora invited Dad's old friends that Mom did not see, and she included my sister Liz. As Grandma helped Dad rebuild friendships with people that had been estranged during his marriage to Mom, his relationship with Mom deteriorated further.

---

18. This was not true. By all accounts, Dora loved Paul's first wife Linda. I think she loved who her son loved.

Even as their relationship soured, Dad supported Mom's interests. She loved to ride horseback. She had done so since she was a young girl on the farm in Boonville, and in California she had participated in dressage competitions. She asked Dad if she could have a horse. He rented a property down the hill from their house and had stables and a riding ring built. It was the first Saddle Club in Tegucigalpa. People rented stables for their horses, and Mom hired a riding teacher so children could take lessons. By the time I was ten, the Saddle Club was my hangout every afternoon after school.

In September of 1974 the deadly Hurricane Fifi tore through the Caribbean, Belize and Honduras, killing eight thousand people. In the mountains of Honduras twenty-four inches of rain fell in thirty-six hours, resulting in devastating floods and landslides. One hundred eighty-two towns and villages were destroyed in one day. Fifty percent of Honduras's food crops were destroyed, including ninety-five percent of the banana plantations, which were still the country's major export.[xciv]

Business in Honduras came to a stop, and bank clients could not make their debt payments. Chito Kafie asked Paul to grant an extension to his business loan. Paul agreed to three years. Chito had heard that Paul gave other businesses a five-year extension and returned home muttering, "That Neapolitan son of a bitch." Chito's son Luis later asked Paul, "Why did you give my dad a shorter period of time to repay than the other businesses in town?" Paul replied, "Because everyone knew Chito was like my brother. I needed for the board of directors to see there was no favoritism towards my brother."[xcv] Paul's family and friends knew he had this philosophy. The closer a person was to him, the tougher he was with them.

Chito Kafie and Paul Vinelli

When I was twelve, a call to a wrong number changed my life. One afternoon after school, the phone rang at our house, and I answered. A girl asked to speak to Elizabeth Vinelli. I replied that there was no person by that name at our number. After hanging up, I was left with a strange feeling, and I told a friend what had happened. He laughed and said, "Gigi, I think Pia and you are the only ones in Tegucigalpa who don't know you have a sister named Elizabeth at the American School."

I was mortified and furious. Rather than confront my parents, I went to my brother Rick. He confirmed that I had a sister named Liz who lived with her aunts, and that Dad and my brothers had a relationship with her. He told me that Mom insisted that Pia and I not be told about Liz. I asked him to arrange an introduction, and he agreed to do so, suggesting we meet her at Grandma's. Dora would be happy to do something that would displease Mom. One day when Mom was out, Rick and I went to Grandma's. Liz was already there when we arrived. It was awkward to be meeting a sibling for the first time at age twelve and fourteen, but we liked each other immediately. Liz, Rick, Grandma and I kept our meeting a secret for some time. I didn't say anything to Pia, who was seven.

At the time I found out about Liz, Bob was getting his MBA at the Harvard extension, INCAE, in Nicaragua. In the summer between his two-year program, he was offered an internship at a sugar mill in rural Nicaragua. There he met a woman named Maria José and they started dating.

In the summer of 1975 Liz turned fifteen and joined other girls in having a *quinceañera*, the traditional coming out party given for girls in Latin America. Traditionally Dad should have been her escort, but he and Mom were on a trip to China. Dad asked Bob to come to Tegucigalpa and be Liz's escort. Bob brought Maria José as his date. Since they were staying at our house, he explained to her that Pia and I did not know about Liz, and therefore she could not tell us what party they were attending. Bob didn't know that I had met Liz, and that I also knew about the party because many of my friends were going to attend. As he and Maria José were leaving the house in their formal clothes I said quietly to Maria José, "Please wish my sister a Happy Birthday from me."

After this I had enough of secrets, and when my parents returned from their trip, I confronted Mom with all the anger a teenager could muster. I told her I should have been at Liz's party, supporting my sister at this pivotal moment in her life. Mom tried to explain that she had absolutely nothing against Liz, and that the circumstances when she first married Dad had put her in a defensive position about his ex-wives. As time passed, not telling Pia and me about our sister had become a habit she didn't know how to reverse.

The climate in our house became charged with blame and frustration. Dad and Mom's relationship was deteriorating rapidly and the evenings and weekends when Dad was at home were very stressful. Pia and I were the only children living at home, and we mostly stayed out of sight of our parents because we never knew when there would be an explosion. Our bedrooms were next to Mom and Dad's and many nights we went to the living room or kitchen to avoid hearing them fight.

They both had a hand in the discord. She was not the supportive kind of wife he wanted but rather was willful and independent. He was fifteen years into his fourth marriage and had no energy nor patience left for nurturing a relationship. Mom's synopsis was that two Scorpios should never marry, it's like putting two scorpions in a basket.

11

GROWING AN INTERNATIONAL BANK:
THE CHASE YEARS
1966 - 1974

Paul's personal life was so complicated and dysfunctional that he craved order and success in the business world. With one hand on the reins of his family life, he focused most of his attention on being an international banker. By the mid 1960s the heirs of the Vaccaro/D'Antoni family, who lived in New Orleans, decided they had no interest in managing the family's businesses in Honduras. They first sold their Standard Fruit Company to Castle & Cooke Corporation, who also bought Dole Food Company and became the world's largest fruit producer.[xcvi]

U.S. legislation prohibited Castle & Cooke from owning a foreign bank, and they weren't interested in it anyway, so the Vaccaro/D'Antoni family asked Felix Lloveras and Paul to help them find a buyer for Banco Atlántida. Whereas the Vaccaro/D'Antoni family owned one hundred percent of the Standard Fruit Company, they had created joint ventures for their multiple sideline businesses in

Honduras, including the bank. They still owned more than fifty percent of Banco Atlántida.

Lloveras and Paul looked for a Honduran buyer for the Vaccaro/D'Antoni shares in the bank but found no local takers for such a large transaction. When the bank board decided to look for an international bank to buy Banco Atlántida, they turned to Paul. This was because of Paul's international banking connections. Since the late 1940s, he had attended almost every World Bank and International Monetary Fund annual meeting. The relationships he had developed made him the more likely person to find a buyer.

Paul made inquiries and two potential buyers emerged: Wells Fargo and Chase Manhattan Bank. Wells Fargo was eliminated because they were only interested in buying twenty-five percent. David Rockefeller was the president and co-CEO of Chase Manhattan Bank at this time. David, together with his brother Nelson, had supported U.S. involvement in Latin America since the 1940s. David had headed the Latin American division of Chase a decade earlier. He had traveled throughout the region extensively and his Spanish was good. By the mid-1960s he had embarked on a campaign to expand Chase Manhattan Bank's presence in Latin America.[xcvii]

From the beginning of their relationship David Rockefeller and Paul understood each other very well. Paul recognized Rockefeller's commitment to Latin America and recommended Chase be the buyer for the bank shares. By the end of 1966 the Vaccaro/D'Antoni families sold their entire majority interest to Chase. Banco Atlántida became the first Central American affiliate of the renowned New York bank. The sale ended the continuous term, since the bank's founding in 1913, of a Vaccaro family member as chairman of the board of

Banco Atlántida. Dr. José Mendoza, who was close to the Vaccaros from his tenure at the D'Antoni Hospital in La Ceiba and had been a director of the bank for years, agreed to become the Chairman of the Board. Months later, on April 22, 1967, Felix Lloveras retired at age seventy-five from his position as CEO of Banco Atlántida. Paul became CEO.

Paul continued his practice of attending the World Bank and the International Monetary Fund annual September meetings. There he reconnected with old colleagues and made new banking relationships. The custom was for the organizations to meet two years in Washington, D.C. and then meet in a member country the third year. Thanks to those meetings Paul and Fran traveled extensively. After the work sessions ended, they visited cities or countries nearby.

David Rockefeller figured prominently in their travels related to the World Bank/IMF meetings. He was an avid traveler and generous host. In 1967, the year after Chase bought the interest in Banco Atlántida, the meetings were held in Rio de Janeiro. One day that week, David chartered a large private plane to fly the heads of Chase's correspondent banks and their wives, including Paul and Fran, to Sao Paulo for a meeting. On the way back, Rockefeller instructed the pilots to circle over Rio for forty-five minutes while they finished a four-course meal. When they landed, it was raining. Rockefeller had transportation waiting for everyone. He walked up and down the line of black cars with his umbrella, making sure all his guests were taken care of before he went to his hotel.

Paul was ever more influential in Honduras's banking and business world, and articles about him were in the newspapers almost weekly. The increased focus on him and the large parties he and

Fran hosted in their new home predictably led to criticism about his lifestyle. One December morning, the Diario La Tribuna newspaper ran a front-page story titled *Los Zapatos del Oligarca*" (the shoes of the oligarch). A picture showed a pile of men's shoes in front of a shoeshine boy in the central park of downtown Tegucigalpa. Some bored reporter looking for a story had seen the shoes and asked the boy who they belonged to. When he learned they belonged to the CEO of Banco Atlántida across the street, he took a picture and ran the story.

Paul often used the phrase "No good deed goes unpunished", and this was an example. He did not need to have his shoes shined in the central park. He owned a shoeshine kit, and I had seen him polish his own shoes. Besides, he had household help at home. But when he walked past the park to the bank, the shoeshine boys always ran after him asking that he give them work. He was a believer in giving people the opportunity to earn a living. He started bringing his shoes downtown for the boys to work on, and he paid them very well for the shines.

The president of La Tribuna was Oscar Flores, a prominent lawyer and journalist who was a friend of Paul's. He regretted that the story made Paul look frivolous. Flores came up with an idea to defuse the awkward situation. A few weeks later Paul and Fran hosted their annual Christmas party. Most everyone in Tegucigalpa society came, as well as many from San Pedro Sula and La Ceiba. Flores attended with his twenty-year-old son Carlos (the future president of Honduras). As they climbed the steps to the front door of the Vinelli house, Paul was standing at the top, greeting guests. La Tribuna journalists followed the Flores father and son. They raised their cameras when Oscar Flores presented his host with a crumpled brown sack. Paul looked inside and found a weathered pair of old shoes. Flores joked they were to add to his collection. Paul laughed, sat down on the front stoop, and removed his shoes to then try on the new shoes. Flores also took his shoes off and a photographer took their picture, both in socks, their arms around each other. The picture ran on the front page of La Tribuna the next day.[xcviii]

Paul's nose for business opportunity wasn't limited to Honduras. Directly north was British Honduras, a colony who had struggled to gain its independence from Great Britain since the 1950s. British Honduras won the right to govern itself in 1964 and by the early 1970s it was on its way to independence. Paul anticipated the new country would have banking needs, and he approached David Rockefeller at Chase about joining forces with Banco Atlántida to create a new bank in Belize City. In 1971, Banco Atlántida, Chase Manhattan Bank, two other banks as well as Belizean investors created Atlantic Bank Belize.[19]

At the inauguration on Saturday August 16, 1971, Paul as chairman of the board of the new bank said in his speech, "Our own experience and philosophy have led us to the conclusion that only what is good for the country is good for the bank. That which makes one grow, will ensure the progress and welfare of the other."[xcix]

Paul's goal was to grow Banco Atlántida from a Honduran bank to an international one with Chase Manhattan Bank's help. Thanks to the American bankers, Banco Atlántida was the first Honduran bank to have banking practices, systems and technology that later

---

19. Chase sold its interest in Atlantic Bank Belize four years later. It was too small an operation for them.

were emulated by all major banks in Honduras. [c] Paul and David Rockefeller introduced the practice of including local business leaders on the bank board. This is something American banks and companies had been doing for years but was not common in Honduras. [ci]

The greatest challenge was finding the right team to lead the expansion. A logical source for talent was the group of economists Paul had trained years earlier at the Central Bank and at the Economics Department at the university. The gathering of his team had started back in 1969 with Macky, who at the time still worked for the Central Bank. The two friends saw each other at a party and, given their common history at the Central Bank, their conversation naturally went in that direction. As Macky talked about work, Paul commented,

"It seems you're bored, Macky."

Macky: "I'm not bored, I'm worn out. My job has me on a plane all the time, to Guatemala, to El Salvador, to Nicaragua. When I get home there's a message from the bank that I need to fly to Costa Rica."

This was during a time when there was an effort to create a Central American Common Market, with one single currency. Macky's schedule would have been punishing for anyone, but more so for her because of her childhood battle with polio. By this time, she needed two canes to walk.

Paul: "This is the moment I've been waiting for. Banco Atlántida's Trust Department only manages three trusts. I need someone to grow the department, someone who knows how to have a relationship with people who have money. You know everyone in town."

Macky: "I'll quit the Central Bank tomorrow."

Paul: "I'm not taking just any employee from them. I need to go speak with Roberto." (Dr. Roberto Ramirez, the chairman of the Central Bank).

The conversation with Dr. Ramirez went well, and Macky took over the Trust Department of Banco Atlántida one month later. [cii]

Adriana Yu Shan had also been Paul's economics student and Central Bank employee in the early 1950s. When Paul insisted that she would benefit from the experience, she went to work for the World Bank in Washington, D.C. Paul often saw her when he traveled to Washington, and he always told her he had a job for her if she returned to Tegucigalpa. She returned at the end of 1973. Soon after, he hired Yu Shan as Head of the Department of Economic Studies of Banco Atlántida. This department performed the same function as the one he headed at the Central Bank, so Adriana had worked for him in that capacity before. Adriana Yu Shan ran the department for almost two decades. [ciii]

Not all the bank's team came from Paul's former students. José Rubén Mendoza was the son of Dr. José Mendoza, then chairman of Banco Atlántida. He had returned to Honduras a year earlier from studying in the U.S. and England and was working in the credit department at the bank. Paul called him into his office and said,

"I want you to take over the management of the International Department of the bank."

José Rubén was very surprised; he only had minor credit experience at this point.

José Rubén: "I don't know anything about running an International Department".

Paul: "Doesn't matter. Jump in the water and get your butt wet."[20]

In 1973 Paul surprised attorney Faustino Laínez by showing up at his office and inviting him to lunch at the Chico Club. He offered him a job as Head of the Legal Department of Banco Atlántida. Faustino's brother had been the previous head of the legal department and had recently resigned to move to San Pedro Sula. Faustino had just accepted an important government ministry position. Because he had political ambitions, he was torn by Paul's offer. His father suggested he give the bank offer serious consideration. He told Faustino, "Paul is a good friend, if he offers you a job, he will give you good opportunities." Faustino agreed, withdrew from the government post and accepted Paul's offer.[civ][21]

Paul rarely closed his office door, which gave him the reputation of being a very accessible boss. At times it got him into trouble, because people felt they could bring him problems that were not his to solve.[cv] But he was sensitive to the misfortunes of others and always tried to help. Many times, he would start a conversation with Macky by saying something like, "There is a man who is having troubles. His wife needs surgery, and he is six months behind on his house payment. I need to see how to help him." Sometimes the help was in the form of a loan extension, other times food was delivered to

---

20. José Rubén remained at the bank for more than 50 years, eventually becoming a director. He retired in 2025.

21. Faustino remained at the bank for more than 50 years, eventually becoming a director. He retired in 2025.

someone's home. He always tried to help, and he never disclosed who needed the help.[cvi]

When the World Bank - IMF meetings were held in Washington, David Rockefeller borrowed his brother Nelson's home to host a party for the heads of Chase's correspondent banks in other countries. Fran remembered that the wives of the Latin bankers were preoccupied with what to wear to a party hosted by David and Peggy Rockefeller. Back then, in Latin America, long gowns were standard for evening parties, so they dressed in their finest gowns for the Rockefeller reception in Washington. Fran was very surprised when their hostess Peggy received them at the door dressed in a simple, short black dress and wearing comfortable flats.

Being associated with Chase gave Paul and Fran extraordinary opportunities. The 1973 World Bank - IMF meeting was held in Nairobi, Kenya. The Rockefeller family owned two luxury photo safari resorts in the area. David Rockefeller invited the foreign bankers and their wives to spend a few days at these properties before the meetings started. They were flown in small planes from Nairobi to the first lodge. Each couple was assigned a private ranger and jeep. Twice that day they drove out to look at the animals. After a gourmet dinner they spent the night in luxurious rooms. The following day Rockefeller had planes waiting to fly them to the second lodge. Here the routine was repeated, and this time they saw different animals. The third day they were flown back to Nairobi for the bank meetings.

Paul and David Rockefeller, 1973

By the mid 1970s the political unrest in Latin America was getting a lot of attention from the international press. David Rockefeller and Chase began to worry about their ownership in Banco Atlántida. By this time, Paul liked the idea of the bank being one hundred percent Honduran-owned for the first time in its history. He did not try to discourage Rockefeller's concerns, and they discussed the possibility of Chase selling its ownership in the bank. Paul began to speak to friends, business associates and Banco Atlántida board members about buying Chase's shares in the bank.[cvii]

Word got out that Colombia was drafting a law that reduced the amount foreign banks could own of local banks. Honduras had not indicated it would pass a similar law, but Chase did not wait. In April of 1974, before the Colombian law was even passed, Chase reduced its ownership of Banco Atlántida down to twenty-five percent. The next year Colombia passed Law No. 55 reducing the amount of foreign ownership permissible in local banks. [cviii] In August of 1975 Chase Manhattan Bank sold the remaining twenty-five percent of its interest in Banco Atlántida. Its investment in Banco Atlántida lasted nine years. The bank was now 100% Honduran-owned.

12

THE COLLECTOR

aul had many personal interests, and his nature was to collect. The love he felt for his adopted country of Honduras turned into a passion for its art and culture. On weekends I often found him at his desk at home, reading books about art, stamps, coins, paper money, and Mayan artifacts. During his decades with Banco Atlántida, he oversaw the creation of important collections in each of these categories. He also built personal collections to the extent his budget allowed.

One of his deepest loves was fine art. Thanks to his years in Honduras he became very knowledgeable about naive and primitivist painting. His journey into this world began in the early 1950s when Paul met José Antonio Velasquez, a painter who earned a living as a barber at the Pan-American Agricultural School in Zamorano, Honduras. Paul met Velasquez through the school's director Wilson Popenoe, who he befriended on his first visit to Honduras in 1949. Popenoe made a great effort to promote Velasquez's primitivist work among the American and international community in Honduras. Paul was impressed by Velasquez's talent and took up the cause as well. He observed that the painter was talented and passionate but used low quality materials. To encourage Velasquez to spend more on his paint, brushes and canvases, Paul started buying his paintings to give as gifts. He became one of Velasquez's market-makers when word spread among his friends and business associates that Paul considered Velasquez to be the best primitivist in Honduras. Later Paul took the painter to New York and introduced him to art dealers. Eventually Velasquez became the most critically acclaimed Honduran artist, with exhibitions all over the world.

The focal point of the living room in our Las Lomas house were three Velasquez paintings. Dad used to challenge Pia and me to search in the paintings for elements that were common in Velasquez's work. The artist depicted the town of San Antonio de Oriente, where he lived for thirty years. Besides red-tiled roofs and cobblestone streets, Velasquez was known to include a woman, a priest, a church and a dog in almost all his paintings.

As Velasquez's fame grew, so did the line of painters outside of the executive offices of Banco Atlántida, each hoping for the opportunity to show Dr. Vinelli his work. As Paul left the office each day, he walked by the artists and pointed at what he liked, setting the price. He bought in quantity, so he didn't pay much. Painters accepted what he offered for their work because Paul was one of the biggest purchasers of art in the country. Even though they didn't make much money selling to him, many artist's careers were launched by his promotion through purchases, word of mouth, and painting exhibitions hosted by Banco Atlántida.[cix]

Painters who have credited Paul as their mentor include Sergio Almendares, Maury Flores, Eduardo Galeano, Carlos Garay, Benigno Gómez, Cesar Ordoñez, Luis H. Padilla, German Durón Lanza,

Hermes Armijo Maltéz, Cesar Rendón, Arturo Lopez Rodezno, Manuel Rodriguez Lazaroni, Miguel Angel Ruiz Matute, and Roque Zelaya. Rodriguez Lazaroni wrote, "Don Paul was one of my great patrons. He had the bank sponsor an exhibition of my paintings and thanks to that, I could stop selling them on the street."[cx]

Over the years Paul amassed a large collection of Honduran paintings for Banco Atlántida as well as for himself. The bank's collection was exhibited throughout the year in their Salon Cultural, a large exhibition room designed to share the cultural heritage of the country with school children and the Honduran public.

In the early 1990s Paul directed the bank to publish several books on Honduran art. They were *El Banco Atlántida en la Historia de la Pintura* by José Miguel Gómez – *Pintor Criollo* by historian Leticia de Oyuela, and *La Batalla Pictórica: Síntesis de la Historia de la Pintura Hondureña*, also by Oyuela.

In 1991 Paul invited a group of young artists to the bank to show him their work. Among them was German Durón Lanza — a twenty-two-year-old artist, self-taught, who was just starting out. His medium was wood carving. Paul looked at his pieces, bought a couple, and told him, "I think that you have what it takes to be a great artist. I suggest you try painting." Durón Lanza was uncertain about a future in art because it seemed Honduran artists could not earn enough to live on. However, he accepted Paul's challenge and returned to his office some months later with paintings. Paul liked them. He said, "Stick with primitivism and you will become great." Paul walked Durón Lanza over to a wall where paintings by José Antonio Velasquez were displayed and told him what those paintings were selling for. Paul looked the artist in the eye and added, "You can be even better than this guy." Durón Lanza told me that Paul's interest in his work gave it real value for the first time.[cxi]

Years later, after Dad had passed away, I was invited to an exhibition of Honduran painters in Houston. As my husband José and I walked around, I was drawn to a small painting of a Honduran landscape. When I asked the exhibition coordinator about the extraordinary detail in the painting, she told me that the artist painted using a magnifying glass and one hair from a donkey tail. She then asked if I would like to meet the painter: German Durón Lanza. He walked over, and as I started to introduce myself, he said, "I know who you are. Your father is the reason I am still painting." My husband bought that painting as my birthday gift and to this day it is my favorite.

When the new Banco Atlántida headquarters was designed in the late 1970s, Paul asked the architect to find a spot for a mural. Together they decided that the twenty-five-foot wall behind the teller stations in the bank lobby was perfect. Paul commissioned a masterpiece by Miguel Angel Ruiz Matute, a renowned Honduran painter who had studied with the masters Diego de Rivera and O'Gorman in Mexico and later trained in Europe. Ruiz Matute worked on the eight panels for five years in his studio in Rome, Italy.

The title of the mural is "Exaltation to Honduras". It depicts important moments in the history of Honduras from the Mayan civilization to the Spanish conquest, to the arrival of the American banana companies, and finally to current days. Mixed in with the cultural history of the country on the mural is the history of the Honduran currency starting with the cacao that the Maya used to the first paper money issued by Banco Atlántida in the early 1900s. The history of Banco Atlántida is also woven into the mural, with all three major bank buildings depicted: the original headquarters in La Ceiba, the building in downtown Tegucigalpa, and the new headquarters. As a tribute to Paul's support of the project, Ruiz Matute painted Paul's face on a Spanish priest accompanying the *conquistadores*.

Honduran journalist and author Elvia Castañeda de Machado wrote that no prominent Honduran nor foreigner deserved a place of as much respect and authority in the world of art as Paul did. She described the altruism and profound sensibility which made him a champion of Honduran culture and art. She pointed out that prior to Paul's arrival in 1949 the country had artists, some budding and some established. But before Paul there was no patron of the arts in Honduras.[cxii]

Since Paul was a prolific letter writer, he received responses from all over the world, and consequently many stamps. Since his first wife Linda introduced him to stamp collecting, he had been fascinated by philately. Over his lifetime he collected stamps from all over the world, but concentrated on building collections of Honduras, Belize, Estonia, Italy, The Vatican, Eritrea and San Marino stamps. Former president Carlos Flores told me that his father Oscar was also a stamp collector and enjoyed talking with Paul about their shared hobby. Oscar told Carlos that at one time Paul owned the rarest Honduran stamp in existence.[cxiii]

Dad tried to pass this interest on to Pia and me. To teach us about stamps, we started a collection of stamps that had been circulated. On weekends, he brought out the envelopes from letters he had received that week and taught us to soak them in the bathroom sink until the glue on the stamps released from the envelope. We then dried the stamps and sorted them into albums. I did not inherit his collector's personality and I'm sorry to say that while I still have the stamps we worked on together, I never pursued the hobby, nor did Pia.

Starting with his days at the Central Bank, and during his decades with Banco Atlántida, Paul urged both banks to collect and exhibit paper money from the colonial and republican history of Honduras. While at the Central Bank in the 1950s, he started a collection of Honduran coins and paper money that, years after his death, became a cornerstone of that bank's exhibition hall.

In February of 1968, Banco Atlántida hosted an exhibition of Honduran and Central American coins from the eighteenth, nineteenth and twentieth centuries. At the inauguration of the exhibit Paul said, "For some time, the bank has been working on buying all the coins minted in Honduras that have been legal tender since the time of the Spanish conquest in 1502, in colonial times, and after independence in 1821. Some have disappeared because of their rarity, but we feel we have accomplished our goal. After an arduous but productive task, the collection now becomes part of the monetary history of this country. The collection is missing only four coins, two of which are owned by the Central Bank."[cxiv] A second exhibition was inaugurated in June of 1988, on the 75th anniversary of Banco Atlántida, this one specifically containing bills and coins issued throughout Honduran history.

Paul also collected coins and bills personally, but he did not have the resources to amass collections of much value in these areas. He did this for his own enjoyment. On weekends I often saw him poring over coin catalogs and stapling coins into coin protector sleeves. He had some original peso coins from Central America and mint condition coins from Honduras, British Honduras and Belize.

Paul was fascinated by the Maya civilization who inhabited northwest Honduras. He was a frequent visitor to the ruins of the Maya city of Copán. The head archeologist at Copán for many years was Ricardo Agurcia, the son of Paul's close friend Jack Agurcia. When Ricardo discovered the famous Rosalila temple, Paul was one of the first people to get a tour inside.[cxv]

Since Honduras had no museum for Mayan artifacts, starting in 1960 Paul had Banco Atlántida purchase Mayan archaeological treasures. The bank bought these from unauthorized excavators and graverobbers so that they would not sell to foreign museums and collectors. Paul felt strongly that these pieces should remain in Honduras. The bank hired a curator/authenticator who filtered out fakes that people tried to sell to the bank. Banco Atlántida assembled a museum-quality collection. Many pieces are on permanent display throughout the bank building. The bank also had frequent exhibitions in the Salón Cultural for the public and for students. Paul had special pieces of Mayan pottery featured in calendars and presentation folders which were distributed to bank clients all over the country. Many Hondurans learned about this civilization, native to their country, thanks to the Italian banker.[cxvi] Paul's hope was that the government of Honduras would eventually build an appropriate museum to house the collection the bank had accumulated.

Honduran historian and art promoter Leticia de Oyuela said of Paul, "He was certain not only of the importance of banking to the Honduran economy, but also of the vision of art and culture, and more than anything knew that without culture it is impossible for men to convert the poorest countries into the rich troughs of identity that permit them to become strong nations."[cxvii]

13

REVOLUTIONARY LEFTIST MOVEMENT
1960s - 1970s

Throughout the 1960s and 1970s Central America experienced a movement to the revolutionary, ideological left. Fidel Castro had been successful in fomenting a revolution in Cuba in 1959, and now the Marxist-Leninist ideas he promoted were spreading throughout the region. The Soviet Union lent financial and military support to this movement. By the 1970s, left-wing guerrillas and paramilitary groups created war-like conditions in many countries.

The ideology took hold in fertile soil, because as in much of the world, there was an unequal distribution of wealth. The economies of Central American countries were controlled by a small number of families who had developed the private enterprise sector. Their businesses were the reason the countries were developing, and they were the job makers which pulled many families out of poverty. But many citizens still had very little, so they saw the successful as the enemy. Those who adhered to Castro's Marxist-Leninist ideology believed that the wealthy only cared about enriching themselves. Capitalism was a bad word.

The Cuban revolution had shown those wanting a different form of government a way to achieve it without participating in the political process. The militant left knew they weren't likely to win elections, and in any case did not want to wait the time it would take to achieve a political turnaround. They decided the solution was to take over governments by force.

Intellectual allies were also necessary. One way the revolutionary leftists expanded their influence was by indoctrinating university professors, who then passed Marxist-Leninist ideas on to their students. At the Universidad Autónoma de Honduras—UNAH—where Paul taught economics, radicalization was occurring. New professors from other countries were teaching a different way of governance. Their lectures conflicted directly with what Paul had been teaching since 1950.

Paul was an experienced student of the world's economies, from his years of studying economics at the University of Michigan and later working for the IMF and interacting with government officials and international bankers at World Bank conferences. He was a believer in democracy, as it restrains political abuse; and in regulated capitalism, as it restrains economic abuse. He did not believe in authoritarianism. His view was that an economy prospered more when the private sector oversaw business, because individual companies were more efficient, creative and motivated than government was. And he further believed that a capitalist society resulted in a better life for all citizens, because when there was prosperity, there were jobs for those who could work, and money for government-sponsored social programs for those who needed help. To balance the freedoms given to the business sector, and to prevent uncontrolled greed and aggressive business tactics, he thought governments should pass laws that protected consumers. He understood that every country would always have a vulnerable segment of society that required protection, and he believed social services should be managed mainly by the public sector.

When Soviet economists reorganized Cuba's economy in the early 1970s to institute central command, Paul was alarmed that Marxist-Leninist policies left over from Stalin's rule were now being adopted in Latin America. He knew well the famine and starvation resulting from centralized communist rule in the Soviet Union and China. If communists gained power, they would want to change how goods and services were distributed and tell citizens what they could and couldn't do. He had lived under Mussolini's authoritarian rule for the first twelve years of his life. What had made him fall in love with the United States, and why he tried so hard to become a citizen, is that the freedom in the U.S. was for anyone. Regardless of wealth or lineage, Americans could succeed if they worked hard. He was a perfect example of this. He could not embrace ideology that would choke entrepreneurship and stifle business investment, which he firmly believed Honduras needed. He could not support an ideology that held that making a profit was illegal. He believed that government resources should come from taxes generated by a growing and competitive economy, not by owning and controlling all means of production.

Late one night in 1973 our doorbell rang. Pia and I heard Dad walk down the hall past our bedrooms to the front door. Curious, we scurried to a window in the living room where we could see what was happening without Dad knowing we were there. Because our house was on a hill, the front door stood high over the driveway. Dad opened the door and walked outside, standing exposed in Bermuda shorts and the V-necked white t-shirt he slept in. There was a line of twenty stone steps between him and a car at the base of the stairway. A young man, clearly drunk, stood next to the car holding a gun.

There was a woman in the passenger seat of the car. She leaned over towards the driver's open door – speaking softly but urgently — trying to convince the man to leave. He ignored her and started yelling at Dad about disagreements he had with Dad's recent lecture on the economy. Pia and I, ages seven and twelve, stared at the man with the gun, and realized that he was one of Dad's students.

Dad didn't do what we hoped he would, which was go back inside and close the door. We watched, hearts pounding, as he stood with no protection between himself and the angry, armed man. He listened quietly as the guy ranted, then he responded calmly. After fifteen minutes, the student ran out of arguments, or steam, or maybe sobered up a bit. The woman was finally able to convince him to return to the car. When they drove off, Dad walked back inside and closed the door. His posture was sad, defeated. Pia and I remained hidden as he slowly walked back to his bedroom.

Stress about Honduras's political climate built up in Paul and he began to experience chronic insomnia. He often called bank chairman José Mendoza, who was a medical doctor, for solutions on how to get to sleep.[cxviii] During this time he slept only a few hours each night, which explains how he kept up with so many obligations and interests. He stayed up reading, grading student papers, or studying about his investments—his stockbroker said Paul never asked for advice on a stock.

His greatest stress reliever had always been exercise, and he did that daily. Every morning began with a vigorous work out: either a brisk two-mile walk up and down the front driveway, or more frequently a tennis match. His regular partners were an American, Rod Saubers, and a Honduran architect, Marco Nuñez. When others showed up, they played doubles. When my brothers or other friends were in town, Paul invited them to play, with the understanding that they would be waking up at 6:00 am to do so. His nephew Armando played with him daily during his annual visits to Tegucigalpa. At one point, Paul injured his right shoulder. Rather than give up tennis while he healed, he switched hands and started playing with his left. This is when his ambidextrous side became apparent – he was almost as good.

Bob, Craig, Paul and Rick

After Paul finished exercising, he showered, and then he watched cartoons on TV while he dressed. We would walk into his room and find Bugs Bunny or the Road Runner on. When he traveled to the U.S., his favorite morning show was not the news, it was Captain Kangaroo.

Over the next two years the leftist movement gained strength. UNAH students traveled to Cuba, became indoctrinated, then returned to their university in Tegucigalpa where they passed out flyers, sprayed graffiti, and marched in demonstrations.[cxix] In 1975, the School of Economics at the university was approaching its twenty-fifth anniversary, which would be that summer. Paul was looking forward to celebrating the milestone, given his role in the creation of the school and because of his twenty-five years of teaching there.

The university had a governing board made up of students, professors, and representatives from each of the professional colleges. Of the fifty-two members on the board, only thirteen were ideologically conservative; the rest were leftist with varying degrees of radicalization.[cxx] This majority did not like Paul's pro-capitalism curriculum and discussed how to oust him. They found a good excuse: Paul's business obligations and frequent travel required that the university often hire a substitute professor, and his busy schedule also made it difficult for him to be available for students. One day in early 1975, Paul walked into his classroom and found another professor teaching. Without any warning, he was kicked out only months before his twenty-fifth teaching anniversary.[cxxi] Paul was deeply hurt.[22]

---

22. The university leadership that removed Paul had a slight change of heart soon after. In November of 1975, Paul was honored for his "twenty-five years" of teaching and for his role in founding the School of Economics. There was no mention of him returning as a professor, however.

He also worried how the changing political climate would impact Banco Atlántida. There was a trend throughout Latin America for governments to take over banks and private sector businesses. Paul recognized that the bank's size, which was much larger than any other in the country, put it at risk for nationalization. He developed a plan to protect bank assets. He enlisted Faustino Laínez, head of the bank's legal department, to help him create holding companies to house the bank's financial, real estate, and service businesses. Paul's thinking was that if a part of the group was nationalized, at least the government couldn't take all the group's businesses.[cxxii]

Paul had been an idea generator for Honduran businesses since the 1950's, and by this time, two decades later, his friends and some Banco Atlántida board members were invested in dozens of companies together. This group of investors was now a major force in the hospitality, insurance, real estate, sugar, soft drink bottling, flour, paper, cement, and information technology industries. In many cases, Paul was the chairman of the board of these companies and held a small interest as well.[cxxiii]

One of the companies Paul chaired was Embotelladora La Reyna, the Pepsi Cola bottling company in Tegucigalpa. At this time labor unions in Honduras were very powerful. Less than a decade before, the union of beverage industry workers, STIBYS, had been created. The lead negotiator for STIBYS was its fiery, headstrong leader Carlos H. Reyes. When Paul and Reyes faced each other across the negotiating table, they both ended up sweating.

Although Paul represented business owners and Reyes represented laborers, the two men worked together well. In fact, Paul had helped Reyes obtain a scholarship to study economics in Russia. At one point, Faustino Laínez asked Paul why he had helped an adversary, and Paul explained, "It helps to sit across the table from him, because he understands economics."[cxxiv] Reyes's training in Russia paid off during labor contract negotiations. When the Pepsi bottler was not performing well and couldn't pay workers higher wages, Reyes knew how to study the balance sheet and explain this to his constituency. His economics education made Reyes unique – very few members of the labor movement could read a balance sheet.

In 2018 I interviewed Carlos Reyes about those labor negotiations. He asked me to come to the STIBYS headquarters. A uniformed guard received me through a gate made of thick black iron bars, and a second guard escorted me upstairs past a large poster of "Che" Guevara, the Marxist revolutionary leader who helped Castro obtain victory in Cuba's revolution. Reyes was meeting with a group in the conference room when I arrived, so he took me next door to the kitchen, where we sat down to talk.

He told me that in the 1970s when he negotiated collective labor agreements with Paul, contracts were negotiated in two months, and the parties kept their word. By 2018, it took three years to reach agreements, required long legal documents, and often the terms were not honored. Reyes told me that despite the contradiction of Paul being a business executive and Reyes a labor union organizer, there was mutual respect and a willingness to come to an agreement that overruled their differences. He and Paul met occasionally to discuss the political and economic situation in the country. Reyes said to me, "He was one of the most well-informed men in this country." They came to trust each other. When Reyes needed a down payment for a house, Paul is who loaned it to him.[cxxv]

As political tensions in the region intensified, bank executives were warned about risks to their personal safety. The Banco Atlántida board determined that Paul should be driven in a bulletproof car. They learned that someone in the military was selling a bulletproof navy-blue Mercedes Benz 450 SEL and bought it for his use.

The left-right conflict that had dominated the news in the neighboring countries of Guatemala, El Salvador, and Nicaragua now moved into Honduras with force. The U.S.-backed right-wing rebel group called the Contras, formed to fight the Sandinista regime in Nicaragua, established a base in Honduras. Backlash from leftist guerrilla groups was one consequence. These revolutionary groups sought to raise money to advance their cause. They collaborated in a wave of terrorist fundraising activities that included bank robbery, assault and kidnapping. Their activity in the previously calm country of Honduras lasted a decade and resulted in hundreds of victims, many of them innocent bystanders.[cxxvi]

The guerilla groups focused on attacking banks and businessmen known to be strong capitalists, both for ideological reasons and because that's where the money was. Paul was an obvious target not only because he was CEO of the largest bank in Honduras. Over his twenty-five years as an economics professor at the university, he had become well-known as a believer in free market economies. There was no doubt that some of Paul's former colleagues and students, who knew this about him, were members of Honduran leftist organizations.

The wave of terror started with bank robberies. In March of 1979, three banks, including Banco Atlántida, were robbed in the town of Catacamas. It was later learned that the perpetrators used some of the funds to buy safe houses and to fund training for members of the FSLN (Frente Sandinista de Liberación Nacional) of Nicaragua.[cxxvii] In June, a Banco Atlántida bank branch in Tegucigalpa was robbed.

On the morning of November 5, 1979, three masked men in civilian clothing appeared at the front desk of the Hotel Honduras Maya, carrying pistols and revolvers. They demanded the reception staff give them the money in the hotel safe, which included the previous night revenues from the hotel casino. They placed the money in a black bag and fled in a waiting taxi. Guerrilla groups from El Salvador, Nicaragua and Honduras claimed responsibility for the robbery on a radio station in El Salvador that was sympathetic to their cause.[cxxviii] In April of 1980, a more personal form of leftist attack began in Honduras. The general manager of Texaco was kidnapped in the northern city of San Pedro Sula.[cxxix]

Banco Atlántida executives met to discuss the risk of one of their own being kidnapped. The most likely candidate was the boss, Paul. At this point Paul and the directors knew the problem was not going away. They needed to take more serious steps to protect bank property and themselves. The bank had a Department of Security, but the personnel was not highly trained—they were basically doormen. While on a trip to Miami, Paul met a former FBI agent who worked with a U.S./British security services company called Wakenhut. They discussed the mechanics of creating a security business in Honduras. They just needed someone to run it.

Juan Ramón Molina was a Honduran army coronel who had studied in the U.S., Europe and South America, including earning a master's degree in business administration in Spain. In August of 1980, Paul invited Molina to the bank and offered him the job of running a security company that would train guards for bank branches and for personal bodyguard services.[cxxx] The bank group created a new company called SISTEC (Sistemas y Tecnologías en Seguridad Industrial de Protección Preventiva).

Paul put my brother Rick on the board of SISTEC. As part of his preparation for board membership, the bank group sent twenty-six-year-old Rick to a training course in Virginia, just outside of Washington, D.C. The course was in bodyguard training and was offered by former U.S. military personnel. One of the training exercises was to kidnap an FBI agent. Rick was along for the ride when his instructors drove to Washington, D.C. where the agent was having lunch at a restaurant. The instructors captured and handcuffed the agent and drove him to a farmhouse. For six hours they threatened him. (No physical harm was done). He was furious and threatened to put all of them in jail. Rick was the only person in the training course who was not in the military nor a police officer. The experience terrified him.

At the end of that day, the head of the school walked in followed by a senior FBI official. They confronted the angry agent who had been taken and acknowledged it was upsetting to be taken by surprise. But they told him, "You're not going to do jack shit to these trainees. This is for your training as much as theirs. You must learn what can happen to you if we send you to a country like Colombia and the guerrilla captures you."

Paul was also being prepared for possible violence. SISTEC assigned him a driver for the heavy bulletproof car as well as a bodyguard. Both men were armed and with him anytime he left the house. He bought a 357 Magnum revolver and SISTEC guards took him out for target practice on weekends.

14

BECOMING HONDURAN
1977-1979

During the years that Honduras was going through ideological turmoil, Paul was experiencing marital turmoil. He and Fran had argued throughout most of their marriage and by 1977, year sixteen, the relationship was very strained. Paul found reasons to be away from home.

When he visited the Banco Atlántida office in La Ceiba he stayed longer than he needed to. On the second floor of the historic building where the bank's original headquarters were, was the former apartment of Felix Lloveras which Paul visited for the first time in 1949. The apartment was now for the use of bank executives traveling from Tegucigalpa to La Ceiba, so Paul used it when he was in town. Paul looked forward to the daily cocktail hour and believed the social anchor of every home was a bar. He had a mahogany one built in the bank's apartment. Many evenings when he was in La Ceiba he visited his friends Bishara and Mary Kawas, and soon had a bar delivered for their house also. Some nights he sent their staff to buy ingredients for *pasta a la puttanesca* so he could cook for everyone.[cxxxi]

When he was home, Dad was conflicted on how to deal with me, the first teenage daughter he spent much time around. Because Linda had died when the four boys were young, Paul was directly involved in raising them—at least when they lived with him. But Liz was raised by her mother and then by her aunts. By the time Pia and I came along, he focused on his professional life and our financial support but did not get involved in the details of parenting. Mom handled our permissions. As their relationship deteriorated, Mom and Dad did not communicate. This meant Dad never knew what my plans were.

One night he decided to exert control over my social life. I was fourteen and had been invited to a *quinceañera*. These parties were large formal dances, a big deal in the social life of a teenager in Latin America. When my date came to pick me up, Dad was in the living room entertaining some friends. Dressed in my long gown, I went to say goodbye to him. He said,

"You need to stay and be our bartender."

"But Dad, Mom gave me permission to go to this party, my date is at the door!"

"You're not going out tonight."

I sent my date away and stayed, furious. After a while Dad seemed to not notice that I was waiting by the bar, so I returned to my room and fumed for the rest of the night about the fun I was missing for no reason other than his capriciousness.

That June when I finished ninth grade, the last grade level Academia Los Pinares offered, I packed to leave home. Dad wanted me to follow the pattern of my three oldest brothers and finish high school in the United States so I would be well prepared for college.

Craig and Bob had attended the all-boys boarding school Choate in Wallingford, Connecticut. By this time Choate had merged with the girls' school Rosemary Hall. Dad had enrolled me for tenth grade at Choate Rosemary Hall. Education had changed Dad's options in life, and he wanted all his children to have the same opportunities. His friend Chito Kafie and he argued more than once over his philosophy. Chito was a protective father who kept his kids very close, especially his daughter Rosemarie. He found it outrageous that Dad wanted to send a fourteen-year-old daughter to another country. Dad debated with his friend that a child's obligation was to get good grades in school, and that otherwise they should be given quite a bit of freedom.

Mom flew me to New England the same month I finished Los Pinares. I was required to first attend summer school since I was coming from an international school system. Mom helped me set up my dorm room and two days later said goodbye. I felt unmoored, almost four thousand miles from home in a cultural environment very different than the one I grew up in. International phone calls were difficult to make on the dorm's one pay phone, so a call was only for extreme emergencies. Mom promised she would write, and that Dad would mail me a plane ticket to come back to Tegucigalpa for Christmas, six months later.

The thought that my brothers had all been sent to the States as young children stopped me from feeling sorry for myself. I drew comfort from the fact that Craig, now a banker in New York City, lived only a few hours away. His wife Carol promised to help me buy warm clothes as soon as the weather turned. I owned nothing for a Connecticut winter.

Now only Pia, nine years old, lived at home. The big house was very lonely for her without Rick nor me there. Mom and Dad were not good company, preoccupied as they were with their lives and their anger at each other. When Pia woke up in the mornings, she usually found our parents' bedroom door closed so she went to the living room and read, waiting for someone to wake up. She wandered around the gardens and climbed onto the house's flat roof from the upper level of the property. At one point that year our black cat Zuzu gave birth to kittens on that roof and Pia often went looking for them. Unless her friend Vicky came to visit, her companions were mostly our maids.

My sophomore year was full of firsts for me. The winter of 1977-1978 was one of the coldest in recorded history, with temperatures below zero and massive snowfall throughout Connecticut. I had never seen a snowflake, so eight-foot drifts outside my dorm were eye-opening. The merger of Choate and Rosemary Hall meant that we had classes on both campuses, so my walks to class could take twenty-minutes in driving snow. I learned that appropriate boots were necessary to avoid freezing cold feet.

Socially I was in a foreign world. The typical Choate-Rosemary Hall student was very privileged and had been exposed to much more than I had. I gravitated to the Latin American students. We banded together because of common culture, common native language, and because we had led a more sheltered life than the American students, who had a sophistication many of us did not.

The academic rigor at Choate was daunting. Academia Los Pinares was a good school but nowhere near the level of one of the top schools in the United States. For the first time in my life, I struggled with grades. My worst nightmare was American History, which I had absolutely no background in. By the time the first semester ended, I had only just managed a passing grade in that class and decent but not impressive grades in everything else but Spanish, which fortunately I had an edge in. Dad was not happy with the grades I brought home in December. My tuition was very expensive, and he expected a better result.

I was thrilled to leave the snow and cold and to return to Tegucigalpa for Christmas. It was fun to reconnect with my friends, although not my parents who were very much on edge. For New Year's Eve, Mom and Dad hosted an open house. My brothers were home and Dad said they and I could invite friends to the party. I invited one boy. By the time people started arriving that evening, Dad had been drinking since early in the day and he was belligerent. When my guest walked in the front door, Dad saw he was not wearing a jacket and told him, "Why don't you go get dressed decently and then you can come in." Mom was embarrassed and said, "Oh for heavens sakes, Paul, many of the people at the party are dressed casually." That set off a major fight in front of our guests.

Just before midnight everyone moved outside to watch the elaborate firework display my four brothers orchestrated down the length of our front driveway. Dad stood at the bottom of the steps with Chito, and Mom was at the top with Nena, trying to hide her tears. At the stroke of midnight, Chito suggested Dad go up and wish Mom a Happy New Year. He did, and she reminded him that they had promised to take Pia and me to another New Year's party hosted by our friends the Alders. Dad informed her nobody was going anywhere.

Mom defiantly packed Pia and me into her car and we left for the Alder house, leaving Dad with the remaining guests. When we returned later that night, rather than go upstairs to our rooms Mom had us sleep in the guest bedroom downstairs. The three of us spent the night in bed together, and near dawn we heard Dad come down the stairs to check if we had gotten home. When I returned to school in January, it was clear to me that my parents' marriage was close to the end.

In February, Dr. Jose Mendoza decided to retire after a decade as chairman of Banco Atlántida. With Chase no longer in the picture, there was no longer a requirement that the roles of board chairman and CEO be held by two different persons. Paul was already CEO. On February 7, 1978, Banco Atlántida's board of directors voted that Paul also be their chairman. (A year later Paul hired an Assistant CEO, Guillermo Bueso, who was Paul's former student and who had most recently been president of the Central Bank.)

Liz finished high school that June. The American School graduation celebration was a formal party called prom. It was different than proms in the United States in that entire families attended. Each senior processed with a parent: daughters with fathers, sons with mothers. Paul attended without Fran, since she still was not involved in Liz's life.

*Liz and Paul Vinelli, American School of Tegucigalpa
senior prom, 1978*

A few weeks later I returned to Tegucigalpa from my first year at boarding school. Dad put me to work at the Hotel Honduras Maya as a switchboard operator. Every day he gave me a ride to the hotel on his way to the bank. He and I sat in the back seat in silence. He was still angry at me about my grades which did not improve much the second semester, and I was afraid to say anything. He wasn't saying much to Mom either—when he did, it was unpleasant. He had taken to referring to her as "*la bruja*", the witch. She was extremely emotional and volatile, her go-to demeanor close to hysteria. When they were both at home, Pia and I stayed downstairs in the game room, out of their way. There was drinking and yelling upstairs in the living room, and occasionally they threw heavy objects that landed on the marble floor and rolled. From where we were, it sounded like they were bowling.

In late July, Dad went on a business trip to New York. After he left for the airport, Mom came into my bedroom and told me she planned to leave him. She asked what I thought. I was only fifteen, but the answer came easily, "Mom, you two are terrible together. I think a good divorce would be better than a bad marriage." She told me she was going to go to Kansas City, Missouri where her sisters Doris and Elizabeth lived. She asked if I would like to come live with her or return to Choate. I chose Kansas City.

She then called ten-year-old Pia into her bedroom. Pia sat on Mom's bed facing her while she leaned against the headboard.

Mom asked, "If you had to choose, who would you like to live with, your father or me?"

Pia: "You. Are you and Dad getting a divorce"?

Mom replied, "I'm not sure, maybe."

Mom had clearly given her plan a lot of thought, because that afternoon there was a moving van hidden behind our house. She told us we would be leaving in two days, and we could not tell anyone, not even our closest friends. This upset me, so she finally said I could let my friends come see me off at the airport, but they couldn't know we were leaving until the night before we left.

Mom went down to the bank the next morning and asked Dad's secretary Marielos to give her access to Dad's and her tax returns and other financial documents. As she was making copies, Dad's colleague Cleto Alvarez walked out of his office next door. He saw what was happening but said nothing to her.

In the afternoon, their friend Coco Alder came to visit unannounced. She walked straight to my parents' bedroom expecting to find Mom in the sitting room. As Coco turned the corner into the bedroom hallway, she saw Mom packing a large trunk, her eyes full of tears. Coco immediately realized what was happening and blurted, "Oh, Fran you are going to be so sorry."

Packers moved from room to room in our house for two days. Mom alternated between sadness about leaving to terror that someone would call Dad in New York. Pia and I stayed out of the way, and I talked up Kansas City as a big adventure for my little sister so she wouldn't cry. Dad's niece Diana was in town, visiting our grandmother Dora two blocks away. Mom worried they might stop by and catch her packing, but since Dad was out of town they didn't come. Ursula, the maids and gardeners didn't say a word, they just watched us with sad faces. Mom told Pia and me we could take only our most special possessions, because shipping to the United States was very expensive. Rather than ship heavy photo albums, she tore the photos she wanted out of them.

The day we left my friends came to Toncontín Airport to see me off. I felt layers of fear. Fear that Dad would be furious. Fear of going to eleventh grade at a huge public high school in Kansas City. Fear of never seeing Tegucigalpa again, because I didn't know if Dad would let us come home after we had left with Mom. The goodbye with my friends felt final.

When we landed in Kansas City, my mother's sister Doris picked us up at the airport. She drove us to her cozy house in Overland Park where her family had made room for the three of us to move in with them. Everything in the house—walls, carpets, bathrooms—was decorated in purple, as was Aunt Doris. I loved everything about the house and charming neighborhood. Honduras and the fighting seemed very far away.

Mom was in an emotional uproar, but full of energy. For the first two days, she took me on manic shopping trips. I followed her through stores, pushing shopping carts piled high with basics for a home. She wanted to buy everything she could before Dad cancelled her credit card. Finally, her card was declined at a cash register. We didn't know if it was because Dad had cut it off or if she had exceeded the limit. In that moment, she lost all the bravado that had taken her this far. All the fire I saw as she packed, organized, and moved us to Kansas City left her. For the next several months, she was in a zombie, tearful state as we registered Pia and me for school, looked for an apartment to live in, and as she started thinking about getting a job.

Someone—we are not sure who—informed Dad about our departure before he returned to Tegucigalpa. From the airport, he went straight to Chito's house. Chito confirmed he had heard a rumor that we had left. Paul asked Chito to call our house. A maid answered. Chito pretended he didn't know where Dad was and said, "Let me speak to Dr. Vinelli". The maid replied that he was out of town. Chito said, "OK, let me speak to Doña Frances." The maid's reply made Dad turn red, "She is in the United States." Dad went home and burst into the house like a raging bull. Ursula later told us that he walked first into my room, then Pia's, then the room he shared with Mom, pulling out drawers to find them empty, slamming open the doors to the bare closets.

At the bank the next day, Paul learned from Cleto that Marielos had given Fran access to the financial documents. He immediately had

Marielos transferred to work for another bank officer. The only other secretary who had experience working for Paul was Mirna Gómez, who worked elsewhere at the bank and substituted for Marielos when she was on vacation. When Mirna was informed that she was now going to be Paul's secretary, she was petrified. Dr. Vinelli terrified her. She told me what the first days were like: "I'd forget my English. He'd speak to me, and I'd answer in Spanish. He'd stare at me, trying to understand what was wrong with me. Others would come and tell me to pull myself together and I'd say, "I can't, that man's presence scares me. He has a look that is so intense."[23] His mood when she first started working for him didn't help. When Fran's credit card bill arrived in Tegucigalpa a few weeks later, there were fireworks coming out of Dad's office. He stormed out to Mirna's desk with the bill in his hand, shouting, "She didn't need a queen-sized bed!"

Two months later, on August 29, 1978, Paul became a Honduran citizen. This was not a minor decision, because it required that he renounce the U.S. citizenship that he had fought for fifteen years to obtain. (Because he was not born an American but was naturalized, once he renounced U.S. citizenship, he could never get it back.) In his statement at the U.S. Embassy in Tegucigalpa, Paul said his reason for taking the action was so he could "represent the government of Honduras at international meetings regarding the economic development of Honduras". Dad gave me another reason. He told me that because he was named chairman of Banco Atlántida earlier that year, and since Banco Atlántida was now one hundred percent owned by Hondurans, he felt it important that the chairman be a Honduran.

---

23. Mirna worked with Paul for the rest of his life and became his biggest fan. She told me, "Working with your father was like being in school. He taught me everything, even accounting." As of 2026, she is still employed by Banco Atlántida.

Around this same time, Paul decided that the downtown location of Banco Atlántida's headquarters didn't work anymore, both because they were outgrowing the space and because of traffic congestion. Tegucigalpa was founded in 1578, exactly four hundred years earlier. Back then, the narrow streets in the city center were designed for horses and carriages. Now the city was growing quickly, and the constant traffic jams downtown made it difficult for bank employees and customers to get there.

Paul convinced the board of directors that the bank should buy a large parcel of land in San Ignacio, an area considered the outskirts of Tegucigalpa, far from any commercial development. He proposed the building of a large modern bank building. The board went along with his suggestion but there were many critics who called the project foolish. Paul was not bothered by the criticism. Similar comments had been made twenty years before when he pushed for the construction of headquarters for the two government banks, the Central Bank and the Banco de Fomento (later called BANADESA). Both of those projects turned out to be good decisions.[cxxxii]

The groundbreaking for the new Banco Atlántida headquarters was on a rainy September day. Paul said in his speech, "Today we are not laying the first brick of a new bank building. We are inaugurating the new financial center of Tegucigalpa." Guests looked dubiously over the vast expanse of empty land behind Paul. Next to it was a garbage dump where buzzards rummaged.

He would prove to be right in this and in many future land purchases. Eventually, the area surrounding Banco Atlántida attracted all the major banks and many other businesses and did, as he predicted, become the financial center of Tegucigalpa. Downtown was eventually abandoned by major businesses. Paul had such an instinct for real estate development that every time Banco Atlántida planned a new branch, they made sure Paul chose the location.[cxxxiii]

A few months after arriving in Kansas City, Mom found us a two-bedroom apartment near Aunt Doris's house. She still hoped for a reconciliation with Dad but didn't want to impose on her sister any longer. My brother John came from Seattle to help us move. Both Dad and Craig criticized John for getting involved. John told Dad, "Fran is the mother I most remember. I will always be there for her."

While Mom was in Kansas City, hoping the separation would make Dad want her back, a woman she thought was her friend was working on replacing her. Maria Mastahinich Perusina lived in San Pedro Sula, the Honduran city where most of the country's industry was based. She owned one of the largest food distribution companies in Honduras. She knew Paul because she was a client of the bank, and through him also knew Mom. In the year prior to Mom leaving Honduras Maria befriended her, and Mom confided her problems with Dad.

Maria was born in the mountainous town of San Marcos, Guatemala. Her parents, Ana and Pablo Mastahinich, had immigrated from Dubrovnik, Croatia. Maria was the oldest of six children. Her father first worked on a coffee plantation and then started his own. Maria first married in 1957. Her husband was a Spaniard by the last name of Granda. Shortly after their wedding, he took her to his small hometown in Spain, where his mother taught Maria exactly how she was to take care of her son. She learned every detail of running a house well: laundry, ironing, setting a table, as well as setting out the clothes her husband would wear every morning.

Then Maria and Granda moved to San Pedro Sula, Honduras where he worked for Nestlé. He had always dreamed of starting his own business, so in 1963 he founded DIAPA. Tragically, less than a year later, Granda died in a small plane accident. Widowed and childless, Maria decided to take over the management of the company and grew DIAPA into a large company. Maria had excellent taste and entertained beautifully, and over the years had befriended the most powerful families in San Pedro Sula.

Everyone in the country knew that Paul's wife had left him. There was a line of women vying to get close to the bank chairman even though he was not divorced. Maria was a shrewd competitor, and she arranged to see Paul through friends whenever he was in San Pedro Sula for business. Paul was attracted to her social skills and her contacts. Fran had never felt comfortable around powerful nor wealthy people so was not helpful to him as his social prominence in Honduras increased. Maria also was different from Fran in that she managed her emotions and always appeared composed and strong. Paul liked being around someone who didn't fall apart. He started visiting San Pedro Sula for reasons other than bank business.

Mom returned to Tegucigalpa in May of 1979, ten months after leaving Dad. On the days leading up to her trip, she was nervous yet excited, hopeful for a reconciliation. I thought she was delusional. Even though I had no idea about the relationship building between Dad and Maria, I knew nobody could publicly humiliate my father the way Mom had and then get him to take her back.

Mom surprised Dad when she returned. He arrived home from the bank one evening to find her sitting in the living room. He recovered from his shock and greeted her distantly but politely. He made them both a drink and turned on some music. They sat in mostly silence until they finished their drinks. Then Dad got up and went out for the evening. Mom was left alone and in tears. Ursula came into the living room and consoled her, urging her to understand that Dad had moved on to a relationship with Maria and that she needed to accept that the marriage was over.

So instead of the reconciliation she hoped for, on May 18, 1979, Fran received divorce papers. Paul was more generous than Honduran law at the time required. He agreed to pay a large settlement in addition to child support for Pia and me as well as our education and medical expenses until we graduated from college. The alimony agreement was for life, as long as Fran did not remarry. She lived many more years than he did and never even dated, so he sent her a monthly check for the rest of his life. And that was the end of marriage number four.

Before leaving Tegucigalpa, my mother visited Liz. It was the first time they had met. Fran apologized for preventing Pia and me from having a relationship with Liz. She made it clear she never harbored ill will towards her and admitted she had handled a complicated social dynamic poorly. Liz was extremely gracious: she told Fran she felt no resentment because her mother and aunts had provided her with a wonderful, loving home environment.

Then Fran got on a plane, leaving her marriage and the country that had been her home for almost twenty years. She flew to Kansas City, carrying with her many regrets. Two months later, on July 18, Paul made Maria his fifth wife, at a small, elegant ceremony at the Camino Real Hotel in Guatemala City.[24]

---

24. None of Paul's five marriage ceremonies took place in Honduras.

Paul and Maria Mastahinich, New York City

When Paul married Maria, Ursula worried about the reaction that Pia and I would have. She knew we planned to visit Dad in Tegucigalpa in August. It would be the first time we saw him since the previous summer when Mom took us out of the country. Ursula sent a letter to Kansas City and included a newspaper clipping of the wedding in Guatemala. Mom was devastated to learn how quickly he moved on after seventeen years of marriage. I was furious that Dad didn't think he should tell me he was married before I went home. I announced to Mom that Pia and I would not go to Honduras that year. Mom sat us down and told us we shouldn't stay away from our father another year, given that our only contact with him were occasional letters. With her encouragement, in late August of 1979 Pia and I flew to Tegucigalpa.

Dad met us at the airport with Maria. He did not know we had been told about his marriage—he intended to surprise us with the news. I was resentful, as a sixteen-year-old would be under the circumstances. When we arrived at our house, we were stunned. Maria had been married to Dad less than a month, yet the house was already transformed. She had repainted everything from beige to white and was in the process of either reupholstering or replacing all the furniture. Her taste was very elegant but not family friendly. It appeared she intended to erase every sign of Mom having lived there.[25]

When I walked into my bedroom, I froze. Maria had removed every trace of the childhood memories I did not have room to pack when we left the year before. Pia and I had bedrooms side by side with a small, shared bathroom in between. Gone was our teenage-looking striped wall décor. Gone were our books and posters. Instead, we now had rooms decorated for little girls, with flowered curtains and bedspreads, and new stuffed animals on the bed. Our old stuffed animals, the ones that mattered, had been thrown away. Everything was pretty but sterile.

Maria did not have children of her own, but she knew how to befriend us. That month she took Liz, Pia and me on a long road trip throughout Guatemala. She asked each of us to bring a friend. We six girls visited Maria's family's coffee plantation, went to the beach in Likín, and ended the trip in Guatemala City where her nieces and nephews took those of us who were older to nightclubs. It was

---

25. I didn't have this context then, but Dad must have been familiar with the situation: twenty years earlier Iris had done the same when she married him and changed all the furniture he and Linda had bought during their marriage.

a wonderful trip. An extra bonus was that for the first time in my sixteen years, I got to know my older sister. Liz and I stayed up late at nights, interviewing each other about the years of each other's lives that we had missed.

After Pia and I returned to Kansas City in late August, Paul and Maria went to Italy for a delayed honeymoon. On the way back, they flew the Concorde from Paris to Washington, D.C. so Paul could attend the World Bank/IMF meetings. Paul loved flying on the supersonic jet, which made the trip across the Atlantic Ocean in three and one-half hours, compared to the normal flight time of seven or eight hours. The flight was extraordinarily expensive, more than thirty times the cheapest fare for the route. It was one luxury Maria did not appreciate. She was nervous on planes and even more so within the confined interior of the Concorde's streamlined design.[26]

Before leaving Paris, Paul sent a message to Rick who had completed his studies in hotel management and now worked as Banquet Manager at a Washington hotel. Paul wanted Rick to pick Maria and him up at Dulles airport. Rick had not met his father's latest wife and surprised them by hiring a black stretch limo to drive them to the Watergate Hotel.

By the end of 1979, Paul's life was in a good place. Maria was extremely attentive to him. The construction of the new bank building was advancing well. His worry was his mother. Dora was sad, still grieving over the loss of Angelo. Even after living in Tegucigalpa

---

26. One of Maria's biggest sacrifices for Paul was to travel with him frequently. She hated flying because so many of her family members, including her first husband, had died in airplane accidents. However, for Paul, she flew all over the world, making sure to take an anti-anxiety pill or a shot of whiskey before boarding. Paul joked that he was glad Maria kept her fingernails short, because she gripped his arm fiercely whenever there was turbulence.

for four years, she was not assimilating well into Latin American culture. Paul asked Rick to move back to Tegucigalpa. He valued the effect Rick had on Dora, who had bonded with him during the two times that he lived with her: in Portland, Maine when he was three (right after his mother died), and later in Rochester New York when he lived with her and Angelo Bufano during fifth and sixth grade. Everyone knew Rick was Dora's favorite grandson.

Our cousin Diana was the closest granddaughter to Dora. Diana described to me the effect Rick had on our grandmother: "When Nononna was in a bad mood, we would all tiptoe around, wondering what was wrong. All it would take was for Rick to walk in, put his arm around her and kiss her cheek, and that scowl would turn into a huge smile." On days when Grandma was especially grouchy, he would greet her with a "Hello sexy!", and that changed her mood immediately.

The Hotel Honduras Maya hired Rick as Banquet Manager. In January of 1980 he moved into an apartment at the hotel. Rick loved organizing events—he was a great host and the life of every party. The Hotel Honduras Maya was still the best hotel in town and had become the hangout for journalists, politicians, and U.S. military personnel. This was the era of the U.S. support of the Contras, who opposed the Sandinista regime in Nicaragua. New York Times correspondent Clifford Krauss wrote in his book *Inside Central America: Its People, Politics, and History*, "The Honduras Maya, Tegucigalpa's only luxury hotel, is a nest of American spies, a Contra rendezvous spot, and a dormitory for American military trainers and soldiers of fortune."[cxxxiv] Rick was in the middle of the action.

Rick moved back to Honduras just before Dora turned eighty-five years old. Paul invited family from Maine and California to come to her birthday party in February. When the mariachis arrived to serenade his mother, Paul got up and danced with her. He was the happiest anyone had seen him in years.

Paul and Dora dancing at her eighty-fifth birthday party, February 1980

15

THEY CAME FOR HIM
1980 – 1981

The terrorist activity that hit Honduras in 1979 increased consistently and by the end of 1980, bank robberies happened almost monthly.[cxxxv] SISTEC personnel knew that both Banco Atlántida's executives and its bank branches were targets. The security company, only a few months old, raced to train personnel and bodyguards.

Security was a priority on the bank executives' minds as Banco Atlántida's new headquarters neared completion. The building was designed to deter robberies and had a separate entrance to protect executives entering the building. Paul went to the construction site several times a week to see the progress. The plan was to move in by January of 1981. He was proud and excited about the first-class building. His large office, in a corner on the executive (third) floor, had a private outdoor patio with a great view of the surrounding area.

In December of 1980, stores in Tegucigalpa dressed up for Christmas. People went about their holiday shopping and entertaining, attempting to ignore the tension caused by the increase in crime.

The living room in Paul and Maria's white house was decorated with several live green pine trees topped with huge red velvet bows. The kitchen staff was kept busy preparing special meals for the many friends they hosted that month. The tree in the downstairs game room had mountains of presents for Paul's children and grandchildren piled around it. The Vinelli siblings who lived in Honduras—Bob, Rick and Liz—were planning to gather in that room with their families for Christmas Day. Pia and I were going to fly to Tegucigalpa on December 19 to join them.

At 8:30 in the morning on Thursday December 18, exactly a week before Christmas, Paul walked down the front steps of the house. His driver held open the back door of a silver Ford Granada. Nothing about this morning was routine. Paul's bulletproof Mercedes 450SEL was in the shop for service. His regular driver, Rolando Garcia, was taking a security training course. His regular bodyguard had called in sick. Consequently, on that morning Paul left for work in a different car—one that was not bulletproof—with a different driver, and with a different bodyguard.[27]

The replacement driver, Roberto Martinez, had been a driver for bank executives for eight years. In the passenger seat next to him was the replacement bodyguard, Demetrio Cedillos. He was a twenty-two-year-old rookie recently hired by SISTEC. Paul sat in the back seat. His gun, a 357 Magnum revolver, was tucked in his open black leather briefcase on the floor. The daily newspapers had been placed on the seat next to him so he could catch up on the news during the drive to work.

---

27. Later investigation into the car's maintenance and the driver and bodyguard's schedules found nothing suspicious.

The car traveled slowly down the long driveway. As it approached the large front gates, a guard opened one for his boss's car to pass through. Paul lifted his hand in greeting to the guards when he passed them. A few hundred yards past the gates, the car turned left up a small hill to Paul's mother's house. Paul visited with Dora for ten minutes. After wishing his mother a good day, he got back in the car and Martinez, Cedillos and he headed to the bank downtown. Paul opened a newspaper.

The Las Lomas del Guijarro neighborhood, situated on a hillside, was now filled with large, elegant homes. The houses were hidden behind high walls, as was necessary for security reasons in most countries in Latin America. Trees lined both sides of the streets. The Ford moved off the smaller road that led to Paul and Dora's houses and turned right onto the main road. A blue car that was parked at the intersection pulled out behind Paul's car. The road wound around the hill then straightened, and the two cars headed down the hill. At the bottom the neighborhood changed from Las Lomas to a modest one called Colonia Pueblo Nuevo.

At the entrance to Colonia Pueblo Nuevo stood a small convenience store, which Hondurans call a *pulpería*. The owner, Doña Alma, sold soft drinks to a young man and woman. They each were carrying a case. School boys were standing at the bus stop in front of the store. Near them stood a woman with a large mole on her cheek, looking up the hill.[cxxxvi] She wore a skirt that came down to her knees and a long sweater over it.

The man and woman in Doña Alma's store finished their soft drinks and walked out to the bus stop. They stood next to the woman with the long skirt. The white van they arrived in was parked next to the store. The vehicle had government license plates, it belonged to a man who worked at the Ministry of Labor. The couple had stolen it at gunpoint an hour earlier.[cxxxvii]

Across the street and slightly higher up the hill was a small market called Magar. In front stood another couple, watching the traffic traveling past. They also carried cases. The woman wore jeans, tennis shoes, a blue sweater and a blue beret. As the Ford Granada drove down the hill past the Magar market, the man and woman waiting there walked out into the street and started following it. The Ford was forced to drive slowly because of the crowd at the bottom of the hill by the bus stop.

Before the Ford reached the bus stop, the man in front of Doña Alma's *pulpería* jumped into the white van and drove it across the road, where it blocked the Ford's path. Martinez slammed on the brakes to avoid hitting the van.

The two women at the bus stop and the one who had walked down from Magar market pulled machine guns out of cases and opened fire on the silver Ford. The woman following behind the car was very close. She shot a constant stream of bullets through the back window, smashing it entirely. Paul threw himself down on the back seat. One of the bullets went through the back windshield, over him, and into the driver's right arm.

The blue car that had been following them pulled alongside the Ford and two men jumped out. They pulled the driver out of the car and shot him in the head twice above his left eye. He fell to the ground, one eye missing, face completely bloodied. The gunmen thought he was dead and left him alone.

Cedillos, the bodyguard, jumped out of the passenger side aiming his .38 revolver. He fired two shots before he was shot in the chest and face by the driver of the van. He dropped to the ground face-up, clutching his face with his hands. The shooter walked over, saw he was still breathing, and shot him in the face again to make sure the job was done.

Paul never removed his gun from the briefcase. The assailants surrounded his car, shot his door open, and violently dragged him out of the car. He tried to resist but one of them knocked him in the head with a machine gun. He was shoved to the ground and felt a woman cover his body with her own while someone tied his hands behind his back and placed a blindfold over his eyes. Bystanders saw him bleeding from the mouth as he was pushed into the van. Doña Alma ran out of her store, thinking someone was shooting off fireworks. When she saw Cedillos lying dead in the street, she realized what had been in the cases her customers were carrying.

Ernesto Mendoza was guarding a construction company across the street. When the shooting started, one of his colleagues instinctively pulled out his gun—but it jammed. Then he saw how many machine guns were on the street, and he jumped back behind their entrance gate. Mendoza, peeking around the gate, saw all seven kidnappers climb uninjured into the two vehicles, taking Paul with them. The incident was over in seven minutes.

Inside the van, someone put cotton in Paul's mouth and ears so he could not speak nor hear. Between the cotton and the blindfold, he had no sense of his surroundings. They drove for about ten minutes. Then Paul was pulled out of the van, spun around multiple times until he became dizzy, and was pushed into a smaller vehicle. This time they drove for what felt like forty or fifty minutes. He thought he was being taken outside of the city. The long drive was to throw anyone who might be following off their trail.

Paul was driven to a modest red brick house in a residential neighborhood called Colonia Alameda. It was located just over a mile from his home, two blocks from where Liz and her aunts lived. The car drove through a black iron gate and parked behind the house, so it would not be visible from the street. Two men pulled Paul out of the back seat, walked him across a backyard and through a back door into a bedroom. The captors had built a wooden cell to hold him. This plywood box measured eight feet on all sides, so was tall enough for Paul to stand in. One of the guards untied his hands, opened a wooden door to the cell, and shoved him inside.

The house in Colonia La Alameda where Paul was held.

In a daze, the fifty-eight-year-old captive removed the blindfold and took the cotton out of his ears and mouth. There was a ventilation system that moved air in and out of the box. This made enough noise that, at first, he could barely hear anything outside. As he calmed down and listened carefully, he thought he could discern three persons talking quietly in the room.

It was morning, but inside the box very little light could enter. A single, fluorescent lightbulb hung from the top of the structure. The only items inside were a small foam *petate* (mat), a thin blanket, a chamber pot, and a roll of toilet paper. At the base of the plywood door was a second, smaller door. Paul realized this was how the kidnappers and he were going to pass food and the chamber pot back and forth. The kidnappers told him to remove his shirt, pants, belt and shoes and to pass them through the opening. They handed pajamas for him to wear back through the little door. He looked around his space and decided the toilet paper roll would be his pillow.

What Paul couldn't know was that during the hour since his kidnapping a commotion was erupting in Tegucigalpa and beyond. These were days prior to the internet and cable news programs, but Paul was well-known, and telephone lines buzzed around the world with the news of the assault and kidnapping. Police checkpoints were set up all around the city—cars leaving Tegucigalpa were carefully inspected. Helicopters manned by the Honduran Air Force were conducting searches, flying low over the mountains surrounding the city.[cxxxviii]

Criminales manchan de sangre conciencia nacional

¡SECUESTRADO PAUL VINELLI!

• Un muerto y un herido saldo trágico del hecho. Fuerzas combinadas del ejército acordonan la capital.

EL HERALDO

LA VERDAD EN SUS MANOS

VIERNES 19 DE DICIEMBRE DE 1980 · No. 551 AÑO II · TEGUCIGALPA, D.C., HONDURAS C.A. EDITADO POR PUBLICACIONES Y NOTICIAS S.A. (PUBLYNSA)

AVISO IMPORTANTE

Microeditorial   LA ZARPA TERRORISTA

El Heraldo front page, December 19, 1980

"Where were you when you heard …?" is a question often asked about life-changing moments in history. Depending on our age, the question might end with: "…President Kennedy was shot? or "…the World Trade Center towers were attacked?" For the Vinelli family, the question is, "Where were you when you heard your father was kidnapped?"

Bob, twenty-eight years old, was the first of Paul's children to be notified. He was at his office at a paper company in San Pedro Sula. Around 9:00 a.m. he received a call from security at the bank in Tegucigalpa. He immediately went to his house and started packing. Bob's wife Maria José had gone to her job at a shrimp company early that morning. At 9:30 she left to run an errand for an office Christmas event. She happened to drive by their house and was surprised to see Bob's car in front. That was unusual, so she stopped and went into the house to find out what was happening. He told her, "They've kidnapped my dad." Right at that moment Bob received a call from Boris Goldstein, his boss and Paul's close friend. Boris was on the board of Banco Atlántida and had been called to Tegucigalpa for a meeting to discuss Paul's kidnapping. He offered to fly Bob on a company plane. Maria José told Bob she would arrange care for their three daughters and would fly to Tegucigalpa that afternoon to be with him.

John, thirty-three years old, was living in Seattle, Washington, pursuing post-graduate studies and doing scientific research for the U.S. government. When Bob called with the news of Paul's capture, he woke up his oldest brother because of the time difference. For John and his wife Linda, the world of kidnapping and guns seemed far away from their peaceful Bainbridge Island neighborhood.

Craig, thirty-two years old, had recently been named Vice President at Chemical Bank in New York City. He was already at his office that morning when Bob called. Craig made a plane reservation for Tegucigalpa and then took the train home to South Orange, New Jersey. His wife and his two-year-old son watched as he packed. His attitude was stoic. He said, "This is not my father who has been taken, it's a business deal to be handled."

Rick was twenty-seven years old. He had recently moved out of the Hotel Maya to an apartment in the same neighborhood where Paul lived. That morning, he was getting into his car to leave for work when a neighbor came outside and told him about the kidnapping on the news. Rick immediately drove to Paul's house.

Liz was twenty years old and in her third year of college in Tegucigalpa. That morning, she was studying at the university library. The librarian rushed over and said, "Your father is the headline on TV". She lent Liz a phone so she could call home to her aunts, who told her what they had heard on the news.

I was eighteen and had just finished my first semester of college in Dallas. It was the holiday break, so I had gone to Kansas City to see Mom. Pia and I were scheduled to travel to Tegucigalpa the next day to spend Christmas with Dad. That morning, I was helping Mom at her flower shop when the phone rang. Mom answered, listened for a minute, shrieked, then hung up. She ran into the stockroom at the back of the store, crying hysterically, and slammed the door. I went into the stockroom and finally got Mom to calm down enough to tell me that Dad had been kidnapped. We went home where twelve-year-old Pia was sorting clothes to pack for the trip. Pia went into Mom's room to ask what she should pack. Mom told her to stop packing. Through tears she explained that Pia and I would not be going to Honduras because Dad had been kidnapped. I had not shown emotion until then for Pia's sake, trying to counterbalance Mom's extreme reaction. I waited in the living room while Mom spoke to Pia. Once my sister knew, I broke down in tears.

Meanwhile, our father sat in his box. Two men came into the wooden cell that afternoon. They were barefoot and wore ponchos with hoods covering their heads and faces. One made Dad hold up a newspaper and warned him not to look at it. The other instructed him to look straight ahead at his camera. They quickly took a picture and left.[28]

Bank executives were called to the bank for an urgent meeting with the Vinelli family. Those that were not in Tegucigalpa found out by news stations covering the story and immediately returned. Maria asked Faustino Laínez, who was head of the bank's legal department at the time, to draft a letter to the kidnappers. The letter stated that Paul took heart medication and that the consequences of going off these meds were heart attack, stroke, or renal failure. That communication was transmitted on television the evening of the kidnapping and published in newspapers the next day.[cxxxix] Later we learned that the kidnappers obtained the medication.

The kidnapping story was reported by UPI news the next day, December 19, and was published in many international newspapers. In the U.S. the story came out in the Washington Post, Chicago Tribune, San Francisco Chronicle and the Miami Herald, among others.

---

28. I have always wondered where the kidnappers had photos of Dad developed, given that this was before the era of digital photography and home photo printers. Either the kidnappers had their own darkroom, or they were paying a photo lab to stay quiet.

That day two letters were delivered to the home of Faustino's father. One letter was addressed to Faustino, the other to Robert Vinelli and family.

Faustino opened his letter.

Honduras, December 19, 1980
Mr. Faustino Laínez Jr.

The organization that has in its power Mr. Paul Vinelli sends you this first communication so that you will hand-deliver this letter to Mr. Robert Vinelli. It is urgent that you take this to him immediately. We remind you that you and your family are in danger. Do not communicate with anyone but the Vinelli family about this.

Signed, The Organization that has in its power Mr. Paul Vinelli.

Faustino was too nervous to drive and had someone take him to the Vinelli house where he showed the family both letters. [29] The picture of Paul holding the previous day's newspaper was included with the family letter. [cxl]

That letter read:

Honduras, December 19, 1980
Mr. Robert Vinelli and family

We are the *Fuerzas Populares de Liberación – FPL - "Farabundo Martí"*, of El Salvador.
At this time our people are waging a decisive battle for their liberation. We are a people with an unbreakable fighting

---

29. Faustino ended up with two ulcers after Paul's kidnapping.

spirit, victoriously on the path to definitive triumph. Currently American imperialism, Central American bourgeoisies, and the puppet governments of Central America are supporting the criminal military Christian-democrat government in its attempts to drown our people's fight.

Currently the bourgeoisie and the puppet government of Honduras have become a bridge of support to American imperialism, and Honduran military troops intervene in the repression along the entire border region between Honduras and El Salvador. This is a crime that cannot remain unpunished and revolutionary justice will arrive where necessary in due time.

Mr. Paul Vinelli, bourgeois exploiter and pillar of American imperialism in Honduras, is an accomplice in this crime.

Thus, we communicate the following:

1. Our organization has Mr. Paul Vinelli in its power.
2. Mr. Vinelli is enjoying good health and is well treated, unlike the treatment given by the enemy to political prisoners.
3. For the security of Mr. Paul Vinelli, the following requirements must be met:

a) The family MUST NOT ask for assistance from the DNI [national police of Honduras], FUSEP [public security force-branch of the military], army nor any other security entity.

b) You must maintain STRICTLY SECRET the identity of the organization that has Mr. Vinelli in its power.

c) The person used as an intermediary must also not know our identity.

d) The family MUST ABSTAIN from looking for Mr. Vinelli or making inquiries about where he is located.

e) The family and all friends MUST STOP ALL INVESTIGATIONS that the security forces are conducting.

f) The media MUST NOT KNOW ANYTHING ABOUT the progress of the negotiations nor anything about our organization and Mr. Vinelli.

g) Our safety AND THAT OF MR. PAUL VINELLI depends on THE EXACT FULFILLMENT OF THESE CONDITIONS.

4. To liberate Mr. Vinelli, we require the payment of a war tax, the amount of which will be made known to you at a later time.

5. If the family is willing to negotiate under these conditions, you must communicate with our organization in the following manner:

On the second page of the CLASSIFIED ADS, in the VARIOUS section, of the La Tribuna newspaper, between the days of December 23 and 27, must appear the ad written on the attached page. THE AD MUST NOT BE CHANGED IN ANY WAY, NOR IN ITS CONTENT NOR IN ITS WORDING.

6. We reiterate that the security of Mr. Vinelli depends on the exact fulfillment of the indications listed above.

Revolution or Death!

The Armed People will Conquer!

Central Command of the *Fuerzas Populares de Liberación – FPL –*

Farabundo Martí

Paul had been kidnapped by a group who was not known at the time. The *Fuerzas Populares de Liberación* – FPL (Popular Liberation Forces) had been formed only two months earlier, in October of 1980, from the merger of five Salvadoran leftist guerrilla groups. They were the Salvadoran faction of the *Frente Democrático Revolucionario* (Democratic Revolutionary Front), a coalition of leftist dissident groups backed by Cuba.

Farabundo Martí was a paramilitary wing of the FPL. They took the name of a former leader of the Communist party in El Salvador, who in 1932 led a peasant uprising that resulted in thousands of indigenous people being slaughtered by the Salvadoran military. They later grew to become the Frente Farabundo Martí para la Liberación Nacional - FMLN (Farabundo Martí National Liberation Front). Their ideology was Marxist-Leninist. Of note: their motto, "Revolution or Death! The Armed People will Conquer!" was strikingly similar to Cuba's motto, "Homeland or Death, We Shall Overcome!"[cxli] The FMLN would become a major force in the civil war waged throughout El Salvador in the 1980's. Eventually they became a successful political party. From 2009-2018, every president of El Salvador was a FMLN party member.[cxlii]

It made sense that Paul had instructed his captors to address their letters to Bob—he was the oldest of Paul's children living in Honduras. At age twenty-eight, Bob became the family's lead negotiator for the release of his father. The next day Bob placed an ad in the newspaper as instructed. He accepted all the kidnappers' conditions.

The bank's security personnel asked Bob, Rick and Liz to live at Paul's house with Maria during the kidnapping. This was so they could keep track of everyone together. Rick and Liz moved in full time. Bob lived there most of the time and occasionally went to San Pedro Sula to be with his family. Craig traveled back and forth from New York. John did not come down until later, and Pia and I obeyed our brothers' request that we not come down at all because security did not want more family members to protect. I stayed in Kansas City with Mom and Pia that Christmas break.

One might think there would be political alignment between the FMLN and Honduran labor unions, who certainly had ideology in common. Many were surprised when, on December 20, the union of workers for the beverage industry (STIBYS) publicly condemned the violent act against Paul in a newspaper announcement. They gave Paul credit for years of fair treatment in negotiating with the Pepsi bottlers union. This must have been the initiative of Carlos H. Reyes, the labor leader Paul had negotiated with for years.[cxliii]

Since the December 18 kidnapping, the police department had multiple teams of five officers patrolling all areas of the city.[cxliv] The various government security forces wanted information about the case. They were under pressure from the public, fueled by the constant media coverage. Bob followed the kidnappers' instructions and asked the police to not intervene. In return, they made him agree to share any communication between the FMLN and the family.

A few days after Paul was taken, two men showed up at the hospital where the injured driver, Roberto Martinez, was recovering from eye surgery. Newspapers had incorrectly reported that Martinez had died, so it was suspicious that someone was looking for him. [cxlv] Even more unusual: the men were inquiring about "Dr. Vinelli's driver" without knowing his name. A hospital employee called the police. Within fifteen minutes, twenty-five officers stormed into the hospital, terrifying patients as they burst into their rooms pointing weapons. The search lasted for hours—the police searched under patients' beds and in bathroom stalls. The two men were gone.[cxlvi] Banco Atlántida executives had Martinez moved to another hospital for his safety.[cxlvii] Later they sent him to Houston for more extensive eye surgery, followed by plastic surgery to repair his damaged face.

He ended up with no left eye and with only five percent vision in his right eye.[cxlviii]

On December 23, day five of captivity, two men came into Paul's box. They again wore hoods over their heads, had ponchos and were barefoot. They brought paper and a pen for Paul to write a letter to his family. They told him exactly what to write.

That day Maria received a phone call. The person told her they knew where Paul was being held, and that they would provide that information in return for L500 ($250). This was the first of many such calls to the family. People claimed to have details about the case and of course wanted to be paid for the information. Some claimed to have seen Paul being mistreated, sick, or in grave distress. The family ignored these informants.

Bank executives were also receiving calls at their homes. Guillermo Bueso, Assistant CEO, received a call saying Paul was found dead in the town of Valle de Angeles. There were simultaneous reports called into the bank and to police that Dr. Vinelli was being held by Nicaraguans and Honduran university students in the Colonia Laguna.

The left-leaning international radio stations reported their versions. The Dec. 23 reports from Radio Havana in Cuba declared Paul was dead. Radio Sandino in Nicaragua reported something closer to the truth—that the kidnappers were leftist revolutionaries, asking for over five million lempiras, four million of which were for the revolutionary cause.

The newspapers knew they had the biggest story in years, but they had no information other than eyewitness accounts of the abduction. Our family said nothing to reporters. To fill space in their newspapers, the press printed information obtained from unreliable sources. Paul was reported to be in the United States, or in Europe. One paper wrote that he had planned his own kidnapping. Another wrote that he was taken by local businessmen as revenge for his refusal to extend banking credit. A third speculated that Anastasio Somoza, the then-dictator of Nicaragua, had hired Guatemalans to kidnap Paul.

On December 23 La Prensa suggested that the kidnappers could not be Hondurans, because the kidnapping followed the style of Guatemalan terrorists. In the same article it was also suggested that the kidnappers must be holding Paul within the city because of the speed in which police checkpoints were set up.[cxlix] This, they got right.

On December 24, El Heraldo reported that Paul was being moved to San Pedro Sula, the second-largest city in Honduras, three hours north of Tegucigalpa. Police set up roadblocks on the outskirts of that city and checked the trunks of many vehicles.[cl] That same day La Prensa reported that an "inside source" claimed that the kidnappers demanded twenty-five million dollars for Paul's return.[cli] (This would have been about $49 million in 2025). A few days later, El Tiempo made fun of that report in an article titled "No Trace Yet of Banker Vinelli", claiming the news about the ransom demand was totally false and that nothing had been heard of from the kidnappers. [clii]

That day, attorney Gautama Fonseca was eating lunch at home with his family. They were discussing the Christmas Eve celebration planned for that evening. The doorbell rang and their maid went to open the door. A man handed her a large white envelope addressed to Fonseca. When she brought it to the table, Fonseca assumed it was correspondence from his office and asked her to put it in his study to review after the holiday.

After a few minutes he mentioned to his wife that the delivery puzzled him, because his office staff was not working that day. She urged him to go see what had come. They went into his study, and he looked inside the envelope. He saw three letters, one addressed to Robert Vinelli. He told his wife, "That's all I needed, to be pulled into this matter." He opened a letter addressed to him, which directed him to immediately deliver the others to the Vinelli family. For a moment he hesitated, wondering if the correspondence was legitimate. He decided it was not his call to make and drove to the Vinelli house.[cliii]

Gautama handed Bob all three letters and left. Maria, Rick and Liz gathered around Bob as he read the two addressed to them. The handwritten note from Paul read,

Maria, Mama and children,
I am very well. My wishes are that you put a stop to the investigations conducted by the DIN[30], the army, and the FUSEP [31] as well as the publicity campaign conducted by the media.
Love, Paul

There was also the formal ransom request, in a typed letter formatted like the one sent on December 19. The FMLN confirmed seeing Bob's ad accepting the kidnapper's initial conditions. The amount the FMLN asked in exchange for Paul's release was twenty-five million dollars. The response was to be sent through a newspaper ad in

---

30. Departamento de Investigación Nacional, the Honduran equivalent of the FBI
31. Fuerza de Seguridad Pública, the uniformed national police of Honduras

three days. They warned that Paul's life was in danger because of the newspaper publicity about the case and the search efforts by "security forces". They also warned that they were not willing to prolong negotiations, and should that occur, the family would be putting Paul's life at risk. Enclosed was a photograph of Paul holding the prior day's newspaper.

The family realized the kidnappers did not know what Paul's financial situation was. Unfortunately for the FMLN and for Paul, they had not captured a wealthy man. Paul was prominent and powerful, but the income he earned as a banker and board member was not enough to support great savings. The travel and lavish parties the public read about in newspapers were primarily paid for by the bank, because his business networking and socializing developed business. The security team and bulletproof car were also paid by the bank. Paul's recent divorce from Fran had meant a financial setback. His support of seven children whose ages spanned twenty-one years had been very expensive, especially because many had studied in the United States at expensive schools.

The ransom letter was addressed to Robert Vinelli, the board of Banco Atlántida, and Chase Manhattan Bank. This told the family that the kidnappers thought they had taken an employee of Chase and that they hoped the international bank would help pay the ransom. The FMLN did not realize that Chase had sold its interest in Banco Atlántida five years earlier.

The family had to convince the kidnappers that they would never see twenty-five million dollars. This was difficult to do given that the kidnappers insisted communication only be through newspaper ads, the wording of which the kidnappers dictated.

Christmas Day was exactly one week after the kidnapping. Paul's holiday feast was one sardine, some rice, a cup of Koolaid, and two cookies. He wondered what the scene at home was. The answer: the decorations were festive, but not the mood.

Paul was becoming stir-crazy from the confinement and lack of stimulation inside the box. He asked the guards for some reading material. The first books they gave him, some in Spanish and some in English, were related to the ideology of his captors. There were books by Lenin, Marx and Engels. *The Mother* by Maxim Gorky. He also read *La Revolución Desconocida*, about the Ethiopian revolution by Raúl Vita Vidas, a Cuban author. Included were some revolutionary fliers edited at the Honduran university that five years before had removed him as a professor. Soldier of Fortune was provided in English. Paul often read standing up to be close to the one lightbulb he had for illumination. He was never given a newspaper because they didn't want him to know what was going on in the world, and because he was often the headline.

He developed an exercise routine. His lifetime habit of working out had always helped calm his racing mind. Paul needed that relief now more than ever. However, inside the box he could only walk eight feet in one direction. The daily schedule he adopted began with thirty minutes of calisthenics. Then he walked in a circle for two to three hours. He calculated that he walked from four to six miles per day

Every day the kidnappers passed a bucket of warm water and a cloth through the little door so Paul could give himself a sponge bath. They made sure he returned the cloth with the bucket each time. On the tenth day of captivity the kidnappers added a razor so he could shave during his sponge bath. He had to return the razor immediately afterwards. The pajamas he lived in were replaced with clean ones weekly.

The meals they passed through the door were bland, but he was well fed considering his circumstances. He had soup, rice, spaghetti, pork, chicken, tortillas, and beans. Salads had no dressing. His breakfast was almost always Corn Flakes. Sometimes he was given Corn Flakes for all three meals—he believed it was so he would lose track of time elapsed. The cereal was always served with hot milk. Once he asked if he might have cold milk and his request was denied. When he asked for more vegetables, that request was granted. Water was always available, and sometimes tea. He was never offered coffee because it could raise his blood pressure.

I could not find the December 27 ad with the family's response to the ransom letter, but I know it did not please the kidnappers because of their reaction. On December 29 they wrote to Bob and the banks that the wording of the ads could not be altered. Apparently, the family had listed a phone number or address for more thorough communication, and the kidnappers shot down the idea. They reiterated their ransom demand of twenty-five million dollars and warned Paul's life was at risk. The family had until December 31 to respond.

A handwritten letter from Paul said,

Dear Maria, Mama, Bob, Rick and family,
Once again I am writing to inform you that I am in perfect health and that I am being treated well. I am not injured nor bruised, nor sick. Apparently, there have been delays in the negotiations. I beg you to be as expeditious as possible as I am the one who loses. Please do not mention phone numbers nor addresses but follow

to the letter the instructions you receive. Being specific as to the numbers for offers or counteroffers. As you know, the most valuable thing we have is the house and it should be mortgaged to the greatest extent possible to be able to respond to any request. I beg that you do not seek the guidance of bad advisers and definitely stay away from the authorities because you could ruin everything.

The separation saddens me, and I am placing all my hopes on that this last effort will be successful and that we will soon be reunited.

I love all of you very much and I feel depressed and inconsolable about not being able to be close to you. The Christmas holidays have been sad, but I harbor hope that all will turn out well. Maria, I love you very much and need you, and you boys are the hope for tomorrow. Follow the aforesaid and we will soon be reunited.

Much affection, Paul

If there are other items that can be sold, also do so.

As 1980 came to an end, Paul didn't feel he could make New Year's resolutions. Instead, he looked back on the fifty-eight years he had lived. He later said that he was not depressed enough to consider suicide. He concluded, "If this is the end, I have had many satisfying things in my life. Having seven children has been a big one – they have brought me much pleasure."[cliv]

The FMLN provided the exact language the family should use in newspaper ads, which were for the sale of either cars, property, or German Shepherd puppies. The Vinellis felt they had to adjust the language slightly to explain Paul's financial circumstances and that Chase no longer was involved in Banco Atlántida. On New Year's Eve they published an ad with the required wording and added one line requesting more direct communication.

The next day the kidnappers sent a letter accusing the family of delay tactics. They emphasized that only the FMLN would dictate how communication occurred. They insinuated Paul might be killed, and if that happened, that they would inform the public it was because the family and the banks valued his life so little. They sent another picture of Paul and a handwritten note in which he pleaded for his family to cooperate with the kidnappers.

On January 3 the family placed an ad with their first counteroffer but still requesting more direct communication. On January 5 the kidnappers reiterated their ransom demand of twenty-five million dollars but said they would entertain other offers if made clearly. They also cryptically stated, "We are aware of the presence of the enemy interfering in the negotiation. This further endangers Mr. Paul Vinelli's situation." It is not clear what they meant by this. The FMLN probably had spies within the Honduran Armed Forces who told them the government was desperate to obtain information about the case even though the family was trying to keep them out of the situation.

News articles began to mention that the family knew that Paul was alive but that they were forbidden by the kidnappers to talk about the case.[clv] On January 7, the Honduran chief of police, Coronel Gustavo Alvarez, confirmed to the press that the Vinelli family was in contact with the kidnappers and were negotiating for Paul's return. He assured the public that the police force was still actively on the case but stayed out of the ransom negotiations to protect Paul's life. Alvarez explained our family's silence about the case with the statement, "They have the right to try to save him."[clvi]

Paul had been a captive for three weeks when the kidnappers upgraded his sleeping conditions. They brought in a small folding bed with a mattress for him. He interpreted this as their acknowledgement that negotiations were going to take longer than expected.

In early January the new Banco Atlántida building was completed. The executive team debated whether it was right to move in while their CEO and chairman was kidnapped. They decided to do so because the message to their clients had to be that bank business was not interrupted.[clvii]

I returned to SMU in Dallas after Christmas break. For John, Pia and me, who stayed in the U.S. during the kidnapping, it was stressful to be away from Honduras and the family. This was prior to cell phones and email. We could not call the land line at our house in Tegucigalpa because we were warned it could be tapped. We spent our days wondering if Dad was safe. Twice a month, Bob had someone who had traveled from Honduras to the U.S.—often it was Craig who went back and forth between New York City and Tegucigalpa—call us with an update.

Throughout January the Vinelli family tried to communicate Paul's financial circumstances to the kidnappers. The FMLN continued to reply with frustration. At one point they threatened to "apply revolutionary justice" to Paul. The guards said to Paul one day, "Your family is not doing anything on your behalf. We're going to have to end up killing you."

Paul overhead as many as ten "Trials by the People", where the kidnappers would debate whether he should be killed or not. One day an argument broke out between his captors. Suddenly a shot was fired. Then he heard muffled movement. He imagined one of them was killed and buried in the backyard. They still weren't prepared to kill their asset, fortunately. They did use sound disorientation techniques on Paul. Loud music, often by Cat Stevens[32], was played repeatedly in his cell. He lost hearing in one ear as a result.

Paul's and Maria's friends stayed in contact with Maria. The family did not disclose the progress of the negotiations but allowed visitors for moral support. Alice Goldstein and her husband Gilbert (Boris's son) were very close to Paul and Maria, and they were also their neighbors. Alice told me that Paul was on her mind constantly. She remembered it was a particularly cold winter in Tegucigalpa that year. She would look out the window at the gray skies and wonder if Paul was warm enough wherever he was being held.[clviii]

On January 20 Paul had been in captivity for over a month. That day, La Prensa reported that Maria was working on raising the ransom money by applying for a loan from the bank, putting up our house as collateral, and by asking friends for small loans. The newspaper reported that the ransom amount was between two and three million lempiras, which equaled between one million and one million five hundred thousand dollars.[clix] From the beginning of the case there were leaks like this. The authorities had demanded the Vinelli family keep them informed and promised in return that they would not jeopardize Paul's life by looking for him. The family gave the minimum information possible. Clearly, someone in the government was not honoring the deal.

The ventilator in the box Paul was kept in made enough noise that he could barely hear his captors speaking, but he occasionally caught something. Spanish was spoken in several accents, telling

---

32. The famous singer had converted to Islam three years prior and was known at this time as Yusuf Islam. He had stopped recording music. I don't know if he had any political ideology that aligned with the FMLN, or if they just liked his music.

him that his captors were from different Latin American countries. He thought he heard Russian, which was plausible because it was known that the Russians were behind insurgent activity in Central America. The conversations were educated and political. The terrorist group's goal was to create a different system of life for the poor of Central America without having to navigate the election process.[clx] Other times Paul's captors talked to him through the wooden box. He found them intelligent and well-read. They had conversations about politics, economics, history and literature.[clxi]

On January 26 the San Francisco Chronicle published a United Press report that Chase Manhattan Bank would not be paying the ransom, because they were no longer affiliated with Banco Atlántida. The New York bank emphasized that Paul's kidnapping was strictly a Honduran matter. The article mentioned that the original sum requested by the kidnappers was "exorbitant" because they thought Paul was a Chase official.[clxii]

On January 30, Banco Atlántida issued a press announcement assuring their depositors that the bank would not be paying the ransom. The announcement also confirmed that Chase Manhattan Bank would not be helping pay the ransom either. From this point on, the kidnappers addressed their letters only to Bob. As letters and ads went back and forth in early February, the ransom amount began to move down into a range that was feasible for the family to pay.

Just as negotiations were becoming fruitful, Paul suffered a health crisis. The kidnappers ran out of his blood pressure medicine and for some reason could not obtain more immediately. He started feeling the symptoms of high blood pressure: headache, dizziness and a general sense of being unwell. It's certain that the anxiety he must have been experiencing did not help.

The captors brought in a doctor and nurse, both wearing hoods, to examine him. The doctor prescribed Valium, and for some days Paul lost track of time. Eventually they resumed his medication and when his head cleared, the kidnappers were much nicer. They urged him to be calm, assuring him that the negotiations were moving forward well. They must have been worried that, after the time and effort they had invested in his capture, Paul might not survive before the ransom was paid. After the health episode, the guards offered him some non-political reading material including issues of *Selecciones*, the Spanish version of *Reader's Digest*. In one edition, he read a story about Elizabeth Blackwell, a British physician who was the first woman to obtain a medical degree in the United States. Paul read the article repeatedly, thinking of his daughter Elizabeth who wanted to pursue a career in medicine. Paul was also given a Spanish tabloid magazine and *Arms and Ammunition* and *Soldier of Fortune* in English.

On February 10, 1981, fifty-five days after Paul was captured, the FMLN sent the family a letter accepting their ransom offer of $1,350,000.[33] The kidnappers gave my brothers ten days to produce the cash in specified quantities of unmarked hundred-dollar, fifty-dollar and twenty-dollar bills.

The family experienced a moment of relief that the negotiating stage of the kidnapping was over. However, ten days was a very limited time to gather the ransom money in dollars. In those pre-internet days, bank transactions had to be done in person. Obtaining that amount of money had required selling assets in Honduras. Now lempiras had to be converted to dollars. It was not possible to obtain

---

33. This was the equivalent of approximately $5 million in 2026 dollars.

such a large quantity of dollars in Honduras. The bills would have to be obtained in the U.S. and transported to Honduras. Craig was in Tegucigalpa when the agreement was reached, so he flew to New York immediately to start the process of obtaining the money.

The family still said nothing about the kidnapping case. It was understandable, then, that the public was ignorant of the progress being made. On February 12, leaders of Banco Atlántida's labor union issued a press statement declaring that they wanted to see Paul released "alive and well", and they protested the act of violence that his kidnapping represented. Their ideology was aligned with that of the kidnappers, and they appealed to them from a humanitarian standpoint, "In Honduras we should avoid acts of violence, no matter the source; instead, we should seek civilized solutions to the economic, political, cultural and social problems the country's population faces. There have been times that there have been labor disputes between the labor union and the bank, but on those occasions Dr. Vinelli has always listened to our claims, and matters have been resolved harmoniously. We offer our assistance as intermediaries, to the extent of our abilities, to achieve his freedom."[clxiii]

Now that an agreement had been reached on the amount of the ransom, the kidnappers asked Paul to select three potential persons to deliver the money. These candidates had to be trusted by both parties, must have proven and unquestionable integrity, and could not have a strong affiliation with any political party.[clxiv] Paul had a difficult time coming up with the names. It was a huge favor to ask anyone to risk their life for him. Finally, he chose Carlos H Reyes (the bottlers' union labor leader), Gautama Fonseca (the attorney to whom the kidnappers had sent the Christmas Eve letters), and Arturo

Medrano, a bank director and Paul's personal attorney. The kidnappers selected Gautama Fonseca. Paul had known Fonseca since the 1950s. He was a very intelligent, left-leaning political leader. [clxv] He was the son-in-law of Marco Batres, the finance minister Paul first worked with when he arrived in Honduras. Fonseca was the Minister of Labor of Honduras in the 1970s. Fonseca's brother-in-law Cesar Batres was a current director of Banco Atlántida.

By mid-February Paul had been gone for almost two months. The board of directors of Banco Atlántida announced in the papers that they planned to name a new board chairman. The election was to be held at a March 18 stockholder's meeting.[clxvi]

Craig was in New York moving as fast as he could, sourcing the cash in the denominations the kidnappers had requested. He got the job done in six days, and on February 16 he called Bob in Tegucigalpa to say that he had the money ready. That afternoon Bob published an ad in La Prensa, using the cryptic language required by the FMLN, informing the kidnappers that the family had the money and were ready to make the exchange.

WE WILL HAVE READY

For barter, first-quality coffee seedbeds.

Ready to plant. Need assurances that

negotiations are being concluded

totally and definitively. What you offer must

be in good condition now and at the hour of

exchange and proof of this will be required at both times.

Information: Las Cumbres farm, KM 448 road to Santa Rosa de Copán.

On Wednesday, February 18, Craig flew from New York through Miami to Tegucigalpa. Special arrangements had been made for Craig's arrival. The bank had sent an armored car to receive the money Craig was bringing, and it was waiting on the tarmac. As the flight was landing, the airport was closed to car traffic. Airport employees were pulled away from their normal stations, presumably to avoid contact with someone who was landing. Word about these unusual measures spread, and it didn't take long for the press to speculate that it was Paul who was flying in. When Craig appeared in the doorway of the plane, rumors flew. He looked so much like his father that fellow travelers, radio stations and newspapers all reported seeing Paul arrive from Miami.

Craig descended the stairs that were rolled up to the plane and he stepped onto the tarmac carrying two heavy small suitcases. A black one was filled with books. He had packed the cash in the other, a bright blue suitcase that belonged to his wife. Craig handed the black suitcase of books to the driver of the armored car. This was so anyone who might be watching him would think the ransom money was in the protection of the bank.

However, the family did not want the money stored at the bank because banks were only open so many hours a day. They didn't know at what hour the kidnappers would ask for the ransom to be delivered. Craig got into a car driven by Paul's guards with the blue suitcase, which looked like it held his personal things. When he arrived at Paul's house, Bob and he stored the cash in the large safe Paul and Maria kept in one of their bedroom closets.

On February 20, Faustino received a letter for Bob from the kidnappers. They instructed the Vinelli family to fill one hundred thirty-five plastic bags with ten thousand dollars each. The bags were to be placed in three muslin fabric bags. Craig, Bob and Rick pulled the $1.35 million out of Paul's safe. They sat on the carpeted floor of his bedroom and counted out the money, wrapping the bills with rubber bands, then putting each bundle in a plastic bag. Soon after, Craig returned to New York. He needed to get back to his wife, his two-year-old son, and his job at Chemical Bank. He took the blue suitcase back home with him.

John flew to Tegucigalpa a few days later to support Bob and Rick for the ransom delivery phase. He left behind in Seattle his wife, who was pregnant with their second son, and their older son.

On February 25, Gautama Fonseca received another letter from the kidnappers for Bob.

Mr. Robert Vinelli and family

The *Fuerzas Populares de Liberación – FPL – "Farabundo Martí"*, communicate:
1. We have decided that Mr. Gautama Fonseca is who should deliver the money to us.
2. Mr. Gautama Fonseca should drive the vehicle Honda Accord, beige color, license plates 53534.
3. The money should be in three muslin bags on the back seat of the vehicle.
4. The vehicle should not have a radio transmitter on board, nor any signal transmitter, nor any electronic device that emits signals.
5. The vehicle should not have any special markings.
6. The vehicle should be in optimum condition with the gas tank full to avoid any foreseen or unforeseen "accidents".

7. The vehicle should have as its only identifying marking a large box of Kellogg's Corn Flakes, placed on the dashboard at the right side of the windshield, above the glove compartment.

8. In the glove compartment of the car you should put all the letters and attachments received, all which are numbered. We will not accept the excuse that they were destroyed or "lost".

9. With regards to Mr. Gautama Fonseca:

a) He must wear a brown suit (pants and jacket), light yellow long-sleeved shirt, light brown tie, and brown loafers.

b) He must not carry a weapon.

c) HE MUST BE ALONE AND ABSOLUTELY NOBODY MUST FOLLOW HIM.

10. The Vinelli family must be gathered at their home, located on Falso Pimiento Street in the Las Lomas del Guijarro neighborhood, on Thursday the 26th, Friday the 27th, and Saturday the 28th of February.

11. Mr. Gautama Fonseca must be located at his home, located in the Colonia Maradiaga No. 218 of Comayaguela, on Thursday the 26th, Friday the 27th, and Saturday the 28th of February. The previously mentioned vehicle must remain at Mr. Fonseca's house those three days and he must have ready the clothing mentioned.

12. Await our instructions.

Revolution or Death!

The Armed People will Conquer!
Central Command of the *Fuerzas Populares de Liberación – FPL –
Farabundo Martí*

The Vinelli family had one day to get everything ready in case they were called to action on the 26th. Fonseca did not own a brown suit, so the family asked him to buy one, promising to reimburse him. They found a light brown tie in Dad's closet and gave it to him as he left for the store.

Early the next morning the kidnappers sent Fonseca precise instructions regarding the delivery of the ransom, which was to take place that same day. He took the letters to the Vinelli house, then returned home to prepare himself for the task ahead. At 4:00 p.m. he went back to the Vinelli house, dressed in the required clothing. Bob, John and Rick had everything ready. As instructed, they put an envelope in the glove compartment. It contained all the ransom notes as well as the photos of Paul holding newspapers. They placed the bundles of cash, divided among the three muslin fabric bags, on the back seat of the Honda. The family thanked Fonseca and wished him well. At 5:00 p.m., he drove down the driveway and out the front gates.

Fonseca followed the instructions exactly. He drove at the prescribed forty kilometers per hour (twenty-five miles per hour) down the Las Lomas hill past where Paul had been captured, then under the bridge to Boulevard Morazán. He drove all the way to the soccer stadium which he circled completely, then headed to Colonia El Prado and arrived at the Los Fierritos restaurant. He got out of the car.[34] His instructions were to find a table marked with an asterisk. It was in the outside seating area of the restaurant. He sat down and ordered a coffee.

Five minutes later he went to the men's bathroom. A note was behind the mirror. He read it, went back to his table, paid the bill and left. Walking out, he noticed that a man and woman were seated

---

34. I had to fact check this, because nobody in Latin America would leave anything visible on the back seat of a parked car, much less bags with more than a million dollars in cash. My brother John, who was there when the car was prepared, assured me these were the instructions. His theory was that the kidnappers were watching Gautama's car from the moment it left Dad's house. Anybody trying to rob the car would have regretted the idea.

in their car in front of the restaurant. The note in the bathroom had instructed him to drive to the seafood restaurant Bocas del Mar, on the road towards the airport. Once there, he ordered a beer and again waited five minutes before going into the men's bathroom. In the trash can he found the next note. Fonseca returned to his table and finished his beer. As he drove away from Bocas del Mar, he noticed he was being followed by a couple in a car. They were probably the same people who were at Los Fierritos, but his nerves didn't allow him to look closely and confirm his suspicion.

After a long, circuitous route, he arrived at the La Colonia supermarket and then went into Chick's restaurant. As instructed, he sat at a booth facing a Sierra Nevada poster, with his back to the window where his car was. In the booth behind him was a young man who had an untouched order of chicken at his place. Fonseca ordered chicken, French fries and a soft drink, and began to eat. According to plan, a man approached him and said, "Today is the 31st. The transaction is going well."[clxvii]

Fonseca handed his car keys to the man and asked him if he needed the car's registration papers which he carried in his pocket. This was not part of the expected communication, and the man nervously replied, "No." It was 6:17 p.m. When the man with his car keys went outside, Fonseca heard the man in the booth behind him stand up and join him. Fonseca turned his head just slightly to see what was happening. He was very nervous – he imagined them catching him looking and returning to put a bullet in his neck.[clxviii]

The two men got into the Honda but couldn't get it to start. A waitress rushed over to tell Fonseca that someone was stealing his car. He had to come up with a story quickly: he told her that all was well, that it was his driver who he had given the keys to. Then the men got the car started and drove away. Fonseca had felt some regret when he first realized the kidnappers planned to take his car with the money in it. But when the Vinelli family assured him that they would replace the car if anything happened to it, he relaxed. As he sat in the booth at Chick's, part of him hoped the Honda would not be found.[clxix]

The kidnappers had told Fonseca to wait thirty minutes before leaving, but he had attracted attention at the restaurant. The workers kept looking at him, probably thinking it was odd that his driver would leave without him. After fifteen minutes of feeling uncomfortable he asked for the check, paid and left. He took a taxi to the Vinelli house and reported completing the handoff. They sent him home with one of their drivers. His relief at the task being over was enormous.

The Vinelli family entered an excruciating period of stress. The ransom had been paid; there was no more action they could take. Would the kidnappers honor their agreement, or would they keep the money and kill Paul? Would another letter arrive saying that the $1.35 million was just a down-payment and negotiations would re-open?

The next day a friend of Fonseca's son called to tell him that he had seen the Honda parked in front of the Supermarket Prisa, a block away from the restaurant. When Fonseca went to recover it, he found in the trunk the three white sacks, and all the rubber bands and plastic bags that the Vinelli brothers had so carefully used to sort the bills.

In her bathroom Maria had lit several candles to the Virgin of Suyapa, Catholic Patroness of Honduras. John spent his nervous energy pacing around the expansive living room, his footprints appearing all over Maria's plush, pristine white rugs. The maids snuck in several times a day to sweep them away. At one point, John turned to his siblings, saying, "All of you need to leave this country and never return." Liz thought, "I'm enrolled in college here, what would I do?"

One long day passed, then two, then three. On Sunday, March 1, Bob returned to San Pedro Sula to be with his family. Monday, March 2 was Paul's seventy-fifth day of captivity. In the afternoon the guards instructed him to shave off his mustache. He did not know his ransom had been paid but could tell something was up. Shortly before 8:00 p.m., his captors passed his clothes, belt and shoes through the small door. He stepped out of his pajamas and dressed in street clothes for the first time in months. His pants were so loose they slipped down on his hips even with his belt buckled to the tightest hole. The captors did not return his watch nor the four hundred lempiras (two hundred dollars) he was carrying when captured.

Men in ponchos and hoods covering their faces came into the cell. They placed a blindfold over Paul's eyes and cotton in his ears. They tied his hands behind his back and bound his ankles. For some reason they did not cover his mouth. The captors pulled him out of the box that had been home for two and a half months and walked him outside to a car parked behind the house. He was made to lie on the floorboard in front of the back seat. They drove around for thirty minutes, which reminded Paul of the day they captured him. They drove to Colonia Miramonte and parked behind a hardware store called Larach y Compañía. The kidnappers removed the cords that restrained Paul's arms and legs, pulled him out of the car, and told him to kneel in some high grass. They stuffed ten lempiras (five dollars) in his shirt pocket and said, "For your taxi."

Paul was told to keep his blindfold on for fifteen minutes, and not to go directly home. He remained frozen in that spot as he heard the car drive away. Just as he was calculating how long fifteen minutes was, he was startled by the voice of a man next to him, demanding to know what he was doing. He tore off his blindfold and was horrified to see the night watchman for Larach y Compañía standing over him, brandishing a *machete*.

He jumped up, tore the cotton from his ears, and ran clumsily to the street and up the hill towards Boulevard Suyapa where he knew he would find a taxi. It was the first time in seventy-five days that he had walked in a straight line for more than eight feet. His many hours of walking in circles had trained his gait to be different. As he reached the boulevard by the Hospital Escuela, he raised his arm. Paul looked terrible, but fortunately a cab driver stopped and picked him up.

A former Banco Atlántida employee named Carmen Neda de Ayón was driving with her husband near the Hospital Escuela when she recognized the chairman of the bank, stumbling and disoriented. She asked her husband to turn around and follow him. By the time they circled back to Paul's location, he was getting into a beat-up taxi. They followed him until the taxi turned up towards the Las Lomas neighborhood, where they knew Paul lived. At that point her husband became nervous about trailing Paul, and the couple drove off in another direction.[clxx]

Paul followed instructions and did not go home. Instead, he had the taxi driver drive to his mother's house, which was not guarded.

He walked up the steps to Dora's door and rang the doorbell. Her maid looked through the peephole, did not recognize him, and refused to open. Paul rang the doorbell again. Dora walked to the door and looked. The man on her front step was barely recognizable as her son. Paul weighed fifty pounds less and his mustache had been shaved off. But when he spoke to her in Italian, despite his weak voice, she knew. Shaking with emotion, she opened the door and hugged her son fiercely. She then called his house.

Maria, John, Rick and Liz were having dinner. The phone rang, and John went into the kitchen to answer. A moment later he burst back through the swinging door to the dining room and said to Rick, "Let's go!" They grabbed their pistols, and without telling the guards outside what was happening, jumped in a car and drove to Dora's. When they walked in Grandma's front door, they found Paul pacing in circles like a caged cougar. He was anxious and disoriented, unable to believe that he was free. And still accustomed to walking in circles like he had been doing for months.

They drove him home. The guards knew their car, so as it approached, they opened the gates and allowed them to speed through. Because it was nighttime, they did not see Paul behind the tinted windows. John backed the car into the open garage under the house, and he and Rick brought Paul inside through the downstairs door without anybody seeing him. As they walked their father up the stairs to the main floor, Maria and Liz were waiting. Paul later said he felt he was in a dream when he walked into the house. He had dreamed of being home so many times during captivity. After hugging him through her tears, all Maria wanted to do was get him into a shower and some clean clothes. He resisted at first—it was difficult to adjust to his new reality.

The phone at the house was kept busy with calls to first family, and then friends. A few of his closest friends came over that night to welcome him home. Paul appeared nervous. He moved constantly using short steps, mimicking the way he moved in his eight by eight-foot jail. He spoke very little. His voice had changed—it sounded much weaker—to the point that friends and family who called him on the phone could not recognize him. Maria, John, Rick and Liz didn't get to sleep until late, and Paul didn't sleep at all.

The next morning, Maria and Paul decided they should go to Houston the following day so he could have a medical checkup. None of Paul's clothes fit, so his friends jumped into action. Alice and Gilbert Goldstein went out and bought him some jogging outfits to wear until he could have clothes altered. [clxxi] Chito Kafie sent over his tailor who measured Paul and took his clothes to alter that same day.

Bob flew in on the first flight from San Pedro Sula. The reunion with his father was emotional: Paul knew what a burden he had placed on his third son in asking that he handle the negotiations. A parade of friends came to visit that day. They observed that Paul was a different man – very thin, sunken eyes, nervous, and without his signature mustache.

*Paul and Jack Agurcia at Paul's house the day
after release from captivity March 3, 1981*

Paul requested that Gautama Fonseca come to visit him. When he arrived, Paul embraced the man who had sacrificed his own safety for Paul's freedom. Fonseca offered to return the tie the family had lent him. Paul laughed and asked him to keep it, at which time Fonseca asked for Paul to autograph the tie. Journalists from radio and print media crowded the front gates of the house hoping to gain entrance, but anyone who was not a close friend was turned away by armed guards.[clxxii]

On Wednesday March 4, before his flight to Houston, Paul was driven to the new bank building where Faustino and other bank executives gave him a tour. He walked into his spacious and elegant corner office, digesting what his new reality would be if he returned to Honduras.

Paul and his family were then driven to the airport in a bullet-proof white van, followed by his brown bulletproof Mercedes Benz, both full of bodyguards. Because Paul's security detail had special clearance, the van and chaser car drove straight onto the tarmac, up to the steep rolling stairs placed at the door of the SAHSA plane. As they left the van, John pulled off the shoulder holster and gun he had been carrying for the entire visit and handed it to one of Paul's guards. Then he, Paul and Maria boarded. (The next day, newspapers identified John as an American bodyguard).

A couple of days after Paul left Honduras, Fonseca received a case of whiskey, a case of champagne, and a case of wine, with a note that read,

"Gautama, I don't have the right words with which to thank you. I hope that we can soon celebrate the experience as an unforgettable memory. Paul." With the letter was a photo taken of Paul and Fonseca the day after Paul was liberated. On the back of the photo Paul wrote: "Gautama, there are times in life when the phenomenon of true friendship occurs in a matter of moments. Despite the long periods of time in which we were not in touch, my admiration for you grew. That allowed me to take advantage of the closeness we developed during a few exchanges in our lives. My gratitude is from my soul, and will last a lifetime, because friends like you gave everything. Paul."[clxxiii]

When they arrived in Houston, Paul, Maria and John checked into a two-bedroom suite at the Warwick Hotel. The next day Paul was admitted to Methodist Hospital for tests. The doctors found him in fairly good shape considering his long captivity. His insistence on maintaining his physical strength in the cramped space had helped.

Besides the weight loss, he had anemia and significant hearing loss in one ear, caused by the loud music his captors played outside his box. Of these physical problems, only the hearing loss was irreversible. It would take time to see what psychological and emotional toll his captivity had taken.

John stayed in Houston for another day until Paul was discharged, and then he flew back home to Seattle. I flew to Houston from Dallas (where I was in college) and moved into the second bedroom of the Warwick suite. Dad looked extremely thin and weak. When I went into the living area late one night, I saw the light on in his and Maria's room and I knew he was having trouble sleeping.

The only conversation Dad ever had with me about the kidnapping was during that visit. He told me that once the Houston doctors had cleared him to travel, he planned to go to Europe for a while to eat well and regain his strength. He then planned to go back to Honduras and work hard – he needed to repay money that friends had lent to get him released as well as rebuild the personal savings used for his ransom. I was scared for his safety. I asked why he would go back. He said, "First of all, I have spent more than thirty years building my professional life in Honduras. What could I possibly do elsewhere that would bring close to the income that I can make there? Second, if I stay away, 'they' will have won." We never spoke of it again.

After Houston Paul and Maria went to Europe. Their first stop was the city where Paul was born, Naples, Italy. They spent three weeks there, staying at Paul's favorite hotel. The Hotel Excelsior faces the Bay of Naples and Mount Vesuvius. This was the view that Paul enjoyed when he was a young child living at the top of the hill in the Vomero district.

Around the corner from the hotel is the famous Caffè Gambrinus, founded in 1860. The café is known for its *sfogliatella* pastry. This is a flaky pastry filled with flavored creamy ricotta fillings such as almond and lemon peel. Paul loved these. Since *sfogliatelle* were not available in Honduras nor the U.S., he often ordered the closest thing, a napoleon. I never understood the origin of his love for flaky pastries until I wrote this book.

In 2018 José and I went to Naples. It was my first visit to Dad's birthplace. Pasquale Faldo's daughter Elsa and her husband Lino toured us around the city to see the building where Dad was born and the church where he was baptized. Then we went to lunch at their club overlooking the Bay of Naples. At dessert time, José asked if we might try a *sfogliatella*, which we had heard was only made well in Naples. Elsa and Lino said there was one place to try that, and it was the Caffè Gambrinus. As we walked there, we passed the Hotel Excelsior, and they pointed out that Dad always stayed there when in town. When we saw the proximity of the café to the hotel, I surmised that's where Dad regained some of weight he had lost during the kidnapping.

While in Naples Paul and Maria spent a lot of time with Elsa's father Pasquale, Paul's former neighbor in Tegucigalpa. Pasquale had retired to Naples. He drove them along the winding Amalfi Coast to Salerno, where Paul had lived from age five to twelve. [clxxiv] During that visit to Naples, Paul investigated regaining the Italian citizenship he had renounced when he became a U.S. citizen. Although he had spoken bravely to me about returning to Honduras, he was considering the option of moving to Italy if necessary.[clxxv] [35]

---

35. He later dropped the efforts to regain the Italian citizenship.

On March 19, La Prensa released a news bombshell. That day and the next, they published copies of every letter the FMLN had written to Bob, Gautama Fonseca and Faustino Laínez. They also printed several ads our family had placed in the paper to negotiate Paul's release, and some photographs of Paul holding newspapers that had accompanied the letters.[clxxvi] Someone in the government had released these documents which the family had surrendered under the condition they be kept out of the public eye. The family worried that the kidnappers would be angered.

Honduran newspapers were full of speculation as to whether Paul would return or not. The president of the Honduran Supreme Court, José Pineda, declared that all affected parties including Paul and Fonseca must appear to testify.[clxxvii] Several crimes had occurred: the murder of the bodyguard Demetrio Cedillos, the serious injury of the driver Roberto Martinez, and the kidnapping of Paul – these needed to be investigated, and the perpetrators found and tried. Three primary witnesses were out of the country, so their testimonies were delayed. While Paul was in Europe, Fonseca was in Washington, D.C. attending an agrarian reform conference.[clxxviii] Roberto Martinez, the injured driver, had been sent by Banco Atlántida to the United States for eye surgery.[clxxix]

Paul and Maria stayed away from Honduras for about six weeks. They coordinated their return carefully, knowing the attention it would attract. Maria arrived in Tegucigalpa first, on April 21. That same day she appeared in court to give her declarations to the judge. She answered questions for two hours. Only she and Criminal Court Judge Victor Manuel Ancheta were present, because she arrived at the courthouse with no announcement. This prevented the press from being notified and having access to her.[clxxx] Bob also testified that day.

The following day, on April 22, Paul flew into Tegucigalpa on TAN airlines. He was received at the base of the airplane steps by his new security detail: six highly trained bodyguards in two cars, including his armored Mercedes. The guards had previously arranged his immigration and customs forms, so they quickly moved him into his car and sped off.

The next morning, Paul made a surprise appearance before Judge Ancheta, frustrating the press's hopes of interviewing him at the courthouse. The judge's questioning lasted three and a half hours.[clxxxi] On Friday, April 24, Paul held a press conference at Banco Atlántida. The event took place on the executive floor of the new Banco Atlántida building. Seated next to him was Cleto Ramón Alvarez, attorney, First Vice-President of Banco Atlántida, and one of his closest advisers. Paul had gained almost half of the lost weight back. His mustache was still growing out.

He started by thanking the press for their interest and attendance, and for the opportunity to set the record straight on several things that had been recorded incorrectly. His demeanor was less confident than people remembered.

He said,

"I have come out of this incident humbler than I was before going into captivity. The experience has had a positive consequence: I feel as if I was reborn, with a greater desire and obligation towards society. I also will be more devoted to my family, especially to my wife."[clxxxii]

Paul confirmed to the audience that the ransom letters published in the papers were the actual ones received by the family. He indicated that the family had been forced to share them with the authorities and had done so under condition of secrecy – unfortunately the authorities had not stuck to the agreement.

"I am certain that the individuals who kidnapped me were not only pursuing financial objectives, they had political aims. These were not common criminals; they were experienced persons who knew what they were doing."

He ended on the positive note he was known for:

"Honduras is a country its citizens should have confidence in. We should leave our fears aside and invest, because only with the contribution of all can we make this nation grow. I am committed to resume my work as CEO of Banco Atlántida, and to lend my assistance in solving the problems of Honduras."[clxxxiii]

This same month, April of 1981, the ideological battle in Central America came to the world's attention when President Ronald Reagan stopped a multi-million-dollar aid package to Nicaragua, to prevent the Sandinistas from shipping arms to leftist guerrillas in El Salvador. Reagan's action began an eight-year showdown of right vs. left between the U.S. and Nicaragua, using Honduras as a middleman, and ended with the notorious Iran-Contra scandal and U.S. congressional hearings.[clxxxiv]

Paul's priority upon his return to Honduras was to thank the people who helped him during the kidnapping. One was Carlos H. Reyes, the labor leader who Paul had proposed to deliver the ransom money. Paul invited him for lunch at the bank where he told him the details about his capture and the conditions under which he was held. This was an unusual move, because Reyes would have possibly known some of the people involved in his kidnapping. Yet Paul kept the door open with him. Reyes told me later that he very much appreciated the level of trust Dad had placed in him.[clxxxv]

After Paul returned to Honduras, his freedom was restricted. From then on, and for the rest of his life, he never went anywhere in the country without six bodyguards, two in his car and four in a chaser car. The guards were a constant reminder that his life was at risk.

Paul was different after his kidnapping. The bon vivant who enjoyed entertaining friends and clients with great food and wines disappeared for a while. The kidnapping had deflated him— there was sadness in his eyes and demeanor. His friends were also sad: for Paul and for the freedom they all had lost. From that point on, there was a collective fear in their social group. Most of his friends increased their security.[clxxxvi]

16

THE NEW NORMAL
1982 – 1986

Paul felt stifled by the security the bank required he have after his kidnapping. The six guards in two cars were assigned to be with him anywhere in Honduras. He began to travel more, attending banking conferences in the U.S. and Europe so that he and Maria could have a break from guards. Instead of vacationing in Roatán, the Honduran island he enjoyed so much, they went to Ambergris Caye in Belize.

Paul's former wife Iris owned several apartments in Coral Gables, an upscale neighborhood in Miami, Florida. He arranged for the bank to rent one of her apartments for the use of its executives when they were in Miami. Maria decorated the apartment in her signature white upholstery and with tables and bar made of Lucite. It was beautiful but made everyone else who used the apartment nervous about staining the furniture.

Paul loved the freedom of moving around independently in the tropical city, which was only a two-hour flight from Tegucigalpa. His favorite places to go were grocery shopping at Publix or to wander around Woolworth on Miracle Mile. He would buy large quantities of basic provisions like socks or toothpaste to take back to Honduras. He loved how inexpensive everything was at Woolworth.

He was especially excited about driving, because he was not allowed to do that in Honduras, where for years he was driven by professional chauffeurs. He had not driven a car in the United States for over thirty years. Unfortunately, he wasn't in Miami often enough to become a good driver. Anytime I visited him, I hoped he wouldn't suggest we drive somewhere.

Maria and Iris started developing a close friendship. When they were both in Miami, Iris taught Maria where the best stores in the city were. The two spent whole days at the elegant Bal Harbour shops where Iris introduced Maria to her personal shoppers at Neiman Marcus. Maria was a quick and grateful student.[clxxxvii] Maria furthered the work Dora had done towards repairing relationships that Paul had lost when he married Fran. Besides befriending Iris in Miami, Maria also got to know Paul's former neighbor Eva Bahr. They got along so well that Iris invited Paul, Maria and Eva on a cruise together.

Once when I visited Dad and Maria in Miami, Dad decided he was tired of eating every meal out (Maria did not cook, and after having a cook for so many years, he rarely did). He asked me to make *pasta a la vongole* (spaghetti with clams). I admitted I had almost no cooking experience. He was irritated and told me to heat up a can of clams and toss it with pasta, how hard could that be? I started by sautéing garlic in oil, because I knew he liked garlic in his pasta. Until you become a cook, some things are not obvious to you. Like: hot oil and liquid from a room temperature can of clams do not mix. When I poured the clams and their juice into the pan, the explosion was magnificent. Clams exploded all over the kitchen: ceiling, cabinets, counters, floors, me. Dad and Maria came running, saw I was alive, grabbed the car keys and went out to dinner. I spent the rest of the evening cleaning.

The time Dad and Maria spent in Miami was a break from the stress in Honduras. The ideological battle continued in Honduras throughout the 1980s. President Suazo Córdova, newly in office in 1982, was incensed by the crimes committed against the business sector. He enlisted the help of the American government in fighting revolutionary factions.

The U.S. Ambassador to Honduras at the time was John Negroponte. He been appointed to the position in 1981 and moved to Honduras months after Paul's kidnapping came to an end. The two men came to know each other well, and Negroponte often sought Paul's advice on the complicated issues facing Honduras. In a 2018 interview Negroponte said to me, "There weren't many wise men in Honduras, so if you wanted a serious opinion Paul was one of the few people you would call to meet over drinks or coffee."[clxxxviii]

On September 19, 1982, a dozen guerrillas kidnapped the entire Chamber of Commerce of San Pedro Sula, approximately one hundred people. They sought the release of members of their cohort, which they considered political prisoners. Among the kidnapped were the Minister of Economics of Honduras, the treasury minister, and the Central Bank president.[clxxxix] Negotiations lasted a week, with some hostages released during that time. On September 26 the government of Suazo Córdova agreed to allow the kidnappers to be flown out of the country in return for a release of the hostages. The captors, the remaining thirty-four hostages, and the mediators were flown to Panama. The guerrillas then boarded a Panamanian Air Force plane for Havana, Cuba, while the Honduran hostages and mediators were flown back to San Pedro Sula.[cxc]

Suazo Cordova's government worked to shut down the guerrilla activity. That year, Honduran police arrested Carlos H. Reyes during a street demonstration. He was questioned under violent circumstances. Paul intervened with the government to obtain his release. Reyes told me the story in 2018, thirty-six years later. The memory of his treatment at the hands of his interrogators was clearly fresh. He said that when he was released, he came out spitting blood. But he was very grateful that Paul, who had a good relationship with the Honduran and the American governments who Reyes blamed for his experience, stepped in on his behalf.

Paul continued to be considered the primary expert on the Honduran economy and served as an unofficial advisor the government of Honduras. Annually he had the Department of Economic Studies of Banco Atlántida prepare an analysis of the Honduran economy, which included current World Bank statistics.[cxci] He was invited to present this report to business groups, the Honduran Congress and the president's council of ministers. Back then Carlos Flores (who was later president of Honduras) was a congressman.

President Flores described these presentations to me when I interviewed him. The economic analysis the bank team prepared was at a very high level. Paul's perspective was always generally optimistic, which was different than that of most Hondurans, whose attitude was to complain about everything in the country. Flores said that Paul was a "glass half full" person. His perspective was particularly well rounded, because he spoke from the point of view of the head of the largest bank in the country and as chairman of companies in different sectors.[cxcii]

Paul socialized in the most important business circles in Honduras because of his position as bank CEO and chairman. Maria worked to cultivate these professional relationships into personal friendships. She was a sophisticated networker and excellent party planner, and soon powerful people including the president of the country and his wife came to the house for meals. Paul and Maria's all-white home was the setting for many beautiful events. (Paul joked that anything not moving at the house would get a coat of white paint.) Every meal was perfection, whether at the glass-topped table in the dining room or on one of the several patios in the gardens. Maria sent her driver David all over town to find her the perfect flowers to match whatever theme she had orchestrated for an event.

Instead of having nighttime Christmas parties like Paul and Fran did in the 1960s and 1970s, Paul and Maria started to host Christmas luncheons. These elaborate events were held in the gardens of their home, started at 1:00 p.m. and lasted through dinner, with guests still dancing after midnight.

Paul was almost sixty years old and Maria was the right wife for this stage of his life. She was a woman of strong character who often got her way, but she also was strategic. She made Paul the boss in their relationship and doted on him. Fran, my mother, was too "American" – she wanted to be an equal partner. While Paul may have enjoyed that kind of relationship with his first love Linda, by his fifth marriage, what he most wanted from a wife was unconditional support. Maria's training from her first mother-in-law in Spain worked well: she made sure his every need was met. Some mornings she ran after him as he left their bedroom, waving a comb, "Paul, Paul, you haven't combed your hair!" He rolled his eyes, but everyone knew that he enjoyed the attentiveness.

Our family had always spoken English with each other, because that's what Dad spoke first with Linda, and then with Fran. Maria did not speak English, so we switched to Spanish when with her. Occasionally she tried out an English word, often with hilarious results. Once she suggested we take the "Surumba" (Suburban) on an outing to the countryside. During a discussion of the stock market, she asked how the "Mazda" (NASDAQ) was doing.

In September of 1982 Paul's mother Dora became ill. She had never been a cheerful woman, but in her eighty-seventh year of life she had been very unhappy, telling friends and family that she wanted to die. She apparently stopped taking her heart medication because her health deteriorated suddenly. One day her maid found her in a critical state, with terrible difficulty breathing, and called Paul. He immediately called her cardiologist, Dr. Alvarez. When he couldn't reach him, he asked Liz to find a doctor. Liz was in medical school at that time, and asked one of her medical school professors, Dr. Velasquez, to come to Grandma's house. When he checked her vitals, he immediately called for an ambulance. Dora protested that she did not want to go to a hospital. Dr. Velasquez suggested Liz go in the ambulance with her grandmother.

Dora arrived at the hospital in very bad shape. Paul met them at Hospital Viera. When Paul walked in her room, her heart had stopped, and doctors were resuscitating her. He walked out, and in the hall encountered Dr. Alvarez who had rushed to the hospital when he heard the news. The doctor took Paul back in to be with his mother for the last half hour until her heart stopped. After she died, Paul wrote to his nephew Armando, "We are still suffering from the shock of your grandmother's passing. A good life means being close to your loved ones. Neither geography nor weather can compensate for that single fact of life."

In early 1983 Paul's close friend Arturo Medrano was diagnosed with pancreatic cancer. Medrano, who had been Paul's attorney and a bank director for many years, refused treatment which, in those days, would have prolonged life for months at most. He pronounced that he wanted to spend his last days in peace with his family. Nobody but his immediate family could visit him, not even Paul. He died within a couple of months. Pia rode with Paul to the Medalla Milagrosa church for Medrano's funeral service. As usual he didn't want to attend the mass, so they waited outside in the car until the service was over. As it ended, he went inside the church to give Medrano's widow, Orfilia, his condolences. He was crying when he got back in the car.

Later that year Paul's friend Chito Kafie also developed pancreatic cancer. Chito agreed to have treatment, but like Medrano, the result was grim. He was gone within six months. A few days before his death, he called his family to his bedside for some final words of wisdom. Someone recorded them. At the end of his talk, he counseled them

"If you ever have a doubt, talk to Paul."[cxciii]

That November of 1984 I flew to Tegucigalpa for Liz's wedding. She and her fiancé José Luis had been dating since they were sixteen years old. Back when Liz informed Dad she was engaged, his response was, "It's your choice. If it doesn't work, don't stay longer than necessary." She probably was expecting some form of "Congratulations!", but Dad was on his fifth marriage and that's all he had to give. I was staying at his house that weekend. When it was time to leave for the church, I walked into his bedroom and found him sitting at the end of his bed, dressed in his tuxedo, looking gloomy. I asked what was wrong and he said, "I don't want to go in the church." I replied, "You have to, Dad. It's for Liz, you aren't making a religious statement." When Pia and I later married, he also walked us down the aisle of a church. It seemed a duty Dad endured with difficulty. While some probably thought he felt sadness about his daughters growing up, I believe it was more about his resistance to the religious ceremony.

Paul was becoming less engaged with the work of running the bank. Since he traveled so often, he left the day-to-day operations to Guillermo Bueso and the other executives to handle. His management style became more authoritarian. Some board members criticized that he no longer allowed much discussion in meetings. This impatience makes sense to me. Paul was sixty-two years old, with far fewer years ahead than behind him. He didn't want to spend hours in a board room, giving everyone time to debate issues interminably, when he knew from experience what the outcome would be.

What he still exhibited interest in was improving the lives of Hondurans. His concern for employees made him a popular leader, and he earned the loyalty of everyone from the executive floor to the pool of drivers in the bank parking lot. Paul encouraged the bank to develop two projects on land next to the Banco Atlántida headquarters. One was a sports club with tennis courts and a pool, for the use of bank employees. Next to the club would be a gated housing development, to be named Residencial Casavola (after his mother, Dora Casavola). He wanted it to be a neighborhood of homes whose front yards were open to the street, American style, which was unheard of in Honduras. (Ultimately the home buyers did put up walls, but to this day the neighborhood is unique. Because of the restricted access and no through traffic, the neighborhood kids can and do play in the street.)

Paul's instinct was to help wherever he saw a need. His bodyguards told us the following story about their boss. Early one morning, they were driving Paul to San Pedro Sula on winding, mountainous roads. As they came around a turn, they saw a naked woman walking on the side of the road. She was likely a mental health patient who had escaped from the nearby Santa Rosita Hospital. Paul instructed his driver to stop, and the chaser car stopped behind them. Slowly both cars backed up on the narrow shoulder, being careful not to hit the woman, who hardly noticed their presence. Paul stepped out of the car, and while pulling off his grey suede jacket, called to her, "Hey! Cover up a bit." After placing the jacket over her shoulders, he reached in his pocket and handed her some money.

One day he was standing on the patio outside of his office at Banco Atlántida, and he saw a homeless woman bathing in the fountain that stood at the building's entrance. He immediately sent staff to give her clothing, food and money. Over the years, the woman returned many times to bathe in the fountain, and when he saw her, he sent people to help her.

17

THERE'S ALWAYS WORSE
1986

On Monday, March 31, 1986, Paul's son Craig was commuting from his home in South Orange, New Jersey to his office at Chemical Bank in New York City. The thirty-seven-year-old banker stood on the crowded train platform reading the newspaper with his back to the tracks. Witnesses say that an express train came on the inside track, which was against regulations because they traveled quickly – only the trains that stopped were supposed to come in on that track. We think that the suction created from the speeding train made Craig lose his balance—and he fell between two cars.

I was at my office at Mercantile Bank in Dallas at the time. Bob called me from Tegucigalpa, and I couldn't understand what he was saying. The poor guy—I made him repeat it three times, "Craig died."

The entire family except Liz who was pregnant and on bedrest, as well as several close friends, flew to New Jersey for the funeral in South Orange. This was the second and last time I saw Dad cry, and it was again about Craig (the first time was when Craig left for

Vietnam). It happened at the funeral home. Despite the damage the train had done to Craig's body, they managed to put him back together and there was an open coffin. I was standing next to him, my hand on his stiff chest, when Dad walked in with Maria and one of my brothers on either side of him. Half-way down the aisle, when he saw Craig's body inside the casket, Dad stopped and broke down crying.

Craig had been a younger replica of Dad: in appearance, personality, career choice, and in his tendency to quiet his intelligent mind with alcohol. Pasquale Faldo later said to me, "Paolo had created a son who WAS him."[cxciv] The loss was also devastating to Craig's widow, to his seven-year-old son, and to us.

After the funeral we went to New York City for a few days. Paul paid for the family to stay at the Helmsley Palace Hotel. Many in the group dealt with the loss by drinking. Rick drank so much that one night the hotel staff found him asleep in the lobby, sitting on the floor leaning against an elegant round upholstered banquette.

Maria dealt with the sadness in her way, by shopping. She announced she was going to "Berguman" (Bergdorf Goodman). I remember being in my hotel room and hearing a knock on the door. I opened, and there was Maria holding an armful of shopping bags from Bergdorf Goodman and Saks Fifth Avenue. She threw all the bags but one in my room and went on down the hall to hers and Dad's room. I knew to hide those bags in my closet until Dad left the hotel, at which time Maria came to collect them.

The woman was a master packer – after every trip she returned to Honduras with twice as much as she had left with, but rarely any additional luggage. Her trick was that when she left home, all her clothes were packed in plastic and tissue from the dry cleaners (this was also so her things wouldn't become wrinkled). As the trip progressed and the clothes were worn, the tissue and paper were replaced by purchases.

When he returned to Honduras Paul created a scholarship in honor of Craig at the School of Economics of the UNAH in Tegucigalpa. It is called Fundación Craig Vinelli and covers the cost of college tuition and books for low-income, qualified students studying economics, accounting or business administration. Craig's widow created a second scholarship at Craig's alma mater, the Wharton School of Business at the University of Pennsylvania.

Craig Douglas Vinelli – 1985

That October, at his annual medical checkup in Houston, Paul learned he had three blocked arteries in his heart. That same week doctors at Houston Methodist Hospital performed a triple bypass surgery. I came from Dallas to visit him afterwards. He was lying in the hospital bed in a thin blue gown. He looked uncharacteristically vulnerable. His sturdy body was bisected by an angry red scar that ran from the top of his chest down the length of his abdomen. Another scar ran down his right thigh. When he referred to the scar, it was clear he felt violated.

After that surgery Paul was changed. He couldn't stand to think about what the doctors had done to him, but he couldn't ignore the reality because his scars reminded him constantly. He had a look of "I remember who I was - where did that person go?" The sadness caused the muscles of his mouth to turn downwards in a frown that lasted months.

After his stitches were removed three weeks post-surgery, Paul returned to Honduras in time for the birth of Liz's first child, a daughter named Maria Esther. When he visited Liz at the hospital, she was startled that he immediately insisted on showing her his scar. It seemed to define who he was at that time, and not in a good way. Fortunately, the birth of a grandchild was the best antidote to his horrible year, and by Christmas he began to enjoy family again.

18

THE GOURMAND

aul knew very well that the massive surgery he had just endured was a consequence of an unhealthy diet. Even though his cardiologist insisted he change his eating habits, food had always been such a source of pleasure and comfort for Paul that he broke the rules regularly. His appetite was tied to his love of travel which started back in the 1950s and which increased as he could afford nicer restaurants and hotels. For decades he carried a small ringed address book with detailed notes he made of his favorite hotels and restaurants around the world. Before the internet, his friends knew that he was the one to ask for the best places to go in any city.

It is hard to imagine now, in this age of celebrity chefs and popular food shows on TV, what the culinary world was in the 1960s. In Tegucigalpa, there were very few places to eat out and none were considered fine dining. Grocery stores and the market carried sad-looking produce in limited quantities. There was no gourmet food for purchase, and imported items of any kind were rare. I remember being grateful when visiting the homes of friends whose parents worked at the U.S. Embassy, because they had access to the embassy commissary and could buy American snacks like potato sticks and candy bars.

Gourmet food was not a big draw in the U.S. either at this time, and few people sought out unusual foods. Paul was an exception. He was ahead of his time about food and was usually planning his next meal. He tried every exotic food item he heard of. When he traveled, he went to all the best restaurants he could. If a dish particularly appealed to him, he charmed his way into the kitchen and asked the chef how to make it. He brought notes back to Tegucigalpa for his cook to learn how to prepare it.

Dad brought seeds home from all over the world and instructed our two gardeners to plant them in the vegetable garden on the top level of our property. Our garden contained items that were odd to many people, like arugula and squash blossoms. People couldn't believe that we ate fried parsley as an appetizer. These tastes had their roots in the southern Italian upbringing of Dad's parents', when his ancestors ate inexpensive things such as wild greens.

His favorite thing to do when traveling was to go to markets and grocery stores. He returned from his trips with his suitcase full of mysterious items. He often brought back canned escargots, which were served at weekend family meals. By age five I knew how to use the special tongs to hold the shell, and then to use the tiny fork to remove the creature—Dad would have said delicacy—inside. The end of this dish was what we anticipated, because who really loves snails? That is when we used crunchy bread to sop up the melted butter loaded with garlic and parsley from the indentations on the round escargot plate.

One time when I was around seven, Dad returned from a trip to Japan and with great excitement pulled a bright orange persimmon out of his briefcase. He had taken great care to protect the delicate fruit over many hours of travel. It was a revelation to try it: I can still remember how sweet and creamy the interior flesh was.

He introduced us to *angulas*, (elvers, baby eels). Dad discovered them in Spain, where they are a delicacy. For years Pia and I thought we were eating bowls of linguine that had black pepper on it. When we were older, we realized the dots of "pepper" were eyes. By then we liked the dish so much we didn't care that eels might as well be small snakes.

After we lost our cook Ursula to cancer, Dad hired a chef for our house and another for the bank's executive floor dining room. He spent a good deal of time training them, teaching them cuisines they had never been exposed to in Honduras. Business associates looked forward to being invited for lunch at the bank dining room because other than our house it was one of the best places to eat in Tegucigalpa. The meals were paired with special wines, usually Italian. Dad's adventurous tastes meant nothing was too strange to appear on the menu. One of his favorite delicacies was iguana, which he ordered whenever he visited Honduran beach towns. One time a friend had a large iguana delivered to him in Tegucigalpa. Dad hosted a large luncheon at the bank and invited bank executives and former economics students of his. When it was announced that iguana was on the menu, some of the guests appeared squeamish at the thought. Iguana is actually very similar to chicken, and delicious cooked in coconut milk over rice. Dad, annoyed, informed them there was also chicken prepared for anyone in the room who "was a chicken".

When people learn I am from Honduras and love to cook, they ask me what my favorite Honduran food is. I have a hard time answering. Dad was not a fan of Honduran food, so the only time I ate it as a child was with our maids, and later the occasions when Maria was in the mood. My favorite was corn tortillas stuffed with melted white cheese, and refried beans with sour cream.

Dad opened our eyes to a much broader food experience. He would have loved the world we inhabit today, where global culinary stories are easily accessible through our television sets thanks to the Food Network and the show Chef's Table. He would have the same bucket list I have, to visit all the restaurants on the list of World's 50 Best Restaurants. What Italians are doing with food would especially thrill him: Massimo Bottura at Osteria Francescana and Corrado Assenza at Caffe Sicilia. He'd want to meet them, to hear their stories and to try to get their recipes to duplicate at home.

His children and grandchildren inherited his love of food. We all care deeply about where our next meal is coming from, most of us are cooks, and several are professionals in the industry.

19

LEGACY
1986-1996

In the Fall of 1986 Liz became both a mother and a doctor. After completing medical school, she wanted to focus on parenting and decided she would not attend her graduation scheduled for the following June. She asked the university to mail the diploma to her instead. She could not have anticipated that the university would choose to honor Paul at the June 1987 graduation ceremony. Liz ended up attending after all—as Paul's guest—and watched her father present diplomas to her medical school colleagues.

Godfather of UNAH graduation -
June 11, 1987

The photo of Paul taken at that ceremony is my favorite.

Paul was very proud of Liz becoming a doctor. He valued education above most things, and she had studied longer than he. Her degree threw him a bit—she was an expert in an arena he knew nothing about. Over time, he leaned on her for medical advice, and she began to go with him to many doctor appointments.

On February 10, 1988, Banco Atlántida celebrated its seventy-fifth anniversary. As part of the festivities, the bank's head of public relations, Marcial Cerrato, suggested that the top executives serve as tellers in the bank lobby for a few hours. Customers who came in that day were amazed to find Paul and the management team at the teller windows. Everyone had a laugh when the cash drawers did not reconcile at the end of the day. Apparently, the executives were better at their desk jobs on the third floor.[cxcv]

This is the year Residencial Casavola, the housing development Paul built near the bank, was completed. Paul's four children who lived in Tegucigalpa joined him at the inauguration.

Paul, Pia, Rick, Liz and Bob - Inauguration Residencial Casavola —
February 1988

Paul and Maria invited the family over monthly for a weekend luncheon at their house. By this time Paul had grandchildren, so they received everyone in the downstairs game room which was more child friendly. Maids in starched uniforms passed fried bread fruit and *yucca*. While the adults talked, Bob's daughters who were the older grandchildren wandered out around the property just as Pia and I had decades earlier.

Outside the game room was an expansive lawn where, in earlier years, Paul's sons had played touch football when home for the holidays. On the lawn was a spectacular *amate* tree that Fran had planted when the house was built. She had planted it upside down, so that its roots formed a wide canopy, like an umbrella. Paul had removed the tetherball and sandbox that Pia and I used as children and replaced them with two enormous white marble heads, copies of work by the Italian sculptor Modigliani.

Paul on the terrace of his Las Lomas house, overlooking Tegucigalpa

One level up, the white marble terrace outside of the dining room was bordered by a white iron fence covered with flowering vines. On the terrace's ivy-covered wall was a marble replica of the statue of the Three Graces. Paul had seen this piece at the Metropolitan Museum of Art in New York and had a local marble company make the copy. Maria jokingly referred to it as "*Las Tres Marias*".

The girls would occasionally walk up to the top level of the property where a gaggle of snowy white geese were kept in a large pen. They made the loudest racket when approached. The geese were for security. Since the grounds were so large, guards could not cover all the perimeter at once. The geese were released at night. Anyone trying to climb the fence would be met with loud quacking and an army of geese rushing at them. Few intruders would have the courage to stand and face them aggressively, which is what one must do to make geese stop charging.

After an hour or so everyone was called in to lunch. The adults sat at a glass-topped table in the dining room. If there was not enough room at that table, which sat ten, grandchildren were seated at a table outside on the patio. Paul and Maria did not spend much time talking with the kids, but Paul clearly enjoyed having the family together. He had always loved making memories, and since his kidnapping had become fastidious about documenting gatherings with his camera, which he always kept close by.

One granddaughter recalled about her grandfather, "Every time you went to Papa Paul's house, you walked out with a gift, it didn't matter if you surprised him with a visit, or if he was waiting for you." Paul kept these gifts in the closet of my former bedroom. There were drawers labeled with gifts for boys, girls and adults. We don't know how involved he was in the purchase of these gifts, but he knew what was in the drawers.

Bob's daughters said it was the same when they visited their father at the bank. Bob worked on the executive floor with Paul, so when they went to see Bob, they would also stop by their grandfather's office to say hello. Paul would pull a chocolate bar out of a drawer, or if he ran out of candy, he might give them a Maya jade bracelet. (This would be a counterfeit piece someone had tried to sell to the bank as authentic. Paul bought these fakes to give away.) Paul also loved giving stuffed animals. His favorite was a small white polar bear that he bought in quantity.

At one family luncheon, the girls were seated with the adults at the dining room table. Paul sat at the head with a mirrored wall behind him. Maria sat at the opposite end of the table. She brought up the subject of Paul's kidnapping, which had never been discussed in front of the girls, who were very young when it happened. Bob and Rick kept trying to change the subject because they could see it made Paul uncomfortable. Maria insisted, asking Paul to talk about the friends who had contributed to the payment of his ransom. Paul finally answered her question, and suddenly his face crumbled. He started to cry. The girls, who had only known a stoic grandfather, were shocked. When Paul recovered, he apologized to the table for breaking down.

Paul's grandchildren saw him as serious and somewhat distant, but as they became older, he surprised them with his interest in their activities. When he heard one liked cheerleading or another liked horseback riding, he would send them a gift or book about that activity. He was this way with everyone he cared about. He took the time to let family and friends know they were on his mind. If someone told him they were curious about something, that person would eventually receive a magazine or newspaper article from Paul about the subject.

Once I expressed an interest in writing a cookbook about Central American cooking. A few months later, I received a box with twenty cookbooks from countries in Central America that he had asked people to gather so I could do research. Maria loved to visit churches during their travels, so Paul began a collection for her of small replicas of churches from all over the world. Rick was interested in owning a restaurant, so Dad brought him menus from restaurants he visited in many countries, usually signed by the chef.

My husband José liked to smoke cigars, and Dad often gave him Honduran cigars. One day a package from Dad arrived at our home in Houston. José was out of town on business, so I opened it. Inside was a box of Honduran cigars with a note that read, "I hope José enjoys these". Dad had clearly packed this himself at his Miami apartment and had used paper towels to pad the box. I threw the paper towels away. Weeks later, Dad asked me how José liked the cigars. I said he liked them very much. Then I asked why he seemed to be making a particular point about these cigars, since they were what he'd given my husband many other times. Dad revealed that, wrapped in the paper towels that I thought were padding, were cigars from the personal collection of Fidel Castro. The Honduran ambassador to Cuba had brought them back from a visit to Havana and given them to Dad. And I had thrown them away. Neither my father nor my husband was happy with me that day.

Even people he was not close to benefited from this thoughtfulness. Paul loved to learn, and for this reason befriended intelligent people who had different ideologies than him. One such person was social historian Rodolfo Pastor Fasquelle. Rodolfo sympathized with the left and criticized Paul for being "a personification of capitalism". He wrote that Paul gave him the best Christmas gift he had received in his life: an antique book to help with some research he was conducting.[cxcvi]

Paul celebrated every holiday, even Halloween which was not a big holiday in Honduras. Every year he invited his grandchildren over to trick-or-treat. He surprised them by opening the front door wearing a black curly wig with red devil horns. They laughed when they saw their serious, almost-intimidating grandfather wearing flashing horns and considered that maybe he didn't take himself so seriously. On Christmas Day he asked the family to come to his house dressed in the loudest Christmas attire they could find. When we were young, he always had an Italian friend dress up as Santa Claus to hand out gifts. Later, it was Paul who sat by the tree, dressed in a red shirt and a Santa hat, calling out our names so we could go up to receive his gifts.

Christmas at Dad's - 1994

Paul wanted the family together even in death. Ever since Craig died, Paul had been thinking about the final resting place for the Vinelli family. In the late 1980s Paul started meeting with Jaime Lacayo, the owner of La Auxiliadora funeral home. Paul wanted to invest in the construction of niches for cremation urns at the local cemetery. Ever since Linda died, he had believed cremation was better than burying a body in the ground. He tried to make Maria understand why he wanted to be cremated. He found a magazine article about what happens when a body decomposes, and asked Mirna to translate it into Spanish for his wife. Both women cringed as they read how soon after death maggots begin to consume a body.[cxcvii] But cremation was not common in Honduras; the only crematorium in the country was in San Pedro Sula. Hondurans, who were almost all Catholic, did not feel comfortable with the process even though the Catholic Church had lifted the ban on cremation in 1963.[cxcviii]

Paul wanted to ensure there would be a place to inter an urn with his ashes when his time came. Lacayo thought the idea a good one and began to study it. The process of obtaining government permits was complex and slow. First the Honduran Catholic Church had to allow for burials that were out of the ground. Then the Ministry of Health put up roadblocks. It took several years before there was approval. Eventually a section of small burial niches for urns was inaugurated at Jardines de Paz Suyapa cemetery. Paul was one of the first purchasers. He also bought larger niches for caskets. This mirrored what his father had done back in 1918, when Angelo bought eight plots at Calvary Cemetery in Maine for the Casavola family.

Paul had Rick and Mirna arrange for Dora's casket to be moved from her grave to a niche. Paul then asked John to have Linda's ashes sent from Michigan, since she no longer had living relatives in Grand

Rapids. John flew to Michigan and made the arrangements with the cemetery for his mother's ashes, in the original square bronze box, to be mailed to him in Florida. Later, Paul met John in Miami and brought the box to Tegucigalpa. He invited Bob and Rick to join him for a small ceremony. Paul told his sons he would like for his ashes to be interred next to their mother. They knew this was unlikely to happen if Maria outlived him. She was already unhappy that he'd brought Linda's ashes back to Tegucigalpa. They doubted she would allow for his final resting place to be by his first wife.

In February of 1992, Pia married Alex Mayr. Dad reserved the presidential suite at the Hotel Honduras Maya for her wedding night. She checked in before the wedding, and Mom and I, who had flown in for the wedding, helped her dress in the suite.

Paul and Pia Vinelli, San Juan Bosco church, 1992

When she was ready, Pia went down the elevator to the lobby. Dad was waiting for her when the doors opened. They walked out to the hotel entry where his Mercedes Benz, driver and bodyguards were waiting. Pia's eyes filled with tears from the importance of what was about to happen. Dad saw her brush the tears away carefully so she wouldn't ruin her eye makeup. He took her hand and held it all the way to the San Juan Bosco church.

That same year in November, our family gathered to celebrate Dad's seventieth birthday. A friend lent us a beautiful resort-style vacation home on the southwest coast of Honduras. The waterfront property faced the gulf and had enough bungalows to accommodate our entire family. All of Dad's children, their spouses, and many of his grandchildren went. Dad's oldest nephew Armando came from California with his wife. Maria oversaw the fantastic three-day party.

A moment stands out. One afternoon we were sitting poolside, listening to a cassette Armando had brought of Italian American comedian Pasquale Caputo (Pat Cooper). Pat's routine was about growing up in Brooklyn's Italian American community. The stories reminded Dad of his family when he was young, and he laughed so hard that tears came. After the tape ended, he grew serious and told us that life was like a tree, with friends the leaves. When one reached his age, too many leaves had fallen, and the tree felt bare. This was weighing on his mind because that weekend his dear friend Jack Agurcia was gravely ill—he died one week later.

Dad loved his grandchildren, but he had an intimidating presence and was awkward at expressing affection, so not all the kids felt comfortable around him. One of Bob's daughters, Linda, did and she liked to rub his balding head when she sat next to him. It made him smile. By the time he was seventy he had more time for grand-children and made an effort to see them. When Pia visited him with her two-year-old daughter Anya, Dad would have Anya sit on his lap while he made funny sounds that made her laugh.

He saw me less because I didn't live in Tegucigalpa, so he made sure we had some days together during his annual medical checkups to Houston. When our oldest daughter Claire was one, he and she had a bonding moment.

Paul and Claire Valera, 1994

When our youngest daughter Alina was born in 1995, Dad surprised me by calling to say he was flying to Houston to meet her. He came without Maria, so for the first time ever stayed at our house instead of at a hotel. During this visit I took the opportunity to interview Dad about his life. I recorded this interview, and it was a great re-source for this book. He revealed that, two months prior, he had stepped down as CEO of Banco Atlántida. He was seventy-two years old. He remained chairman of the board, and Guillermo Bueso took over as CEO.

One of his closest colleagues ended his career at the bank that year. In November, Paul was walking out of a board meeting with the bank's legal advisor Cleto Alvarez when suddenly Cleto slumped over the desk of Paul's secretary Mirna. He asked her to call his driver to take him home. Paul insisted Cleto be taken to a hospital.[cxcix] A while later they learned that Cleto's prostate cancer had metastasized to his brain and lungs. Paul was very upset by the news – Cleto had been his close friend for years. A few weeks later, another leaf dropped off Paul's tree.

Pia lived on a farm outside of Tegucigalpa with her husband and daughter. She noticed how hard it was for the farm employees to buy food and clothing. They had to walk long distances to the closest town that had a market. She mentioned this to Paul, and he built her a *pulperia* (small convenience store) on the farm. Every Friday she drove forty minutes into Tegucigalpa from the farm to buy groceries and supplies for the small store.

Paul began to worry about the old Land Cruiser he had bought for Pia some years earlier. When Pia drove to town for supplies, she usually returned to the farm the same day, which meant driving on sharp winding roads through the mountains after dark. Two-year-old Anya sat in a car seat in the back. It would have been dangerous for a woman alone with a child to have her car break down. One day Mirna called Pia to ask her to come into town to the bank. When Pia arrived, Paul wasn't there but he had left her a gift in the parking lot: a white, used Subaru Legacy station wagon with a big red bow on it.

It had been fifteen years since his kidnapping, but there were still security concerns. One Sunday after lunch at Paul's, the family was sitting out on the front terrace at white wrought iron tables. Spread out in front of them was Tegucigalpa, the city now growing up the mountainsides. The population of the city had multiplied nine times to 650,000 in the forty-five years Paul had lived there.[cc]

As they lingered over post-lunch drinks, a maid came out to tell Paul he had a phone call. After taking the call he came back out to the terrace. His mood was melancholic. He returned to his seat next to Pia and confided to her that the call was to warn him not to go on a trip he had planned to El Salvador, because a threat had been made against him. He was misty-eyed when he said it. Pia teared up also. Others at the table asked them "Are you two OK?" Paul replied, "Oh, just love".

Paul had his annual medical checkup in Houston in June of 1996. He learned that he had an aortic aneurysm that was seven centimeters in diameter. Surgery to repair it was performed immediately. The repair of the aneurysm was successful, but during surgery the doctors found significant atherosclerosis in all his arteries—years of eating rich foods had made them very hard. After a week in the hospital Paul returned home to Tegucigalpa, worried about the condition of his arteries.

Pia and her husband were talking of moving from the farm to Tegucigalpa. Paul wanted Pia to become a property owner—he had always been preoccupied by the idea of a woman owning her own home. He once told Liz, "A woman must own her own home, so she'll always have a roof over her head no matter what happens. A man can settle anywhere, but a woman, especially with children, must have a home." Around this time, two women Paul was close to had suffered break-ins at their homes: Mirna, his secretary, and Rita, the head of special events at the bank.

He wanted to make Pia a property owner, and he wanted Mirna and Rita to live somewhere safe. He thought of a way to resolve all three of his concerns at once. He owned land adjacent to the Casavola neighborhood that the bank had developed eight years earlier. He hired an architect to design a building that would house a three-bedroom apartment for Pia's family upstairs, and two apartments for her to rent to Mirna and Rita downstairs.

He was involved in every detail of the construction. Early on, Paul had the architect walk him through the site. When Paul pointed to an area adjacent to the master bedroom, the architect told him it would be a balcony. Paul insisted that instead it be turned into a walk-in closet. He had learned from Maria how important closets were to a woman. Pia was later grateful for his intervention, because she filled every inch of the space.

Mirna and Rita were not sure they wanted to move because they liked their houses despite the robberies. Paul tried to persuade them by pointing out that the rent they would pay Pia was much less than what they could receive in rent for their homes. The difference could be used to help pay for their children's education and health expenses (both were single mothers). He added that their commute would be easy, because the apartments were a short walk from the bank. What he did not say, but they knew, was that he wanted them there to support Pia. She would be moving into town from the farm with her husband and daughter, and he liked the idea of there being someone he trusted living nearby in case her young family had any problems. Mirna and Rita were still hesitant but told him they would think about it. As construction advanced, he brought the subject up to them repeatedly.[cci]

In September of 1996 Paul and Maria traveled to New York City after Paul attended the IMF-World Bank meetings in Washington. Paul called Bob's youngest daughters, Linda and Maria Jose (Pepina), who attended college in the area. He and Maria took them to his favorite Italian restaurant, Grotta Azzura. Many of the waiters knew him. That evening Paul was jovial and relaxed, and appeared younger than they remembered him.

Paul had recently been named the Honduran Ambassador to the FAO, the Food and Agriculture Organization of the United Nations. This agency of the U.N. leads international efforts to combat world hunger. He was pleased to accept the appointment by Honduran President Carlos Roberto Reina because the mission was of interest and because the position involved traveling to Rome, a city which he and Maria enjoyed visiting. His first assignment was to attend the World Food Summit at the FAO headquarters in Rome, which would take place from November 13-17, 1996.

On November 4, Paul and Maria flew from Miami to Rome. They were offered beluga caviar and champagne to start their meal in the first-class cabin. The sodium content of caviar combined with alcohol were not a good idea a for a heart patient, but Paul never turned down a special meal.

The following day, Paul formally presented his credentials to Jacques Diouf, Director-General of the FAO. He and Maria then headed to the beautiful Tuscan town of Montecatini Terme, known worldwide for its thermal water spas. Their plan was to spend a few days celebrating Paul's seventy-fourth birthday which was on November 7. They then would return to Rome for the summit which started on November 13.

We don't know what therapeutic baths Paul enjoyed while in Montecatini, but we know that the waters are salt-sulphated. [ccii] Presumably he also drank the mineral water offered at the spa, which would have added to his sodium intake. On November 10, Paul suddenly couldn't breathe. The hotel staff called an ambulance, which took him to a nearby hospital in Pescia. When he arrived at the emergency room, his blood pressure was extremely high, 220/110. He was diagnosed with pulmonary edema, fluid in the lungs. Several of his heart exams were not normal. It took doctors four days to stabilize him in the hospital. Paul pushed doctors to discharge him because he was anxious to attend the World Food Summit.

On the 14th, Paul and Maria left Tuscany and returned to Rome on the second day of the summit. Paul had missed the opening remarks given the first day by Pope John Paul II, which probably would have been the least interesting part for him. One hundred eighty-six countries were members of the FAO at that time, and forty-one were represented at the meeting by their head of state, including Oscar Luigi Scalfaro, President of the Italian Republic. Paul felt honored to represent Honduras at such a high-level gathering in the country of his birth. The experience was worth how tired he felt.

After the summit, Paul and Maria returned to Honduras, and Paul began to schedule doctor appointments in Houston. Liz translated the discharge report from the Italian hospital so he could take it to his doctors. Both Paul's internist and cardiologist in Houston had become Paul's friends over the years. When they saw him at the end of November, they were professionally and personally concerned by how much his health had deteriorated in the five months since his surgery for the aortic aneurysm. October had marked the tenth anniversary of his bypass surgery. Bypasses were only supposed to last for ten years. When they mentioned this to him, he joked that he was "living on borrowed time."

After a series of tests, his cardiologist told Paul he had stenosis of the aortic valve. He needed that valve replaced, plus another bypass surgery. Paul asked if the surgery, which he knew was major, could wait until after the holidays. The doctors thought that would be fine. Paul scheduled the surgery for February of 1997, three months later. When we said goodbye before he left Houston, he hid the surgery plans from me. His story was that doctors had discovered minor arrythmia in his heart and had prescribed medication to alleviate it. He said he would return in February for a checkup.

20

THE LAST CHAPTER
1996-1997

When he returned to Honduras, Paul told almost nobody what the doctors in Houston had said. He put his secretary Mirna to work organizing his personal papers. She placed labels with each of his children's names on the albums containing his stamp and coin collections. Paul had kept organized files with every letter we ever wrote him, all our school grades, and even records of money he sent us over the years, such as tuition payments. He instructed Mirna give the files to us if he didn't return after his surgery.

That December he flew all over Honduras to attend the board meetings and Christmas parties of each of the seventeen companies of which he was board chairman. He was determined to stick to the punishing schedule, but everyone could see he felt bad. He had always been punctual, even though few people in the country shared that priority. This did not change despite the deterioration of his health.

For Christmas he and Maria hosted the traditional family celebration. There were gifts from Paul and Maria and from Santa, even for the adult grandchildren. As they sat together, he asked Liz how someone with stenosis of the aortic valve would die. She answered, "It would be a sudden death." He became pensive.

As January arrived Paul was still hiding the fact that he was going to have heart surgery in mid-February. Maria knew, of course, and she confided in a few of their closest friends. Those she had told were alarmed when Paul made a point of visiting many friends that month. His gloomy demeanor made his visits feel like farewells, and those who knew he was having surgery worried that doctors in Houston had given him poor odds of surviving.[cciii] Actually, both his surgeon and his cardiologist had given him good odds—almost eighty percent—of a successful surgery. But Paul's behavior showed he felt differently.

He had told Liz about his surgery because he wanted her to accompany him to Houston for the procedure. He even obtained permission from the Houston heart surgeon for Liz to be present during the surgery. He requested Liz not tell her siblings because he didn't want to be fussed over. In preparation for surgery, Paul needed to have an echocardiogram. Liz went with him to see his Honduran cardiologist, Dr. Zacapa. After the test he met privately with Dr. Zacapa. When he walked out of his office, he told Liz, "I'm very sad. I asked the doctor if I can avoid having surgery. He said I could, but he wouldn't want me to play tennis. And that I should only work half days. I'm the head of seventeen companies. How do I choose?"

He asked Adriana Yu Shan to come see him. They had been friends for almost fifty years, as she was in his first economics class at the university in 1950 and was also one of the first employees after the Central Bank was created. After she retired from seventeen years as head of Banco Atlántida's Economic Studies Department, Adriana helped Paul with some of his side interests of promoting Honduran art and culture. On this day in January of 1997, he asked to her work on publishing a bilingual book about the bank's art collection. He particularly wanted younger painters to be included, to promote their talent.[cciv][36]

That month he also visited Maria Isabel Martel, another former student in his first economics class. He brought her a book about ten persons who had received the Nobel Prize in Economic Sciences. When she saw what the topic was, she asked him, "Are you lending it to me or is this a gift?" He responded with a great deal of emotion, "I want you to read it, it's a great book, I liked it very much and I'm sure you'll enjoy it also." She felt that the moment was a goodbye, and the book was a gift to remember him by.[ccv]

On January 23, Liz hosted a party for her husband José Luis's birthday. They prepared Peking duck, a favorite of Paul's. He came, but he ate little. He appeared down and overly tired.

Paul was pushing hard for Pia's apartment building to be completed. He stopped by the construction site in the mornings on the way to the bank. He would walk upstairs to Pia's apartment and stare out her windows at the mountains of Tegucigalpa. He had his secretary Mirna call Pia to come to town and select paint, appliances and beds. Pia and Alex were not planning to move with their daughter Anya until that summer, but Paul did not want to leave for Houston without seeing Pia's place completed. By early February, construction was mostly complete.

---

36. The book, *Catalogo de Pintores: Colección Banco Atlántida,* was completed that year and was dedicated to Paul.

Paul was weaker than anyone had ever observed. His bodyguards carried his heavy briefcase for him and sometimes even had to push him in a wheelchair down the long hallway to his office.

The son of Paul's longtime attorney and friend, Arturo Medrano, had succeeded his father as Paul's personal attorney. Paul had Arturo Medrano Jr. update his will. On February 5 they met for Paul to sign. As Paul was leaving the office Arturo said:

"I hope everything goes well!".

Paul turned at looked at him with annoyance:

"What are you saying: that things might not go well?"[ccvi]

Paul was scheduled to fly to Houston on Saturday, February 15. One week before, there was a knock at Mirna's door. A truck from Maria's company DIAPA was outside, sent by Paul to move Mirna into one of Pia's apartments. Mirna still hadn't committed fully to the plan and had not packed. She rushed around her house, throwing clothes in garbage bags, while the movers picked up her furniture and loaded it into the truck. Paul did the same to Rita.[ccvii]

The week before going to Houston, Liz couldn't stand being the only one of Paul's children that knew he was going to have surgery. She decided to tell everyone but Pia, who she worried would get upset and confront Paul. Rick and his wife decided to fly to Houston also. José and I lived there so we made plans to receive everyone.

Paul had instructed Rita to organize a housewarming party for Pia's new apartment building, where Rita and Mirna were now moved in as Pia's tenants. Rita arranged the event for the Thursday prior to Paul's departure.[ccviii] The party was held outside on the patio. Paul gave Pia a table made of a large tree core, setting on an iron base. His second gift was a painting from Haiti. Paul saw Faustino over by the food table, holding a fresh chicharron (pork rind) wrapped in a corn tortilla. He circled him, put his arm around him, and said, "What do you have there?"

Faustino replied, "I'm eating a chicharron taco."

"Don't eat that, let me have it."

Faustino looked at him doubtfully, knowing the condition of Paul's heart.

Paul took the taco out of his hand and said, "Hand it over and don't let anyone see me eating it."

Earlier that day, Liz had received the news that she had passed transfusion medicine board exams that she had recently taken at the Royal College of Physicians in Edinburgh, Scotland. She had faxed the report to Paul at his office. In the afternoon, Liz drove to Pia's housewarming party. When she walked through the gate, everyone on the patio started clapping. She was confused until she saw that Paul was leading the applause, and realized he was congratulating her for passing the exam.

Friday night was the eve of Paul's trip to Houston and the engagement party of Bob's oldest daughter, Muriel with Fernando Medina. Paul and Maria attended. At one point, Paul asked the couple,

"Are you planning on having children?"

They replied, "Papa Paul, we're just getting engaged, we haven't given that thought yet."

Paul suggested, "Have a lot of them."

Saturday, February 15, Paul woke up knowing he had several stops to make before his noon flight to Houston. Maria had already packed their bags. While he was getting dressed, a maid knocked on the door to say that Bob's wife Maria José and her newly engaged daughter were there. This was unusual, because they had never come to say goodbye when he was going on a trip. He greeted them at his bedroom door. As the three headed down the hall together, Paul walked slowly, taking in every detail. The first room to the right was Pia's childhood bedroom. The two women watched as he stopped and looked in. He then moved on to my former bedroom, staring in the doorway.

At the end of the bedroom hallway, he turned and stopped at the entrance to the enormous living room to look around. The women realized he was saying goodbye to his house. They waited by the front door as he walked, alone, through the dining room and into the kitchen. He walked back to the front door and said goodbye to them. In that moment Maria José had a premonition that he was not going to return.

The guards drove him to the bank. He had asked Faustino to meet him at his office. Paul told him, "This is what the cardiologist told me. If I don't have surgery: no tennis, no wine, no exertion. That's not life." When they parted ways, Paul said, "Goodbye" to Faustino in a meaningful way.

Faustino said, "Doctor, are you thinking you will not return?"

"That's right, I don't think I'm coming back."

"And if you think that, why are you going? You have a lot of life here."

"I like quality of life, not just life."[ccix]

That day was his granddaughter Anya's fourth birthday. Paul's next stop was the bank club where Pia was setting up for the birthday party in the gardens. Since it was the day after Valentine's Day,

Pia had ordered an enormous, heart-shaped piñata. Fran, who had moved back to Tegucigalpa a few years before to be close to Pia, was also there helping.

The bulletproof Mercedes Benz arrived at the bank club, the chaser car behind it. The six bodyguards jumped out—one to open Paul's door, the rest standing guard. Pia and Anya went up to give him a hug, and they pointed across the lawn to the piñata. He asked two of his bodyguards to go pick it up and bring it to where he was standing. When he saw the large heart up close, he turned to Anya and asked, "Is that the size of your heart?"

Fran was hanging balloons in the garden on a lower level. When she saw Paul, she walked up to the sidewalk where he was standing. He greeted his former wife of seventeen years with a quick kiss on the cheek.

Pia had heard rumors that Paul was going to Houston for surgery, and as she walked with him towards his car, she asked,

"Dad, are you going to have surgery?"

"No no no, I'm just going up for a checkup."

He hugged her goodbye, and Pia watched as he walked slowly towards his car, his white comfortable shoes making a crunching sound on the gravel. The bodyguards opened the heavy back door, and he got in. Pia kept watching until the car drove away to the airport.

When he arrived in Houston, Dad called me. He sounded tired but asked me to make a reservation in the private dining room at the Ritz Carlton for brunch the next day. He also invited José and me to bring our daughters to see him at his hotel that afternoon. Claire was three years old, and Alina was one. We visited for about an hour. He had brought stuffed animals for both girls. On the dining table of his hotel suite was a bowl of fresh fruit. He laughed when Alina tried to fit an enormous strawberry in her mouth. That night when I returned home, I called Pia. I felt it only right that she be aware of what really was happening. On Sunday Jose and I met Dad and Maria for brunch. Always the host, he also invited that daughter of a friend who was a nurse in Houston. Dad clearly wasn't feeling well, but he ate a nice meal and didn't skip the mimosa.

Monday, the day prior to surgery, Liz went with him as he entered the hospital for pre-operative tests. Doctors needed to perform a catheterization to map out the condition of his arteries. When preparing Paul for the procedure, the nurse could not find his vein for the IV. Liz saw that he was hurting and took over to insert the IV herself. During the catheterization procedure, Paul's blood pressure shot up to critical levels. When the doctor saw Liz's concern, he said, "Don't let this worry you – we have plenty of ways to lower high blood pressure. You can worry if the pressure gets too low."

That night José and I took dinner to Dad's hospital room. He requested fettuccine Alfredo from Prego, an Italian restaurant nearby. Not a heart-healthy choice, but we weren't going to argue.

Surgery day, Tuesday February 18, also happened to be Maria's birthday. That morning, the family was feeling nervous but hopeful. Paul had come through his aortic aneurysm repair seven months before just perfectly. His doctors felt strongly he would do well this time also.

Rick stood near Dad's hospital bed as a nurse shaved the thick, black hair off his chest, stomach, and thigh. The scar from his bypass surgery ten years before was still visible. Soon another would follow the same path down his chest and stomach, but this time down the left thigh—the surgeon would take veins from this other leg for the bypass.

Rick looked down at his father—once so strong and dominant—and thought he saw tear drops on his eyelashes. Rick told me he imagined the tears were of regret, for things Dad had not said to him. There had been many times throughout his life when Dad knew Ricky was in trouble and he didn't get involved.

A male hospital attendant came to wheel Dad's hospital bed to the operating room. Maria, Rick, Veronica, Liz, José, and I walked next to the gurney as it rolled through the hospital hallways. At the door to the operating area, the attendant stopped to let us wish Dad well. Maria leaned over the bed and Dad gave her a kiss on her forehead. He lifted his hand halfheartedly to wave to the rest of us and said, "Goodbye". The attendant said to him cheerfully, "It's not goodbye! Say, 'See you later!'"

Dad then said, without conviction, "See you later".

Liz went through the pre-op cleansing procedure and as she was about to walk into the operating room, she saw Paul was naked on the operating table, being prepped. She held back and waited. She heard him say to the OR nurses, "Is my daughter here?" They looked confused—they didn't know that she was going to be present and must have thought Paul had a problem with his mind as well as his heart. Liz waved to them from the doorway. When they realized she was who he was asking for, they pointed to her and told Dad, "She's here, she's here!" Paul looked over to the doorway and raised his arm to let Liz know he saw her.

Surgeons, the anesthesiologist and nurses poured into the room. Surgery started around 9:00 a.m. Liz stood off to one side as they sawed through his sternum. They spread apart the cut halves with a retractor until Paul's heart was accessible. The anesthesiologist called Liz over to stand next to him at Paul's head, so that she could see the valve replacement. She was amazed by the number of threads used to connect the new valve. Once this part of the surgery was complete, Liz moved away and again stood off to one side.

After the valve replacement, two bypasses were done, also successfully. Surgically the operation was a success. But when doctors took Paul off the cardiopulmonary bypass pump, his heart beat very weakly, then stopped. They revived him and reconnected the pump. Each time they took him off the pump, his heart stopped, requiring an electric shock to re-start it. The surgeon called Paul's cardiologist, who ran to the operating room from the adjacent medical tower. He made some recommendations, but none worked.

It was now 3:00 p.m., and the surgery had been going on for six hours. The operating room atmosphere was very tense, in part because the patient's daughter was present. One of the nurses suggested to Liz that this might be a good time for her to take a break. She was relieved to walk out of the operating room.[37] When Liz returned to the waiting area where the rest of us were, I felt sure something was wrong. But I knew my sister had just been through something extremely stressful, so I did not bother her with questions.

Turning to José, I said, "Dad's not going to make it."

---

37. When we thought about this later, we knew that the doctors were surprised by what was happening. If they had thought there was a chance Dad's heart was not strong enough, they never would have allowed Liz to be present during the surgery.

His response was, "Why do you say that? You don't know that!"

"Yes, I do. Liz wouldn't have left the operating room if things were going well. Besides, he's already been in there longer than planned."

Liz leaned against a wall in the hallway and called her husband José Luis. She told him, "It's not going well." Then she called Bob, who was at home in Tegucigalpa with Pia, waiting to get an update. She explained that Paul's heart couldn't beat without assistance.

Bob called the bank and asked to be connected to the board room, where executives had gathered and waited for updates. After receiving Bob's report, CEO Guillermo Bueso ran to his office and called Liz from his private line. He insisted Paul have a heart transplant. Of course, it doesn't work that way: hospitals don't have hearts laying around waiting for such an occasion. After Liz finished the calls, she realized she had not eaten all day. Maria, Rick and Veronica went with her to the basement cafeteria. José and I stayed in the waiting room.

The battle inside the operating room continued. When it was apparent there was no way Dad's heart could beat on his own, he was moved to a recovery area with a portable bypass pump connected. Liz and the rest of the group were returning from the cafeteria when they saw the surgeon walking slowly towards the waiting room. He looked defeated, exhausted. He asked us to join him in a private room next to the waiting area. I followed him reluctantly. From the hours of being in the waiting room I knew that this room was where doctors gave families bad news.

The surgeon explained that Dad's heart was not strong enough to beat on its own. He said Dad was still alive, but not conscious and not for long. He invited us to come into the adjacent area and sit with Dad during his last minutes of life. Only two persons were allowed in at a time. Liz and Maria went in first. While they were with him, his heart stopped. The nurses asked them to step outside while they revived him. They did so to allow the rest of his children the chance to say goodbye while he was still technically alive. Rick and I went into the room next. Dad looked like he was sleeping. I placed my hand over his while Rick looked down over my shoulder at him.

We might not have known the exact moment when he died, because there was no loud alarm from the monitor like there would have been in a movie. But at 9:07 p.m. the nurse who was looking at his monitor looked up at us and said, "That's it."

21

THE FUNERAL
1997

Bob sat in his living room in Tegucigalpa with Pia, waiting for news about the surgery outcome. In Liz's first call, she reported that Dad's heart had stopped mid-surgery, but his doctors had managed to get it going again. When Bob told Pia what had happened, she concentrated furiously on keeping her hopes high. The tension she felt was excruciating. At age twenty-nine, she was the youngest and the most emotional of Dad's six living children. An hour or so later, Bob's phone rang again. He picked it up, listened for a minute, and said softly, "When will they bring the body?"

Pia lost control. She ran into the backyard screaming, "No, no - not my dad, no!" She hit her head repeatedly against the stone wall that surrounded the garden. Bob quickly finished his call with Liz and followed Pia. He wrapped his arms around her tightly, his six-foot-two frame both hugging and restraining her.

A neighbor heard the screams coming from Bob's house and thought someone was being assaulted. He fired off some shots with his gun to scare away whoever was hurting the person next door, then he called Mirna, Paul's secretary. She called Bob to find out what was going on, and that's when she learned her boss had died. [ccx]

The following day, my father's death was the headline of every newspaper and the lead story of every television newscast in Honduras.[38] People from all walks of life were moved by the news. Dr. Paul Vinelli, as most Hondurans knew him, had made an impact on a wide cross-section of people with his generosity, vision and leadership. The entire country seemed to be waiting for the body of the chairman of Banco Atlántida to be returned home so that people could pay their respects.

News reporters described him as a businessman who had been helpful to local and foreign businessmen, governments, artists, and ordinary citizens. They recognized the tremendous work he did to advance Honduras. He was described as a visionary, a leader with an eye always toward modernization, the greatest contributor to the development and growth of banking in Honduras.

Guillermo Bueso, CEO of Banco Atlántida, spoke on television about Paul Vinelli's contributions to banking and economics in Honduras. He told Hondurans that the International Monetary Fund had sent Paul to Honduras in 1949, where he guided the team that founded the Central Bank in 1950, which gave the country sovereignty over its currency for the first time. That same year Paul helped create the National Development Bank which developed agricultural lending in Honduras. In 1950 he also helped establish the Economics Department of the University of Honduras.

---

38. For the following week, newspapers were full of hundreds of notices of condolence, many of them full-page ads. These were taken out by companies that were bank clients, private sector business councils, and foreign organizations he had collaborated with.

Bueso spoke of the attention to detail Dr. Vinelli gave to the opening of each bank branch, wanting them to be beautiful additions to Honduran cities and towns, along with bringing essential banking services to citizens. It was a shame Paul would miss the inauguration of Banco Atlántida's one hundredth branch, scheduled for the following month.

Faustino Laínez, the bank executive who had helped Paul plan his final matters, called Maria in Houston to tell her he would get the appropriate papers in order. He also reminded her of Paul's wish to be cremated. Maria told him, "Faustino, his body is mine now. I'm taking him to Honduras in a casket."[ccxi]

Since my husband José and I lived in Houston, it was up to us to make the arrangements to get Dad's body to Honduras. José went to the Honduran Consulate to process the necessary paperwork.

I took Maria to George Lewis & Sons, a stately Houston funeral home. She visibly relaxed as we walked through the heavy entrance doors which were held open by a white-gloved porter. I had chosen the right place: elegance soothed my stepmother.

Maria asked to see their caskets. I reminded her that Dad asked to be cremated. She shook her head. At that moment I reasoned, "I suppose funerals are for the survivors; the widow should get to decide." Maria selected the largest, grandest casket they had, made of polished walnut wood and brass handles.

Of course, Dad was not in a position to enforce his will. I felt the decision Maria was making was a mistake and soon learned it would not be the only one made, regarding his final act.

Maria instructed the funeral home to charter a private plane to fly the body to Honduras the following day. The rest of the family would fly on Continental Airlines and land in Tegucigalpa shortly after.

The small white jet carrying Paul's body landed in Tegucigalpa at 11:45 a.m. on February 20, two days after his death. Bob was waiting on the tarmac, as were his wife Maria José, our sister Pia and her husband Alex, and Liz's husband José Luis. Paul's drivers and bodyguards – six in total - were there, solemn looks on their faces. Representatives from the local funeral home and the bank were also waiting.

When the pilots saw how many observers surrounded the plane, the captain stuck his head out the door and quietly explained to Bob what was about to happen. In those days, U.S. law required that human remains transported in an airplane be contained in a plain metal casket. Paul's body was not going to come out of the plane in the beautiful wooden casket Maria had selected.

Press was everywhere, cameras clicking. The La Auxiliadora funeral home had sent a hearse. Bob asked their personnel to use the hearse to help shield the plane's entrance from view of the observers. The bodyguards and friends also helped him maintain some privacy.

Pia had been crying for two days, so somebody had given her a pill to calm her down. She walked up next to Bob and looked through the open door of the jet. She saw a metal box. Several men began the laborious process of moving the heavy metal box down the tiny steps of the plane, and Pia asked Bob, "Will I get to see him?"

Bob simply answered, "No."

He didn't take time to explain that she couldn't see their father at that moment because they had to hurry and get the crowd off the tarmac. Within half an hour, the Continental Airlines flight the rest of us were on from Houston would be landing. Soon afterwards, an American Airlines flight from Miami was due, carrying our oldest brother John and his family, as well as Bob's two college-aged daughters.

Pia thought Bob meant she was never going to see her father. She ran to Guillermo Bueso, Banco Atlántida's CEO, who was standing off to one side. She asked him desperately,

"What can we do for them to open the box? They're saying I can't see him."

Bueso replied, "It would be best that you speak with Jaime Lacayo" (the owner of the funeral home).

Pia ran frantically inside the airport where Lacayo was managing his staff. She begged him to help her see her father. He reassured her that the box would be opened, but at the bank, where the viewing would take place.

Behind the metal box in the plane was the wooden casket, in three pieces: the base, and the two halves of the lid. It was too large to fit in the jet whole. The funeral home staff assembled it on the tarmac and then lifted the metal box containing Paul into the casket. They draped a large Honduran flag over the casket before loading it into the hearse.

Family, friends and press followed the hearse to Banco Atlántida, the largest bank in Honduras, which Paul had run for forty years. The Salón Cultural, an event space where large meetings and art exhibitions were held, had been transformed for Paul's wake. There were hundreds of white wooden chairs lined up in rows, all facing inwards where a space was made for the trolley that would wheel the casket in. Huge arrangements of white roses surrounded the central space. Some had been sent by Paul's sister Elizabeth, who lived in Portland, Maine and was not well enough to travel to Honduras for the funeral.[ccxii]

Nobody had been allowed in the room earlier except for Paul's secretary Mirna and Rita, the bank's event planner. Rita had prepared the room for the viewing. Guards stood before the glass entry doors, looking down a flight of stairs to a parking lot in front of the Salón Cultural.

The hearse drove slowly into the parking lot, which was lined with dozens of bank employees dressed in black and white, standing at attention. Behind the hearse was a car bringing Bob, Maria José, Pia and Alex, and Liz's husband José Luis. When the procession stopped, Bob and José Luis left the car and walked to the hearse, while Maria José and Alex escorted Pia up the steps and into the room where the wake would be held.

The team from the funeral home pulled the heavy casket out of the hearse. Bob, José Luis, and Paul's bodyguards helped the funeral home employees carry the casket up the stairs and into the Salón Cultural. Photographers from various newspapers followed closely but were prevented from entering by bank guards. Mirna stayed in the far corner of the room, fighting to control her emotions. Alex held Pia back while Paul was readied for the viewing.

Bob lifted the two halves of the heavy wooden casket lid. The funeral home team pried the metal box open. Paul's body lay inside. He looked like a sardine stuffed in a tin can. Bob had seen his father alive just days earlier. He froze for a moment, needing time to process the sight.

Maria José said, "We can't leave him in that metal box. This is the last memory people will have of him, and he needs to look dignified. We've got to take him out."

She went to the door and asked three men to come inside: her brother Guillermo, her cousin's husband Wilson, and one of the bank guards. She directed the three men and Bob to lift Dad's rigid body up and out of the metal box. While they balanced the body in the air, the funeral home personnel pulled the metal box out of the casket and set it to one side.[ccxiii]

The four men gently laid Dad back onto the cream satin padding of the wooden casket.

The caps placed in Dad's nose by the Houston embalmer had popped out when they lifted the body. A bit of fluid seeped out of his nose. Maria José called over to Mirna, asking for some Kleenex. Mirna brought the tissues, avoiding looking at the body. Maria José wiped Paul's face clean and replaced the nose caps. They closed the bottom half of the casket.

Bob turned to Mirna and said, "Come see how my dad looks." Mirna replied, "No, no, I prefer to remember him alive."[ccxiv]

Finally, Pia was allowed to approach the casket. Tears flowed – hers and everyone else's – as she bent down and kissed her father over and over.

It was fitting that Dad's wake was in this room. Years before, he had instructed that it be built to exhibit the various collections he amassed on behalf of Banco Atlántida: paintings, Mayan artifacts, stamps, bills, and coins. Over decades he sponsored many art exhibits so that Honduran painters would be better known. Some of the artists he mentored were waiting outside to pay tribute. They knew he cared deeply about their work. In a speech he once said, "Our art is the purest face of our nation."

While this was happening, our plane landed from Houston. Maria, Liz, Rick, Veronica, José and I were met by some of Dad's guards at the bottom of the airplane stairs. My cousin Armando and his wife had come from San Francisco for the funeral and were on our flight as well.

The plane from Miami carrying Paul's oldest son John, his wife, and their three sons, as well as two of Bob's daughters, landed just after us.

Television stations had announced the time of Paul's wake for 2:00 p.m., so by the time we drove up in front of the large white bank building, crowds of people were gathering for the viewing. The guards had to move people out of the way for us to go up the stairs and into the Salón Cultural. Maria and I walked over to Dad's open casket. She checked to make sure it was the one she had chosen in Houston.

When I looked down at my father, I felt sad and still shocked by the suddenness of his death. But I also felt like my goodbye with Dad had been in the hospital during his last minutes of life. I had said a second goodbye in Houston the night before, when George Lewis & Sons called the family to come see him after his body was prepared and in the casket. There we were able to sit with him in the calm viewing room and silently tell him all he meant to us.

Here, he belonged to everyone. He looked alone and exposed, lying in that box in the crowded room. More than a thousand people filed by and stared down at his expressionless face.[ccxv]

It was a true cross-section of Honduran society. The country's most successful businessmen, diplomats and politicians stood in line with artists, housekeepers and cooks. There were the bank employees who had looked to him for guidance, the industry leaders who had called for advice, the clients who depended on his optimism to make loans in a country always plagued by political unrest and economic crisis. It was revealing to observe how many people had been profoundly affected by having known him. As the line passed in front of us, I greeted drivers, nuns, gardeners, bankers, sculptors, security guards and some of his former university students. Many had tears in their eyes.

Carlos Roberto Reina, the president of Honduras, and Carlos Roberto Flores, the president of Congress, walked up and solemnly told Maria what Dr. Paul Vinelli had meant to the country.

A moment that caught the room's attention was when my mother Fran, wife number four, walked up and gave Maria, wife number five, a quick hug. For that second, the women suspended years of animosity. They shared something unique: they were the only two of his five wives still alive to witness his death. Mom was married to him for seventeen years, Maria for eighteen. Mom always said he was an impossible act to follow. It could be why none of his former wives ever remarried.

Bishara Kawas, a businessman from the northern city of La Ceiba and one of Dad's closest friends, walked up. He looked down at his friend of more than four decades with tears in his eyes. He turned to me and asked if he might place his rosary in the casket. Bishara was a devout Catholic, and I knew how much parting with his special rosary meant to him. I also knew how much Bishara had meant to Dad. Even though I sensed another mistake was being made, I agreed. Funerals are for the survivors, right?

Liz told me later that, after Bishara, she also slipped her rosary into his casket.

Dad's bodyguards and drivers, hired to risk their lives in the protection of his, stood stoically outside. Everyone knew them, because they had been part of his security detail for years. As people came in from the bank parking lot, many stopped to offer their condolences to Neto, Rolando, José, Cristobal, Edíl and Arambú. They wore sunglasses to hide their tears.

Maria was from Guatemala, and her family flew in from that country on a private plane just before the wake. They brought an enormous rosary made of fragrant yellow roses, sized to cover the entire length of the casket. It ended up being hung in the viewing room because bank executives decided the Honduran flag should continue to cover the casket. When I think back, they were faithful to what Dad would have wanted, despite Maria's intention to have a religious burial.

Three rosaries. For the man who wanted no religious symbols at his funeral. Mistake number two.

After the viewing, which lasted for two hours, Dad's casket was carried out of the Salón Cultural and down the steps to the hearse. Rick and Bob were the pallbearers at the head of the casket, followed by John, his son, my husband José, Liz's husband José Luis, and our cousin Armando.

The funeral procession did not head to the cemetery as I had expected. Instead, we drove to San Juan Bosco Catholic Church. Maria had approved this from Houston, unbeknownst to us. I didn't think it a good idea to have a mass for the man who had resisted entering a church for more than fifty years. (He made an exception for the weddings of his three daughters and sometimes could be seen standing against the back wall of a church at the funeral mass for a close friend).

Even though I knew Dad would not have approved, I understood Maria's thinking. Most Hondurans are Catholic, and Dad was a public figure. Most people would have considered it inappropriate if a mass had not been held. As I sat in the front pew with Maria, my siblings, and President Reina, I stared at Dad's casket. I thought how uncomfortable Dad must be in that box and in this place, and how he was powerless to sneak out the back of the church like he did at friends' funerals. The mass was mistake number three.

By the time we arrived at the Jardines de Paz Suyapa cemetery, stretched out in the shadow of the beautiful Basilica, the crowd had doubled to almost two thousand.[ccxvi] People stood gingerly on the grass—trying to avoid graves and the flowers placed on them by mourners.

Dad didn't want flowers. This was years before it became common to request charitable donations instead. He had left instructions that, in the event of his death, he wanted donations to be sent to the Fundación Craig Vinelli. This was a foundation established by Dad in the name of my brother Craig, who died ten years earlier at age thirty-seven. It provides scholarships to qualified, low-income business students studying at the university in Honduras.

Cameramen for newspapers and television stations were stationed at all angles of the entrance to the narrow burial niche area. A tent had been placed in front—Dad's casket underneath. The crowd pushed closer, straining to hear Guillermo Bueso's eulogy.[ccxvii] When he finished, it was 6:00 p.m. and turning dark. Pia asked that the casket be opened for a last time, and - just as she had done during the wake - bent down to hug and kiss Dad many times.

Then it was time for the interment. Traditionally, a funeral in Honduras would have meant a burial in the ground. Dad had wanted to have a cremation urn placed in the wall of burial niches built for urns. Since a casket arrived from Houston, the funeral home changed the plan. It so happened that Dad had also bought larger niches in another section. These were sized to hold a casket, for family members who preferred not to be cremated. He would be placed in one of these.

The niche chosen was directly beneath his mother Dora's place of rest. It was located ten feet high, so the casket had to be loaded onto a hydraulic lift. Everyone was mesmerized by the sight of the casket slowly lifting. The lift stopped at the top, and the attendants moved the casket towards the open hole.

It didn't fit.

Tras darle el último adiós al doctor Paul Vinelli, su féretro fue ingresado al nicho respectivo en Jardines de Paz Suyapa, en presencia de sus familiares, amigos y compañeros.

Paul's son Bob (in glasses), trying to find a solution
Photo: La Tribuna, February 21, 1997 "Paul Vinelli cumplió la misión de su vida"

A reluctant smile replaced my tears. Dad didn't want to be buried in a casket, and he was resisting until the end. I felt he was showing us, from wherever his spirit now was, that his instructions should have been followed. The casket was slowly brought back down.

After long deliberations, an awkward solution—the only solution if we were to bury him that day—was chosen. The funeral home team removed the top halves of the lid and flipped them, so the arched parts were pressing down against Dad's body. As the lift was raised for a second attempt, those who were Catholic prayed, and those who weren't, crossed their fingers.

This time the partially-open casket slid into the niche—just barely.

Dr. Paul Vinelli was buried, but not in the way anyone—including him, his children, or Maria—had envisioned.

APPENDIX

DECORATIONS AND AWARDS

1951 - Recognition by President of Honduras Juan Manuel Gálvez for Paul's contribution to Honduran banking and monetary reform.

1967 - U.S. Department of State Honor Scroll, for Paul's contribution to the relationship between Honduras and the United States.

1968 - Order of Merit of the Italian Republic, Commendatore. Senior order of knighthood conferred by the President of Italy, Aldo Moro, for Paul's contributions in economics and humanitarian endeavors.

1975 - Honor of Merit by the Universidad Autónoma de Honduras for founding the School of Economics.

1978 – Hoja de Liquidambar en Plata, Grado de Oficial, presented by the Tegucigalpa Metropolitan Council.

1987 - Godfather of the graduation ceremony of the Universidad Autónoma de Honduras in recognition of Paul's social and cultural support of Hondurans.

1991 - Commander of the Order of Vasco Nuñez de Balboa by the government of Panama for Paul's contribution to relations between Panama and Honduras.

1993 - Order of José Cecilio del Valle, Gran Cruz, Placa de Plata, presented personally by President of Honduras Rafael Leonardo Callejas, for Paul's diplomatic services to the country.

1994 - Order of Bernardo O'Higgins by President of Chile Eduardo Frei Ruiz-Tagle. The highest civilian honor awarded to non-citizens, it was for Paul's contribution to humanitarian and social cooperation between Honduras and Chile.

1996 - Brassavola de Oro, Museo del Hombre Hondureño.

1997 - Zamorano Agricultural School – Posthumous recognition for Paul's decades of support.

ACKNOWLEDGEMENTS

Paul Vinelli, my father, gets the credit for this book. He lived a seventy-four-year life that was so inspiring it merited a book. He was a sentimental man, meticulous in documenting his life. When he died in 1997, he left neatly organized scrapbooks and files full of photos, newspaper articles, letters and awards. He kept all the letters his children and family members wrote to him, cards showing his membership in organizations, and even his high school notebooks and college transcripts. All this gave me a close look at his life, and often in his words from the letters he wrote to his first wife Linda.

I am extremely grateful to my five living siblings: John Vinelli, Robert (Bob) Vinelli, Richard (Rick) Vinelli, Dr. Elizabeth (Liz) Vinelli, and Pia Vinelli. All sat with me for interviews and were patient with my many follow-up questions. John shared a box full of Dad's scrapbooks and years ago brought back from Grand Rapids, Michigan the many letters Dad and his first wife Linda wrote to each other. These letters told the story in their words. Bob and his wife María José were the most familiar with Dad's life in Honduras and were gracious to share their perspectives with me. Bob let Liz and me spend days doing research in the room where he keeps Dad's archives. María José recommended several people for me to interview and, together with her son-in-law Gabriel Prats, obtained access for me to meet people with important perspectives. Rick brought me Dad's high school notebooks and first told me about the many letters Linda wrote. Liz and her husband José Rivera opened their home in Tegucigalpa to me when I traveled there for interviews. They suggested interviewees and helped me make appointments with those people. Liz helped me research, went with me to some interviews, and performed other interviews for me. Pia contributed pictures and filled in the blanks about our childhood days in Honduras as well as of Dad's later years. Her sharp memory amazes me.

Several of Paul's grandchildren sat for interviews and suggested sources for reading or interviews. Papa Paul thanks you for your contributions, Muriel Vinelli Medina, Linda Vinelli Prats, María Jose Vinelli Sanchez, José Luis Rivera Vinelli, and Alessandra Mayr. And to Fernando Medina, Gabriel Prats and Marcio Sanchez, thank you for your ideas and encouragement.

My mother, Frances Smith Vinelli, was the only one of Paul's five wives still living when I wrote the book. She was a vibrant ninety-five-year-old and although she and Dad had divorced many years prior, she was able to give me an intimate perspective on my father that only a spouse could. Thanks Mom, for opening up.

Many cousins from the Vinelli-Casavola family helped me piece together the history of our family that began in Castellaneta, Italy in the 1800s and continued in Portland, Maine. Thank you for agreeing to be interviewed, answering follow-up questions, sending me family photographs, letters and genealogy charts, and helping me find others who could complete the story. My gratitude to Janet Giampetruzzi Blessing, Judy and Dave Cavalero, Anna Santoro Davis, Hilda Santoro Emerson, Diana Romano Flaherty, Antoinette

Casavola Going, Nina Giampetruzzi Kamman, Anita Linnell, Terri Linnell, Dianne Davis Manning, Armando Romano, and to my very special cousin Lisa Emerson Stoclet.

To the many people I interviewed who knew Paul through friendship or business—it was usually both—thank you for sitting down with me to share your stories. He clearly has stayed alive in your memories, Anny Bahr Lucker, Jorge Bueso Arias, Dr. Lino Califano and Elsa Faldo Califano, Marcial Cerrato, German Durón Lanza, Pasquale Faldo, President Carlos Roberto Flores, Alice Goldstein, Mirna Gómez, Luis Kafie, Schucry and Marlene Kafie, Juan Kawas, Faustino Laínez, Arturo Medrano, Ela Mejía, José Rubén Mendoza, Deborah Mills Agurcia, Colonel Juan Ramón Molina, Ambassador John Negroponte, Jacqueline de Pierrefeu, Carlos H. Reyes, Janeth Romero, Sor María Rosa, Macky Salinas, Rita Sosa, and Adriana YuShan.

To those who helped me obtain permissions for the use of photographs and newspaper articles in the book, I am very grateful for your help navigating a complex process: Maria José and Robert Vinelli, Alessandra Mayr, Gabriel Prats, Lisa Stoclet, Jacqueline de Pierrefeu, Diana Villeda, Carlos Villeda, Pia Vinelli, Axel Uclés, and the excellent team at Mayora IP.

There were those who did not know Paul, but who supplied information for the book. Thank you for your time and contributions, Sandra Bástidas, Manuel Dávila, Billy Joya, and María Fernanda Lacayo.

Claire Valera helped with photo editing and designed the cover of the book. She also created and manages my website: gigivalera.com. Alina Valera Mitchell wrote the back cover copy and guided me on social media and the launch of the book. Thank you for letting me lean on you. I know Papa Paul is happy we worked together.

The writing professors of the Inprint Writing workshops I took in Houston helped me tremendously in getting this book off the ground. Thank you to Will Burns, Leah Lax, and Caroline Leech, as well as to the workshop friends I made, for your guidance and encouragement. The writing coach Suzette Mullins also helped tremendously with structuring the book.

To the patient readers of the many manuscript versions, thank you for your careful reading and recommendations—you caught mistakes, made my writing clearer, and improved the structure of the book: Consuelo Duroc-Danner, Bob and María José Vinelli, Liz Vinelli, Pia Vinelli and José Valera, whose legal eye was excellent at catching errors.

Special thanks go to Colin Graham of Graham Publishing Group for your expertise in book design. This was the last step in a long process, and you made it easy.

To the brother we lost too soon: Craig, we remember you always and know that Dad and you are enjoying a good laugh together.

My most heartfelt thank you to José, Claire and Alina who lived through the creation of this book with me, and whose love and support kept me going.

NOTES

The majority of the information in this book came from:

1 – Personal interviews and telephone/email/text communications conducted by the author with Vinelli-Casavola family members between 2018-2020. Their names are listed in the Acknowledgements.
2 – The recording of an interview with Paul Vinelli conducted by the author in July 1995, two years before Paul's death.
3 – Personal, unpublished papers/letters belonging to Paul Vinelli (in the possession of Robert Vinelli).
4 – Personal, unpublished letters from Linda Laine Reisman Vinelli to her family (copies in the possession of Richard Vinelli).
5 - Personal, unpublished papers/letters belonging to the author. Information from the above is not cited.

All interviews were conducted by the author unless otherwise specified.

ENDNOTES

i Jerre Mangione and Ben Morreale. *La Storia: Five Centuries of the Italian American Experience* (New York: Harper-Collins Publishers, 1992), xiii.

ii Barrie Lillie, "The Italian Ritual of 'fare la scarpetta'", *Italy Magazine*, February 11, 2014, https:///www.italymagazine.com/news/italian-ritual-fare-la-scarpetta.

iii Mangione and Morreale, *La Storia*, 77.

iv Marco Rovinello, "The Draft and Draftees in Italy." In *Fighting for a Living, A Comparative Study of Military Labour 1500-2000*, edited by Erik-Jan Zurcher, 488. Amsterdam University Press, 2013.

v "Battle of Adwa," *Encyclopaedia Britannica*, accessed November 19, 2019, www.britannica.com/event/Battle-of-Adwa.

vi Mangione and Morreale, *La Storia*, 94.

vii Mangione and Morreale, *La Storia*, 93.

viii Mangione and Morreale, *La Storia*, 102.

ix Mangione and Morreale, *La Storia*, 111.

x Paul Vinelli, Personal interview, July 1995.

xi "Italy in WWI," *History*, accessed June 9, 2020, https://www.history.co.uk/italy-in-wwi.

xii "Benito Mussolini Biography: Italian Dictator & Leader of the National Fascist Party," *Biographics*, accessed September 9, 2020, https://biographics.org/benito-mussolini-biography-italian-dictator-and-journalist-who-was-the-leader-of-the-national-fascist-party/.

xiii Mangione and Morreale, *La Storia*, 36.

xiv "Historical Boys Uniforms," Histclo, accessed May 10, 2020, https://www.histclo.com/youth/youth/org/nat/ita/natit.htm.

xv Wendell Johnson and Lucile Duke, "Changes in Handedness Associated with Onset or Disappearance of Stuttering: Sixteen Cases", *The Journal of Experimental Education*, Volume 4, No. 2 (December 1935): 112–132. https://www.jstor.org/stable/20150391.

xvi "Historical Boys Uniforms," Histclo.

xvii P. W. L. Cox, "Opera Nazionale Balilla: An Aspect of Italian Education," *Junior-Senior High School Clearing House* 9, no. 5 (1935): 267-70. accessed June 10, 2020. http://www.jstor.org/stable/30176386.

xviii "Paul Vinella Chosen Portland Swim Pilot," *Portland Press Herald*, 1939.

xix "World War II Enemy Alien Control Program Overview," *National Archives*, accessed July 12, 2018,
www.archives.gov/research/immigration/enemy-aliens-overview.

xx "Japanese American Internment," *Britannica*, accessed July 22, 2020,
https://www.britannica.com/event/Japanese-American-internment.

xxi Marjory Collins, "Why America Targeted Italian-Americans During World War II," *History*, January 14, 2019,
https://www.history.com/news/italian-american-internment-persecution-wwii.

xxii "Italian War Prisoners Housed in Law Quad", *The Michigan Alumnus*, Volume 50, October 2, 1943 – September 23, 1944, 396.

xxiii "IQ Percentile and Rarity Chart," *IQ Comparison Site*, accessed July 15, 2020, https://www.iqcomparisonsite.com/IQtable.aspx.

xxiv "Camp Stoneman," Wikipedia, accessed August 10, 2019, https://en.wikipedia.org/wiki/Camp_Stoneman.

xxv "C-54 Skymaster Long Range Transport," *World War 2 Headquarters*, accessed May 20, 2020, http://worldwar2headquarters.com/HTML/aircraft/ americanAircraft/skymaster.html#:~:text=The%20Douglas%20C%2D54%20 Skymaster,the%20Pacific%20or%20European%20Theaters.

xxvi "The IMF and The World Bank," International Monetary Fund, March 25, 2020, https://www.imf.org/en/About/Factsheets/Sheets/2016/07/27/15/31/IMF-World-Bank.

xxvii "Honduras," Wikipedia, accessed June 23, 2019, https://en.wikipedia.org/wiki/Honduras.

xxviii "Contrata los servicios de dos técnicos," *La Época*, Honduras, January 27, 1950.

xxix César Indiano, *Los Oligarcas: De Donde Salieron Los Ricos?*, (Tegucigalpa, Honduras: Zafra Editores, 2014), 151-158.

xxx "Zamorano," Wikipedia, accessed July 6, 2019, https://en.wikipedia.org/wiki/Zamorano.

xxxi "Saboteada la fundación del banco nacional por la comisión de la ONU", *Prensa Libre*, Honduras, August 15, 1949.

xxxii Darío A. Euraque, *Reinterpreting the Banana Republic, Region and State in Honduras 1870-1972* (The University of North Carolina Press, 1996), 91.

xxxiii "Miembros de la comisión organizadora," *La Época*, Honduras, March 19, 1950.

xxxiv "Miembros de la comisión organizadora," *La Época*.

xxxv "Organización de la banca nacional," *El Día*, Honduras, March 23, 1950.

xxxvi "Breve charla con los miembros de la comisión organizadora de la banca," *La Época*, Honduras, April 15, 1950.

xxxvii "Dos economistas del país partirán hacia Honduras," *El Diario de Hoy*, El Salvador, April 14, 1950.

xxxviii "Economista salvadoreño en Tegucigalpa," *La Época*, Honduras, April 19, 1950.

xxxix "Choluteca y San Marcos de Colón serán visitadas hoy por el Ministro de Hacienda y Crédito Público," *Diario Comercial*, Honduras, May 13, 1950.

xl "Expertos para la organización bancaria", *El Día*, Honduras, April 28, 1950.

xli "Escogencia de los sitios para emprender el trabajo de crédito rural," *Diario Comercial*, Honduras, May 3, 1950.

xlii Paul Vinelli, Javier Márquez, Alexander McLeod, and Julio Gonzalez del Solar, *Estudio Sobre La Economía de Honduras*, IMF for Banco Central de Honduras, June 23, 1950.

xliii "Cordialísimo agasajo a las misiones bancarias," *Diario Comercial*, Honduras, May 12, 1950.

xliv Paul Vinelli, "The Currency and Exchange System of Honduras," *IMF Staff Papers*, 1951, Vol. 1, Issue 1, 420-431, 422.

xlv Guillermo Bueso, "Semblanza de Paul Vinelli," *El Heraldo*, Honduras, February 24, 1997.

xlvi Oscar Acosta and Vicente Machado Valle, *Doctor Paul Vinelli: Biografías Ilustradas* (Tegucigalpa, Honduras: Evensa, 1997), 32-33.

xlvii President Carlos Flores, Personal Interview, April 30, 2018.

xlviii Macky Salinas, Personal Interview, April 30, 2018.

xlix Bueso, "Semblanza."

l Bueso, "Semblanza."

li "Roatán," Wikipedia, accessed June 13, 2020, https://en.m.wikipedia.org/wiki/Roat%C3%A1n.

lii Jorge Bueso Arias, Personal Interview, September 13, 2018.

liii "Centro Social", *El Día*, Honduras, August 30, 1981.

liv Salinas, interview.

lv Salinas, interview.

lvi Salinas, interview.

lvii Salinas, interview.

lviii "Chronology," United Fruit Historical Society, accessed March 10, 2020, http://unitedfruit.org/chron.htm.

lix Adam B. Siegel, "Use of Naval Forces in the Post-War Era", Naval History and Heritage Command, accessed October 10, 2020, https://www.history.navy.mil/research/library/online-reading-room/title-list-alphabetically/u/use-naval-forces-post-war-era.html.

lx Donald E. Schulz and Deborah Sundloff Schulz, *The United States, Honduras, and the Crisis in Central America* (Boulder: Westview Press, 1994), 25.

lxi Lucker, Anny Bahr, Personal Interview, May 2, 2018.

lxii Lucker, interview.

lxiii Thomas P. Anderson, *The War of the Dispossessed: Honduras and El Salvador* (Lincoln: University of Nebraska Press, 1969), 60.

lxiv Salinas, interview.

lxv Salinas, interview.

lxvi Salinas, interview.

lxvii César Indiano, *Luis "Chito" Kafie, Un Viaje Por La Vida*, (Tegucigalpa, Honduras: Lithopress, 2018), 198.

lxviii César Indiano, *Luis "Chito" Kafie, Un Viaje Por La Vida*, (Tegucigalpa, Honduras: Lithopress, 2018), 199.

lxix Salinas, interview.

lxx Ela Mejía, Phone Interview, September 8, 2018.

lxxi Thomas L. Karnes, *Tropical Enterprise: The Standard Fruit and Steamship Company in Latin America*, (Louisiana State University Press, 1978), 269.

lxxii José Rubén Mendoza, Personal Interview, May 2, 2018.

lxxiii Mendoza, interview.

lxxiv Lucker, interview.

lxxv Salinas, interview.

lxxvi Lucker, interview.

lxxvii Salinas, interview.

lxxviii Lucker, interview.

lxxix Lucker, interview.

lxxx Salinas, interview.

lxxxi Lucker, interview.

lxxxii "History", *The MMA Bugler,* accessed May 4, 2020, themmabugler.wordpress.com/history.

lxxxiii Lucker, interview.

lxxxiv Kirk Bowman, "The Public Battles Over Militarization and Democracy in Honduras, 1954-1963," *Journal of Latin American Studies,* Volume 33, Issue 3 (Cambridge University Press, 2001), 555.

lxxxv Lucker, interview.

lxxxvi "Palabras del Dr. Paul Vinelli en la colocación de la primera piedra de Escuela Americana", El Pueblo, Honduras, March 6, 1961.

lxxxvii Pasquale Faldo, Personal Interview, May 2, 2018.

lxxxviii Luis Kafie, Personal Interview, September 11, 2018.

lxxxix Kirk Bowman, *Militarization, Democracy, and Development: The Perils of Praetorianism in Latin America,* (Pennsylvania State University Press, 2002), 174.

xc César Indiano, *Luis "Chito" Kafie, Un Viaje Por La Vida,* (Tegucigalpa, Honduras: Lithopress, 2018), 195.

xci Jacobo Goldstein, "Adios a Paul Vinelli," *La Tribuna,* Honduras, February 20,1997, 87.

xcii Mirna Gómez, Personal Interview, May 1, 2018.

xciii Sor Maria Rosa, Personal Interview, September 12, 2018.

xciv "1974 - Hurricane Fifi," Hurricanes Science and Society, accessed February 12, 2020, www.hurricanescience.org/history/storms/1970s/fifi.

xcv Kafie, interview.

xcvi Dan Koeppel, *Banana: The Fate of the Fruit that Changed the World* (New York: Hudson Street Press, Penguin Group (USA) Inc., 2008), 170.

xcvii David Rockefeller, *David Rockefeller: Memoirs* (New York: Random House, Inc., 2002), 133, 196, 201, 421.

xcviii Flores, interview.

xcix "Central Bank of Belize Quarterly Financial Information for Commercial Banks," *Atlantic Bank Limited Bulletin*, Quarter ending September 30, 2010.

c Faustino Laínez, Personal Interview, September 13, 2018.

ci Juan Kawas, Personal Interview, April 26, 2019.

cii Salinas, interview.

ciii Adriana Yu Shan, Email Interview, June 26, 2018.

civ Laínez, interview.

cv Mendoza, interview.

cvi Salinas, interview.

cvii Laínez, interview.

cviii "Foreign Bank Operations and Acquisitions in the United States," Hearings Before the Subcommittee on Financial Institutions Supervision, Regulation and Insurance of the United States Congress House Committee on Banking, Finance and Urban Affairs, 96th Congress-Second Session, (U.S. Government Printing Office, September 24 and 25, 1980. Serial No. 96-97.), 592.

cix Laínez, interview.

cx Sabino Gámez, "Manuel Rodriguez, Uno de los más grandes pintores," *La Prensa*, Honduras, January 2, 2018.

cxi German Durón Lanza, Phone Interview, September 10, 2018.

cxii Acosta and Machado, *Doctor Paul Vinelli, Biografías Ilustradas*, 71.

cxiii Flores, interview.

cxiv "Exhiben colección de monedas hondureñas", *La Prensa*, Honduras, February 8, 1968.

cxv Mariela Tejada, "Rosalila, el templo mejor preservado, cumple 30 años de su descubrimiento", *La Prensa*, Honduras, June 26, 2019.

cxvi Jacobo Goldstein, "Adios a Paul Vinelli," 87.

cxvii Acosta and Machado, *Doctor Paul Vinelli, Biografías Ilustradas*, 77.

cxviii Mendoza, interview.

cxix Billy Joya, Personal Interview, September 11, 2018.

cxx Laínez, interview.

cxxi Laínez, interview.

cxxii Laínez, interview.

cxxiii Bueso, "Semblanza."

cxxiv Laínez, interview.

cxxv Carlos H. Reyes, Personal Interview, September 12, 2018.

cxxvi Billy Joya, *El Informe BJ*, 21.

cxxvii Joya, *El Informe BJ*, 20.

cxxviii Joya, *El Informe BJ*, 21.

cxxix Joya, *El Informe BJ*, 15.

cxxx Juan Ramón Molina, Personal Interview, September 13, 2018.

cxxxi Rita Sosa, Personal Interview, April 26, 2019.

cxxxii Bueso, "Semblanza."

cxxxiii Laínez, interview.

cxxxiv Clifford Krauss, *Inside Central America: Its People, Politics and History*, (New York: Summit Books, Simon & Schuster, 1991), 181.

cxxxv Joya, *El Informe BJ*, 21-24.

cxxxvi "Banquero Vinelli - Sangre fría y precisión demostraron secuestradores", *El Tiempo*, Honduras, December 19, 1980.

cxxxvii "En libro secreto anotan secuestro de Paul Vinelli", *La Tribuna*, Honduras, March 7, 1981.

cxxxviii Laínez, interview.

cxxxix Laínez, interview.

cxl Laínez, interview.

cxli "Cuba," Wikipedia, last modified August 27, 2020, https://en.wikipedia.org/wiki/Cuba.

cxlii "Farabundo Martí National Liberation Front," *Encyclopaedia Britannica*, accessed April 17, 2019, https://www.britannica.com/topic/Farabundo-Marti-National-Liberation-Front.

cxliii "Sindicalistas repudian el acto criminal," *El Tiempo*, Honduras, December 20, 1980.

cxliv "Férreas medidas de seguridad pone en práctica la policía," *El Tiempo*, December 20, 1980.

cxlv "Muere conductor de Paul Vinelli," *La Prensa*, Honduras, December 20, 1980.

cxlvi "Espectacular operativo en caso de Vinelli," *El Tiempo*, Honduras, December 20, 1980.

cxlvii "Policía no sabe aún si han solicitado rescate," *La Tribuna*, Honduras, December 24, 1980.

cxlviii "Terroristas han destruido mi vida!" *El Heraldo*, Honduras, December 23, 1982.

cxlix "Comando guerrillero extranjero habría secuestrado a Vinelli", *La Prensa*, Honduras, December 23, 1980.

cl "La policía intensifica la búsqueda del plagiado banquero Paul Vinelli", *El Heraldo*, Honduras, December 24, 1980.

cli "Veinticinco millones estarían pidiendo plagiarios de Vinelli", *La Prensa*, Honduras, December 24, 1980.

clii "Ningún rastro todavía del banquero Vinelli", *El Tiempo*, Honduras, December 27, 1980.

cliii "Gautama Fonseca: Mi vida estuvo en riesgo en el caso de Vinelli", *El Heraldo*, Honduras, March 21, 1981.

cliv "Primer aparición pública de Vinelli", *El Tiempo*, Honduras, April 25, 1981.

clv "Paul Vinelli está con vida", *La Prensa*, Honduras, January 2, 1980.

clvi "Piden rescate por P. Vinelli", *El Tiempo*, Honduras, January 7, 1980.

clvii Laínez, interview.

clviii Alice Goldstein, Phone interview, September 13, 2018.

clix "Esposa de Vinelli reúne dinero del rescate", *La Prensa*, Honduras, January 20, 1981.

clx "Banca privada debe invertir para rescatar la economía de la nación", *El Heraldo*, Honduras, April 25, 1981.

clxi "Liberado Paul Vinelli", *La Prensa*, Honduras, March 4, 1981.

clxii "Chase Bank won't pay ransom", *San Francisco Chronicle*, January 26,1981.

clxiii "Sindicalistas del banco se ofrecen como intermediarios en caso Vinelli", *La Prensa*, Honduras, February 12, 1981.

clxiv "En peligro familia Vinelli por infidencia atroz e irresponsable", *La Tribuna*, Honduras, March 21, 1981.

clxv Euraque, *Reinterpreting the Banana Republic*, 91.

clxvi "Paul Vinelli ya no regresa a la presidencia de Bancatlan", *La Tribuna*, Honduras, February 13, 1981.

clxvii "Se encargó de entregarles a los guerrilleros el dinero del rescate", *La Prensa*, Honduras, March 20, 1981.

clxviii "Gautama Fonseca: Mi vida."

clxix "Gautama Fonseca: Mi vida."

clxx "Otra versión sobre la liberación de Vinelli", *El Tiempo*, Honduras, March 5, 1981.

clxxi A. Goldstein, interview.

clxxii "Cercana vio la muerte banquero Paul Vinelli", *La Tribuna*, Honduras, March 4, 1981.

clxxiii "En peligro familia Vinelli, *La Tribuna*, March 21, 1981."

clxxiv Faldo, interview.

clxxv Faldo, interview.

clxxvi "Terroristas salvadoreños planificaron y ejecutaron secuestro del Dr. Vinelli", *La Prensa*, Honduras, March 19, 1981.

clxxvii "Vinelli y Gautama comparecerán a declarar sobre caso de secuestro", *El Heraldo*, Honduras, March 4, 1981.

clxxviii "En cuanto regrese del exterior Fonseca será llamado a declarar", *La Tribuna*, Honduras, March 25, 1981.

clxxix "En cuanto regrese."

clxxx "Esposa de Paul Vinelli declara ante juzgados", *El Tiempo*, Honduras, April 21, 1981.

clxxxi "Paul Vinelli declaró ante los tribunales", *La Prensa*, Honduras, April 24, 1981.

clxxxii "Primera aparición pública de Vinelli", *El Tiempo*, Honduras, April 25, 1981.

clxxxiii "Primera aparición."

clxxxiv Roy Gutman, *Banana Diplomacy: The Making of American Policy in Nicaragua 1981-1987*, (New York: Simon and Schuster, 1988), 16,18.

clxxxv Reyes, interview.

clxxxvi Alice Goldstein, interview.

clxxxvii Lucker, interview.

clxxxviii Ambassador John Negroponte, Phone Interview, June 28, 2018.

clxxxix Richard J. Meislin, "Honduran Guerrillas Release 14 of their Hostages," *New York Times*, September 19, 1982.

cxc Jesús Ceberio, "Termina el secuestro de Honduras con la salida de los guerrilleros hacia la Habana por vía aérea," *El País*, México, September 26, 1982.

cxci Yu Shan, interview.

cxcii Flores, interview.

cxciii César Indiano, *Luis "Chito" Kafie, Un Viaje Por La Vida*, (Tegucigalpa, Honduras: Lithopress, 2018), 270.

cxciv Faldo, interview.

cxcv Marcial Cerrato, Personal Interview, May 1, 2018.

cxcvi Rodolfo Pastor Fasquelle, "Chao Don Paolo", *El Tiempo*, Honduras, February 22, 1997.

cxcvii Gómez, interview.

cxcviii "Piam et Constantem," Holy Office, Vatican, May 8, 1963, accessed March 15, 2020, https://www.catholicculture.org/culture/library/view.cfm?recnum=11422.

cxcix Gómez, interview.

cc "Tegucigalpa, Honduras, Metro Area Population 1950-2020," Macrotrends, accessed June 2, 2020, https://www.macrotrends.net/cities/21136/tegucigalpa/population.

cci Sosa, interview.

ccii "Montecatini Terme (Italy)", European Historic Thermal Towns Association, 2017, https://ehtta.eu/portal/montecatini-terme/.

cciii A. Goldstein, interview.

cciv Adriana Yu Shan, Email Interview, July 7, 2018.

ccv Acosta and Machado, *Doctor Paul Vinelli*, 34.

ccvi Arturo Medrano, Personal interview, May 2, 2018.

ccvii Gómez, interview.

ccviii Sosa, interview.

ccix Laínez, interview.

ccx Gómez, interview.

ccxi Laínez, interview.

ccxii Sosa, interview.

ccxiii Gómez, interview.

ccxiv Gómez, interview.

ccxv Janeth Romero, Telephone Interview, June 6, 2018.

ccxvi Romero, interview.

ccxvii Bueso, "Semblanza".

BIBLIOGRAPHY

BOOKS

Acosta, Oscar. *Paul Vinelli - Biografías Ilustradas*. Tegucigalpa, Honduras: Evensa, 1997.

Britannica, The Editors of Encyclopaedia, "Battle of Adwa." *Encyclopaedia Britannica,* Chicago: Encyclopaedia Britannica, Inc. 22 Feb. 2018, www.britannica.com/event/Battle-of-Adwa. Accessed June 15, 2018

Cohen, Rich. *The Fish that Ate the Whale.* New York: Farrar, Straus and Giroux. 2012.

Euraque, Darío A. *Reinterpreting the Banana Republic, Region and State in Honduras, 1870-1972.* The University of North Carolina Press, 1996.

Gutman, Roy. *Banana Diplomacy, The Making of American Policy in Nicaragua 1981-1987.* New York: Simon and Schuster, 1988.

Indiano, César. *Los Oligarcas ¿De dónde salieron los ricos?* Tegucigalpa, Honduras: Zafra Editores, 2014.

Joya, Billy F. *El Informe BJ: Un Rayo de Luz en el Camino.* Self-published, 1996.

Karnes, Thomas L. *Tropical Enterprise: The Standard Fruit and Steamship Company in Latin America.* Baton Rouge: Louisiana State University Press. 1978.

Koeppel, Dan. *Banana: The Fate of the Fruit that Changed the World.* New York: Hudson Street Press, Penguin Group (USA) Inc., 2008.

Krauss, Clifford. *Inside Central America.* New York: Summit Books, 1991.

Mangione, Jerre and Ben Morreale. *La Storia: Five Centuries of the Italian American Experience.* New York: Harper-Collins Publishers, 1992.

Rockefeller, David. *David Rockefeller: Memoirs.* New York: Random House. 2002.

Rovinello, Marco. The draft and draftees in Italy, 1861-1914. In Zürcher, Erik-Jan (Ed.) *Fighting for a Living: A Comparative Study of Military Labour 1500-2000.* Amsterdam University Press, 2013.

Sleeper, Frank H. *Images of America – Portland.* Charleston, South Carolina: Arcadia Publishing, 1996.

NEWSPAPER ARTICLES

Lardizábal, Patricia D'Arcy, "Donde El Corcho Se Hunde y El Hierro Flota". *La Tribuna* Oct 23, 2016.

MAGAZINE ARTICLES

Ortez, Brenda "Maria Vinelli – He realizado todos mis sueños". *Estilo*, June 2002.

PHOTO CREDITS

Cover: Paul Vinelli senior yearbook photo, 1944 (age 21), *The Michiganensian*, Volume 48, p. 85.

p. 3: Courtesy of the Vinelli family.

p. 6: Courtesy of the Vinelli family.

p. 11: Courtesy of the Vinelli family.

p. 14: Courtesy of the Vinelli family.

p. 19: Courtesy of the Vinelli family.

p. 20: Courtesy of the Vinelli family.

p. 31: "Portland High's Interscholastic League Swimming Champions", *Portland Press Herald*, Winter 1939.

p. 52: Courtesy of the Vinelli family.

p. 70: Courtesy of the Vinelli family.

p. 108: Courtesy of the Vinelli family.

p. 124: Foto Artistica Tegucigalpa, April 1954.

p. 140: Foto Artistica Tegucigalpa, November 1956.

p. 148: Courtesy of the Vinelli family.

p. 152: Courtesy of the Vinelli family.

p. 156: Courtesy of the Vinelli family

p. 162: Courtesy of the Vinelli family.

p. 169: Courtesy of the Vinelli family.

p. 177: Courtesy of the Vinelli family.

p. 180: Courtesy of the Vinelli family.

p. 183: Courtesy of the Vinelli family.

p. 192: Courtesy of the Vinelli family.

p. 204: Courtesy of the Vinelli family

p. 219: Courtesy of the Vinelli family.

p. 233: Courtesy of the Vinelli family.

p. 242: Courtesy of the Vinelli family.

p. 246: Courtesy of the Vinelli family.

p. 252: Courtesy of the author.

p. 254: "¡Secuestrado Paul Vinelli!", *El Heraldo*, No. 331, Honduras, December 19, 1980.

p. 287: Courtesy of the Vinelli family.

p. 307: Courtesy of the Vinelli family.

p. 313: Courtesy of the Vinelli family.

p. 314: Courtesy of the Vinelli family.

p. 315: Courtesy of the Vinelli family.

p. 319: Courtesy of the Vinelli family.

p. 321: René y Margarita Soto, Tegucigalpa, Honduras.

p. 323: Courtesy of the Vinelli family.

p. 354: "Paul Vinelli cumplió la misión de su vida, *La Tribuna*, Honduras, February 21, 1997, p.16.

About the Author: Courtesy of the Vinelli family.

ABOUT THE AUTHOR

Gigi Vinelli Valera is Paul's daughter and biographer.
She was born and raised in Tegucigalpa, Honduras.
She now lives with her husband in Houston, Texas.
gigivalera.com
For more about Paul: https://en.wikipedia.org/wiki/Paul_Vinelli

encendía cuando cruzaba hacia el área de atención al cliente. Ella creía firmemente que vender no era solo entregar un producto, sino interpretar el deseo de quien lo buscaba. Desde el mostrador observó a uno de los empleados nuevos. Se veía tenso, intentando convencer a un cliente que miraba con escepticismo un fardo de cuero rústico color tabaco. El hombre, de unos cincuenta años y manos callosas de artesano, negaba con la cabeza, visiblemente indeciso y a punto de marcharse. Valentina vio la oportunidad. Se ajustó la blusa, acomodó su cabello detrás de los hombros y caminó con la seguridad que sus hermanos siempre habían admirado.

—Permíteme, Roberto —dijo con voz suave pero firme, tomando el control de la situación.

El empleado, aliviado, dio un paso atrás. Valentina se colocó frente al cliente, le dedicó una sonrisa cálida y lo miró directamente a los ojos.

—Muy buenos días. Mi nombre es Valentina —se presentó, extendiendo la mano con elegancia—. He notado que busca algo especial. Para el tipo de calzado que suele fabricar, imagino que necesita resistencia, pero también un acabado que gane carácter con el tiempo. ¿Me equivoco?

El hombre, sorprendido por la perspicacia de la joven, se detuvo.

—Así es, señorita. Pero este cuero me parece muy rígido. No quiero que se agriete al trabajar el doblez.

Valentina no discutió; en lugar de eso, buscó en un estante bajo una pieza de cuero curtido vegetal en un tono miel profundo. Lo desplegó sobre la mesa de madera con un movimiento fluido.

—Toque esto —le indicó, señalando la fibra—. Este cuero no es solo materia prima; es historia. Tiene la flexibilidad del aceite integrado en el proceso de curtido. Observe cómo reacciona al calor de mis manos.

Comenzó a masajear una esquina del cuero, demostrando cómo la piel se volvía maleable bajo sus dedos.

—Si utiliza este, sus clientes no solo comprarán un zapato; adquirirán algo que se adaptará a su pie como una segunda piel. Si lo que busca es excelencia y que su nombre sea sinónimo de calidad, este es el fardo que su taller necesita.

El cliente pasó los dedos por la superficie, asombrado.

—Tiene usted razón, señorita Valentina. Me llevaré tres fardos.

Valentina asintió con profesionalismo, mientras por dentro sentía esa descarga de adrenalina que solo el éxito de una venta le otorgaba.

—Excelente elección. Roberto le ayudará a cargarlo y yo misma me encargaré de que su factura esté lista en un momento. Gracias por confiar en nosotros.

Mientras caminaba hacia la caja, sintió la mirada de orgullo de su padre desde la oficina vidriada. Valentina no era solo una joven de rasgos llamativos; era una fuerza en los negocios, una estratega que sabía que, para conquistar un mercado, primero había que conquistar la confianza del cliente. Después de una jornada intensa en la empresa, donde el peso de los fardos de cuero y el rigor de los inventarios habían consumido sus horas, la noche caía como un bálsamo. Valentina necesitaba sacudirse el polvo de la oficina y los negocios. Frente al espejo de su habitación, se preparó con un entusiasmo eléctrico; se delineó los ojos con precisión, resaltando su sello personal y enrizó su cabello café oscuro dejándolo caer con libertad sobre sus hombros. Ella y sus dos amigas llegaron al karaoke, un lugar vibrante, lleno de luces de neón y el murmullo de risas que cortaban la monotonía de la semana. Para Valentina, ese ambiente no era solo diversión; era su escenario. Mientras muchos se sentían intimidados por el micrófono, ella se sentía como pez en el agua, moviéndose al ritmo de la música con una fluidez que parecía natural en su piel canela. Mientras Diana y Karina, sus amigas inseparables, subían al pequeño escenario para cantar un dueto cargado de energía, Valentina se quedó a un lado, cerca de la mesa. No podía quedarse quieta; el ritmo la habitaba. Comenzó a bailar al son de la canción, con movimientos elegantes y precisos que delataban su pasión por el baile y la música. En ese momento, no tenía responsabilidades que cumplir, era simplemente una joven disfrutando del arte de vivir. Sin embargo, la armonía de su momento se rompió cuando un chico, que la había estado observando con una intensidad invasiva desde la barra, se le acercó. Sin pedir permiso, invadió su espacio personal y le puso una mano en el brazo para invitarla a bailar.

—Oye, preciosa —le dijo al oído, con un tono cargado de una confianza vulgar—, con ese cuerpo y esos ojos, no deberías estar bailando sola. Ven conmigo y te enseño lo que es disfrutar de verdad, no te pierdas con esas niñitas.

Las palabras, cargadas de un irrespeto evidente, encendieron de inmediato el temperamento que Valentina había forjado entre tres hermanos mayores. La música del karaoke pareció quedar en segundo plano mientras su carácter fuerte tomaba el frente. Valentina se zafó del agarre con un movimiento seco y se plantó frente a él, irguiendo su figura esbelta. Sus ojos marrones, que hace un segundo brillaban con alegría, ahora lanzaban chispas de acero.

—Primero, quítame la mano de encima —le contestó con una voz brusca y firme que cortó cualquier intento de galantería barata—. Segundo, no estoy sola, estoy con mis amigas y no necesito que un extraño venga a decirme cómo disfrutar mi noche. Si crees que por decir una frase vulgar me vas a impresionar, te equivocaste de mujer. Aprende a respetar y vete por donde viniste antes de que pierda la paciencia.

El chico, sorprendido por la dureza y la determinación de aquella "jovencita" que parecía tan delicada, retrocedió un paso, balbuceando una disculpa inexistente mientras se alejaba hacia la oscuridad del local. Valentina respiró hondo, se acomodó el cabello y, sin dejar que el incidente le amargara la noche, volvió a mirar a sus amigas en el escenario. Ella era una mujer de contrastes: capaz de escribir el poema más dulce, pero también de levantar una muralla de hierro cuando alguien intentaba sobrepasar sus límites. Su dignidad no estaba en venta, ni en el negocio de sus padres ni en una pista de baile. Para Valentina, los hombres no eran un pasatiempo, ni el amor un juego de azar. La educación de sus padres había sido muy clara desde que era niña: el noviazgo era la antesala del matrimonio, un camino serio que no debía recorrerse con cualquiera ni repetirse con demasiados. Cuando Diana y Karina bajaron del escenario, entre risas y aplausos, encontraron a una Valentina radiante.

—¡Lo hicieron increíble! —exclamó, abrazándolas mientras el DJ ponía una canción con un ritmo más bailable.

A Valentina le apasionaba el arte en todas sus formas. Para ella, el karaoke no era solo ir a ver a otros cantar; era una oportunidad para que su cuerpo y su voz se expresaran. Cuando llegó su turno, no eligió una canción cualquiera. Eligió una que le permitiera jugar con los matices de su voz, esa que practicaba mientras cocinaba en casa de su abuela o mientras diseñaba en la universidad. Al subir al escenario, la luz de los reflectores destacó el brillo de su piel radiante y la profundidad de su mirada. Valentina no solo cantó; interpretó. Cada gesto de sus manos, cada paso que daba sobre la tarima, era un reflejo de su formación en el modelaje y su amor por el baile. Era una mujer que disfrutaba ser el centro de su propio universo artístico. En ese momento, rodeada de música y de sus mejores amigas, Valentina se sentía invencible. Disfrutaba el desestrés de la noche, riendo con Diana y Karina sobre las ocurrencias del día, sintiendo que la rutina del negocio familiar se disolvía entre versos y melodías. Esa era la verdadera Valentina: una joven que podía ser una estratega implacable en una venta de cuero por la mañana, una estudiante de diseño detallista por la tarde, y una artista vibrante y empoderada por la noche. Una mujer que amaba su cultura, que honraba a su familia y que, sobre todo, se respetaba a sí misma por encima de cualquier cosa. Al día siguiente, el domingo en el hogar de Valentina no era un día de descanso absoluto, sino un día de rituales compartidos donde las personalidades de los cuatro hermanos se entrelazaban como los hilos de un tapiz árabe. En esa casa, el aire de la mañana olía a café con cardamomo y a la promesa de una tranquilidad que solo se encuentra entre quienes se conocen desde siempre. Valentina, con su habitual energía, solía ser la primera en despertar el espíritu de la casa, pero pronto se encontraba con las tres columnas que habían custodiado su crecimiento: sus hermanos. Joaquín, apenas tres años mayor que ella, era quizás con quien más chispas saltaban.

Él vivía inmerso en su mundo *gamer*, entre pantallas y estrategias digitales que a veces lo hacían parecer distante. Sus caracteres chocaban con frecuencia; la determinación de Valentina y la testarudez de Joaquín creaban tormentas pasajeras en los pasillos. Sin embargo, detrás de esa fachada de indiferencia y controles remotos, Joaquín era su sombra protectora. Valentina sabía que, si el mundo se ponía difícil, él dejaría cualquier partida a medias para estar a su lado. No necesitaba palabras; su presencia era un contrato silencioso de lealtad. Por otro lado estaba Javier, él era su cómplice de salidas. Javier era la persona a la que Valentina acudía cuando necesitaba desconectarse del mundo; con él podía ir a comer un helado, disfrutar de una tarde en el cine o sentarse a platicar de negocios durante horas. Javier era metódico y tranquilo, lo que lo convertía en el contrapunto ideal para la energía desbordante de Valentina. Entre ellos no había juicios, solo una amistad profunda de hermanos que compartían la visión empresarial y el gusto por los pequeños placeres de la vida. Pero era con Julio, el mayor, con quien Valentina compartía una conexión casi mística. A pesar de la diferencia de edad, ambos hablaban el mismo lenguaje: el del arte. Julio poseía esa sensibilidad que solo tienen los que ven el mundo a través de la belleza y la creación. Eran confidentes, dos mitades de una misma moneda creativa. Cuando estaban juntos, el tiempo parecía detenerse; podían pasar horas discutiendo desde la composición de un cuadro hasta la armonía de una canción. Los momentos más mágicos ocurrían en la sala, cuando la estructura conservadora de la casa se relajaba. Joaquín, dejando por un momento sus videojuegos, se unía a sus hermanos mientras Julio tomaba la guitarra y comenzaba a rasgar las cuerdas con una habilidad que sorprendía a quien no lo conocía. Enseguida, Valentina cerraba los ojos, dejaba que el ritmo fluyera por su cuerpo esbelto y comenzaba a cantar.

Su voz llenaba el salón, elevándose sobre las notas de la guitarra, mientras sus padres los observaban con orgullo, simplemente disfrutando de la pureza del momento. En esas mañanas de domingo, Valentina no era la empresaria ni la estudiante de carácter fuerte; era la hija y la hermana menor, la artista, la joya de la familia que florecía bajo el cuidado de sus tres guardianes y sus dos pilares, sus padres.

Capítulo 2:

Un rostro nuevo

Todo comenzó con una fotografía y un amigo en común que servía de puente entre dos mundos. William, al ver la imagen de Valentina en la pantalla de un celular, sintió una curiosidad inmediata. Había algo en su sonrisa, en la serenidad de su mirada, que lo impulsó a buscarla en las redes sociales.

La notificación llegó al teléfono de Valentina como un susurro moderno:

"William V te ha enviado una solicitud de amistad." Ella, tras revisar el perfil y reconocer los vínculos compartidos, aceptó. No pasaron muchos minutos antes de que el primer *"Hola"* iluminara su pantalla.

Las semanas siguientes fueron un intercambio constante de mensajes que acortaban la distancia. Entre textos que volaban de un lado a otro, descubrieron con sorpresa que no solo compartían amigos, sino también el mismo campus universitario. La curiosidad digital pronto se transformó en el deseo de un encuentro real, de ponerle voz a las palabras y profundidad a las imágenes.

El día señalado, Valentina se encontraba sumergida en el ritmo monótono de la universidad en el laboratorio de computación. El sonido rítmico de las teclas y el brillo azulado de los monitores la rodeaban mientras se concentraba en terminar un trabajo pendiente. En medio de su concentración, su teléfono vibró sobre la mesa.

"Estoy cerca del laboratorio de cómputo.
¿Nos vemos?"

—decía el mensaje de William.
Valentina sintió un ligero vuelco en el corazón. Guardó sus archivos, cerró su sesión y se colgó el bolso al hombro. Caminó hacia la salida, sintiendo esa mezcla de nervios y anticipación que vibraba por todo su cuerpo. Al empujar la pesada puerta del laboratorio, el aire del pasillo la recibió de golpe, y con él, la figura de William. Él estaba allí, apoyado cerca de la entrada, esperándola. Valentina se detuvo en seco. Las fotos no le habían hecho justicia. Al verlo de frente, lo primero que la impactó fue la intensidad de su mirada: unos ojos azul cielo que parecían capturar toda la luz del campus. Por un segundo, el bullicio de los estudiantes a su alrededor se desvaneció. La imagen de aquel chico alto y apuesto, con su sonrisa tímida y sus ojos magnéticos, quedó grabada en su memoria como un cuadro nítido.
—Hola, Valentina —dijo él, y su voz terminó de romper el hechizo del silencio.
Ese encuentro fortuito a la salida del laboratorio fue el inicio de algo que fluyó con naturalidad. Lo que empezó como una amistad nacida entre clases y cafés, pronto se convirtió en algo más profundo. William se volvió una presencia constante para Valentina.
William era un joven deslumbrante de diecinueve años, era el tipo de hombre que hacía que las conversaciones se

detuvieran a su paso. Con el paso del tiempo iniciaron un noviazgo que para muchos era el ideal: dos jóvenes guapos, con la vida por delante, compartiendo los días entre clases y risas. El noviazgo comenzó con la dulzura propia de la juventud universitaria. Caminaban por el campus compartiendo risas y planes inmediatos. Sin embargo, Valentina no era una joven que se dejara llevar solo por la superficie. Su mente, entrenada en la lógica del negocio familiar y en la estructura de sus valores, necesitaba saber hacia dónde se dirigía ese camino. Una noche, Valentina terminó de retocarse frente al espejo. Sus ojos árabes brillaban con una ilusión genuina mientras esperaba el sonido del motor frente a su casa. Cuando William llegó, no se limitó a pitar; bajó del coche y caminó hacia la entrada con una presencia que irradiaba seguridad y respeto. La caballerosidad de William no era una pose, era su naturaleza. Al llegar al vehículo, se adelantó con paso firme y, con una sonrisa que desarmaba cualquier tensión, le abrió la puerta del carro a Valentina, esperando a que ella se acomodara antes de cerrarla con suavidad.

—Te ves muy guapa, Vale —le dijo al entrar al asiento del conductor, mirándola con una sinceridad que la hacía sentir la mujer más especial del mundo.

El trayecto al restaurante fue una extensión de esa armonía. Iban conversando y riendo todo el camino; la risa de Valentina, esa que recordaba al trino de un pájaro, se entrelazaba con la voz armoniosa de William. No había silencios incómodos, solo la fluidez de dos personas que disfrutaban genuinamente de la compañía del otro. Sentados en una mesa acogedora, el mundo exterior pareció desvanecerse. La conversación fluyó sin esfuerzo hacia los temas que los apasionaban. Hablaron de la universidad, de los retos de las clases de diseño de ella y de los complejos números que William manejaba en su carrera de finanzas.

—A veces los balances no cuadran a la primera —decía él entre risas—, pero es como en la cancha: si pierdes un punto, te concentras más para el siguiente saque. Valentina lo escuchaba con fascinación. Admiraba profundamente la disciplina de William. Él no solo era un estudiante brillante; era un atleta dedicado al voleibol. Ella veía en sus ojos la chispa de la competitividad sana y el rigor del entrenamiento. Le encantaba cómo él lograba equilibrar la frialdad de las finanzas con la adrenalina del deporte. Para Valentina, ver a William esforzarse en el juego era ver un reflejo de su propia determinación empresarial. Pasaron un momento agradable, celebrando las pequeñas victorias académicas y compartiendo sus metas. En William, Valentina sentía que había encontrado a alguien que no solo respetaba su carácter fuerte y sus sueños de independencia, sino que los impulsaba. Una tarde, William llegó a la casa de los padres de Valentina a visitarla. El tocó el timbre y ella entre ansiosa y alegre abrió la puerta con rapidez. Entraron y pasaron a la sala. El ambiente en la casa de los padres de Valentina era tranquilo, impregnado de esa sensación de hogar que solo dan los años de estabilidad y las costumbres compartidas. William estaba sentado frente a ella, luciendo tan impecable como el primer día que lo vio en la universidad. La luz de la tarde entraba por la ventana, haciendo que su mirada brillara con una claridad casi irreal. Para cualquier espectador, eran la imagen de la pareja perfecta. Sin embargo, Valentina sentía una inquietud que no podía ignorar. Su mente, siempre acostumbrada a planificar con la precisión de una receta de repostería, necesitaba respuestas que el silencio del noviazgo ya no podía sostener.

Con la franqueza que siempre la caracterizó, Valentina le hizo la pregunta que definiría su futuro:

—William —comenzó ella, rompiendo la calma del momento—, hemos estado juntos un tiempo y creo que es importante saber qué pensamos. ¿Hacia dónde va lo nuestro? ¿Cómo te proyectas tú con nosotros en el futuro?

William se recostó en el sofá, relajado, la miró con calma, con esa confianza de quien siente que tiene todo el tiempo del mundo. No detectó la seriedad en el tono de Valentina.

—Vale, yo estoy muy bien contigo —respondió él con una sonrisa ligera—. Pero si me preguntas por el matrimonio... yo me veo casado hasta los veinticinco años. No antes. —respondió él con naturalidad.

El silencio que siguió a sus palabras fue ensordecedor para Valentina. Ella tenía dieciocho; William, diecinueve. Siete años. En su mente, Valentina hizo el cálculo rápido: siete años de un noviazgo que, según sus valores, solo debía ser la preparación para algo más grande. Siete años esperando a que él decidiera que era "el momento".

Para William, siete años de espera eran un suspiro; para Valentina, eran una eternidad de incertidumbre. En su esquema de vida, si un camino no conducía al destino deseado en un tiempo razonable, no era el camino correcto. Ella no buscaba un pasatiempo, buscaba un proyecto de vida. Con una madurez que sorprendió a ambos, Valentina comprendió que estar con él sería como intentar hornear un pan sin fuego: una espera inútil.

La tarde caía sobre la sala, tiñendo las paredes de un tono ámbar que hacía juego con la melancolía del momento.

—No puedo perder mi tiempo —se dijo a sí misma.

Valentina, sentada con la espalda recta pero la mirada cargada de una honestidad valiente terminó de hablar. Había puesto las cartas sobre la mesa con la claridad que la caracterizaba: sus sueños de independencia y sus metas personales necesitaban un espacio que, en ese momento, la relación no podía ocupar. William la escuchó en un silencio respetuoso, con las manos entrelazadas y la mirada fija en el suelo, procesando cada palabra. El dolor era evidente en su rostro, pero su nobleza le permitió mantener la compostura.

—Valentina... —comenzó él, con la voz un poco más grave de lo habitual—. No te voy a mentir, esto me duele. Yo no quiero que terminemos. Siento que todavía tenemos mucho por construir, y me cuesta imaginar mis días sin nuestras pláticas o no volverte a ver con los ojos de un enamorado.

Hizo una pausa, buscó los ojos marrones de ella y, al ver la determinación inamovible en su mirada, suspiró con resignación.

—Pero te entiendo —continuó él con un rastro de tristeza—. Comprendo tu punto de vista. Siempre he admirado esa fuerza que tienes para saber exactamente hacia dónde vas. Si sientes que nuestros relojes internos marcan horas distintas y que necesitas este espacio para tus metas, no soy quién para encadenarte. Lo último que querría es ser un obstáculo para tu brillo.

Se hizo un silencio breve, cargado de un cariño que mutaba de forma. William se levantó del sofá con la misma elegancia con la que se retiraba de las canchas cuando la partida ya se había acabado. No hubo gritos, ni reproches, ni intentos desesperados de manipulación.

—Gracias por ser tan sincera conmigo, Vale. Me quedo con lo mejor de nosotros —dijo él, extendiéndole la mano primero y luego dándole un abrazo cálido que sellaba el final de un capítulo.

Terminaron su relación en buenos términos, con el respeto de dos personas que se aprecian profundamente. Aquella tarde, mientras lo veía caminar hacia la puerta, Valentina aprendió su primera gran lección de madurez: el amor, por muy "guapo" o "simpático" que fuera el compañero, necesitaba tener un norte claro y compartido. Sin dramas ni resentimientos, transformaron el romance en una amistad respetuosa. Al cerrar la puerta, Valentina sintió tristeza, pero a la vez un peso menos en el alma. Ella había honrado sus propios sueños por encima de la inercia del corazón.

Capítulo 3:

El caballero de la noche

El tiempo pasó y Valentina continuó enfocada en sus metas, moviéndose entre las aulas de la universidad y las oficinas de la empresa familiar. Sin embargo, una noche de sábado, decidió que era momento de un respiro. Acompañada de su amiga Graciela, se sumergió en el ambiente vibrante de una fiesta local. La música y las luces creaban un paréntesis en su rutina de disciplina. En medio de la noche, Valentina se encontró con otro grupo de amigas y, por un par de horas, se dejó llevar por la charla y las risas. Pero el instinto de cuidado de Valentina, aquel que habían cultivado en ella sus padres nunca se apagaba del todo. De repente, se dio cuenta de algo: Graciela no estaba. Recorrió el lugar con la mirada, buscó entre la multitud y salió a los pasillos, pero su amiga parecía haberse esfumado. El rastro de mensajes y llamadas que Valentina dejó en el teléfono de Graciela no obtuvo respuesta. Preocupada, pero consciente de que debía cumplir con su propio horario en casa, Valentina decidió marcharse solo cuando la búsqueda resultó inútil. La música y las risas de la fiesta se habían quedado atrás, pero la preocupación seguía martillando en la cabeza de Valentina mientras manejaba hacia su casa. Ya en la seguridad de su habitación, el ritual de desconexión comenzó: se desmaquilló frente al espejo y se puso el pijama, pero la inquietud por Graciela seguía latiendo en su pecho. Se sentó en la cama y marcó el número de su amiga una vez más, dispuesta a insistir hasta obtener una señal de vida. Al tercer tono, alguien contestó. Pero no era la voz de Graciela.

—¿Aló? —una voz masculina, profunda y desconocida, resonó en el auricular.

El cuerpo de Valentina se tensó de inmediato. El miedo, frío y punzante, la hizo ponerse a la defensiva.

—¿Quién eres tú? ¿Por qué tienes el teléfono de mi amiga? —preguntó ella con una firmeza que ocultaba el temblor de sus manos.

—Tranquila —respondió el hombre. Su voz era dulce, pausada, cargada de una amabilidad que desarmaba a cualquier soldado—. Me llamo Federico.

Valentina escuchó en silencio, con los dedos apretando el teléfono.

—Me encontré a tu amiga hace un rato —continuó Federico con un tono casi paternal—. Estaba muy ebria, apenas podía mantenerse en pie. Le pregunté si quería que la llevara a su casa y ella me dirigió. De hecho, ya estamos llegando a su dirección.

La tensión en los hombros de Valentina comenzó a disiparse. A través del receptor pudo escuchar el motor del coche detenerse y el sonido de una puerta al abrirse. Federico hablaba con una educación impecable, como alguien que entendía perfectamente la gravedad de la situación.

—Mira, para que te quedes más tranquila —agregó él con suavidad—, voy a guardar tu número. En cuanto me asegure de que tu amiga entre a su casa y cierre la puerta, te enviaré un mensaje de texto confirmándote que está a salvo. Así podrás dormir sin preocupación.

Valentina aceptó, agradecida por el gesto de aquel extraño que parecía comprender su angustia.

—Muchas gracias, Federico. De verdad, te lo agradezco mucho —respondió ella, suavizando el tono por primera vez.

—No es nada. Es lo que cualquier persona debería hacer —concluyó él con sencillez antes de colgar.

Al colgar, se recostó en la almohada pensando en la suerte que había tenido su amiga de toparse con un "caballero" en medio de la noche. Minutos después, la pantalla se iluminó con un mensaje corto:

"Ya entró a su casa. Está segura. Buenas noches."

Ella suspiró con alivio. Cerró los ojos pensando que, después de todo, todavía quedaban hombres nobles que entendían el valor de la seguridad y el respeto. El sol de la mañana siguiente trajo consigo una sensación de gratitud renovada. Valentina, fiel a sus modales y a su educación, no quiso dejar pasar el gesto de la noche anterior. Tomó su teléfono y le escribió a Federico un mensaje sencillo pero sincero, agradeciéndole una vez más por haber cuidado a Graciela y por haberse tomado la molestia de avisarle. Lo que empezó como un mensaje de cortesía se transformó, casi sin darse cuenta, en un diálogo fluido que se extendió durante todo el día. Las palabras de Federico fluían con una facilidad asombrosa. Cada texto abría una nueva puerta: hablaban de metas, de estudios y de sus visiones de vida. Valentina descubrió en él a un hombre que sabía escuchar y parecía compartir ese mismo sentido del orden y la responsabilidad que ella tanto valoraba. La conversación era tan amena que el tiempo entre clases se pasaba volando, y Valentina se encontró sonriendo frente a la pantalla más de lo habitual. Después de varios días de mensajes constantes, llegó la invitación natural. Federico le propuso verse para tomar un café al terminar su última clase en la universidad. Valentina aceptó, sintiendo una mezcla de curiosidad y la seguridad que él le había transmitido desde aquella primera llamada. El lugar elegido fue una pequeña cafetería, un refugio de aroma a grano tostado y luz cálida que contrastaba con el ajetreo del campus. Valentina llegó puntual y, al entrar, buscó con la mirada al hombre de la voz pausada. Cuando finalmente lo vio, la primera impresión fue inesperada. Tras haber conocido a alguien tan físicamente impactante como William, el aspecto de Federico no le causó ningún revuelo. Su físico no le resultó atractivo en absoluto; no hubo ese flechazo visual ni esa admiración inmediata por sus rasgos. Era un hombre común, alguien que fácilmente podría pasar desapercibido en una multitud.

Sin embargo, en cuanto se sentaron a la mesa y comenzaron a hablar, el entorno cambió.

—Es un gusto ponerle rostro a la voz —dijo Federico con una sonrisa amable, manteniendo un contacto visual que no era agresivo, sino reconfortante.

A medida que avanzaba la tarde, Valentina se dio cuenta de que la falta de atracción física estaba siendo compensada por algo mucho más poderoso para ella en ese momento: su carisma. Federico era una compañía extraordinariamente agradable. Tenía el don de hacerla sentir escuchada y comprendida. Cada comentario que él hacía reforzaba la imagen de un hombre maduro, centrado y, sobre todo, confiable. A medida que las semanas se convertían en meses, Federico se volvió una pieza fundamental en la vida de Valentina. Lo que había comenzado con un café después de clases se transformó en una rutina de mensajes, confidencias y un apoyo constante. Sin embargo, para Valentina, el sentimiento era transparente y tranquilo: Federico era un gran amigo. Su compañía le resultaba amena. A su lado, no había la presión de las apariencias ni el agotamiento de los juegos románticos. Ella se había encariñado con su presencia, con la seguridad de saber que él siempre estaba ahí, listo para escucharla o para ofrecerle un consejo sensato sobre el negocio familiar o sus estudios. Federico se había convertido en un refugio. Ella lo quería, pero lo quería con la pureza de la amistad, sin verlo realmente como "su hombre". El punto de inflexión llegó una tarde en la que la calma habitual se rompió. Federico, con una seriedad que Valentina no le conocía, decidió poner las cartas sobre la mesa. Le declaró su amor con palabras intensas, asegurándole que ella era la mujer con la que quería construir todo lo que alguna vez habían platicado. Valentina, sorprendida y con un nudo en la garganta, fue honesta con él: —Federico, te quiero muchísimo, pero no puedo corresponderte de esa manera. Te veo como mi mejor amigo, no me sale sentir algo más...

En ese momento, la amabilidad de Federico dio paso a una táctica mucho más fría y calculada. No hubo comprensión, sino una retirada estratégica.

—Entiendo —dijo él, bajando la mirada con una tristeza que parecía genuina—. Pero yo no puedo ser "solo tu amigo", Valentina. Verte todos los días, hablar contigo y saber que nunca serás mía me causa un dolor que no puedo soportar. Si no somos algo más, prefiero alejarme de tu vida por completo. Es mejor que no nos volvamos a ver.

Aquellas palabras cayeron sobre Valentina como un balde de agua fría. La idea de un mundo donde Federico no estuviera, donde no hubiera mensajes de buenos días, ni cafés reparadores, ni ese apoyo incondicional, le provocó un miedo repentino y profundo. Se sintió egoísta por no querer perderlo, pero al mismo tiempo, se sintió acorralada. ¿Cómo iba a dejar que se fuera el único hombre que parecía entenderla y protegerla? El miedo a la soledad y a la pérdida de ese "lugar seguro" que Federico había construido a su alrededor fue más fuerte que su falta de atracción física. Bajo la presión de ese vacío inminente, Valentina cedió.

—No te vayas —susurró—. Está bien... intentémoslo.

Esa tarde, Valentina permitió que la amistad se transformara en un compromiso. No entró en esa relación empujada por el deseo o por la convicción, sino por el temor a perder la seguridad que él le ofrecía. Federico había ganado la primera gran batalla: consiguió que ella aceptara estar a su lado no por amor, sino por el miedo a perderlo. Sin saberlo, Valentina acababa de entregar su libertad a cambio de no sentir el dolor de la ausencia. El inicio del noviazgo fue, en apariencia, la consolidación de todo lo que Valentina había aprendido a valorar: estabilidad, respeto y un compromiso que no temía al futuro. Federico no tardó en integrarse en la dinámica de su vida con una habilidad pasmosa. Se ganó la confianza de sus tres hermanos —una tarea que Valentina consideraba casi imposible— y mostró un respeto impecable hacia sus padres. Para el mundo exterior, Valentina había encontrado al fin al hombre que William no pudo ser: alguien con un plan, alguien que no huía del "para siempre". Sin embargo, bajo esa superficie de perfección, las primeras grietas comenzaron a aparecer, camufladas bajo el disfraz del amor protector. La transición de amigos a novios trajo consigo un cambio sutil en la atmósfera. Al principio, Valentina se sentía halagada por la atención constante de Federico. Después de la frialdad de su ruptura anterior, la intensidad de él se sentía como un refugio. Pero, poco a poco, ese refugio empezó a estrecharse.

Capítulo 4:

El dulce engaño del control

Una tarde, mientras Valentina se preparaba para salir a cenar con Graciela y sus otras amigas de la universidad, recibió una llamada de Federico. Minutos antes, como solía hacer para evitar malos entendidos, le había enviado una selfie frente al espejo: una foto sencilla, sonriendo, con el vestido puesto y el cabello suelto, buscando compartir el momento y, de paso, tranquilizarlo.

—¿A dónde vas con ese vestido, Vale? —preguntó él. Su voz seguía siendo dulce, pero había una nota de rigidez que ella no había notado antes.

—Es solo una cena, Fede. El vestido es normal —respondió ella, extrañada.

—Es que no conoces a la gente como yo, mi amor. Hay muchos hombres ahí fuera que no saben respetar, y me angustia pensar que te miren de más. Lo digo porque te amo y quiero cuidarte.

Valentina, acostumbrada a la protección de sus hermanos, interpretó aquel comentario como un gesto de cariño. No vio el hilo que empezaba a enredarse en su muñeca; solo vio a un hombre que la valoraba tanto que temía por ella. Esa noche, por primera vez, se cambió de ropa para "no preocuparlo". Fue una pequeña renuncia, una concesión insignificante en apariencia, pero fue el primer territorio que Federico conquistó. Pronto, el objetivo de Federico se centró en su círculo social. Empezó con comentarios aislados sobre Graciela, la misma amiga a la que él había "rescatado" la noche que se conocieron.

—Me parece que Graciela es un poco irresponsable, ¿no crees? —le decía mientras tomaban café—. No me gusta que te rodees de personas que no tienen tus mismos valores. Tú eres una mujer de hogar, de negocios, con metas… ella solo busca fiestas. Me da miedo que su mala influencia termine afectando tu reputación.

Federico utilizaba los propios valores de Valentina —su conservadurismo, su ética de trabajo— para aislarla. Lo hacía de forma tan persuasiva que ella empezó a sentir que, efectivamente, pasar menos tiempo con sus amigas era una señal de madurez. Él se estaba convirtiendo en su único espejo, el único que validaba quién era ella. Sin embargo, Federico no se detuvo en las amistades femeninas; su control pronto se extendió al ámbito digital. Durante una plática aparentemente casual, sacó a relucir el nombre de William.

—He visto que William aún te sigue en las redes sociales —soltó Federico, endureciendo el gesto—. Me parece una falta de respeto total hacia nuestra relación y hacia mí como tu pareja. Ese hombre no tiene por qué estar en tu lista de amigos si ya me tienes a mí. Si de verdad me valoras, lo borrarás ahora mismo.

Valentina, queriendo evitar un conflicto y convencida de que su "sacrificio" era una prueba de amor y lealtad hacia él, cedió. En ese mismo instante, bajo la mirada vigilante de Federico, buscó el perfil de William y lo eliminó de su vida digital. No se dio cuenta de que, con cada clic, estaba borrando también una parte de su propia identidad y autonomía, entregándole a Federico las llaves de su dominio.

En la empresa de sus padres, donde Valentina pasaba gran parte del día, el teléfono se convirtió en una presencia constante. Federico necesitaba saber cuándo entraba, cuándo salía y con quién almorzaba.

—Solo quiero saber que llegaste bien —repetía él.

Pero si ella tardaba cinco minutos en responder porque estaba atendiendo a un cliente o revisando un inventario, el siguiente mensaje llegaba cargado de una tristeza manipuladora:

"Siento que ya no soy tu prioridad".

Valentina se encontraba disculpándose por trabajar, por estudiar, por vivir. La "compañía agradable" de los primeros meses estaba siendo reemplazada por una vigilancia silenciosa que ella, en su inocencia y lealtad, seguía llamando amor. Federico era un experto en la arquitectura del control: construía paredes tan altas que ella ya no podía ver el horizonte, pero las pintaba de colores tan bonitos que Valentina todavía creía que estaba en un palacio cuando, en realidad, los cimientos de su prisión ya estaban terminados.

Para Valentina, el trabajo nunca había sido una carga, sino una forma de realización. Por eso, cuando Federico decidió abrir su propia tienda de camisas deportivas, ella sintió que al fin estaban hablando el mismo idioma. Verlo dar ese paso alimentó la admiración que sentía por él; era, a sus ojos, el reflejo de lo que ella misma soñaba para su futuro. El local olía a plástico nuevo y a cartón seco. Era un espacio rectangular, apretado, donde las paredes estaban ocultas tras hileras infinitas de percheros que sostenían camisetas de poliéster de colores brillantes. Bajo la luz blanca y zumbante de los tubos fluorescentes, Valentina pasaba las horas doblando prendas, alineando costuras y etiquetando precios. Sus manos, que en casa solían estar cubiertas de la calidez de la harina, aquí se sentían ásperas, resecas por el contacto constante con las fibras sintéticas.

—Vamos a construir nuestro imperio. —le decía él mientras acomodaban los estantes—. Esto es por nuestro futuro.

Valentina se entregó al proyecto con una dedicación absoluta. Pasaba días enteros y horas interminables tras el mostrador, organizando inventarios, atendiendo clientes y puliendo cada detalle de la tienda. Lo hacía sin cobrar un solo centavo, convencida de que cada hora de sudor era una inversión en la vida que tendrían juntos. Para ella, esa tienda no era solo un local de ropa; era el campo de entrenamiento para la empresaria que siempre había querido ser. Ver a sus padres haber logrado su propia empresa le daba la certeza de que este era el camino correcto. Se visualizaba a su lado: dos emprendedores luchando hombro a hombro. Su amor se traducía en esfuerzo, y Federico recibía ese sacrificio con una sonrisa que Valentina interpretaba como gratitud.

—Esta es la nueva tanda de la Champions, Vale. Si las acomodamos bien en la vitrina, volarán —decía Federico desde el mostrador, sin levantar la vista de la pantalla de su computadora.

Valentina se secó una gota de sudor de la frente. Eran las ocho de la noche y el aire acondicionado del local apenas podía contra el calor húmedo del exterior. A sus pies, una montaña de cajas vacías esperaba ser llevada a los estantes. Le dolía la espalda y el eco de sus clases de la mañana todavía resonaba en su cabeza, pero al mirar a Federico sentía un fogonazo de orgullo. Su hombre era un emprendedor. Y ella, como le habían enseñado en casa, era su mano derecha, el cimiento silencioso sobre el cual se construiría su futura prosperidad.

Un martes, el ambiente en la tienda se sintió especialmente denso. Federico no hablaba mucho; caminaba de un lado a otro, golpeando rítmicamente un bolígrafo contra el mostrador de vidrio. El sonido —clic, clic, clic— ponía nerviosa a Valentina.

—¿Qué pasa, Fede? —preguntó ella, dejando de organizar las tallas de las camisetas de la selección.

—Es el inventario de la próxima temporada, amor —suspiró él, frotándose las sienes—. Tengo la oportunidad de comprar un lote grande a un precio increíble, pero el proveedor quiere el efectivo ya. Si no aprovecho esto, la tienda se va a quedar vacía el próximo mes.

Valentina lo observó. Se veía vulnerable, cargando solo con el peso de la "empresa". Recordó el sobre que guardaba en el cajón de su escritorio en casa: sus ahorros de meses, dinero que había ganado trabajando con sus padres y privándose de lujos. Pero al ver a Federico, sintió que ese dinero no era suyo, sino de ambos. Al día siguiente, Valentina entró al local con el sobre oculto en su bolso. Al entregárselo a Federico sobre el mostrador de vidrio, el roce del papel madera contra el cristal sonó como una sentencia definitiva.

—Toma. Es para que el negocio no se detenga —dijo con una sonrisa tímida.

Federico tomó el sobre y, por un segundo, un destello de luz cruzó sus ojos. La rodeó con los brazos y la besó en la frente. En ese abrazo, rodeada del olor a caucho de los balones nuevos y el poliéster de las estanterías, Valentina se sintió la mujer más importante del mundo. La vida de Valentina se había convertido en un laberinto de compromisos sin fin. El cansancio era una sombra constante bajo sus ojos marrones y el ligero hundimiento de sus ojeras; sus días se fragmentaban en mil pedazos: la exigencia creativa de la universidad por la mañana, el rigor operativo en el negocio de cuero de su familia por la tarde y las noches interminables en la tienda deportiva de Federico. Ya casi no tenía vida social; el baile, el canto y los paseos con su hermano Javier habían sido desplazados por facturas, percheros y la presión de un "imperio" que recaía sobre sus hombros. Aquel viernes, el peso de la rutina se sentía más pesado de lo normal. A las seis de la tarde, mientras Valentina doblaba minuciosamente una fila de camisetas, su teléfono vibró.

Era un mensaje de Diana y Karina:

"Vale, no aceptamos un no por respuesta.
Te esperamos a las 8:00 p. m. para cenar.
Necesitas respirar. ¡Te extrañamos!"

Valentina sonrió por primera vez en el día. La idea de una cena, de risas sin hablar de inventarios, se sintió como un oasis. Federico estaba en la parte de atrás del local y ella se acercó con cautela.

—Fede, las chicas me invitaron a cenar hoy al salir —dijo, intentando sonar entusiasta—. Me vendría bien distraerme un poco; he estado muy cansada esta semana.

El aire en el local cambió de inmediato. Federico dejó de anotar en su libreta y la miró, no con alegría por ella, sino con una decepción ensayada. Suspiró profundamente, dejando caer los hombros con un gesto de amargura.

—¿A cenar, Vale? ¿Precisamente hoy? —preguntó, bajando la voz a un tono herido—. Yo pensé que estábamos juntos en esto. Mañana entra el pedido grande que tú misma ayudaste a financiar y pensaba que nos quedaríamos hoy hasta tarde organizando todo para que mañana sea un éxito.

—Solo serán un par de horas, Fede. Mañana puedo venir más temprano… —intentó explicar ella.

Federico se acercó, tomándola suavemente de los hombros, usando esa mirada que Valentina aún confundía con amor protector.

—No es solo el trabajo, mi amor. Me preocupa que andes sola de noche con ellas. Sabes cómo está la situación y tus amigas… bueno, ellas no tienen las mismas responsabilidades que tú. Ellas solo piensan en divertirse, pero tú y yo estamos construyendo un futuro —hizo una pausa dramática—. Me duele que prefieras irte a reír por ahí mientras yo me quedo aquí matándome por nuestro sueño. Pero ve, si sientes que tu diversión es más importante que lo que estamos haciendo juntos, ve. Yo me encargo de todo solo, aunque no sé a qué hora termine.

El nudo en la garganta de Valentina se apretó. La manipulación, disfrazada de sacrificio y preocupación, surtió efecto. Ella se sintió egoísta por querer un par de horas para sí misma.

—No digas eso, Fede. No es que sea más importante… —susurró, sintiendo cómo el entusiasmo se evaporaba ante el sentimiento de culpa.

—Es que lo parece, Vale. Si me amaras como dices, entenderías que este no es momento de distracciones. Quédate conmigo; cenamos algo rápido aquí mientras trabajamos y así nos cuidamos el uno al otro. ¿No es eso lo que hace una pareja de verdad?

Valentina bajó la mirada hacia las camisetas que acababa de doblar. Tomó su teléfono y, con los dedos temblorosos, escribió a sus amigas:

> *"Lo siento, chicas. No podré ir.*
> *Hay mucho trabajo en la tienda. Pásenlo lindo."*

Al ver que ella guardaba el celular, Federico cambió su expresión de inmediato por una sonrisa satisfecha y le dio un beso en la frente.

—Esa es mi mujer. Sabía que podía contar contigo. Somos un equipo, ¿recuerdas?

Valentina asintió mecánicamente, pero mientras volvía a sus tareas bajo la luz fría del local, sintió una punzada de soledad. El olor a tela nueva ya no le parecía el aroma de un sueño, sino el de una jaula que empezaba a cerrarse. Y, por primera vez, su carácter fuerte no encontró las palabras para defender su propio espacio. La noche ya había avanzado cuando Valentina hizo girar la llave en la cerradura de su casa. El silencio del vecindario contrastaba con el zumbido que aún sentía en sus oídos por las luces fluorescentes y la música ambiental de la tienda. Entró arrastrando los pies, con los hombros caídos y el agotamiento físico mezclado con un vacío emocional que no lograba descifrar. Al entrar a la sala, se sorprendió al encontrar las luces encendidas. Sus tres hermanos estaban allí, como si la hubieran estado esperando en una guardia silenciosa. Joaquín estaba en un rincón, con la mirada clavada en su consola, pero con los auriculares al cuello, atento a la puerta; Javier revisaba unos reportes en el comedor y Julio, con su guitarra descansando sobre las piernas, fue el primero en romper el silencio con un acorde suave y melancólico.

—Hasta que apareces, Vale —dijo Julio, dejando de acariciar las cuerdas para mirarla con una preocupación que le nublaba los ojos—. Te guardamos comida, pero ya debe estar fría.

Valentina dejó su bolso sobre el sofá y forzó una sonrisa que no llegó a sus ojos.

—Gracias, chicos. Había mucho que hacer en la tienda de Fede. El pedido grande llega mañana y…

—Siempre hay algo que hacer en esa tienda, Valentina —la interrumpió Javier, dejando sus papeles a un lado y cruzándose de brazos—. Es viernes por la noche. Hace meses que no salimos por un helado. Ni siquiera te hemos visto en las últimas cenas familiares. Estás dividida en mil pedazos y parece que el pedazo más grande se lo está llevando un negocio que ni siquiera es tuyo.

Joaquín soltó el control de su videojuego y se unió a la conversación, con su brusquedad habitual pero cargada de ese afecto protector que siempre mostraba cuando ella lo necesitaba.

—Incluso tus amigas llamaron a la casa preguntando por ti. Dijeron que les cancelaste a última hora. Vale, pasas metida en ese local desde que sales de la universidad hasta que cierran. ¿Dónde quedó tu tiempo para cantar?

Julio dio un rasgueo seco a la guitarra, captando la atención de todos.

—Ya ni siquiera nos sentamos aquí a sacar canciones, Valentina. Tu voz es lo que le da vida a esta casa, pero ahora solo hablas de inventarios de otros. Nosotros te conocemos. Eres alguien muy social y una artista... pero te estás convirtiendo en el soporte de un hombre que no parece preocuparse por si tú también tienes sueños. Mira tus ojos; ya no brillan igual.

—Es que Federico me necesita —respondió ella, tratando de recuperar su carácter fuerte, aunque su voz sonó débil—. Él está empezando y, como pareja, tengo que apoyarlo. Estamos construyendo algo juntos.

—¿Juntos? —replicó Javier—. Vale, tú eres la que hace las ventas, la que diseñó el orden del local, la que incluso puso sus ahorros. Que ahora nos digas que "él te cuida" prohibiéndote ver a tus amigas porque son una "distracción"... eso no suena a protección. Suena a que te está quitando tu mundo para que solo exista el de él.

Valentina miró a Julio, esperando encontrar apoyo en su hermano artista, pero él solo sostuvo la guitarra con tristeza.

—Él no está cuidando tu talento, Vale. Lo está usando —susurró.

El silencio que siguió fue pesado. Valentina miró a sus tres guardianes, los hombres que le habían enseñado a ser fuerte, y por un segundo se sintió pequeña. La manipulación de Federico había sido tan sutil que ella la había disfrazado de amor, pero frente a la honestidad de sus hermanos y la guitarra silenciosa de Julio, la venda empezaba a deshilacharse.

—Solo estoy cansada, eso es todo —dijo finalmente, evitando la mirada de Javier—. Mañana será un día mejor.

Se retiró a su habitación, pero mientras subía las escaleras, el eco de una nota solitaria de la guitarra de Julio la siguió, recordándole una melodía que ya no recordaba cómo cantar. Los meses se convirtieron en una marea monótona que arrastró a Valentina hacia un destino que ella misma ya no reconocía. Llevaba casi tres años de noviazgo, tres años en los que su brillo se había ido diluyendo entre las facturas de la tienda y las expectativas de Federico. Una tarde, mientras Valentina estaba en la universidad, Federico decidió dar un paso decisivo a espaldas de ella. Se presentó en la casa familiar para hablar con sus padres y, siguiendo las costumbres que sabía que ellos valoraban, les pidió formalmente la mano de su hija. En la sala, el ambiente se tornó denso. Por dentro, los padres de Valentina no estaban del todo convencidos; sus ojos de empresarios y de padres protectores detectaban grietas en el carácter de Federico y dudaban profundamente que él fuera el hombre capaz de hacerla feliz. Sin embargo, fieles a su principio de respetar la autonomía y el corazón de su hija, tragaron sus reservas.

—Lo que nuestra hija decida, nosotros lo apoyaremos —dijo su padre con voz grave—. Solo te pedimos una cosa: cuida de ella.

Al día siguiente, Federico preparó el escenario perfecto. Le anunció a Valentina que harían un viaje corto por carretera para pasar el día en la playa. Ella, agotada por la rutina asfixiante, sintió un alivio genuino; pensó que, por fin, tendría un respiro de la monotonía y que Federico estaba siendo el hombre detallista del que se había enamorado al principio. Al llegar al restaurante frente al mar, el sonido de las olas se mezcló de repente con el estruendo de los mariachis. Los músicos rodearon la mesa entonando la canción que él siempre le había dedicado, esa melodía que antes le parecía romántica y que ahora, inexplicablemente, le pesaba en el pecho. Federico se puso de pie, buscó el centro de la atención de todos los presentes y, con un movimiento ensayado, se arrodilló sobre la arena. Sacó una pequeña caja aterciopelada y la abrió, revelando un anillo que brillaba bajo el sol del mediodía.

—Valentina, ¿te quieres casar conmigo? —preguntó con una seguridad que la dejó sin aliento—. Ayer hablé con tus padres y les pedí tu mano formalmente.

En ese instante, el tiempo se detuvo para ella, pero no por la alegría, sino por un temor silencioso que le recorrió la espalda. Valentina se paralizó. Al mirar el anillo y la expresión expectante de Federico, su mente se convirtió en un torbellino de pensamientos. Cruzó por su mente la idea de que ya había invertido demasiado tiempo, demasiado esfuerzo y demasiado dinero en esa relación; sentía que había llevado las cosas demasiado lejos como para retroceder ahora. Muy en el fondo, en ese rincón de su alma que aún conservaba su voz de artista, sabía que no era realmente feliz. Pero la presión de los tres años, la bendición que él ya había buscado de sus padres y los ojos de los extraños que esperaban un final perfecto en el restaurante la acorralaron. Se sintió comprometida, casi obligada por la inercia de su propia entrega.

—Sí… —susurró, con una sonrisa que no nacía de su corazón, sino de su sentido del deber—. Sí, acepto.

Mientras él le deslizaba el anillo en el dedo, su mente se llenó de una resolución forzada. En ese instante ya no había espacio para más dudas, solo para la aceptación. Pensó, con una frialdad que la sorprendió, que había tomado una decisión y que, desde ese momento, ya no había vuelta atrás.

Capítulo 5:

La voz que rompió el silencio

El zumbido de las lámparas fluorescentes parecía más fuerte en el silencio de la tarde. El local estaba vacío, sumido en ese aroma a caucho y tela nueva que ahora formaba parte del inventario diario de Valentina. Aprovechando un momento de calma en la tienda, se acercó a él para compartirle su decisión de comenzar una rutina de ejercicio, esperando que, como su futuro esposo, se alegrara por ella. Valentina se acercó despacio, alisándose el cabello café. A pesar del cansancio, sus ojos marrones tenían un brillo de ilusión; después de meses de entregarse a los sueños de otros, por fin había decidido reclamar un pequeño espacio para sí misma.

—Fede, decidí que voy a entrar al gimnasio —le dijo con firmeza mientras él revisaba unos documentos—. Hay uno muy bueno aquí cerca del local comercial; me queda perfecto para ir después de la universidad. Ya es hora de que me dedique algo de tiempo.

La reacción de Federico fue inmediata y visceral. Dejó lo que estaba haciendo, se cruzó de brazos y su rostro se ensombreció.

—No, Valentina. Definitivamente no vas a ir a ese lugar —sentenció con un tono de autoridad que nunca antes había usado de forma tan directa—. Tú no sabes cómo son esos gimnasios. Los entrenadores solo están ahí para coquetearles a las mujeres y los hombres no quitan la vista de encima. No voy a permitir que estés expuesta a ese tipo de faltas de respeto.

En ese instante, algo se rompió dentro de Valentina. La joven que durante tres años había cedido, la que había prestado sus ahorros y cancelado cenas con amigas, sintió que el aire le faltaba. Esa última prohibición fue la chispa que encendió la fiera que había tenido dormida por años. Su carácter fuerte, el que sus hermanos tanto admiraban, despertó con una fuerza volcánica.

—¿Que no me vas a permitir? —le contestó ella, con una voz que vibraba de indignación—. Yo no te estoy pidiendo permiso, Federico. Te estoy informando. Es mi salud, es mi tiempo y es mi dinero. He dado todo por este negocio y por ti, pero no vas a decirme qué puedo o no hacer con mi propio cuerpo.

La discusión escaló rápidamente. Lo que antes eran sugerencias "protectoras" se transformaron en reclamos hirientes. Federico intentó usar la culpa, acusándola de serle infiel con el pensamiento, mientras ella le recordaba cada sacrificio que había hecho. Por primera vez, Valentina le gritó las verdades que había callado, dejando en evidencia la toxicidad de un noviazgo que ya no tenía retorno. Cansada de las ofensas, tomó su bolso y se marchó.

—No quiero hablar más. No me busques —le advirtió antes de salir del local.

Llegó a su casa temblando de rabia y agotamiento. Se encerró en su habitación, buscando el refugio del silencio, pero la paz no llegó. Federico comenzó a hostigarla: el teléfono no dejaba de vibrar sobre la mesa de noche. Eran llamadas tras llamadas perdidas y una ráfaga de mensajes cargados de una insistencia enfermiza:

"Contéstame ahora mismo."

"Tenemos que hablar de lo que pasó."

"No puedes dejarme así después de todo lo que
he hecho por ti."

Valentina miraba la pantalla iluminada en la oscuridad de su cuarto, sintiendo por primera vez que ese anillo en su mano no era un símbolo de amor, sino una marca de propiedad que ya no estaba dispuesta a cargar. Las horas pasaban y el teléfono sobre la mesa de noche parecía un animal inquieto que no dejaba de vibrar. Finalmente, con el pulso acelerado y la paciencia agotada, deslizó el dedo para contestar. No hubo saludos.

—¡Valentina, por fin! ¿Por qué me ignoras? Sabes que odio que me hagas esto —la voz de Federico sonaba cargada de una mezcla de angustia fingida y reclamo.

—No te estoy haciendo nada, Federico —respondió ella, tratando de mantener la voz firme a pesar del temblor en sus manos—. Te dije que no quería hablar. Lo del gimnasio fue la gota que derramó el vaso. No puedo seguir viviendo bajo tus reglas.

—¡No son reglas, es amor! Te cuido porque eres mi mujer y nos vamos a casar —insistió él, elevando el tono—. Esa actitud de rebeldía no te queda, Valentina. Mañana mismo vas a la tienda y arreglamos esto, pero olvídate de ese gimnasio. No voy a quedar como un tonto frente a todos mientras tú te expones.

—Ese es tu problema, Federico: siempre se trata de ti, de cómo te ves tú, de lo que tú quieres —replicó ella—. Yo soy una persona, no un accesorio de tu tienda. No vamos a llegar a ningún acuerdo porque tú no quieres una compañera, quieres una mujer sumisa y obediente. ¡Ya basta!

Sin esperar respuesta, colgó y lanzó el teléfono sobre la cama. Pero el silencio que siguió no fue liberador; fue aplastante. Se dejó caer y, de repente, la "fiera" que había salido horas antes se desmoronó, dando paso a una fragilidad desgarradora. Comenzó a llorar, un llanto silencioso y amargo que le quemaba el pecho. Se sentía atrapada en un callejón sin salida. Miraba el anillo y lo sentía como un grillete.

—No quiero esto para mi vida —se repetía entre sollozos.

La imagen de un matrimonio con Federico se le presentaba como una condena de días grises y discusiones infinitas. Sin embargo, el miedo —ese enemigo invisible— comenzó a paralizarla. En su mente, la presión social pesaba más que su propia infelicidad: tenía miedo al qué dirán. Sus padres ya le habían dado la bendición, la noticia del compromiso se había extendido y ella sentía la carga de una lealtad mal entendida. Creía que, si rompía el compromiso, estaría defraudando a sus padres, a quienes tanto respetaba. Se sentía perdida, navegando en un mar de culpas y expectativas ajenas. ¿Cómo iba a explicar que el hombre caballeroso que todos veían era, en realidad, su carcelero? Valentina, la mujer fuerte, la diseñadora creativa, la empresaria astuta, se sentía en ese momento como una niña pequeña en la oscuridad, sin saber qué dirección tomar para recuperar su libertad sin romper el corazón de su familia. En medio de la oscuridad de su habitación y con el rostro empapado en lágrimas, Valentina comprendió que su fuerza humana ya no era suficiente. Recordó los valores de fe que sus padres le habían inculcado y decidió acudir a su refugio más sagrado. Se levantó de la cama con movimientos lentos, como si cargara un peso invisible, y se arrodilló frente a su cama. Apoyó las manos entrelazadas sobre el borde del colchón e inclinó la cabeza. En ese rincón de intimidad, su voz, quebrada pero decidida, comenzó a elevarse en una oración profunda:

—"Señor, tengo miedo de defraudar a mis padres, tengo miedo del que dirán si rompo mi compromiso... he dado tanto tiempo a este noviazgo, no sé qué hacer. Ilumíname, dame fuerzas para romper este compromiso y que no me importe lo que digan los demás. Por favor, muéstrame el camino".

El silencio de la habitación se volvió como una melodía de paz, casi solemne. En ese preciso momento, algo extraordinario sucedió. Valentina sintió un aire fresco que surgió de la nada, naciendo desde su espalda. No era una corriente fría, sino un soplo de vida que rociaba su cabello con suavidad, descendiendo con una caricia sobrenatural por sus hombros.

Ese roce invisible disolvió el nudo en su garganta. Instantáneamente, la angustia fue reemplazada por una paz y una tranquilidad que sobrepasaban todo entendimiento. Sintió cómo le entraba la fuerza que necesitaba, una determinación de acero que quemaba cualquier rastro de duda. En ese instante, ya no le importaba la opinión de la sociedad, ni las críticas, ni las expectativas ajenas; solo importaba su libertad y su verdad. Se puso en pie, ya no como una víctima, sino como la mujer poderosa que siempre fue. Con un movimiento seco y liberador, se quitó el anillo de compromiso, sintiendo cómo el dedo finalmente descansaba de aquel peso. No hubo más llanto. Salió de su habitación con paso firme, sus hermanos y padres, que estaban en las áreas comunes, se volvieron hacia ella sorprendidos por la transformación de su semblante. Valentina, con la mirada fija en el horizonte de la calle y la mano apretando el metal que ya no la encadenaba, anunció en voz alta para que todos escucharan:

—"Ya vuelvo, iré a entregar este anillo".

Sin esperar respuesta, con el aire fresco aún guiando sus pasos, salió a la noche dispuesta a recuperar el control de su vida. Valentina llegó a la tienda de Federico con el paso de quien ya no carga cadenas. Al entrar, el aroma a tela y vinil ahora le resultaba indiferente. Federico no estaba, pero ella no necesitaba verlo para cerrar ese ciclo. Se acercó al mostrador con determinación y, bajo la mirada confundida del empleado que custodiaba la caja registradora, deslizó el anillo sobre la mesa.

—Entrégale esto a Federico, por favor —sentenció con una voz clara y sin rastro de duda.

Como una ráfaga, sin siquiera mirar a los ojos al hombre y sin dar espacio a preguntas, dio media vuelta y salió del local. El aire de la calle nunca le había parecido tan puro. Caminó de regreso a casa sintiendo que cada paso la devolvía a su centro, a la Valentina que amaba diseñar y soñar.

Al cruzar la entrada de su hogar, el ambiente era de una tensión eléctrica. Sus padres estaban de pie cerca de la sala y sus tres hermanos, encabezados por Javier, daban vueltas inquietos. En cuanto la vieron entrar sin el brillo del metal en su mano izquierda, el silencio se rompió.

—"¡Vale! Por Dios, nos tenías con el corazón en la mano" —exclamó su madre, acercándose para tomarle las manos—. "¿Qué fue lo que pasó? ¿Estás bien?".

Valentina suspiró, pero esta vez fue un suspiro de alivio. Los miró a todos, uno a uno, y con la honestidad que solo da la libertad recobrada, comenzó a hablar.

—"Ya terminó. Fui a entregar el anillo" —dijo con serenidad—. "Siento mucho si sienten que los defraudo, pero no podía seguir así. Federico no me quería como compañera, quería una marioneta. Me prohibió ir al gimnasio, me alejó de mis amigas... incluso me hizo sentir que mi esfuerzo en su tienda era una obligación y no un apoyo, me tardé demasiado en darme cuenta y dejé que las cosas llegaran muy lejos, pero ya abrí los ojos".

Javier dio un paso al frente, con la mandíbula apretada pero los ojos llenos de orgullo. —"¿Defraudarnos? Vale, te estábamos perdiendo. Ese tipo te estaba apagando el alma. Lo único que nos dolía era verte aceptar algo que no te hacía feliz".

—"Es cierto, hija" —intervino su padre, poniendo una mano en su hombro—. "Te dijimos que te apoyaríamos en tu decisión, y nuestra mayor alegría es que hayas decidido respetarte a ti misma. Ningún 'qué dirán' vale más que tu paz".

Julio, que sostenía su guitarra como si fuera un escudo, soltó una nota vibrante y alegre. —"No te sientas mal, hermanita. Lo importante es que te diste cuenta antes de dar el siguiente paso y luego fuera peor".

Valentina soltó un suspiro profundo, sintiendo cómo la carga pesada que había sostenido sobre sus hombros durante años finalmente se desvanecía, dejándola con una extraña sensación de ligereza. Sin embargo, junto a esa liberación, un mar de nervios le inundó el estómago. Se sentía desorientada; después de tres años enfocando cada uno de sus planes, ahorros y visiones en una vida junto a Federico, de repente el mapa que seguía se había borrado. Ahora debía cambiar su visión por completo y encontrar una nueva dirección, un reto que la asustaba tanto como la emocionaba. Esa noche, tras fundirse en un abrazo largo y sanador con sus padres y hermanos, Valentina subió a su habitación. Lo primero que hizo fue tomar su teléfono, que vibraba sin descanso con las incontables llamadas y mensajes hostigantes de Federico; con un movimiento decidido, lo apagó. En lugar de ese ruido, buscó una lista de reproducción con música suave, melodías que le daban paz a su alma y la ayudaban a relajarse. Las notas llenaron el espacio, envolviéndola en una calma que le hacía mucha falta. Cuando por fin logró poner la cabeza en la almohada, cerró sus ojos y oró nuevamente desde lo más profundo de su ser:

—"Señor, gracias por la fuerza y la valentía que me diste para terminar este compromiso. Por favor, guía mis pasos de ahora en adelante, muéstrame el camino".

Con esa entrega, el agotamiento la venció y se durmió profundamente. A la mañana siguiente, al abrir los ojos, no se levantó de inmediato. Se quedó un rato atenta, viendo hacia el techo de su habitación en un estado de calma absoluta, mientras repasaba en su mente el sueño vívido que había tenido: en él, Valentina visualizaba con total claridad el nombre y el logo de una cafetería y repostería que sentía, con una certeza inexplicable, que "era suyo". Impulsada por una energía renovada, se bajó de la cama con rapidez y se sentó frente a su escritorio. Abrió la computadora y, con las manos volando sobre el teclado y la tableta gráfica, comenzó a apuntar cada detalle y a diseñar aquel logo que había visto en sus sueños. No tenía idea de por qué estaba creando eso en ese preciso instante, ni de dónde saldría el capital o el local, pero sentía un impulso incontrolable por trabajar en ello. Era como si su creatividad, tanto tiempo amordazada, finalmente hubiera encontrado el cauce por el que Dios le indicaba que debía caminar.

Valentina se enfocó de lleno en su nueva visión. Aquella chispa que nació en su sueño se convirtió en una hoguera que consumía sus días y noches. Con la precisión de una arquitecta de sueños, trabajó sin descanso en el logo hasta que cada trazo reflejó su esencia. Una vez listo, no se detuvo: pasó horas investigando la maquinaria industrial necesaria, contactando proveedores de granos de café de altura, experimentando con recetas de repostería que llenaban su cocina de aromas a vainilla y canela, y cuadrando presupuestos con la rigurosidad que solo una futura empresaria posee. Sin embargo, mientras ella estaba enfocada en un proyecto que no entendía aún porque lo hacía, Federico intentaba anclarla al pasado. El hostigamiento no cesaba; las llamadas, aunque bloqueadas, se convertían en correos y mensajes a través de terceros. Una mañana, esa sensación de alivio se vio interrumpida. Valentina salió de una de sus clases de diseño, con el portafolio bajo el brazo y la mente repasando costos de hornos de convección, cuando lo vio. Federico estaba apoyado contra una columna, con el rostro desencajado y la mirada fija en ella. En cuanto la vio, se abalanzó hacia ella, interceptándola en mitad del pasillo.

—"Valentina, tenemos que hablar. Ya basta de este juego de ignorarme" —dijo él, bloqueándole el paso con el cuerpo—. "No puedes tirar tres años a la basura por una rabieta de un gimnasio".

—"No es una rabieta, Federico, es mi libertad" —respondió ella, tratando de rodearlo, pero él volvió a interponerse—. "Te devolví el anillo. Todo está dicho. Por favor, vete, tengo otra clase ahora mismo".

—"¡No te vas a ir a ningún lado!" —exclamó él, elevando la voz y atrayendo las miradas de otros estudiantes—. "¿Quién te crees que eres? Después de todo lo que invertí en ti, de cómo te cuidé... ¡Me debes una explicación de verdad! Ese anillo no se tira así como así".

Valentina sintió que la rabia le quemaba el pecho, pero mantuvo la frente en alto. Su voz salió fría y cortante:

—"Yo no te debo nada, Federico. Al contrario, fui yo quien puso sus ahorros y su trabajo gratis en tu tienda. Si hablamos de inversiones, tú saliste ganando. Ahora, hazte un favor y mantén un poco de dignidad. Se acabó. No quiero estar contigo, no me siento feliz a tu lado y no voy a ser tu prisionera".

—"Es por alguien más, ¿verdad?" —escupió él con veneno, cerrando los puños—. "Seguro ya tienes a algún imbécil del gimnasio o de esta facultad de artes llenándote la cabeza de estupideces. Por eso me dejaste, ¡porque eres una ingrata!".

—"Me dejé a mí misma por ti durante tres años, y eso es lo que no me perdono" —sentenció Valentina con una calma que lo enfureció aún más—. "Por favor, vete. No me obligues a llamar a seguridad".

Federico intentó tomarla del brazo, pero ella dio un paso atrás con una agilidad que lo dejó en el aire. Sin darle tiempo a reaccionar y sin dedicarle una sola mirada más, Valentina giró sobre sus talones y entró al salón de su siguiente clase, cerrando la puerta tras de sí. Se sentó en su pupitre, con el corazón latiendo a mil por hora, pero sin una sola lágrima. Escuchó los pasos de Federico alejarse por el pasillo mientras él gritaba algo que ya no le importaba. Abrió su cuaderno y, en lugar de tomar notas de la clase, dibujó en una esquina una pequeña taza de café humeante. Federico era el ruido, pero su proyecto era la melodía que ahora guiaba su vida.

Capítulo 6:

La máscara caída

La música retumbaba en el pecho de Valentina, un ritmo que por fin se sentía libre. Entre risas con sus amigas y el frío del vaso en su mano, el compromiso roto con Federico parecía una sombra que finalmente se disipaba. Pero la libertad era un espejismo. Entre la multitud, unos ojos fijos la vigilaban: Julián, el amigo de Federico, un centinela de su obsesión ya estaba tecleando la traición en su teléfono. Minutos después, el aire del lugar se volvió pesado, como si la presión atmosférica hubiera caído de golpe. Federico irrumpió como una tormenta fuera de control, con la ropa desaliñada y el rostro encendido por una mezcla tóxica de alcohol y furia. Sus ojos, que alguna vez le transmitieron paz a Valentina, ahora eran dos brasas oscuras que buscaban una sola presa.
Ebrio y lleno de ira, alzó la voz:
—¡Te vas de aquí conmigo ahora mismo!
El grito, ronco y cargado de una autoridad violenta, cortó el aire con la fuerza de un latigazo. En los oídos de Valentina, la música no se detuvo, pero se transformó en un zumbido lejano. La risa de sus amigas se extinguió y fue reemplazada por un silencio sepulcral que cayó sobre ella con el peso de una condena pública, dejándola desnuda ante el juicio de

quienes la rodeaban. Valentina sintió cómo la sangre se le retiraba del rostro, dejándola fría bajo la luz estridente del salón. En ese vacío de sonido, cada segundo se estiraba como una tortura. No eran solo sus amigas las que callaban; era todo el lugar.

Podía sentir los ojos de los extraños clavándose en su nuca, en sus manos temblorosas que intentaban inútilmente sostener su dignidad. Para una mujer que había crecido bajo los pilares del honor y el esfuerzo, aquel silencio era un foco encendido que iluminaba su humillación. Valentina buscó refugio en las miradas de su grupo, pero solo encontró una lástima punzante o un asombro que la hacía sentir pequeña, casi insignificante. Era la hija de los empresarios, la estratega, la mujer que siempre tenía el control, ahora reducida a ser la protagonista de un espectáculo bajo y violento. Por miedo a que el escándalo la consumiera frente a todos, cometió el error de acceder.

—Está bien… Vámonos. Por favor, baja la voz —susurró, con las palabras apenas logrando escapar de unos labios que habían perdido todo el color.

Al entrar al vehículo, el golpe de la puerta al cerrarse sonó como el martillazo de un juez. Dentro, el aire era escaso, viciado por el olor acre del alcohol que Federico exhalaba y por un calor denso que parecía emanar del tablero. Valentina se hundió en el asiento del copiloto, intentando hacerse pequeña, como si así pudiera evitar que la furia de él la alcanzara. Tenía un nudo en la garganta tan sólido y punzante que cada intento por tragar saliva era una batalla. Sentía que el oxígeno no llegaba a sus pulmones; el pecho se le oprimía bajo un peso invisible y el cinturón de seguridad, que siempre le había dado confianza, ahora le recordaba una atadura. Federico arrancó de forma violenta. El chirrido de las llantas sobre el asfalto fue el último sonido del mundo conocido.

Mientras el coche ganaba velocidad, Valentina miraba por la ventana cómo las luces de la ciudad se alejaban. Quería hablar, quería calmar a la fiera que bufaba a su lado, pero la voz se le había quedado atrapada en ese nudo de angustia. No podía respirar bien; el aire entraba en ráfagas cortas y desesperadas. De repente, sin previo aviso, el movimiento cesó. Federico giró el volante con brusquedad y se desvió hacia un camino lateral, lejos de la ruta principal. El coche se detuvo en seco. El sonido del motor apagándose fue lo más aterrador que Valentina había escuchado jamás. El silencio que lo reemplazó era absoluto, un vacío ensordecedor que hacía que el latido de su propio corazón retumbara en sus oídos como un tambor de guerra.

No había faroles de calle ni luces de casas lejanas. El camino estaba desierto. Valentina no se atrevía a girar la cabeza. Sus ojos estaban fijos en el parabrisas, donde la negrura de la noche se fundía con el miedo que ya le desbordaba el alma. Federico estaba ahí, a centímetros de ella, sumergido en esa misma sombra. En ese rincón olvidado del mundo, donde nadie podía oírla y nadie podía verla, Valentina comprendió que su estrategia de "evitar el escándalo" la había llevado directamente al encuentro de su peor pesadilla. Federico permanecía inmóvil, con las manos aferradas al volante de tal manera que sus nudillos se veían blancos, incluso en la penumbra. Valentina no se atrevía a mirarlo directamente; mantenía la vista al frente, pero por el rabillo del ojo veía la silueta rígida de su mandíbula tensa. Finalmente, él rompió el silencio. No gritó. Su voz fue un susurro áspero, una vibración baja que erizó los vellos de la nuca de Valentina.

—¿Te divertiste mucho, Valentina? —la pregunta flotó en el aire como una navaja.

Valentina tragó saliva, sintiendo que el nudo en su garganta era ahora una piedra filosa. Intentó que su voz sonara estable, apelando a la cordura que siempre había sido su refugio.

—Fede… solo estaba con mis amigas. No estábamos haciendo nada malo —respondió ella. Sus palabras sonaron pequeñas, casi infantiles, dentro de la inmensidad del coche.

—¿Nada malo? —Él giró la cabeza con una lentitud mecánica. En la oscuridad, Valentina solo podía ver el brillo de sus ojos, nublados de toda la dulzura que alguna vez la cautivó.

— Me hiciste quedar como un estúpido. Me obligaste a ir a buscarte. Tú no perteneces a ese lugar. Tú eres mía, y parece que se te olvida quién te ha cuidado todo este tiempo —dijo Federico.

—No se me olvida —dijo ella rápidamente, intentando apaciguar la fiera—. Yo te agradezco todo, pero me estás asustando. Por favor, volvamos a casa. Mañana podemos hablar de esto con calma…

Federico soltó una carcajada seca, un sonido carente de alegría que rebotó contra los cristales cerrados. Se inclinó hacia ella, invadiendo su espacio vital de forma tan brusca que Valentina se pegó instintivamente a la puerta, sintiendo el frío del vidrio en su espalda.

—¿Calma? ¿Quieres calma ahora? —su voz empezó a subir de tono, cargada de una amargura que Valentina no lograba comprender—. Terminaste nuestro compromiso y ahora tú estás ahí, exhibiéndote, dejando que todos te miren como si fueras un premio.

—Yo no me estaba exhibiendo, Federico. No digas eso —susurró ella y, por primera vez, una pizca de la indignación de su crianza afloró en su voz—. Mis padres me enseñaron a respetarme, y eso es lo que hago.

Esa mención a sus valores pareció ser el detonante. Federico golpeó el volante con la palma de la mano, un estruendo que hizo que Valentina saltara en el asiento.

—¡Tus padres! ¡Tus valores! —escupió él—. ¡Estoy harto de tu perfección, Valentina! Siempre tan correcta, siempre tan "la hija ideal". Pero esta noche vas a aprender que aquí la única voluntad que cuenta es la mía. No estás en la cocina de tu mamá ni en la oficina de tu papá. Estás conmigo.

El eco del golpe en el volante aún vibraba en el reducido espacio del coche cuando Federico hizo un movimiento brusco. Valentina, con los ojos apretados y el cuerpo encogido contra la puerta, escuchó un sonido seco, metálico: el roce de algo pesado saliendo de debajo del asiento. Cuando abrió los ojos, el aire se congeló en sus pulmones. Federico no la miraba a ella; miraba el objeto que ahora sostenía en su mano derecha. El cañón de la pistola brillaba con un destello opaco y aceitoso bajo la tenue luz del tablero. Valentina sintió un escalofrío que no nació de la piel, sino del centro mismo de sus huesos. No podía gritar. No podía llorar. Su cuerpo entró en un estado de parálisis absoluta. El mundo se detuvo. El tiempo, que antes corría frenético con los gritos y la velocidad del coche, se congeló en un instante eterno y macabro. Valentina fijó la vista en aquel objeto: el cañón oscuro de la pistola parecía un abismo negro capaz de tragarse toda su luz. Federico la miraba con una fijeza que le helaba la sangre. Sus ojos, que alguna vez le transmitieron una falsa paz, estaban ahora nublados por el alcohol y una posesividad enferma. Su respiración era un fuelle acelerado, ruidoso, que llenaba el habitáculo con un hedor a aguardiente y furia contenida.

—Eres mía, Valentina. No vas a ser de nadie más —sentenció él.

Las palabras salieron de su boca de forma pastosa, arrastradas por la embriaguez, pero cargadas de una determinación asesina. No era una amenaza vacía; era una sentencia que retumbaba contra los vidrios cerrados del coche. Valentina sintió nuevamente el movimiento brusco de Federico y luego el contacto: el cañón de la pistola, gélido y pesado, se hundió contra la suavidad de su frente. Ese roce metálico fue como un choque eléctrico que le recorrió la espina dorsal, una frialdad que parecía querer congelar sus pensamientos. Federico la sostuvo allí, fijamente, con el pulso errático de quien ha perdido el rastro de su propia humanidad. Por fuera, Valentina parecía una estatua de sal bajo la luz tenue del tablero. Pero por dentro, su cuerpo era un epicentro de sismos. Sentía que sus órganos tiritaban, que su sangre golpeaba las paredes de sus venas con un pánico líquido. Buscando un ancla en medio de ese mar de sombras, entrelazó sus manos en su regazo. Las apretó con una fuerza desesperada, hundiendo sus uñas en la piel, sosteniéndose a sí misma con tanta intensidad que sentía que sus propios dedos iban a deshacerse bajo la presión de su angustia. Era la única parte de su cuerpo que podía controlar, el único pedazo de realidad al que podía aferrarse. Y entonces, desde lo más profundo de su ser, emergió su verdadera armadura. No era la estrategia, ni el negocio familiar, ni su reputación. Era su fe.

«Todo lo puedo en Cristo que me fortalece», comenzó a susurrar en su mente, como un mantra que se repetía en un eco infinito. En ese segundo, algo cambió dentro de ella. El pánico se transformó en valentía y un instinto de supervivencia gélido y calculador nació en ella. Valentina dejó de ser la víctima que temblaba para convertirse en la estratega que siempre fue, pero ahora el tablero de ajedrez era su propia vida. Comprendió con claridad que la única salida de ese camino desierto no era la fuerza, sino la manipulación. Tenía que darle a Federico la única droga que lo calmaría: la sensación de dominio total. Valentina comprendió que para salvarse

tenía que convertirse en la mejor actriz de su propia vida. Con el cañón de la pistola todavía hundido en su frente, realizó un esfuerzo de voluntad sobrehumano. Obligó a sus hombros a descender y a sus manos a soltar la presión que ejercían entre sí.

—Tranquilo, amor… —susurró, forzando una dulzura que le quemaba la garganta.

La palabra "amor" emergió de sus labios envuelta en una seda falsa. Una caricia verbal que le producía náuseas físicas, pero su voz no tembló. Sabía que su vida dependía de la frecuencia de ese susurro. Forzó una expresión de entrega, de falsa comprensión, permitiendo que sus ojos se suavizaran como si estuviera mirando al hombre que alguna vez creyó conocer, y no al monstruo que la apuntaba. En su mente, Valentina empezó a mover las piezas. "Si lloro, me mata. Si grito, me mata. Si lo desafío, me mata", razonó con una frialdad mecánica.

La única opción era convertirse en el espejo de lo que él necesitaba ver: una mujer sumisa, devota y asustada solo de perderlo a él, no a su vida. Federico, con los ojos nublados y la respiración aún pesada por el alcohol, pareció vacilar ante ese cambio de frecuencia. El poder que él buscaba ejercer a través del terror se encontró de pronto con un muro de aparente ternura. Valentina observó, con la agudeza de un halcón, cómo la tensión en el dedo de Federico sobre el gatillo cedía apenas un milímetro. El interior del coche se convirtió en un escenario de pesadilla donde Valentina, con el alma blindada por una fe inquebrantable y una inteligencia de acero, ejecutó su papel. Para Federico, aquel cambio era una victoria; para ella, era una operación de rescate de su propia vida.

—Lo siento, Fede… tienes razón, no lo debí hacer —decía ella, armando frases que eran como hilos de seda diseñados para amarrar la furia del animal.

Federico, sintiéndose de nuevo el dueño de la voluntad de Valentina, bajó el arma, pero no la alejó. El metal quedó allí, un recordatorio gélido descansando sobre el asiento, mientras él buscaba en ella una validación que no merecía. El movimiento de Federico fue lento, viscoso, cargado de una confianza renovada por la aparente rendición de Valentina. Él se acercó; la mano que aún sostenía el arma se movió de forma errática y, por un segundo, el frío del metal rozó de nuevo su piel antes de descansar contra su muslo. Valentina no se apartó. Se obligó a ser una estatua de carne que aceptaba el avance del depredador. Él puso una mano en su nuca, apretando con una fuerza que no era de afecto, sino de propiedad. Sus labios se estrellaron contra los de ella de forma torpe, húmeda y violenta. No era un beso; era una marca de territorio. Valentina sintió lo áspero de su barba descuidada raspando su piel y el calor sofocante de su aliento inundando sus sentidos. Por dentro, experimentaba una repulsión que le recorría la espina dorsal como una descarga eléctrica. Sentía náuseas, un deseo primitivo de gritar y limpiarse la boca hasta que la piel le ardiera. Pero su instinto frío y calculador mantuvo sus manos quietas en su regazo.

En lugar de rechazarlo, cerró los ojos y se desdobló. Dejó que su cuerpo estuviera ahí, recibiendo la humillación, mientras su mente se refugiaba en la oración y en la cuenta regresiva. Para que la fiera se calmara, ella debía responder. Con un esfuerzo que le costó parte de su dignidad, le devolvió el contacto con una suavidad mecánica, fingiendo que esa cercanía no la estaba matando por dentro. Él se separó apenas unos milímetros, sus frentes casi tocándose, y Valentina pudo ver el brillo turbio y triunfante en sus pupilas. En ese espacio mínimo entre sus rostros, el aire era escaso y tóxico.

—Así me gusta, Vale… que entiendas quién te ama de verdad —dijo él, con esa voz pastosa.

Estaba comprando su vida segundo a segundo, dejando que él creyera que sus besos habían borrado el terror, cuando en realidad cada roce solo alimentaba la llama de su determinación por escapar y no volver jamás. Valentina soportó sus besos, el olor a alcohol y el roce del arma, devolviéndole palabras bonitas como quien doma a una fiera hambrienta. Cada caricia era una ficha que apostaba para lograr llegar a casa. Con el arma ya descansando entre los dos como una serpiente dormida, Valentina aprovechó el silencio que siguió a sus besos. Sabía que Federico estaba en ese estado de euforia tóxica que sigue al ejercicio del poder; era el momento exacto para atacar con la dulzura.

—Fede, mi amor… —comenzó ella, usando un tono de voz suave, casi arrullador, que contrastaba violentamente con los latidos desbocados de su corazón—. Estamos muy cansados y este no es el lugar para nosotros. Es peligroso, está muy oscuro. Mañana, cuando estemos más tranquilos y hayamos descansado, vamos a sentarnos a hablar de todo. Vamos a arreglar esto, ¿sí? Tú sabes que yo quiero estar contigo, pero necesito ir a mi casa ahora.

Federico la miró de reojo, con los párpados pesados. El alcohol y el cansancio de su propia explosión de ira empezaban a pasarle factura. Valentina no esperó a que él cuestionara su oferta; se inclinó ligeramente hacia él, invadiendo su espacio de forma no amenazante, apelando a su ego.

—Llévame a casa —insistió, forzando una sonrisa tímida en la oscuridad—. Mis papás se van a preocupar si llego más tarde y no quiero que sospechen nada de nuestra discusión. Mañana será un día nuevo para los dos.

Federico soltó un suspiro largo, un bufido de animal domesticado por la vanidad. Las palabras de Valentina —"lo que tenemos", "mañana", "arreglar"— funcionaron como una anestesia. Al mencionar a sus padres, ella tocó la fibra de la respetabilidad que él tanto se esforzaba por mantener ante la familia de ella. Él metió la llave y el motor rugió de nuevo. Ese sonido, que antes le había causado terror, ahora era para Valentina la música de su liberación. Mientras el coche se ponía en marcha y salía de la oscuridad del camino desierto para reincorporarse a la carretera principal, Valentina mantenía su mano sobre el brazo de Federico, dándole pequeñas y rítmicas caricias. Era una tortura física; cada contacto le quemaba la piel, pero era el precio de su pasaje de vuelta. Cuando las primeras luces de la ciudad empezaron a reflejarse en el parabrisas, Valentina sintió que el aire volvía a entrar en sus pulmones, aunque fuera a cuentagotas. Cada poste de luz que dejaban atrás era una victoria silenciosa. Ella seguía alimentando el espejismo, hablando de planes inexistentes para el día siguiente, prometiendo llamadas y encuentros, mientras por dentro su mente ya estaba cerrándole con candado todas las puertas de su vida. Él la miraba de vez en cuando, creyéndose el vencedor de la noche, el hombre que había "puesto en su sitio" a su mujer. No sospechaba que detrás de esa máscara de dulzura y esas promesas de arreglo, Valentina lo estaba desterrando para siempre. Ella ya no era su prometida, ni su socia, ni su amiga; era una sobreviviente que estaba contando los metros que faltaban para que el neumático tocara el asfalto frente a su casa y ella pudiera, finalmente, soltar la mano del hombre que casi le arrebató la vida. El neumático rozó el bordillo de la acera con un sonido seco, marcando el final de la travesía. La fachada de su casa se alzaba frente a ella como un bastión de orden y luz en medio de la negrura de la noche. Federico detuvo el motor y, por un instante, el silencio volvió a ser amenazante. Valentina no esperó a que él se despidiera. No le dio espacio para otra caricia ni tiempo para decir una palabra. Se bajó del coche con un paso firme, una columna vertebral de acero que ocultaba la tormenta que arreciaba en su interior. Sus piernas, que minutos antes se sentían como gelatina, ahora respondían con una precisión militar. Sin embargo, en el hueco de su pecho, su corazón palpitaba con una violencia salvaje, un tamborileo frenético que parecía querer romperle las costillas; era la adrenalina de un atleta que acaba de cruzar la meta tras una carrera contra la muerte. Caminó hacia la entrada sin mirar atrás, sintiendo los ojos de Federico clavados en su espalda. Al girar la llave en la cerradura, el sonido del cerrojo fue la nota más dulce de toda su vida. Entró, cerró la puerta y apoyó la espalda contra la madera fría y sólida. Solo entonces, rodeada del olor a hogar y de la protección de sus muros, Valentina se permitió soltar el aire que parecía haber estado retenido desde la carretera. Subió las escaleras hacia su habitación como quien huye de un incendio. Al cerrar la puerta de su cuarto, el santuario de su intimidad, la máscara de "la mejor actriz de su propia vida" se resquebrajó y cayó al suelo. Pero no fue el llanto lo que surgió de sus grietas; fue la rabia. Una ira pura, incandescente y purificadora inundó sus venas, reemplazando el frío del miedo. La humillación de los besos forzados, el asco del olor a alcohol y el insulto del metal en su frente se transformaron en un fuego que le devolvió el mando de su existencia. Sentada en el borde de su cama, con las manos aún temblorosas pero la mente más lúcida que nunca, tomó el teléfono. Sus dedos volaron sobre la pantalla. Marcó el número de Federico con la determinación de quien firma un decreto irreversible. Cuando él contestó, probablemente esperando escuchar de nuevo la voz dulce y sumisa que lo había "domado" en el coche, se encontró con un muro de hielo. Valentina habló con una voz que él no reconoció: una voz profunda, cortante, despojada de cualquier rastro de la niña que él creía poseer. Era la voz de la estratega, de la mujer de negocios, de la sobreviviente.

—Jamás volverás a apuntarme con un arma —dijo, y cada palabra cayó como una guillotina en el aire—. Y jamás, Federico, volverás a tener un sitio en mi vida.

No esperó respuesta. No necesitaba su explicación, ni sus disculpas borrachas, ni sus promesas de cambio. Presionó el botón de finalizar llamada con una fuerza definitiva. En ese pequeño clic, Valentina no solo terminó una relación; cortó los hilos de una marioneta que se negaba a seguir bailando al ritmo del terror. El silencio que siguió en su habitación ya no era aterrador; era el silencio de un nuevo comienzo, el aire limpio que queda después de que la tormenta, finalmente, se ha marchado.

El silencio que siguió al "clic" del teléfono fue más pesado que los gritos de Federico. Valentina se quedó inmóvil, todavía sosteniendo el celular con un agarre de hierro, como si el aparato fuera el único escudo capaz de mantener a raya el mundo exterior.

Sus manos, que habían permanecido engañosamente firmes durante su "actuación" magistral en el coche, finalmente la traicionaron. Empezaron a temblar con una rapidez eléctrica que le recorrió los brazos, los hombros y terminó sacudiéndole todo el cuerpo. No era solo el miedo residual; era una náusea visceral y profunda. Sentía en sus labios el rastro del alcohol de él y, en su frente, la marca invisible pero ardiente del cañón de la pistola. El asco de haber tenido que besar y acariciar al hombre que, segundos antes, calculaba su muerte la golpeó como una ola física. Sin fuerzas para sostenerse, se deslizó lentamente hasta el suelo, abrazando sus rodillas contra el pecho en un intento desesperado por contener el temblor. La luz de la luna entraba por la ventana en láminas plateadas y frías, dibujando sombras alargadas sobre la alfombra que ahora le parecían dedos negros que la alcanzaban, tratando de arrastrarla de vuelta a la oscuridad de la carretera. Cerró los ojos, pero no hubo alivio. En su mente se proyectaba, en un bucle infinito, la imagen de Federico: sus ojos turbios, el sudor en su frente y ese brillo metálico y letal apuntándola. Podía sentir de nuevo el frío del acero rozando su piel, una sensación que sabía que tardaría años en borrarse. De pronto, la pantalla de su teléfono se iluminó de nuevo, rasgando la penumbra de la habitación con un brillo blanco y agresivo. Valentina contuvo el aliento, sintiendo que el corazón se le subía a la garganta.

No era una llamada. Era un mensaje de un número desconocido, pero la redacción, el tono y la obsesión eran inconfundibles:

"Esto no acaba aquí, yo sé que me amas como yo te amo".
El aire se escapó de sus pulmones. El mensaje en la pantalla fue como un disparo, esta vez directo a su sentido de seguridad. Se quedó inmóvil por un segundo; su mente se congeló. Miró a su alrededor y, en ese momento, se dio cuenta de que, en un parpadeo, las paredes que antes representaban su fortaleza se habían vuelto traslúcidas. Su casa, su refugio sagrado, se había transformado de repente en una pecera de cristal frente a un depredador que conocía cada uno de sus movimientos, sus horarios y sus miedos. Se sintió expuesta, exhibida bajo una luz vulnerable, mientras él acechaba desde las sombras del exterior. El mensaje no era una declaración de amor; era una amenaza envuelta en un delirio. Valentina comprendió en ese instante que Federico no solo era un

hombre violento, sino alguien que habitaba una realidad distorsionada donde el control era sinónimo de afecto. La "sentencia final" que ella acababa de dictar por teléfono no había cerrado un capítulo; había iniciado una guerra. Soltó el teléfono como si el aparato quemara, dejándolo caer sobre la alfombra, pero el silencio que inundó la habitación no le trajo la paz que buscaba; era un silencio cargado, espeso, que amplificaba el eco de la amenaza de Federico. Valentina giró la cabeza hacia la puerta de su habitación. Sabía que, a solo unos metros, al final del pasillo, sus padres y sus tres hermanos mayores descansaban, sumergidos en el ritmo tranquilo de una noche normal. El impulso de correr hacia ellos fue una marea física, una presión insoportable en el pecho. Visualizó la escena: irrumpir en sus cuartos, sentir el abrazo protector de sus hermanos —aquellos guerreros que la habían cuidado siempre— y sollozar hasta que las palabras salieran: *"Federico me apuntó con un arma"*.

Deseaba, con cada fibra de su ser, deshacerse de esa carga, entregarles a ellos el miedo y que su fuerza de hombres la pusiera a salvo. Pero el miedo la detuvo. Conocía a sus hermanos; sabía que, si se enteraban, el orgullo y la rabia los llevarían directo a buscar a Federico. Se imaginó sus reacciones, la furia ciega de hombres que no permitirían que nadie tocara a su hermana, y el rastro de sangre y dolor que vendría después si ellos salían a buscar justicia. No podía arriesgar sus vidas. La carga era solo suya. Con las piernas todavía entumecidas, Valentina se obligó a ponerse de pie. Cada movimiento le pesaba, como si la gravedad hubiera duplicado su fuerza sobre ella. Cruzó la habitación en penumbra hacia el baño privado, moviéndose con la inercia de un fantasma. Al entrar, la luz blanca del espejo la golpeó con una crueldad necesaria. Se quedó allí, observando su reflejo como si mirara a una desconocida. Tenía el maquillaje corrido, los labios ligeramente hinchados y una palidez que la hacía parecer de mármol. Pero lo que más le dolió fue verse los ojos: quedaba en ellos un rastro del terror animal que Federico había desatado. Se despojó de la ropa de esa noche con movimientos mecánicos y casi con asco. Cada prenda que caía al suelo se sentía como una capa de suciedad que se desprendía de su piel. Se puso ropa de dormir, buscando el refugio de la tela suave y limpia, intentando desesperadamente recuperar una sensación de normalidad que se le escapaba entre los dedos. Se acercó al lavamanos y abrió el grifo. El sonido del agua corriendo fue el único permiso que necesitó para quebrarse. Al principio, solo fueron espasmos silenciosos que le sacudían los hombros, pero en cuanto el agua fría tocó su rostro, la contención se rompió. Mientras se lavaba la cara con una urgencia casi maníaca, frotando su frente justo donde había sentido el metal frío de la pistola, el llanto surgió desde lo más profundo de sus entrañas. No era un llanto delicado; era un desahogo amargo, una purga de toda la carga, la humillación y el terror que había tenido que tragar para sobrevivir. Lloró por la Valentina que creyó en el amor, lloró por el asco de los besos forzados y por la traición del hombre que juró cuidarla. El agua se mezclaba con sus lágrimas, lavando el rastro del aliento de Federico. Se sostenía de los bordes del lavabo con tanta fuerza que sus nudillos volvieron a blanquearse, mientras sollozaba en voz baja, ahogando los gritos en la toalla para no despertar a su familia. En ese pequeño espacio iluminado, Valentina se permitió ser vulnerable por última vez esa noche. Cada gota de agua que caía por el desagüe se llevaba un poco de la "actriz" que había tenido que ser, dejando solo a una mujer herida que, en medio del llanto, empezaba a comprender que ya no quedaba nada de su antigua vida. El espejo le devolvía la imagen de alguien que acababa de pasar por el fuego; estaba quemada, sí, pero seguía en pie. Sintiéndose pequeña, casi quebrada por el peso asfixiante del secreto que cargaba, Valentina se dejó caer de rodillas en medio de la habitación. El suelo de madera se sentía sólido bajo ella, el único punto de apoyo en un mundo que acababa de desmoronarse. No buscó llamar a la policía ni justicia en los hombres; buscó ayuda de algo más alto.

—Por favor… —susurró con los ojos cerrados, hundiendo la barbilla en su pecho. Sus manos estaban entrelazadas con tanta fuerza que los nudillos le dolían, como si quisiera estrujar de su propia alma una respuesta—. Dios, dame una señal. Ilumíname. Dime cómo salir de esto sin que nadie más salga herido. Necesito irme, necesito poner tierra de por medio.

Se quedó allí, en una quietud absoluta, dejando que el eco de su súplica llenara el vacío de la habitación. Poco a poco, el temblor de su cuerpo cedió y su respiración, antes errática y rota, se calmó hasta volverse un ritmo constante. Al abrir los ojos, la habitación seguía igual, pero su percepción había cambiado. En la oscuridad, su mirada se posó en un pequeño punto de luz: la luz LED intermitente de su computadora sobre el escritorio. Como si una mano invisible pero firme la guiara desde el centro de su espalda, Valentina se levantó. Caminó hacia el escritorio y, con un movimiento lento, abrió la tapa de la laptop. El resplandor de la pantalla iluminó su rostro cansado, bañándolo en una luz azulada que parecía traer consigo una claridad nueva. Ahí, frente a ella, estaba el archivo en el que había estado trabajando durante meses, casi como un sueño lejano: el plan de negocios para una cafetería y repostería artesanal. Lo que empezó como un proyecto de pasión se iluminó en su mente como la llave de su celda. En ese instante de claridad absoluta, su mente de estratega conectó los puntos a gran velocidad. Se dio cuenta de que ese documento no era solo una meta profesional: era una herramienta legal de extracción. El rigor con el que había detallado cada inversión y la viabilidad del concepto eran los requisitos exactos para una Visa de Inversionista en Estados Unidos. Valentina recorrió con los dedos la pantalla, acariciando las palabras que ahora eran su promesa de supervivencia. La idea la golpeó con la fuerza de una revelación divina. Comprendió que Dios le había permitido construir su propia salida mucho antes de que ella supiera que la necesitaría. La cafetería dejó de ser un sueño para convertirse en una misión de rescate. No era solo un negocio; era su salvoconducto. Era la distancia necesaria para que Federico no pudiera volver a tocarla nunca. Mientras el cursor parpadeaba, Valentina pasó en vela toda la noche ultimando los detalles de su propuesta de inversión. Esa noche no solo diseñó un negocio; diseñó su libertad. Valentina finalmente encontró tierra firme en su propio ingenio. Con el plan de negocios brillando en la pantalla como una promesa, cerró la laptop con una suavidad que contrastaba con la violencia de la noche. Se movió hacia la cama y, por fin, sintió que sus músculos dejaban de ser cuerdas tensas a punto de romperse. Al recostarse, cerró los ojos. El contacto de su cabeza con la almohada no trajo las imágenes del cañón del arma de fuego, sino el aroma imaginario del café recién tostado y el azúcar glas de su futura repostería. Una ilusión eléctrica, vibrante y nueva empezó a correrle por las venas. Ya no era la adrenalina del miedo; era la energía del propósito. En la oscuridad de su cuarto, Valentina empezó a tejer la red que la sostendría.

Capítulo 7:

El sueño en marcha

En la mañana siguiente, frente al desayuno familiar, no habría rastro de la mujer quebrada. Al amanecer les presentaría a sus padres la propuesta de su vida. Les hablaría de expansión, de mercados internacionales y de la oportunidad única de llevar su talento a Estados Unidos.

Sabía que necesitaba su apoyo, no solo emocional, sino también financiero. Una parte dolorosa de su realidad era que gran parte de sus ahorros estaban atrapados en el negocio de Federico, un dinero que él le había "pedido prestado" y que ahora funcionaba como una cadena más. Recuperar ese capital sería una batalla perdida o peligrosa, por lo que presentar este nuevo proyecto a sus padres era su jugada maestra.

A pesar de la oscuridad que la había rodeado horas antes, el amanecer entró en la habitación de Valentina con una claridad casi profética. Cuando abrió los ojos, no hubo el peso de la derrota, sino el impulso eléctrico de un nuevo propósito. La luz del sol que se colaba por las cortinas traía consigo la frescura de una página en blanco.

Se levantó con una firmeza renovada, como si el suelo bajo sus pies fuera ahora tierra conquistada. Mientras se preparaba, cada gesto era un acto de guerra contra su pasado reciente. Se lavó la cara con agua helada, se cepilló los dientes y se miró al espejo con la cabeza en alto. La mujer que veía no era una víctima; era la arquitecta de una fuga maestra.

Su motivación no nacía solamente del deseo de huir, sino de la pasión por emprender. La idea de su cafetería, del aroma a canela y café en un lugar donde nadie conociera su miedo, le devolvió el brillo a su mirada. Su mente estaba enfocada en la meta con la precisión de quien apunta a la mira sin parpadear. Al bajar las escaleras, el sonido de la casa despertando —el tintineo de las cucharas, las voces tranquilas de sus hermanos— la llenó de una energía vibrante. Sentía una urgencia positiva, un entusiasmo que le quemaba en el pecho. No iba a bajar a pedir refugio; iba a presentar una oportunidad de oro.

Caminaba con la espalda recta, cargando su laptop como quien porta un tesoro. Sabía que ese día marcaría el antes y el después. El miedo seguía siendo una cicatriz, pero su visión del porvenir era un faro. Valentina comprendió que Federico pudo haberle apuntado con un arma, pero jamás pudo tocar su capacidad de soñar, y era precisamente ese sueño el que le daría las alas que necesitaría para volar tan lejos que él nunca la pudiera alcanzar.

El sol de la mañana se filtraba por las ventanas del comedor, creando una atmósfera de paz que contrastaba violentamente con la tormenta que Valentina acababa de sobrevivir. Sobre la mesa, entre el café y el pan recién horneado, abrió su computadora y desplegó los planos de su futuro. En ese momento, no era la mujer que había temblado frente a un arma; era la estratega, la artista y la empresaria. Sus padres y sus tres hermanos se inclinaron hacia la pantalla, cautivados por la claridad de su visión.

Con una determinación que emanaba de cada poro, Valentina comenzó a desglosar el proyecto. No era un sueño vago; era un estudio de mercado impecable. Les mostró el análisis de la competencia en Estados Unidos, el flujo de caja proyectado y los detalles técnicos de la maquinaria de alta gama que ya había cotizado: hornos de convección especializados, batidoras industriales y máquinas de espresso de última generación.

—No es solo una cafetería, papá. Es una experiencia artesanal —decía mientras les enseñaba el logo que ella misma había diseñado: elegante, limpio y con un nombre que evocaba hogar y sofisticación a la vez.

Les habló del tipo de repostería que servirían: recetas familiares elevadas con técnicas modernas, masas madre fermentadas con paciencia y postres que eran pequeñas obras de arte. Cada vez que mencionaba un detalle, su voz ganaba una convicción tan poderosa que el aire en el comedor parecía vibrar. Su emoción era contagiosa, pero era su preparación técnica lo que realmente los dejaba sin aliento. Sus padres, que conocían bien el talento de su hija pero nunca la habían visto con esa mirada de acero, quedaron desarmados. Vieron en ella no solo a la "hija ideal", sino a una líder lista para conquistar un mercado extranjero.

—Hija, esto no es solo un plan de negocios. Es una obra maestra —comentó su padre, ajustándose los lentes mientras revisaba las tablas de inversión.

La determinación que había nacido en el coche la noche anterior se traducía ahora en una pasión profesional que no dejaba lugar a dudas. La urgencia que Valentina sentía por escapar se disfrazaba de una ambición empresarial brillante. Sus padres, convencidos por la solidez del proyecto, no dudaron.

—Si vamos a hacer esto, lo haremos bien. Vamos a contactar a un abogado de inmigración hoy mismo —sentenció su madre, conmovida por la fuerza de Valentina—. Queremos ver si esta propuesta es el camino acertado para esa visa de inversionista. Si el abogado da el visto bueno, tienes nuestro apoyo total.

Valentina asintió, manteniendo una sonrisa profesional mientras por dentro lanzaba un grito de alivio. Al ver a su familia unida, planeando el contacto con el abogado y discutiendo los detalles legales de la inversión, supo que su plan estaba funcionando.

Sus padres ya tenían la idea de que invertirían en un negocio en el extranjero, pero lo que no sabían era que con cada llamada y cada documento que revisaban estaban construyendo el muro que la protegería de Federico. Su inteligencia había logrado lo imposible: transformar su tragedia personal en una oportunidad de éxito, comprando su libertad con la moneda de su propio talento. Cruzar la frontera no sería solo un viaje; sería interponer un océano de leyes, aeropuertos y miles de kilómetros entre su cuello y las manos de Federico. Estados Unidos no era solo un mercado nuevo; era el territorio donde él no tendría jurisdicción, donde su nombre no significaba nada y donde su rastro se perdería en la inmensidad de una nueva vida. Aquel día, el aire en la casa tenía un peso distinto, una electricidad silenciosa que lo cargaba todo. Valentina apenas había probado bocado; su mente era un cronómetro que contaba los segundos hacia la cita que definiría su existencia. Cuando el reloj marcó la hora acordada, ella y sus padres se dirigieron, casi en procesión, hacia la oficina de la casa para esperar la llamada con los abogados que tanto habían ansiado. Sabían que de esa conversación dependía lograr cumplir el sueño que estaban anhelando. La oficina en casa de los padres de Valentina era un refugio de madera oscura, estantes repletos de libros de contabilidad y un suave aroma a papel viejo y cera de muebles. Era el lugar donde se tomaban las decisiones importantes de la familia, el santuario donde se planificaba el futuro con rigor y prudencia. Valentina estaba sentada frente al escritorio de caoba, flanqueada por sus padres, quienes mantenían la vista fija en el teléfono celular situado en el centro, como si de aquel pequeño aparato fuera a emanar su destino. El dispositivo vibró sobre la madera noble y el corazón de Valentina dio un vuelco. Sus padres intercambiaron una mirada de determinación antes de presionar el altavoz. Al otro lado de la línea, desde Estados Unidos, la voz de la abogada de inmigración rompió el silencio con una seguridad que caló hasta los huesos de Valentina.

—He analizado cada página del proyecto que Valentina envió —dijo la abogada, y su tono cambió de lo profesional a una genuina admiración—. Y quiero ser muy sincera: es impresionante. Valentina, me cuesta creer que alguien de tu edad haya desarrollado una estructura de costos y un plan de marketing tan maduros. Es un proyecto increíble y sumamente prometedor.

Hubo una pequeña pausa, y la abogada bajó el tono, hablando con la honestidad de quien conoce bien los pasillos de inmigración.

—Miren, les hablaré con total transparencia. Lo único que tenemos "en contra" es la corta edad de Valentina. A los ojos del consulado, ella es muy joven para manejar una inversión de esta magnitud en un mercado extranjero. Es un factor que ellos siempre miran con lupa. Pero... —hizo énfasis en la palabra— la solidez de lo que ella creó es tan impactante que ese riesgo vale la pena correrlo. No les puedo prometer al cien por ciento que lo aprobarán debido a su juventud, pero les aseguro que este proyecto tiene la fuerza suficiente para dar la pelea. Vale la pena arriesgarse e intentarlo porque es un negocio excepcional.

En ese instante, Valentina sintió un calor ascendente que reemplazó el frío que Federico había dejado en su piel. Sus padres se miraron. En el rostro de su padre no hubo duda, solo la confirmación de que su hija era capaz de eso y más. La palabra "arriesgarse" no asustó a Valentina; después de haber sentido un arma en su frente, cualquier riesgo empresarial le parecía una bendición.

—Si la abogada dice que vale la pena, nosotros no vamos a dar un paso atrás —sentenció su padre con firmeza, mirando a Valentina con un orgullo que casi la hizo llorar—. Si el riesgo es su edad, nosotros seremos su respaldo hasta que vean de lo que ella es capaz.

—Procedamos entonces —añadió su madre, apretando la mano de Valentina—. Queremos iniciar los trámites hoy mismo.

Para Valentina, el sonido de sus padres discutiendo términos legales y financieros era la melodía más hermosa que había escuchado. Federico creía que la tenía atrapada en su red de deudas y amenazas, pero en esa habitación, protegida por el amor de sus padres y la fuerza de su propia inteligencia, Valentina ya se visualizaba cruzando el océano. La inversión no era solo dinero; era la construcción de un nuevo horizonte donde el eco de la pólvora seca jamás volvería a escucharse.

Capítulo 8:

La arquitectura del escape

Los meses que siguieron fueron una coreografía perfecta entre la ambición empresarial y un plan de fuga meticuloso. Para el mundo, y especialmente para sus tres hermanos mayores, Valentina estaba simplemente conquistando sus sueños. Solo ella sabía que cada documento firmado y cada maleta empacada eran ladrillos de un muro que estaba construyendo entre su vida y el cañón de una pistola. La preparación de la visa de inversión se convirtió en su obsesión y su refugio. Valentina pasaba noches enteras frente al monitor, perfeccionando los planos de la que sería su cafetería en Estados Unidos. El aroma de la repostería, que antes era solo un placer, ahora olía a libertad. Cada receta, cada estudio de mercado y cada trámite legal eran piezas de un rompecabezas que la alejaba de su verdugo. Mantener el secreto frente a sus hermanos era la parte más difícil. Sus tres hermanos, protectores por naturaleza, a menudo le preguntaban por la prisa repentina. Sabían que ella era ambiciosa, pero la urgencia en sus ojos les resultaba inusual.

—¿Por qué tan rápido, Vale? Quédate unos meses más —le decía Javier durante una de las cenas, mientras la observaba revisar documentos en su teléfono—. Ni siquiera hemos celebrado bien tu decisión. Aquí tienes todo, no hay necesidad de salir corriendo.

Julio asintió, dejando los cubiertos a un lado.

—Tiene razón. Un proyecto de esta magnitud requiere tiempo. No queremos que te vayas a lo loco, hermanita. Si es por el dinero que le prestaste a Federico, nosotros podemos ayudarte a recuperarlo para que te vayas con más tranquilidad después.

Joaquín, el más observador de los tres, no dejaba de notar cómo Valentina esquivaba ciertas preguntas.

—Parece que estuvieras huyendo de algo, no solo yendo hacia algo.

Valentina les sonreía, forzando una calma que era puramente interpretativa, ocultando un miedo que la devoraba por dentro. No podía decirles que cada vez que un coche frenaba bruscamente frente a la casa, ella contenía la respiración, temiendo que fuera Federico bajando con la misma mirada desquiciada de aquella noche. No podía contarles que Federico seguía enviando mensajes, a veces suplicantes, jurando que "cambiaría", y a veces cargados de una furia pasivo-agresiva que le helaba la sangre.

—Es por el mercado, de verdad —mentía Valentina, sintiendo que la lengua le pesaba—. La abogada dice que los tiempos de la visa son caprichosos. Si no tomo acción ahora, pierdo el cupo del local que tengo visto. Solo quiero que mi futuro sea sólido.

Sabía que, si pronunciaba el nombre de Federico en el contexto real, si mencionaba el arma o el olor a alcohol sobre su rostro, sus tres hermanos se convertirían en una fuerza destructiva que terminaría con ellos en la cárcel o con Federico muerto. No podía permitir que la toxicidad de su exnovio manchara la vida de los hombres que más amaba. Cada pregunta de sus hermanos era un recordatorio de la burbuja en la que ellos vivían y de la guerra solitaria que ella libraba. Mientras ellos hablaban de logística y despedidas, ella solo pensaba en el sello de la visa como el escudo definitivo. El proyecto no era solo su éxito profesional; era la única forma de mantener a sus hermanos a salvo de su propia protección.

El asedio de Federico no se detuvo con el silencio de Valentina; al contrario, se volvió una sombra invisible que la perseguía en cada rincón de su rutina. Su teléfono era un campo de batalla: las notificaciones de llamadas perdidas se acumulaban como advertencias silenciosas. Ella no contestaba, pero el simple brillo de la pantalla con su nombre le provocaba una sacudida de náuseas. Cada salida de casa, incluso un trayecto tan mundano como ir al supermercado, se sentía como una misión de infiltración en territorio enemigo. El mundo exterior ya no era un lugar seguro; era un espacio abierto donde ella estaba expuesta. Esa tarde, mientras Valentina manejaba de regreso, el instinto que nació la noche que Federico la amenazó se activó de golpe. Por el espejo retrovisor divisó dos motocicletas con los conductores totalmente cubiertos por cascos oscuros. Vio cómo se emparejaban por un segundo, intercambiando lo que parecía ser una instrucción rápida, antes de colocarse estratégicamente detrás de su vehículo. Valentina sintió que se le iba a salir el corazón por la garganta, pero su mente se puso en guardia.

"«No entres en pánico. Piensa», se ordenó. Aceleró ligeramente, y las motos aceleraron al unísono. Cambió de carril sin poner la luz de giro, intentando tomarlas por sorpresa, pero los conductores imitaron su movimiento con precisión. La estaban siguiendo. En ese instante, el aire empezó a faltarle. Sentía que sus pulmones se cerraban, como si la cabina del coche se estuviera quedando sin oxígeno, pero Valentina no se permitió el lujo de desmayarse. Su mente, decidida a salvarse, tomó el volante: analizó las calles, los semáforos y los posibles desvíos. Vio una luz ámbar a punto de cambiar a rojo en una intersección concurrida. Aceleró con prisa, hundiendo el pie en el pedal, y en el último microsegundo dio un giro brusco hacia la derecha, metiéndose por una calle estrecha y en sentido contrario por apenas unos metros. Escuchó el chirrido de los neumáticos y el rugido de las motos intentando maniobrar tras ella, pero el tráfico del cruce se interpuso entre ellos. Manejó por callejones que conocía desde niña, doblando en cada esquina posible, con los ojos inyectados en adrenalina, vigilando cada sombra. Solo cuando estuvo segura de que el rugido de los motores se había perdido en la distancia, enfiló hacia su casa a toda velocidad.

Al llegar, frenó de forma errática, bajó del coche y entró a la casa como un vendaval. Sus padres estaban en la cocina, pero ella no se detuvo. Subió corriendo las gradas, evitando cualquier contacto visual, ignorando las llamadas de su madre, que preguntaba si todo estaba bien. Se encerró en su cuarto, girando la llave con una urgencia maníaca. Solo entonces, apoyada contra la puerta, se permitió derrumbarse. Se deslizó hasta el suelo y se puso a llorar, un llanto roto y seco que nacía del agotamiento absoluto. Las piernas y las manos le temblaban con una violencia tal que tuvo que abrazarse a sí misma para no sentir que se desarmaba. El terror de la persecución se mezclaba con la rabia de sentirse presa en su propia ciudad. En ese suelo, rodeada de la paz de su habitación, que ahora se sentía tan frágil, Valentina comprendió que no le quedaba tiempo. Federico no iba a dejarla ir por las buenas. Cada sollozo era una confirmación: necesitaba esa visa, necesitaba ese avión, necesitaba que el océano se interpusiera entre ella y el hombre que la estaba cazando. Los días que siguieron a la persecución se convirtieron en una especie de arresto domiciliario autoimpuesto. Valentina transformó su habitación en un búnker de alta tecnología y emociones contenidas. El mundo exterior ya no le parecía atractivo. Solo se permitía salir para trayectos cortos y controlados: la casa de su abuela, donde el olor a jazmín y café árabe le daba un respiro momentáneo, o las casas de sus amigos más íntimos, quienes la recibían sin hacer demasiadas preguntas sobre su palidez. Evitaba cualquier centro comercial, restaurante o plaza pública. Para ella, cada rostro desconocido en una esquina era un informante potencial de Federico, y cada motor de motocicleta que rugía a lo lejos le provocaba un sismo interno que intentaba disimular con una sonrisa fría. Dentro de su casa, Valentina mantenía una fachada perfecta. Se instalaba en el comedor o en la oficina con su laptop, rodeada de libretas llenas de anotaciones, presupuestos y catálogos de mobiliario para su futura cafetería.

—Estoy aprovechando cada segundo para que, cuando llegue la cita en la Embajada Americana, no haya ni un solo error —les decía a sus padres y hermanos cuando pasaban junto a ella.

Ellos la veían con admiración. Javier, Julio y Joaquín comentaban entre ellos lo orgullosos que estaban de su disciplina. No sospechaban que detrás de ese enfoque desmedido en el plan de negocios, Valentina estaba escondiendo un terror paralizante. No era solo ambición; era una carrera contra el tiempo. Cada vez que estudiaba un gráfico de rentabilidad, en realidad estaba contando los días que le faltaban para ser libre. Su "preparación" era su armadura; mientras ellos veían a una empresaria, ella estaba siendo una sobreviviente que construía su propia balsa de rescate. Sin embargo, conseguir esa visa no era lo único que ocupaba su mente. Tenía otra preocupación constante. El teléfono celular, que descansaba sobre el escritorio junto a sus planos de diseño, era una fuente constante de ansiedad. Federico no paraba de buscarla y presionarla; era obsesivo. Las llamadas llegaban a cualquier hora: a las tres de la mañana, cuando la casa estaba en un silencio sepulcral, o al mediodía, interrumpiendo sus pensamientos. Valentina mantenía el teléfono en silencio, pero el brillo de la pantalla iluminando el techo o la mesa era como una puñalada visual. Los mensajes eran un carrusel de manipulación hostigante que le helaba la sangre:

"¿Crees que puedes ignorarme para siempre? Sabes que nadie te conoce como yo".

"Vi tu coche ayer cerca de casa de tu abuela. Te ves hermosa, pero te ves sola".

"No me obligues a ir a buscarte a tu casa, Valentina. Solo quiero hablar".

Valentina los leía con la respiración contenida, sintiendo que él podía verla a través de la cámara, que su presencia era una niebla tóxica que se filtraba por las rendijas de las puertas. En esos momentos, se ponía las manos frente a la cara, hundiendo los dedos en sus sienes y cerrando los ojos con una preocupación que le tensaba cada músculo del cuello. Miraba el logo de su cafetería en la pantalla y repetía para sí misma: *"Falta poco. Resiste".*
Su vida se había reducido a eso: fingir frente a su familia y sostener un duelo silencioso contra un acosador, mientras esperaba que el gobierno de otro país le otorgara el papel que, finalmente, le devolvería el aire.

Capítulo 9:

El boleto a la libertad

El día que parecía una meta inalcanzable finalmente había llegado. El calendario marcaba la fecha de la cita en la Embajada Americana, el punto de inflexión entre su pasado de sombras y su futuro de libertad. Esa mañana, Valentina madrugó antes de que el primer rayo de sol tocara su ventana. No hubo dudas ni pereza; se movió con la certeza de quien sabe que está a punto de jugar la partida más importante de su vida. Revisó una última vez la carpeta que contenía su destino: el plan de negocios, los certificados bancarios, la carta de la abogada y cada documento que probaba su visión. El estómago se le había encogido tanto por los nervios que la simple idea de probar bocado le resultaba imposible. Salió de su casa directo a la cita, sin desayunar, con el corazón latiendo con fuerzas contra sus costillas, pero con la espalda más recta que nunca. Mientras manejaba hacia la embajada, el trayecto se convirtió en un santuario. Valentina comenzó a orar con una devoción profunda. No era una súplica desesperada, sino un pacto de confianza.

—Señor, aquí estoy —susurró mientras sus manos apretaban el volante—. Si este es el camino que tienes para mí, abre todas las puertas. Te entrego mi miedo, te entrego a mi familia y te entrego este sueño. Que se haga Tu voluntad.

En ese instante, una sensación casi física de alivio la recorrió. Fue como si un peso de toneladas se desprendiera de sus hombros y se lo entregara a Dios. El nudo en su garganta no desapareció del todo, pero la carga ya no era solo suya. Se encomendó a su fe y, por primera vez en semanas, sintió que no estaba sola frente a la adversidad. A pesar de que llegó mucho antes de la hora acordada, al acercarse a la embajada se encontró con una larga fila que serpenteaba fuera de las puertas de hierro. Valentina se colocó al final de la hilera, abrazando su carpeta de documentos contra el pecho como si fuera un escudo de oro. Cada segundo que pasaba se sentía eterno, una gota de tiempo que caía lentamente en un océano de ansiedad. Para distraer su mente de la presión, comenzó a observar los detalles a su alrededor con una nitidez absoluta. Miraba los carros pasar por la avenida, escuchaba a los pájaros cantar en los árboles cercanos y sentía la brisa de la mañana en su rostro. Sin embargo, detrás de esa observación tranquila, su mente trabajaba a mil por hora. Repasaba mentalmente cada gráfico de su proyecto, cada respuesta sobre su inversión y la logística de su repostería. Imaginaba al oficial consular frente a ella y ensayaba, una y otra vez, las respuestas claras y seguras que daría. No iba a permitir que su corta edad fuera un obstáculo; iba a demostrar que su determinación era más grande que cualquier cifra o prejuicio. Estaba allí, en la fila, pero en su mente ya estaba cruzando la frontera hacia su nueva vida. El cansancio físico empezaba a pasarle factura, pero su voluntad era de piedra. Después de haber permanecido de pie por horas bajo el sol intermitente, avanzando centímetro a centímetro en aquella fila que parecía no tener fin, Valentina finalmente cruzó el pasillo de seguridad. El aire acondicionado del gran salón de la embajada la recibió con un golpe de frío que le erizó la piel, refrescando su rostro, pero no sus nervios. Se sentó en una de las hileras de sillas metálicas, apretando su carpeta contra las rodillas.

A su alrededor, el salón era un murmullo constante de voces bajas, el tecleo de las computadoras y el sonido de los turnos siendo anunciados por los altavoces. Valentina se obligó a respirar profundo, tratando de relajar los músculos de sus piernas, que todavía le dolían por el esfuerzo de la espera. Miró a las personas a su alrededor: rostros cargados de ansiedad, familias enteras esperando una respuesta, empresarios revisando documentos.

En ese espacio, todos eran iguales ante la ley, pero ella sentía que su lucha era distinta; para ella, ese turno no era solo un trámite, era su salida de emergencia. Mantuvo la mirada fija en las pantallas, esperando ver su nombre. Cada vez que un oficial llamaba a alguien, su pecho se oprimía por dentro. Se sentía pequeña en ese salón inmenso, pero, a la vez, sentía una fuerza interna que nunca antes había experimentado. Repasó mentalmente sus argumentos por última vez, visualizando el éxito, hasta que finalmente la voz del altavoz pronunció con claridad su nombre completo. Era su turno. El eco de su nombre resonó en el gran salón de la embajada como una campana que anunciaba el juicio final. Valentina se puso en pie, sostuvo la carpeta contra su costado y caminó hacia la ventanilla con una elegancia que ocultaba el hecho de que sus pies apenas sentían el suelo. Al llegar, se encontró frente a un hombre de mediana edad, con el rostro curtido por años de evaluar destinos. Sus ojos, enmarcados por unas gafas metálicas, eran dos rendijas de escepticismo. No hubo saludos cordiales. El agente extendió la mano, tomó el folder y, con un movimiento mecánico, comenzó a hojear la vida de Valentina: sus ahorros, su estudio de mercado, el diseño de su marca. El silencio en ese cubículo era tan espeso que Valentina podía oír el roce del papel contra los dedos del oficial. De repente, él cerró el folder con un golpe seco y levantó la mirada. Fue una mirada firme, directa, diseñada para resquebrajar a los que mienten o a los que dudan. Sin preámbulos, comenzó el interrogatorio. Valentina contestó cada pregunta mostrándose totalmente segura de sí misma, aunque por dentro sentía una corriente que recorría todo su cuerpo: explicaba los costos de operación, la selección de la maquinaria y la visión de expansión futura. Su voz era clara, sin un solo quiebre. Entonces, el agente se reclinó en su silla, cruzó los brazos y lanzó la estocada final, la pregunta que colgaba en el aire desde que ella entró:

—Valentina, tienes apenas 21 años. Es una inversión importante y un mercado difícil. ¿Cómo es que alguien tan joven va a tener la experiencia suficiente para manejar un negocio como este?

El aire pareció detenerse. En cualquier otra circunstancia, una joven de su edad se habría encogido, pero Valentina recordó el frío del arma en su frente, recordó las motos persiguiéndola y recordó que el fracaso no era una opción porque significaba volver al terror. Sin titubear un segundo, con la espalda recta y los ojos fijos en los del oficial, contestó:

—Desde que tengo uso de razón sé lo que son los negocios. Me crié en el rubro del negocio de mis padres; no es solo teoría para mí, es mi lengua materna. Es algo que siempre me ha apasionado y, en cuanto tuve la edad suficiente, asumí un cargo en su empresa. Con fervor me dediqué a aprender, a crecer desde adentro y a desenvolverme lo suficiente para hoy poder hacerme cargo de mi propio proyecto y llevarlo al éxito.

Mi edad no es una falta de experiencia; es mi mayor ventaja: tengo la energía, la formación y la determinación que este negocio exige.

El agente la observó en silencio durante unos segundos que parecieron siglos. Buscaba un rastro de arrogancia o de duda, pero solo encontró una convicción inquebrantable. Era una "jovencita" físicamente, pero la mujer que le hablaba tenía la madurez de quien ha sobrevivido a una tormenta. Lentamente, el hombre tomó el pasaporte de Valentina. Abrió una gaveta, sacó el sello y, con un movimiento cargado de fuerza y rapidez definitivas, lo estampó sobre la página en blanco. El sonido del sello golpeando el papel fue, para Valentina, el sonido de las cadenas rompiéndose.

El oficial, con una sonrisa medio cerrada —esa expresión de quien se ve obligado a admirar la audacia de la juventud, aunque no quiera admitirlo—, le deslizó el documento de vuelta.

—Aprobado —dijo con un tono de respeto apenas disimulado.

Valentina tomó su pasaporte. Sintió el calor del sello fresco a través de la cubierta. No solo tenía una visa; tenía las llaves de su libertad. Al darse la vuelta para salir, el aire de la embajada ya no se sentía pesado. Ahora, cada paso que daba la alejaba de Federico y la acercaba al primer día del resto de su vida.

Cuando Valentina cruzó las puertas automáticas de salida y sintió el sol de la mañana en su rostro, el aire ya no era el mismo. Lo que sentía no era solo alivio; era una alegría desbordante que parecía vibrar en cada una de las partículas de su cuerpo. Sus hombros estaban ligeros y el nudo de hierro que Federico había instalado en su pecho se había desatado por completo.

Caminó hacia el estacionamiento con un paso elástico, casi flotando. Al entrar a la seguridad de su coche, cerró la puerta y se quedó un segundo en silencio, observando el pasaporte con el sello fresco. Había logrado el paso más difícil, el cimiento sobre el cual construiría la muralla que la mantendría a salvo. Sabía que aún quedaban meses de trabajo duro: firmar el contrato para el local comercial, decorarlo, montarlo y completar una gran cantidad de trámites bancarios, además de una mudanza internacional. Pero el obstáculo que parecía una montaña infranqueable —la aprobación legal— ahora era un camino abierto.

Inmediatamente, con las manos aún temblorosas, pero por pura emoción, encendió el motor y tomó su teléfono celular. Necesitaba gritarlo, necesitaba compartir esa chispa de esperanza con los únicos que la habían sostenido sin saber el peligro real que corría. Mientras manejaba de regreso a casa, con la mirada fija en la carretera, pero el corazón puesto en el horizonte, marcó el número de sus padres.

—¡Mamá, papá… me aprobaron la visa! —exclamó Valentina, y su voz, antes contenida y profesional, se quebró en una risa cargada de lágrimas de felicidad—. ¡Todo salió bien! Ya es oficial. Debo comenzar a empacar y organizar absolutamente todo antes de partir; no hay tiempo que perder.

Al otro lado de la línea, el estallido de júbilo fue instantáneo. Pudo escuchar el suspiro de alivio de su madre y la voz vibrante de su padre, quien probablemente estaba dando saltos de alegría en la oficina.

—¡Gracias a Dios, Valentina! ¡Qué bendición tan grande! —exclamó su madre con una emoción que traspasaba la señal—. ¡Sabíamos que podías hacerlo, hija! ¿Te esperamos en casa para que nos cuentes cada detalle, sí? ¡Vente con cuidado, aquí estamos todos!

Valentina colgó con una sonrisa que le dolía en las mejillas. Al mirar por el retrovisor, ya no buscaba motocicletas ni sombras; miraba el camino que la llevaba a su casa para empezar a cerrar maletas. La palabra "partir" tenía un sabor dulce, como la repostería que soñaba crear.

Esa tarde, el miedo a Federico empezó a desvanecerse, sustituido por la logística de su triunfo. Él pensaba que la tenía acorralada en su ciudad, pero Valentina ya estaba poniéndose las alas para volar alto.

Cuando Valentina finalmente cruzó el umbral de su casa, la atmósfera era de triunfo absoluto. No hubo necesidad de palabras; al ver su rostro iluminado, sus padres y hermanos la rodearon en un abrazo colectivo que se sintió como el escudo más sólido del mundo.

Esa noche, la mesa del comedor se vistió de gala. El brillo de la cristalería y el aroma de una cena preparada con amor llenaban el ambiente. Su padre descorchó una botella de champán, y el sonido del "pop" resonó como un grito de alegría, borrando el eco de las amenazas de los meses pasados. Antes de probar el primer bocado, se tomaron de las manos. La oración de esa noche fue profunda; dieron gracias por la protección divina y encomendaron el futuro de Valentina en esta nueva etapa. Para ellos, el logro no era solo de ella; en esa familia tan unida, el éxito de uno era el oxígeno de todos.

Capítulo 10:
La partida de una valiente

Al día siguiente, el pragmatismo de la mudanza se impuso. Valentina sabía que no podía irse sin despedirse de las raíces que la sostuvieron en la oscuridad. Contactó a sus amistades más cercanas y los citó esa misma tarde. Se reunieron en el patio de la casa, un rincón verde y tranquilo donde el viento mecía las hojas de los árboles. Allí, rodeada de Matías, Karina y Diana, Valentina finalmente soltó la carga. Les contó sobre la persecución, el acoso incesante y, finalmente, la noticia bomba: se iba del país en apenas un par de días. El silencio que siguió a sus palabras fue sepulcral. Sus amigos, que habían sido testigos mudos de la toxicidad de Federico, quedaron paralizados.

—¿En un par de días? —exclamó Karina, con los ojos humedecidos y la voz temblorosa—. Sabíamos que necesitabas alejarte de ese tipo, pero… irte así, tan lejos… es como un balde de agua fría, Vale. Te vamos a extrañar demasiado.

Matías se frotó la nuca, mirando hacia el suelo con una mezcla de tristeza y alivio.

—Es una locura, pero es la mejor locura que podías hacer. Ese imbécil no se va a detener, y aquí todos estaríamos siempre con el corazón en la mano. Si te quedas, él te va a encontrar. Si te vas... eres libre.

Diana, que siempre había sido la más práctica, tomó las manos de Valentina con fuerza.

—Nos duele en el alma que el precio de tu seguridad sea la distancia, pero este proyecto de la cafetería es tu sueño. No dejes que el miedo a Federico sea lo único que te mueva; deja que tu talento sea el motor. Te mereces una vida donde no tengas que mirar atrás cada vez que caminas por la calle.

La charla se extendió por horas, entre anécdotas compartidas y planes de visitas futuras. Hubo risas nostálgicas y algunas lágrimas que el viento de la tarde se encargó de secar. Al caer el sol, el grupo se puso en pie para el adiós definitivo.

—Suerte en tu nueva vida, Valentina —dijo Matías, dándole un abrazo que olía a despedida y a hermandad.

—Esperamos verte pronto, aunque sea por videollamada —añadió Diana con una sonrisa triste, pero llena de esperanza. Se fundieron en un último abrazo grupal, un círculo de protección que Valentina se llevaría grabado en el corazón. Mientras ellos cruzaban el portón de su casa, ella se quedó en el patio observando cómo las sombras crecían. Ya no tenía miedo de la oscuridad; ahora sabía que el sol que saldría en un par de días no sería el mismo de siempre, sino el sol de un nuevo comienzo. Esa misma noche, el aire se sentía cargado de una solemnidad dulce y dolorosa. Sus padres, queriendo sellar su partida con la bendición de la sangre, habían organizado una cena de despedida en el lugar que para Valentina representaba el centro de su universo emocional: la casa de su abuela. Se montaron al coche en silencio, un trayecto corto que Valentina recorrió grabando en su memoria cada poste de luz y cada esquina de su ciudad. Al llegar, la casa de la abuela los recibió con esa calidez que ninguna otra arquitectura en el mundo podría imitar. Era un refugio de paredes blancas, cuadros antiguos y ese olor cálido a café recién colado, mezclado con el aroma de las especias y las recetas secretas que solo las manos de su abuela sabían ejecutar con perfección.

La mesa estaba rodeada de rostros amados. Tíos, primos y hermanos se turnaron para dedicarle palabras que eran como ungüento para sus heridas invisibles.

—Lleva nuestro apellido con orgullo, Valentina. Eres la más valiente de nosotros —le dijo un tío mientras le estrechaba la mano.

Cenaron entre risas que intentaban tapar la nostalgia. Brindaron por el éxito de la cafetería, por la visa aprobada y por el futuro brillante que le esperaba en el norte. Cuando llegó el momento de partir, el nudo en la garganta de Valentina se volvió casi insoportable. Se acercó a su abuela, cuyo rostro era un mapa de ternura, y se hundió en su abrazo. Inhaló profundamente ese aroma a hogar, sabiendo con una punzada en el corazón que pasarían meses, años, o que quizás nunca volvería a disfrutar de esas cálidas noches bajo ese mismo techo, rodeada de todos ellos al mismo tiempo. Valentina recorrió el salón con la mirada, abrazando uno a uno a los miembros de su familia. Cada abrazo era un "gracias" silencioso por haberla amado tanto que, sin saberlo, la estaban ayudando a huir de un monstruo. Al llegar a la puerta, se detuvo y se giró. Con la voz entrecortada, pero con una fuerza que nacía desde lo más profundo de su ser, les dijo:

—Los amo a todos. Los extrañaré.

Salió por la puerta de la casa de su abuela y el contraste fue total. Afuera, la noche era oscura y fresca, pero su rostro estaba iluminado por las luces de la calle y por la chispa de su nueva libertad. Sus ojos, nublados por las lágrimas, eran un espejo de sentimientos encontrados: el dolor desgarrador de la despedida y la euforia eléctrica de quien sabe que acababa de dar el primer paso para ganar una gran batalla. Sin mirar atrás, se subió al coche con el corazón dividido, dejando el refugio de su infancia para convertirse en la mujer que, a partir de ahora, dictaría sus propias reglas en una tierra desconocida.

Capítulo 11:

El inicio de una nueva vida

El sol de la mañana se filtró nuevamente por las rendijas de las cortinas, pero Valentina ya tenía los ojos abiertos antes de que la alarma sonara. Un cosquilleo eléctrico le recorría la columna vertebral: ¡había llegado el día! El día que durante meses pareció un espejismo en medio del desierto de su miedo finalmente se materializaba bajo sus pies. No era solo un viaje; era el despegue hacia su independencia, el inicio de la obra maestra que era su propia vida. Con un entusiasmo renovado, se alistó con movimientos ágiles y precisos. Terminó de cerrar las maletas, escuchando el satisfactorio sonido de las cremalleras que guardaban no solo ropa, sino sus sueños, sus herramientas y su libertad. Al bajar las escaleras, la casa, que tantas noches fue su refugio silencioso, parecía vibrar con ella. Valentina entró en la cocina, el santuario donde tantas veces ideó sus recetas, y comenzó a preparar su último café en casa. Mientras el agua hervía y el aroma del grano molido inundaba el espacio, de su garganta brotó una melodía espontánea. Se escuchaba el cantar de Valentina como si fuese un pajarillo cantor que celebra el fin del invierno; era un canto ligero, fresco, que brotaba desde un lugar de su pecho que Federico no pudo marchitar. Con una energía radiante, puso su taza de cerámica y su plato con pan sobre la mesa. Con una sonrisa que iluminaba hasta los rincones más oscuros de la cocina, exclamó en voz alta:

—¡Buenos días, buenos días a todos!

Su entusiasmo y buena vibra eran casi tangibles, expandiéndose por los pasillos como una brisa cálida. Sus padres y sus tres hermanos, contagiados por esa fuerza vital, bajaron de inmediato para compartir esos últimos instantes de cotidianidad. En la mesa, el vapor del café subía perezoso mientras la familia se acomodaba en sus lugares de siempre. Sin embargo, antes de dar el primer sorbo, se hizo un silencio sagrado. De forma natural, como lo habían hecho toda la vida pero con una intensidad nueva, se tomaron de las manos formando un círculo inquebrantable. Cerraron los ojos y, en una comunión de almas, oraron con fervor. Pidieron por el vuelo de Valentina, para que los ángeles custodiaran su camino entre las nubes; oraron por cada paso que ella daría en tierras extrañas, por la sabiduría para manejar su negocio y por la protección de su futuro. En ese momento, Valentina sintió que las manos de sus hermanos y sus padres le transferían toda la fuerza necesaria para enfrentar lo desconocido. Ese desayuno no fue una despedida triste, sino un lanzamiento. Entre el sabor del pan caliente y las miradas de orgullo de su familia, Valentina comprendió que se iba físicamente, pero que ese círculo de amor sería el ancla invisible que la mantendría firme, sin importar cuán lejos volara. El trayecto al aeropuerto fue un desfile de paisajes conocidos que Valentina despedía con una serenidad nueva. Sus tres hermanos cargaron las maletas en el carrito con una eficiencia protectora, mientras sus padres caminaban a su lado, formando un muro de amor que la escoltaba hasta el final. Al llegar al mostrador de la aerolínea, el bullicio de la terminal —el anuncio de los vuelos, el rodar de las maletas y el murmullo de los viajeros— no la abrumaba; al contrario, era la música de su libertad. Tras los abrazos finales, cargados de promesas de videollamadas y prontas visitas, Valentina cruzó el control migratorio. No miró atrás. No lo hizo porque sabía que, si volteaba a ver sus rostros una última vez, rompería en llanto; un llanto que no sería de tristeza, sino de una emoción incontenible y de la certeza de que, aunque iba al inicio de una aventura emocionante, los extrañaría con cada fibra de su ser. Mientras caminaba por el pasillo de abordaje, a punto de entregar su ticket, Valentina sintió de repente una mirada punzante, una energía que le recorrió la nuca. Al ver de reojo, su corazón dio un pálpito incontrolable: a unos metros de distancia, en una puerta de embarque vecina, reconoció a uno de los primos de Federico. El hombre la observaba con fijeza, con una expresión de sorpresa maliciosa, mientras sostenía su propio pase de abordar. En ese instante, Valentina lo supo: Federico no tardaría más de unos minutos en recibir una llamada. Sabría que ella estaba en el aeropuerto, que llevaba maletas, que se iba. Por un segundo, el viejo nerviosismo intentó apoderarse de ella, acelerando su pulso. Pero, mientras ponía un pie dentro del avión y el aire presurizado de la cabina la recibía, una calma absoluta descendió sobre ella. Se relajó, soltó un suspiro profundo y pensó para sí misma que ya no importaba lo que él supiera. Ya no había nada que Federico pudiera hacer para detenerla. Caminó por el pasillo, buscando su número de asiento con una calma que le sorprendía a ella misma. Cuando finalmente llegó, se acomodó con cuidado, deslizó su bolso bajo el asiento delantero —asegurándose de que su pasaporte y documentos estuvieran a la mano— y se abrochó el cinturón de seguridad. El clic metálico del cierre fue el sonido final de su compromiso con el pasado; ahora estaba sujeta únicamente a su propio viaje. Se recostó en el asiento, sintiendo la textura de la tela contra su espalda. A su alrededor, el murmullo de los demás pasajeros y el sonido de los compartimentos superiores cerrándose creaban una sinfonía de partida. Valentina apoyó la cabeza en el respaldo y exhaló un suspiro que parecía haber estado contenido durante años. Ya no había vuelta atrás. El avión comenzó su lento carreteo hacia la pista de despegue. Valentina miraba por la pequeña ventana ovalada, viendo cómo los edificios del aeropuerto se alejaban. Entonces, el piloto anunció la salida. El rugido de los motores vibraba bajo sus pies. Mientras el aparato tomaba impulso sobre la pista, ganando velocidad, ella cerró los ojos y apretó con fuerza los apoyabrazos. Sintió el tirón en el pecho, esa presión gravitacional que indicaba que las ruedas habían dejado de tocar el suelo. Estaba en el aire. Ella ya estaba fuera del alcance de Federico. Cuando la señal de cinturones se apagó y el avión se estabilizó en su altitud, Valentina sacó su teléfono del bolso. Lo encendió solo para revisar la hora, pero al desbloquear la pantalla, sus ojos se clavaron en la fecha del calendario. Un escalofrío —esta vez no de miedo, sino de asombro— le recorrió la espalda.

—Hoy… —susurró—. Hoy era la fecha en que me iba a casar con él.

Según el plan que Federico y la inercia de una relación tóxica habían trazado, en ese preciso momento ella debía estar vistiéndose de blanco, rodeada de azahares, preparándose para caminar hacia un altar que, ahora lo sabía, habría sido su tumba en vida. En lugar de un velo, llevaba auriculares; en lugar de un anillo que la encadenara, sostenía un pasaporte que la liberaba.

—Gracias, Dios… —susurró, pegando la frente al frío cristal de la ventanilla—. Gracias por traerme hasta aquí.

No era coincidencia. Era redención. Valentina aterrizó en Estados Unidos con el corazón latiendo a un ritmo nuevo. Al bajar del avión, el aire acondicionado del aeropuerto se sentía como un preludio de la frescura que la esperaba afuera. Se dirigió con paso firme hacia la zona de migración, donde una fila alargada avanzaba con eficiencia. Cuando finalmente fue su turno, se paró frente al oficial con una sonrisa en su rostro.

—Good afternoon. Passport and travel documents, please —dijo el agente con un tono neutro y profesional.

—Good afternoon, officer. Here you go —respondió Valentina con un inglés fluido y seguro, entregándole su pasaporte.

El agente abrió el documento; sus ojos recorrieron las páginas hasta detenerse en el sello de la visa de inversionista. Al ver que todo estaba en orden y que ella venía con un propósito claro de emprendimiento, el oficial estampó el sello de entrada sin hacer más preguntas.

—Welcome to the United States —dijo él, devolviéndole el pasaporte.

—Thank you —sonrió ella.

Todo estaba fluyendo a su favor, como si el universo mismo estuviera abriéndole paso. Al salir del aeropuerto, el impacto fue inmediato. Esta no era una ciudad de concreto y caos; era un paisaje vivo, una ciudad abrazada por montañas imponentes, árboles frondosos, ríos y lagos que reflejaban la luz de un cielo inmenso. El aire no solo era limpio; tenía un aroma a libertad. Valentina cerró los ojos por un segundo y respiró profundamente, sintiendo cómo ese aire fresco llenaba sus pulmones de una paz y una seguridad que no experimentaba desde hacía mucho tiempo. Se sintió en casa antes de conocer su propia dirección. Rentó un carro pequeño y moderno, colocó su teléfono en el soporte con la dirección del que ahora sería su refugio y comenzó a conducir. Durante el trayecto, Valentina iba impresionada; el paisaje parecía sacado de una postal, con colinas verdes que se sucedían una tras otra. Finalmente, llegó a su destino: la casa que sus padres habían adquirido años atrás como una inversión, pero que ella nunca había visitado. Era una construcción acogedora, rodeada de naturaleza. Al abrir la puerta y entrar, el olor a madera y a hogar la recibió. Buscó la que sería su habitación principal y comenzó a meter sus pertenencias una a una. Aunque el día había sido agotador y el viaje largo, la felicidad no le cabía en el pecho. La adrenalina era tan grande que sentía que sus energías eran inagotables; cada maleta que abría, cada prenda que colgaba en el armario, era un acto de soberanía sobre su propia vida. Se entregó a la tarea de organizar cada rincón, transformando ese espacio en su santuario. Trabajó con una sonrisa persistente hasta que el reloj marcó la medianoche. Solo entonces, cuando el silencio de las montañas envolvió la casa, Valentina accedió a ceder al cansancio. Se recostó en su nueva cama, miró el techo con una gratitud infinita y, por primera vez en mucho tiempo, cerró los ojos sabiendo que el mañana no le pertenecía a nadie más que a ella misma. A la mañana siguiente, Valentina se despertó antes de que el sol terminara de escalar las montañas. No había rastro del cansancio del viaje; la determinación era su nuevo motor. Con una precisión que ya era su marca personal, llamó a la dueña del local comercial, con quien ya había mantenido negociaciones meses antes de despegar. Quedaron de verse en una hora. Valentina se montó en el carro, bajó un poco la ventanilla para dejar que el aire puro de la mañana la terminara de espabilar y pasó por un café local. Con el vaso humeante en la mano y el corazón acelerado, se dirigió hacia la dirección que tanto había estudiado en mapas satelitales. Sin embargo, antes de llegar a su cita con el local de sus sueños, sabía que debía cerrar una última puerta que aún golpeaba con fuerza a sus espaldas. Se detuvo frente a una tienda de telefonía. Al entrar, pidió un cambio inmediato de número y un dispositivo nuevo; necesitaba que nada de su antigua vida tuviera un puente hacia su presente. Mientras el técnico preparaba la nueva tarjeta SIM, Valentina encendió su viejo teléfono por última vez. La pantalla se iluminó con una ráfaga de notificaciones: Federico no se había rendido. Entre la marea de textos, abrió el último mensaje.

Era una nota cargada de una obsesión asfixiante:

"Ya me enteré de que te fuiste del país, Valentina.
Crees que puedes escapar, pero sé dónde estás.
Iré a buscarte. No me vas a dejar así".

En ese instante, Valentina no sintió miedo; sintió una rabia fría y clarificadora. Sus dedos volaron sobre el teclado, armada con una valentía que ya no conocía dudas.

"Si te atreves a poner un pie en este país para buscarme,
lo primero que haré será poner una orden de restricción
en tu contra y te denunciaré ante las autoridades migratorias.
Aquí las leyes sí funcionan. Aléjate de mí para siempre."
—escribió con firmeza—.

La respuesta fue casi instantánea. Federico, cuyo ego y estatus siempre habían sido su prioridad, mostró su verdadera cara.

"No voy a arriesgarme a que me cancelen
la visa por una malagradecida como tú.
Te odio por lo que me hiciste."

—contestó él.

Valentina miró la pantalla y vio los tres puntos suspensivos que indicaban que él seguía escribiendo, probablemente volcando más veneno y reproches. Pero ella ya no necesitaba leer más. Sin esperar a que el mensaje llegara, con un movimiento seco y definitivo, apagó el teléfono. Entregó el aparato viejo para reciclaje, tomó su teléfono nuevo con su número recién asignado y salió de la tienda. Al cruzar la puerta, sintió que el hilo invisible que la unía a su pasado se había cortado para siempre. Federico era ahora solo un mal recuerdo atrapado en un dispositivo apagado. Valentina subió a su auto, puso su música favorita y aceleró hacia la cita que tenía, lista para ser, finalmente, quien siempre quiso ser. Cuando finalmente estacionó frente al lugar, se quedó unos segundos en silencio. El local estaba ubicado en una zona estratégica, con grandes ventanales que dejaban entrar la luz dorada de la mañana. Al bajar del auto y caminar hacia la entrada, sintió que sus pasos tenían un propósito que nunca antes habían tenido. La dueña la recibió con una sonrisa amable y, al girar la llave, la puerta se abrió hacia su nueva realidad. Al entrar, Valentina se detuvo en seco para absorber el lugar. El aire dentro del local tenía un aroma particular: una mezcla de limpieza, el olor metálico y frío del acero inoxidable de los electrodomésticos industriales y un sutil rastro de harina y azúcar de lo que seguramente fue una pastelería anterior. No era un olor a viejo, sino un aroma a "posibilidad". Sus ojos recorrieron el espacio con la velocidad de una experta: ahí estaban ya un horno de convección impecable, una cafetera profesional de tres grupos y un refrigerador industrial de doble puerta. Era tal como lo había visualizado; el espacio era exacto, las dimensiones eran perfectas para el flujo de clientes que ella ya había diseñado en su mente.

No era solo un local comercial; era el lugar donde su sueño dejaría de ser papel para convertirse en ladrillos y aroma a café.

—*Es perfecto* —susurró Valentina, más para sí misma que para la dueña.

Confirmó cada detalle técnico: las tomas de agua, la ventilación, el espacio para las mesas frente a los ventanales. Todo encajaba. Sin titubeos, miró a la mujer y, con la seguridad de quien sabe que está en el lugar correcto, cerró el trato de palabra ahí mismo.

—No quiero esperar más —dijo con firmeza—. Estoy lista. Acordemos la firma del contrato para esta misma tarde.

Esa tarde, Valentina regresó al local para el encuentro definitivo. Se sentó frente a la dueña con el documento que representaba su futuro. Al tomar el bolígrafo, no le tembló la mano; al contrario, sentía una firmeza que venía desde lo más profundo de su ser. Mientras deslizaba la pluma sobre el papel para estampar su firma, algo llamó su atención. Levantó la vista hacia los grandes ventanales transparentes que daban a la calle y se quedó sin aliento. Pequeños cristales blancos, ligeros como plumas, comenzaban a descender del cielo grisáceo. Había comenzado a nevar. Valentina jamás había conocido la nieve. Para ella, ese espectáculo silencioso y puro que cubría el asfalto no fue un evento climático cualquiera; fue una señal de bendición absoluta sobre el paso que estaba tomando. Sintió que el cielo mismo estaba celebrando su valentía, lavando con blanco su pasado para dejarle un lienzo nuevo donde escribir su historia. Al soltar el bolígrafo, sintió que el círculo finalmente se cerraba. Ya no estaba al alcance de Federico ni era la sombra de los sueños de otro. Con el contrato bajo el brazo, caminó hacia la salida con una emoción que le desbordaba el pecho. Al cruzar la puerta, se detuvo bajo el frío acogedor de la tarde. Extendió sus manos y cerró los ojos, dejando que los copos de nieve aterrizaran sobre su piel y su cabello. Sintió la nieve por primera vez, ese frío delicado que se derretía al contacto con su calor, y no pudo evitar sonreír hacia el cielo.

El aire fresco le llenó los pulmones de una vitalidad renovada. Ya no había marcha atrás. El futuro de Valentina acababa de poner su primera piedra bajo un manto blanco cargado de hambre de triunfar. Valentina no perdió ni un segundo. Durante las semanas siguientes, el local se convirtió en su taller y su campo de batalla. Con una visión clara, decidió que la decoración sería de estilo rústico industrial: una fusión elegante de texturas que se sentía moderna pero profundamente acogedora. Ella misma supervisó la instalación de las vigas de madera recuperada y eligió una paleta de colores minimalista, dominada por el negro mate y el blanco puro, que resaltaba la calidez de los detalles en madera y el brillo del acero de sus máquinas. Trabajó día y noche, a menudo con las manos manchadas de pintura o polvo de madera. Instaló repisas flotantes donde colocó frascos de vidrio con granos de café y especias, y diseñó una iluminación tenue con lámparas colgantes de estilo vintage que creaban una atmósfera de refugio. Mientras el lugar tomaba forma física, su mente trabajaba en el alma del negocio: el menú. Valentina volcó toda su creatividad en recetas únicas, fusionando la técnica que aprendió con tantos años de práctica en la cocina de la casa de sus padres y utilizando sabores que evocaban su esencia. Inventó cada postre como una obra de arte y cada bebida con un equilibrio perfecto, escribiendo a mano las descripciones de una carta que prometía una experiencia sensorial completa. Una vez tuvo definidos los detalles, se sentó frente a su computadora y diseñó la imagen de lo que sería el menú visual frente al mostrador. Cuando faltaban apenas unos días para la gran inauguración, ocurrió algo inesperado que aceleró su pulso: una importante televisora de noticias local la contactó. El rumor sobre el nuevo concepto que estaba naciendo en la ciudad, bajo el mando de una joven inversionista latina, había despertado un enorme interés. Querían entrevistarla, grabar el interior y anunciar la apertura en el segmento estelar de la mañana. Valentina se sintió abrumada por la emoción. Ver que el apoyo de la comunidad y de los medios locales era real, y que estaban genuinamente interesados en su visión, fue la validación que su alma necesitaba.

El día de la entrevista, Valentina se preparó con una dedicación impecable. Se vistió con un atuendo que reflejaba su nueva identidad: profesional, segura y elegante. Antes de que llegaran las cámaras, preparó la barra: el aroma a café recién molido inundó el espacio y una selección de sus mejores postres lucía perfecta en la vitrina bajo las luces cálidas. Cuando el equipo de grabación llegó, Valentina sintió un breve destello de nervios. Respiró profundo, pensó en positivo, se sacudió la ansiedad y, sin pensarlo más, se acercó a las cámaras. La entrevista fue un éxito rotundo. Valentina habló con una elocuencia y una pasión que traspasaban la pantalla; describió su concepto no solo como una cafetería, sino como un espacio de conexión y arte. Mostró los detalles rústicos del local, explicó el origen de sus granos y, cuando el periodista le preguntó qué la había llevado hasta ahí, ella simplemente sonrió con la seguridad de quien ha recuperado su vida.

—Sé que suena increíble y que mucha gente se ríe o no lo cree cuando lo digo —confesó Valentina con una sonrisa genuina frente al lente—, pero este negocio nació literalmente de un sueño. Una noche, tras pedir dirección para mi vida, soñé con este nombre, con este logo y con este lugar tal como lo ven hoy. Para mí, estar aquí hoy no es coincidencia; es el resultado de creer en los sueños propios y tener la valentía de empezar de nuevo.

Al terminar la grabación, el equipo de noticias estaba impresionado. Valentina sabía que, tras esa emisión, la inauguración no sería solo un evento, sino el inicio del proyecto más importante de su vida. El día de la gran inauguración, Valentina se levantó mucho antes de que saliera el primer rayo de luz, impulsada por una mezcla de nervios y una alegría eléctrica que no la dejaba dormir. Sin embargo, al llegar a su negocio, se dio cuenta de que el impacto de la entrevista había superado cualquier expectativa: la ciudad, cautivada por su historia, ya se había volcado a las calles. Antes de que ella pudiera siquiera girar la llave en la cerradura, una extensa fila de personas ya se extendía a lo largo de la acera, ansiosas por conocer a la mujer que había "soñado su negocio" y probar su famosa repostería. Apenas abrió las puertas, el local se llenó del tintineo de las tazas y de murmullos de admiración hacia la decoración rústica. En medio del ajetreo, mientras Valentina servía con manos expertas los primeros cafés, su teléfono personal comenzó a vibrar con una intensidad especial. Era una videollamada grupal. Se apartó un segundo hacia la parte trasera de la barra y contestó. En la pantalla aparecieron los rostros de sus padres y sus tres hermanos: Javier, Joaquín y Julio. Todos estaban amontonados frente a una computadora, con los ojos rojos y pañuelos en las manos.

—¡Vale, te vimos! ¡Saliste en las noticias internacionales, hija! —exclamó su madre entre sollozos de alegría—. ¡Te veías tan hermosa y tan segura hablando de tu sueño!

—Esa es mi hermana —dijo Javier, con la voz quebrada pero llena de un orgullo feroz—. Les dijimos a todos en el barrio que esa empresaria que sale en la televisión es nuestra Valentina. ¡Mira ese local, es increíble!

Julio, siempre el más sensible, apenas podía hablar.

—Lo lograste, Vale. El aire de libertad te sienta de maravilla. Estamos celebrando aquí como si estuviéramos contigo.

Valentina sintió que las lágrimas también asomaban a sus ojos, pero esta vez eran lágrimas de triunfo y plenitud.

—Gracias por creer en mí cuando yo misma tenía miedo —les dijo, mostrando con la cámara del celular el local lleno de clientes y la nieve que aún decoraba el paisaje exterior—. Todo lo que soñé esa noche es real ahora. Los amo.

Cortó la llamada con el corazón rebosante. Regresó al mostrador con una energía imparable, atendiendo a cada persona con una sonrisa que ya no era forzada ni por compromiso. Esa tarde, mientras el sol se ponía tras las montañas, Valentina se dio cuenta de que no solo había construido una cafetería; había construido su propio reino sobre los cimientos de su valentía.

Los meses siguientes fueron una danza constante entre el cansancio y la plenitud. Valentina se sumergió por completo en la rutina diaria: desde hornear los primeros pasteles antes de que saliera el sol, hasta cuadrar las cuentas al final de la jornada bajo la luz de las lámparas industriales. Aunque sus pies dolían al final del día y el agotamiento físico era real, cada gota de sudor le sabía a gloria porque estaba haciendo crecer su propio negocio. Ver cómo los clientes regresaban por su nombre y cómo la comunidad adoptaba su espacio como su favorito era el combustible que mantenía su fuego encendido.

Con el paso de los meses, la disciplina y el éxito de la cafetería dieron sus primeros frutos tangibles. Valentina logró lo que poco tiempo atrás parecía un sueño lejano: comprar su primer carro propio. No era simplemente un vehículo; para ella representaba un gran logro de independencia y la prueba física de que podía sostenerse por sí misma sin depender de nadie. El día que recibió las llaves, se quedó un momento en silencio frente al volante, recordando las veces que Federico la hacía sentir pequeña o incapaz. Sintió un orgullo profundo que le recorrió el cuerpo; ese carro, comprado con el fruto de sus desvelos y su talento, era un trofeo a su resiliencia. Ahora, al conducir por las carreteras rodeadas de pinos y montañas, cada kilómetro le recordaba que era libre, exitosa y que el camino que Dios le había mostrado en sueños apenas estaba comenzando. A medida que el negocio se consolidaba, las visitas de sus seres queridos dejaron de ser un anhelo lejano para convertirse en una constante que llenaba de luz su vida en el extranjero. Valentina se encargaba de organizar cada detalle para que, al menos un par de veces al año, los suyos pudieran tomar un avión y encontrarse con ella; a veces eran sus padres, otras veces alguno de sus hermanos, y así mantenían viva la convivencia familiar a pesar de la distancia. Cuando su familia llegaba, la cafetería se transformaba por completo. No venían solo como invitados; llegaban con el deseo profundo de ser parte de su mundo. Ver a sus padres y hermanos ponerse el delantal y moverse con agilidad detrás de la barra era para Valentina una de las experiencias más conmovedoras de su nueva vida. Mientras atendían a los clientes, Valentina sentía que el tiempo se detenía. Al ver a su madre organizando los postres con delicadeza o a sus hermanos bromeando con los clientes mientras servían el café, revivía con intensidad los momentos de su infancia y juventud cuando trabajaba en la tienda de sus padres. Aquella esencia de negocio familiar, donde el servicio se daba con el corazón, se había trasladado desde su país natal hasta su nuevo horizonte. Había algo profundamente sanador en ver a su padre dar las gracias con una sonrisa o ver a sus hermanos Javier, Joaquín y Julio compitiendo por quién despachaba más rápido. En esos días de trabajo compartido, Valentina no solo veía crecer su negocio, sino que sentía que estaba honrando sus raíces. Su local ya no era solo una cafetería en tierras lejanas; era una extensión de la tienda donde todo comenzó, un pedazo de su historia que ahora florecía con fuerza gracias al esfuerzo de todos.

Capítulo 12:

Lo que es para ti, ni aunque te quites

Los años pasaron como una corriente de agua cristalina, transformando a Valentina en una mujer de éxito, serena y dueña de su destino. A sus 23 años, ya no quedaba rastro de la muchachita temerosa que alguna vez huyó de las sombras del control; ahora era una mujer con una visión clara y prioridades inamovibles. Su vida se había vuelto un refugio de orden y bienestar: su rutina se dividía entre el crecimiento de su cafetería, sus sesiones en el gimnasio, donde fortalecía tanto su cuerpo como su mente, y la calidez de su casa. Una noche, después de varios meses desde la última visita de su familia, la espera terminaba: sus padres y sus tres hermanos llegarían juntos para pasar las festividades de Navidad y Año Nuevo. Por fin, después de tanto esfuerzo y distancia, estarían todos bajo el mismo cielo de nuevo y en el mismo lugar. Valentina llegó al aeropuerto con el corazón palpitando a un ritmo que no sentía desde hacía meses. Se estacionó y caminó hacia la terminal de llegadas internacionales, sintiendo que el aire frío de la noche apenas la rozaba gracias a la adrenalina que recorría sus venas. Se colocó frente a las puertas automáticas, ajustándose el abrigo, con los ojos fijos en el flujo de pasajeros que comenzaba a salir. Cuando las puertas se deslizaron una vez más, los vio. Al frente venían sus padres, con pasos cansados por el viaje pero ojos alertas, y justo detrás, Javier, Joaquín y Julio, cargados de maletas y de esa energía ruidosa que tanto extrañaba. En el momento en que sus miradas se cruzaron, el protocolo del aeropuerto desapareció. Valentina corrió hacia ellos con un impulso que la hizo sentir de nuevo como una niña. Se fundieron en un abrazo colectivo, una masa de seis personas que se apretaban con una fuerza desesperada, como queriendo recuperar cada segundo perdido. Valentina hundió su rostro en el hombro de su madre, respirando el aroma que para ella significaba "hogar", mientras sentía las manos fuertes de su padre rodeándola y las carcajadas de sus hermanos que la levantaban del suelo.

—¡Mírate, Valentina! ¡Qué linda estás, hija! —exclamó su padre con la voz quebrada por la emoción, apartándola un poco para admirar a la mujer que tenía enfrente, tan segura y radiante.

—Por fin estamos juntos, Vale. No puedo creer que estemos de nuevo todos aquí —decía Javier, mientras Joaquín y Julio se turnaban para abrazarla y bromear sobre el frío inevitable del invierno.

Mientras caminaban hacia el estacionamiento, Valentina lo hacía con la frente en alto, guiando a su familia hacia su vehículo. Al subir todos al auto, el silencio de los últimos meses fue reemplazado por un caos bendito de voces, anécdotas y risas. Con el carro lleno y el corazón rebosante, Valentina condujo hacia casa, mientras su madre le apretaba la mano con ternura desde el lugar del copiloto. Valentina sonreía en silencio, consciente de la magnitud de aquel momento. Sabía que esa Navidad no sería simplemente una fecha más en el calendario; era el reencuentro más esperado, la prueba viviente de que, aun a la distancia, seguían siendo una familia unida, lista para celebrar la alegría de estar reunidos. Durante una de esas tardes mágicas de víspera de Navidad, mientras el local estaba decorado con luces cálidas y el aroma a canela flotaba en el aire, una notificación inusual iluminó la pantalla de su celular. Era una solicitud de amistad. Al abrirla, por un segundo pensó que no estaba viendo bien; tuvo que parpadear dos veces para confirmar que el nombre en la pantalla era real. Pero, a diferencia del pasado, esta vez la sorpresa no venía acompañada de miedo o culpa, sino de una sensación dulce y nostálgica. Valentina observó la foto de perfil: aquel chico apuesto con el que había compartido un noviazgo ligero, tierno y genuino hacía ya cinco años, antes de que la sombra de Federico lo oscureciera todo. Su rostro reflejaba la misma bondad que ella recordaba. Con una sonrisa pura, sintiendo que era el cierre perfecto para sus heridas, presionó el botón de "Aceptar".

Casi en el acto, como si él hubiera estado esperando ese momento durante años, entró un mensaje que iluminó la pantalla. William la saludó con una cordialidad impecable y ese respeto que siempre lo había caracterizado. Valentina, con los dedos volando sobre el teclado y una alegría que le iluminaba el rostro, leyó las palabras que marcaban el inicio de este nuevo capítulo. William le explicó que, mientras navegaba en sus redes sociales, el algoritmo del destino hizo de las suyas: el nombre de Valentina apareció en su sección de "Personas que quizás conozcas". Al ver su foto, el corazón le dictó que no podía dejar pasar la oportunidad, y aprovechó ese instante para enviarle la solicitud que ella acababa de aceptar.

El mensaje decía:

"Hola, Valentina. ¡Qué alegría que hayas aceptado mi solicitud! Me saliste como sugerencia y no dudé en agregarte. Estuve viendo tu perfil y no pude evitar sonreír... te ves radiante."

"¡Feliz Navidad, William! ¡Qué sorpresa tan linda! Hace tanto tiempo que no sabía de ti; me da muchísimo gusto volver a conectar contigo. Gracias por tus palabras sobre mi negocio; ha sido un esfuerzo grande, pero ha valido la pena. Me alegra mucho saber de ti", escribió.

La conversación fluía con una velocidad asombrosa, como si estuvieran recuperando el tiempo que les fue robado.
Entre anécdotas y risas digitales, William soltó una noticia que hizo que Valentina soltara el aire que no sabía que estaba reteniendo.

"Vale, hay algo que no te he contado —escribió William junto a un emoji de asombro—. Yo también estoy viviendo en Estados Unidos desde hace un par de años. Estoy en Florida. Me vine buscando nuevas oportunidades y aquí me he establecido. Cuando vi en tus fotos que tú también estabas de este lado, no lo podía creer."

Valentina se quedó mirando la pantalla, procesando la información con una mezcla de sorpresa y alegría.

"¡No puede ser, William! ¿En serio estás en Florida? —respondió ella con el corazón acelerado—. Yo también estoy acá en el sur, pero vivo entre montañas y un clima totalmente distinto al sol de Florida. ¡Qué pequeño es el mundo! Siempre pensé que seguías allá, en nuestra tierra."

William le contestó de inmediato y, esta vez, se atrevió a enviarle una nota de voz. Su tono era maduro y profundo, pero conservaba esa dulzura que Valentina recordaba perfectamente:

"Pues sí, aquí estamos los dos, Vale. Tú en el frío y yo en el calor de Florida, pero me da mucha alegría saber que estamos en el mismo país, luchando por lo nuestro."

A partir de ese mensaje, el tiempo pareció detenerse y acelerarse a la vez. No pararon de escribirse ni un solo día. La dinámica entre ellos fluyó con una naturalidad asombrosa: Valentina despertaba ahora con un mensaje de "buenos días" de William que le iluminaba el rostro antes de salir de la cama. Durante el día, mientras ella dirigía su cafetería, mantenía esa chispa de ilusión, esperando ansiosa el momento de cerrar el negocio y regresar a casa. Una vez en su refugio, se entregaba por completo a textearle, contándole los pormenores de su jornada y descubriendo, mensaje a mensaje, que la conexión que Federico intentó destruir seguía intacta, pero ahora era mucho más madura y profunda. Tras el estruendo de las celebraciones de Año Nuevo y con la satisfacción de haber compartido el inicio de un nuevo ciclo junto a sus padres y hermanos, la paz de enero trajo consigo una sorpresa inesperada. El 31 de diciembre, mientras Valentina disfrutaba de la calma de la tarde, su celular vibró con un mensaje de William que cambiaría el rumbo de su invierno.

¡Hola, Vale! ¡Feliz Año Nuevo! Espero que lo hayas pasado increíble con tu familia. Oye, te escribo porque surgió un viaje de trabajo por carretera y, revisando el mapa, me di cuenta de que pasaré exactamente por tu ciudad este fin de semana. No quiero parecer atrevido, pero me encantaría pasar a saludarte. Sería increíble verte después de tanto tiempo, ¿qué opinas?

Valentina leyó el mensaje con el corazón acelerado, pero con la madurez que le daban sus 23 años. Pensó que ver a una vieja amistad, a alguien que conocía su esencia desde antes de la tormenta, era una idea maravillosa en un país que, aunque ya era su hogar, seguía siendo ajeno.

Valentina:

"¡Hola, William! ¡Feliz Año! Qué coincidencia tan grande. Pues me parece una idea genial. Como dices, ha pasado una eternidad y sería muy lindo ver una cara conocida por acá. ¡Claro que puedes venir!"

William:

"¡Qué bueno leer eso! Me hace mucha ilusión. Estaré por allá el sábado por la tarde. Si te parece bien, pásame tu dirección y llego a saludarte un momento. Prometo no quitarte mucho tiempo; sé que debes estar disfrutando a los tuyos."

Valentina:

"No te preocupes, mi familia estará encantada de recibirte también. Te mando la ubicación de mi casa. Avísame ese día cuando estés cerca para salir a recibirte."

Valentina soltó el teléfono con una sonrisa nerviosa pero genuina. No había rastro de la culpa que Federico solía sembrar en ella; esta vez se sentía libre. Se puso de acuerdo con él para que llegara directamente a su casa, donde la presencia de sus padres y hermanos le daba un marco de seguridad y calidez. Para ella, aceptar esa visita era un acto de justicia con su propio pasado: era la prueba de que ya nadie dictaba quién podía entrar o salir de su vida.

Esa tarde, el 2 de enero la expectativa se transformó en realidad cuando el sonido del timbre rompió el murmullo de la casa. Valentina se levantó, sintiendo una mezcla de curiosidad y calma, y abrió la puerta. Al verlo ahí de pie, una sonrisa se dibujó en su rostro. Sus ojos recorrieron su figura y, por un instante, su mente se llenó de pensamientos veloces: se veía diferente, más maduro, con la presencia de un hombre que también había crecido en la distancia, pero, al mismo tiempo, seguía siendo exactamente la persona que ella recordaba en su esencia.

—¡William! Qué gusto verte —dijo ella, invitándolo a pasar.

Se sentaron en la sala a platicar, intentando resumir años en pocos minutos. Al poco tiempo, los padres de Valentina se acercaron. La atmósfera era cálida, pero el aire cambió sutilmente cuando el padre de Valentina, con ese instinto protector que nunca se pierde, se sentó frente a él. Sin pensarlo dos veces y con la franqueza que lo caracterizaba, lanzó el primer dardo en forma de pregunta:

—Y bien, William… ¿qué haces por aquí?

William, sintiendo el peso de la mirada del hombre, guardó la compostura y contestó con otra pregunta, intentando ganar un segundo para organizar sus ideas:

—¿Aquí en esta ciudad o aquí en Estados Unidos?

El papá de Valentina esbozó una sonrisa que era mitad sarcástica y mitad pícara, de esas que solo los padres saben hacer cuando están analizando a alguien.

—Las dos —sentenció, cruzándose de brazos, pero manteniendo ese brillo divertido en los ojos.

William se acomodó en el asiento, visiblemente nervioso, pero manteniendo la educación. Se aclaró la garganta y comenzó a explicar su situación, bajo la atenta mirada de toda la familia que, desde la cocina, también prestaba atención.

—Bueno, pues… trabajo en una empresa de electrodomésticos en Florida —explicó William, gesticulando un poco más por los nervios—. Justo ahora voy a unas reuniones importantes con unos proveedores de partes y, como la ruta pasaba por esta ciudad, no quise dejar pasar la oportunidad de ver a Valentina.

Valentina observaba la escena desde un costado, divertida por el nerviosismo de William y la "audacia" de su padre.

Al ver que William estaba empezando a sudar bajo la mirada inquisidora del señor, los hermanos decidieron que era el momento justo para intervenir y romper el hielo. Julio, el hermano mayor, entró a la sala con paso firme, pero con una sonrisa relajada. Se acercó a William y le dio una palmada amistosa en la espalda, una de esas que sirven para liberar tensiones.

—Ya deja al muchacho,, papá. No lo vas a asustar en la primera visita, ¿o sí? —bromeó Julio, mientras Javier y Joaquín se acomodaban en los sillones laterales con gestos de complicidad—. William, no le hagas caso. Mi papá todavía no procesa que Valentina ya no es la niña que ayudaba en la tienda, pero aquí todos somos amigos.

La tensión se rompió de inmediato. El padre de Valentina soltó una carcajada sonora, relajando finalmente su postura y dándole un sorbo a su café.

—Está bien, está bien —dijo el señor, levantando las manos en señal de tregua—. Solo quería asegurarme de que este "floridano" supiera que Valentina tiene quien la cuide aquí en el sur.

A partir de ahí, la plática dio un giro total. William, sintiéndose mucho más cómodo al ver que el "interrogatorio" se había convertido en una bienvenida cálida, empezó a soltarse. Julio recordó anécdotas de hace años, cuando ellos eran apenas unos jovencitos en su tierra natal.

—Yo me acuerdo de que tú eras de los pocos que se atrevía a llegar a la casa cuando nosotros tres estábamos en la puerta —comentó Joaquín entre risas—. Tenías valor desde entonces, William.

William se rió, esta vez de forma relajada, y empezó a contarles cómo había sido su experiencia trabajando en la empresa de electrodomésticos y lo mucho que le había costado adaptarse al sol constante de Florida después de venir de su pueblo. Los padres de Valentina, conmovidos por su historia de esfuerzo —que guardaba tantos paralelismos con la lucha de su propia hija—, terminaron tratándolo como a uno más de la familia, ofreciéndole comida y compartiendo historias de su viaje.

Después de un largo rato de risas y anécdotas en la sala, Valentina sintió que era el momento de rescatar a William del nido familiar y compartir un momento más personal. Quería mostrarle el lugar que la había acogido y del cual se sentía tan orgullosa.

—"Oye, William, ya que estás aquí, no puedes irte sin ver lo mejor de esta ciudad" —dijo Valentina, levantándose con entusiasmo—. "El centro es un espectáculo, especialmente porque tenemos unas cataratas que pasan justo por en medio de la ciudad. Es algo que no se ve todos los días".

William aceptó de inmediato, agradecido por la oportunidad de estirar las piernas y, sobre todo, de pasar un tiempo a solas con ella. Valentina se giró hacia sus padres y sus hermanos, quienes los observaban con curiosidad.

—"Papá, mamá, voy a llevar a William a que conozca un poco el centro y las cataratas. No tardamos; le doy un tour rápido y regresamos para seguir conviviendo" —avisó con esa seguridad que ahora la definía.

Sus padres asintieron con una sonrisa, y Julio, como el hermano mayor, solo les lanzó un gesto de despedida con la mano, dándoles el visto bueno implícito.

Salieron a la calle y el aire frío del invierno los recibió de golpe, contrastando con el calor de la casa. William se puso al volante de su auto mientras Valentina lo guiaba, y condujeron hacia el corazón de la ciudad. Mientras él manejaba, ella le iba señalando sus lugares favoritos, pero cuando llegaron al centro, William se quedó mudo. El estruendo del agua cayendo empezó a llenar el ambiente. Caminaron juntos hacia el majestuoso puente colgante, una estructura diseñada especialmente para que los visitantes pudieran suspenderse sobre el abismo y admirar el paisaje en toda su gloria. Al llegar al centro, el puente se mecía sutilmente con el viento, ofreciendo una vista privilegiada: desde allí, las cataratas caían con una fuerza imponente, rodeadas de árboles cuyas ramas, cubiertas por una fina capa de escarcha, enmarcaban el agua como si fuera un cuadro pintado a mano. El escenario era tan perfecto que parecía irreal, una obra maestra de la naturaleza en medio de la ciudad.

—"Es increíble, Vale" —dijo William, rompiendo el silencio mientras se sujetaba de los cables del puente y contemplaba la caída del agua—. "Nunca imaginé que vivirías en un lugar así de imponente. Te define mucho… tiene esa fuerza que tú siempre has tenido, aunque antes no te dejaran mostrarla".

Valentina lo miró de reojo, sintiendo cómo la estructura colgante vibraba suavemente bajo sus pies, armonizando con la paz que sentía en su interior. La brisa fresca que soplaba desde la caída del agua les acariciaba el rostro, trayendo consigo el sonido puro de la naturaleza que parecía aislar el resto del mundo, creando un momento de absoluta conexión entre ellos y el paisaje. Estar ahí, con un amigo de su pasado en su nueva ciudad y sobre ese puente que parecía flotar entre los árboles, era la confirmación de que su mundo finalmente era tan grande como ella siempre soñó.

—"A veces me detengo aquí solo para recordar lo lejos que he llegado" —respondió Valentina, dejando que el aire frío le rozara el rostro—. "Este lugar me dio la libertad que necesitaba".

William se quedó observándola un momento, más impresionado por la serenidad de Valentina que por la majestuosidad de las cataratas.

—"Se nota en tu mirada, Vale. Estás en el lugar que te pertenece".

Se quedaron un momento más en silencio, suspendidos sobre el rugido del agua, dejando que la belleza del paisaje, pintado a mano, sellara ese reencuentro que el destino había tardado años en preparar. Buscaron un lugar donde sentarse, resguardados por la vista del puente y el murmullo de las cataratas, y comenzaron a desenterrar el pasado. Habían pasado cinco años desde la última vez que se vieron, desde aquel tiempo en que fueron novios. Con una madurez que solo dan los años y los golpes de la vida, recordaron lo corto, pero profundamente significativo, que fue su noviazgo. Valentina, sintiéndose en un espacio seguro, le abrió su corazón y le contó todo lo que vivió con su exnovio: las sombras, el control y el largo camino que tuvo que recorrer para sanar y encontrar su propia voz. William la escuchó con un respeto absoluto y luego, con la misma honestidad, le contó de una relación que él tuvo, una novia con la que duró dos años, compartiendo las lecciones que ese tiempo le dejó. Las horas se sintieron como simples minutos. La química entre ellos era inexplicable; era como si aquellos muchachitos que se quisieron años atrás aún estuvieran ahí, pero habitando cuerpos y mentes diferentes. Ahora eran adultos, maduros, situados en una etapa de plenitud. Esa noche, sentada a su lado, Valentina sintió una paz y una tranquilidad que hacía años no experimentaba con nadie. No había presión, no había juicios, solo dos almas reconociéndose en la distancia. De repente, Valentina sacó su teléfono para revisar la hora y la realidad la golpeó de pronto. Tenía un mensaje de su madre preguntándole:

"¿Todo bien?".

Al ver la hora, Valentina pegó un brinco, totalmente sorprendida.

—"¡No puede ser! ¡William, mira qué tarde es!" —exclamó con los ojos muy abiertos—. "Se me fue el tiempo volando, no me di cuenta de nada. Mi mamá ya me escribió preocupada. ¡Tenemos que volver a casa ya mismo!".

William se levantó de un salto también, soltando una risa nerviosa pero encantada.

—"¡Es verdad! Cuando la plática es buena, el reloj se detiene" —dijo él, ayudándola a recoger sus cosas—. "Vámonos, no quiero que tu papá piense que te secuestré en mi primer día de visita".

Caminaron de regreso al auto casi trotando, compartiendo una última risa cómplice. El frío de la noche ya no se sentía tan intenso; el calor de esa conexión renovada los acompañó durante todo el trayecto de vuelta, dejando en el aire la promesa silenciosa de que este era solo el principio de algo nuevo. William la dejó en la puerta de su casa, despidiéndose con una mirada que decía mucho más que cualquier palabra, y arrancó su vehículo, perdiéndose en la oscuridad de la calle. Esa noche, Valentina se acostó y se quedó mirando el techo de su habitación por largo rato, procesando el torbellino de emociones. No sabía qué esperar después de esa visita ni qué dirección tomarían sus pensamientos, pero lo que sí tenía claro era la paz mágica que la envolvía. Hacía años que no experimentaba esa sensación de seguridad y alegría sin sombras; lo único que sabía era lo bonito que se sentía volver a ser ella misma frente a él. A la mañana siguiente, mientras Javier preparaba el café, el sonido del timbre interrumpió el desayuno familiar. La mamá de Valentina, con esa curiosidad natural de madre, se adelantó a abrir la puerta. Se encontró con un mensajero que sostenía un espectacular arreglo de flores frescas, cuyo aroma inundó la entrada de inmediato. La señora entró a la casa con una sonrisa pícara, cargando el detalle, mientras los hermanos de Valentina —Julio, Javier y Joaquín— asomaban la cabeza desde la cocina para ver de qué se trataba.

—"¡Valentina! ¡Ven rápido, te trajeron algo!" —exclamó su madre con voz cantarina.

Valentina bajó las escaleras y se quedó sin aliento al ver el ramo. Sus manos temblaron un poco al tomar la pequeña tarjeta blanca que venía escondida entre los pétalos. Al abrirla, sus ojos recorrieron una caligrafía firme que dictaba una frase que la hizo suspirar:

"Lo mejor de mi viaje fue volver a verte".

No hacía falta firma; el corazón de Valentina supo de inmediato quién enviaba ese mensaje. La frase caló hondo porque reconocía que, por encima de sus negocios y sus reuniones en Carolina del Norte, el verdadero propósito de esos kilómetros recorridos había sido ella.

Sus hermanos, que no podían contener la curiosidad, se acercaron de inmediato. Julio, como el mayor, intentó leer la tarjeta por encima de su hombro con una sonrisa burlona.

—"A ver, a ver… ¿qué dice el galán de Florida?" —bromeó Julio, mientras Javier y Joaquín soltaban una carcajada—. "Parece que las cataratas no fueron lo único que lo dejó impresionado ayer".

Valentina guardó la tarjeta en el bolsillo de su suéter, tratando de ocultar, sin éxito, el sonrojo de sus mejillas. Su madre, desde la cocina, la miraba con una ternura profunda, sabiendo que ese brillo en los ojos de su hija era algo que no veía desde hacía mucho tiempo.

Ese arreglo de flores no era solo un regalo; era la declaración de que William no la veía simplemente como una "vieja amistad", sino como la mujer increíble en la que se había convertido a sus 23 años. Valentina se acercó a la ventana, mirando hacia la calle por donde él se había ido la noche anterior, sintiendo que el nuevo año realmente traía consigo promesas que nunca se atrevió a imaginar.

Valentina hundió su rostro en los pétalos frescos del arreglo, aspirando profundo ese aroma que parecía limpiar el aire de cualquier duda pasada. Con el corazón latiendo a un ritmo distinto, sacó su celular e inmediatamente le escribió a William para agradecerle el detalle, confesándole que las flores habían alegrado su mañana.

La respuesta de él no se hizo esperar y, esta vez, William decidió ser directo, dejando claro que su interés iba más allá de un simple saludo.

> *"Me alegra que te gustaran, Vale. La verdad es que me quedé con ganas de más tiempo contigo.*
> *¿Estarías de acuerdo si me organizo para seguirte visitando?"*

Valentina leyó el mensaje y sintió una calidez recorrerle el cuerpo. No había presiones, solo una pregunta respetuosa. Con una sonrisa segura, tecleó su respuesta:

> *"Sí, me encantaría".*

Capítulo 13:

De la amistad al amor

Las semanas siguientes pasaron volando, marcando un ritmo nuevo en la vida de Valentina. Ella seguía férreamente enfocada en sus pilares: el crecimiento imparable de su negocio y su bienestar personal en el gimnasio, donde cada levantamiento de pesas reafirmaba su fortaleza física y mental. Sin embargo, ahora había una constante dulce en su rutina: William.

Estaban en contacto día y noche. Él se convirtió en su primer mensaje al despertar y el último antes de dormir. Una de esas noches, justo antes de que Valentina apagara la luz, su teléfono sonó. Era él. Hablaron durante horas, perdiendo la noción del tiempo entre risas y confesiones, hasta que William, con tono entusiasmado, le soltó la noticia:

—"Vale, he estado revisando mi calendario y logré acomodar todo. Voy a ir a visitarte de nuevo, pero esta vez quiero hacerlo bien, con tiempo".

Valentina, quien solía poner su trabajo por encima de todo, no lo dudó ni un segundo.

—"Avísame las fechas exactas" —le respondió con dulzura—. "Voy a organizar mis turnos en la cafetería para tener un par de días completamente libres. Quiero que aprovechemos el tiempo al máximo".

A los pocos días, William cumplió su palabra. Tomó un avión desde Florida hacia las Carolinas, aterrizó en la ciudad y rentó un auto para tener total libertad de movimiento. Esa misma tarde pasó por ella a su casa. Al verlo bajar del carro, Valentina sintió esa familiaridad reconfortante de quien llega a un lugar seguro. William la llevó a almorzar a uno de sus restaurantes favoritos. El restaurante que Valentina había elegido era un rincón con un encanto particular, de esos que parecen esconderse del ruido del mundo. El ambiente era cálido y acogedor, con una decoración que mezclaba lo rústico y lo moderno: paredes de ladrillo visto, vigas de madera en el techo y una iluminación tenue proveniente de lámparas de filamento que bañaban todo con una luz dorada y suave. A pesar de ser un lugar concurrido, las mesas estaban lo suficientemente distanciadas como para crear una burbuja de intimidad. Se escuchaba de fondo un jazz suave que se mezclaba con el murmullo de las conversaciones y el tintineo ocasional de las copas de cristal. Sentados en una mesa cerca de un gran ventanal que daba a una calle arbolada, el contraste era perfecto: afuera, el aire fresco de la tarde; adentro, el calor de una buena charla. Sobre el mantel de lino, los platos de comida gourmet lucían como obras de arte, pero para ellos eran solo el acompañamiento de algo más importante. Estaban frente a frente; la comida pasó a segundo plano ante la fluidez de su conversación. Rieron a carcajadas recordando anécdotas de su adolescencia, reviviendo historias de cuando vivían en su país natal, con ese humor y códigos que solo dos personas con las mismas raíces pueden entender. La conexión entre ellos era indudable; no necesitaban forzar nada, simplemente fluían. En un momento de la charla, el tema giró hacia lo profesional. William comenzó a explicarle su experiencia con los clientes y profundizó en temas sobre su trabajo en la ingeniería de electrodomésticos, describiendo con pasión los procesos y los retos que enfrentaba con los proveedores. Valentina lo escuchaba atentamente, observando cómo le brillaban los ojos al hablar de su carrera. Cada vez que William se inclinaba hacia adelante para explicarle algún detalle técnico de su trabajo, el brillo de las velas en la mesa se reflejaba en sus ojos, resaltando su entusiasmo. Valentina, apoyando la barbilla en su mano, lo observaba fascinada. Había algo en la forma en que él movía las manos al hablar y en la seguridad de su voz que llenaba el espacio. En ese restaurante, rodeados de extraños, pero sintiéndose más cerca que nunca, la atmósfera se volvió eléctrica. No era solo el reencuentro de dos personas que se conocieron de niños; era el encuentro de dos adultos exitosos que, en medio de la elegancia del lugar, se daban cuenta de que su conexión seguía siendo tan real y potente como la primera vez, pero con la profundidad que solo la madurez les podía otorgar. Lejos de aburrirse, Valentina se sentía fascinada. Quedaba admirada no solo por su inteligencia y dominio del tema, sino por esas ganas genuinas de prosperar que él demostraba. Veía en William a un hombre trabajador y visionario que, al igual que ella, había llegado a ese país para comerse el mundo. En esa mesa, entre risas y admiración mutua, Valentina confirmó que William no solo era un recuerdo bonito del pasado, sino un hombre a la altura de su presente. El tiempo en el restaurante se diluyó entre miradas y sonrisas hasta que el sol comenzó a ocultarse, tiñendo el cielo con matices púrpuras y anaranjados. Fue entonces cuando William, notando la energía vibrante de Valentina, la miró con complicidad y le hizo una invitación que ella no pudo rechazar: ir a bailar. Valentina amaba el baile; para ella, era la forma máxima de expresión y libertad. Al llegar al lugar, la atmósfera cambió por completo. El ambiente estaba cargado de una energía eléctrica, con luces tenues que cortaban la penumbra y un ritmo envolvente que marcaba el pulso de la noche. En cuanto pisaron la pista, la conexión que habían sentido durante el almuerzo se transformó en algo físico y tangible. Salieron chispas. William, con una seguridad que Valentina no le conocía, la tomó por la cintura y la mano con la firmeza justa. Desde el primer paso, ella supo que él sabía exactamente lo que hacía. William la guiaba con una precisión técnica impresionante, marcando cada giro y cada pausa con una sutileza que permitía a Valentina lucirse. Ella, que siempre había sido una mujer independiente y fuerte, encontró un placer inmenso en dejarse guiar, fluyendo al ritmo de la música como si sus cuerpos hubieran ensayado esa coreografía durante los cinco años que estuvieron separados. Sus manos se desplazaban de un lado al otro, encontrándose y entrelazándose con una naturalidad asombrosa. En cada giro, el roce de sus dedos y el calor de sus palmas enviaban una descarga de adrenalina por la columna de Valentina. Él la acercaba hacia sí en los momentos lentos y la soltaba con gracia para que ella girara, solo para recibirla de nuevo con una seguridad que la hacía sentir protegida y libre al mismo tiempo. Mientras bailaban, el ruido del lugar desapareció. Sus miradas estaban clavadas la una en la otra; Valentina veía en los ojos de William esa mezcla de inteligencia que la había cautivado en el restaurante y una pasión nueva que la hacía vibrar. Él la miraba con absoluta admiración, reconociendo en sus movimientos a la mujer empoderada y radiante que tenía frente a él. El sudor ligero, el aroma del perfume de William mezclado con la cercanía y el vaivén de sus cuerpos crearon una burbuja de intimidad en medio de la multitud. En esa pista de baile no había pasado doloroso ni sombras del ayer; solo existían ellos dos, redescubriéndose a través del lenguaje universal del movimiento. Valentina se sintió viva, deseada y, sobre todo, en perfecta sintonía con un hombre que no solo admiraba su mente, sino que sabía seguirle el paso en cada sentido de la palabra. Al finalizar la noche, con el eco de la música aún vibrando en sus cuerpos y el aire frío de la madrugada recibiéndolos a la salida del lugar, llegó el momento de regresar. El trayecto en el auto fue tranquilo, envuelto en una atmósfera de complicidad que no necesitaba muchas palabras. William estacionó frente a la casa de Valentina. Con la caballerosidad que lo había distinguido durante todo el día, se bajó del coche, rodeó el vehículo y le abrió la puerta a ella. Caminaron juntos por el pequeño sendero hasta llegar al umbral de la entrada, donde la luz tenue del porche creaba un círculo de intimidad que los aislaba del resto del vecindario.

Frente a la puerta, el silencio se volvió denso, cargado de todo lo que no se habían dicho en la pista de baile. Valentina se giró para agradecerle, pero antes de que pudiera hablar, William se acercó para despedirse. Él inclinó el rostro y le dio un beso en la mejilla, pero lo hizo con una lentitud deliberada, dejando que sus labios rozaran peligrosamente la comisura de la boca de ella. En ese instante, el mundo de Valentina se detuvo. Sintió una corriente eléctrica, un chispazo repentino que le recorrió la columna y le erizó la piel de inmediato. Fue una sensación tan intensa que la tomó por sorpresa, desarmando cualquier defensa que hubiera construido. Valentina, aturdida por la magnitud de lo que acababa de sentir y sin saber exactamente cómo reaccionar ante esa descarga de adrenalina, intentó recuperar el aliento y la compostura. Disimulando el impacto, dio un pequeño paso hacia atrás, creando una distancia segura que la ayudara a procesar el momento. Le dedicó una sonrisa dulce, algo nerviosa, y se despidió con la voz un poco más suave de lo normal:

—"Nos vemos mañana, William… que pases buenas noches"
—dijo, mientras su corazón seguía latiendo con fuerza contra su pecho.

William la miró fijamente, con una chispa de triunfo y ternura en los ojos, asintió y esperó a que ella entrara. Valentina cerró la puerta y se apoyó contra ella, exhalando el aire que no sabía que estaba reteniendo. Se tocó la mejilla, justo donde el roce de él todavía se sentía como un rastro de fuego, dándose cuenta de que esa corriente eléctrica acababa de cambiar las reglas del juego para siempre. La mañana siguiente, Carolina del Sur amaneció transformada. Valentina se despertó temprano y, al abrir las cortinas, soltó un suspiro: el jardín y los árboles estaban sepultados bajo un manto de nieve blanca y reluciente. El silencio era absoluto, roto solo por el crujido del hielo.

Casi al instante, su teléfono vibró. Era un mensaje de William:

> *"Mira hacia afuera. Creo que el destino quiere que me quede un rato más en tu ciudad".*

Un par de horas después, William llegó a la casa de Valentina. Esta vez no vestía formal, sino ropa abrigada y una bufanda que le daba un aire más relajado. La familia de Valentina, al ver el clima, lo recibió con una calidez natural. Salieron al patio trasero, donde la nieve llegaba casi a los tobillos. Entre risas, comenzaron una pequeña guerra de bolas de nieve, pero pronto la competitividad se convirtió en ternura. William ayudó a Valentina a caminar por las zonas más resbaladizas, sosteniéndola de la cintura con una firmeza que a ella ya no la ponía nerviosa, sino que la hacía sentir protegida. Cuando el frío se hizo sentir en las mejillas, entraron a la casa. Valentina, en su elemento, preparó un chocolate caliente especial, utilizando sus conocimientos de la cafetería. William la observaba apoyado en la barra, admirando la destreza de sus manos.

—"Ayer te vi bailar, hoy te veo en la cocina… me pregunto cuántas versiones más de ti me faltan por descubrir" —le dijo él en un tono bajo, mientras el vapor del chocolate subía entre los dos.

Se sentaron juntos en un rincón cerca de la ventana, viendo cómo los copos seguían cayendo. Hablaron de sus sueños a largo plazo. William le confesó que su éxito en Florida se sentía incompleto y Valentina le contó que su cafetería era solo el primer paso de un imperio que quería construir. No hablaban como extraños, sino como dos personas que estaban alineando sus mundos. En un momento de silencio, William tomó la mano de Valentina. Sus dedos se entrelazaron con naturalidad sobre la mesa.

—"Ayer, cuando nos despedimos, sentí que algo cambió" —comenzó él, bajando la voz mientras el vapor de su aliento se mezclaba con el aire frío—. "Ver todo este paisaje detenido por la nieve me hace pensar que no es casualidad que esté aquí hoy. Después de cinco años, la vida nos puso en el mismo camino y, sinceramente, no tengo ninguna prisa por irme. Me gusta el lugar donde estás, pero me gusta mucho más la mujer en la que te convertiste".

Valentina no retrocedió esta vez. Al contrario, apretó su mano. El contraste entre el frío gélido que se veía por el cristal y el calor que emanaba de William creó una atmósfera de absoluta seguridad. En ese día de nieve, Valentina comprendió que ya no tenía que defenderse del amor; con William, el amor no era una cárcel, sino un refugio.

—"Yo también siento que el tiempo se detuvo, William. Y me gusta lo que veo ahora" —respondió ella con sinceridad.

Pasaron el resto de la mañana así, compartiendo sueños bajo el cielo gris, admirando cómo la nieve lo cubría todo, excepto la calidez que empezaba a crecer entre ellos. Era un día de quietud, pero para Valentina, era el día en que su corazón finalmente se sentía a salvo. La nieve seguía cayendo con insistencia tras los cristales, convirtiendo la casa en un refugio cálido y acogedor. Ante la imposibilidad de salir, decidieron que el plan perfecto sería simplemente disfrutar de la compañía del otro. Se acomodaron en el sofá, envueltos en una manta cálida, para ver una película que terminó quedando en segundo plano; la verdadera trama estaba en los comentarios en voz baja, las risas compartidas y esa cercanía que se sentía cada vez más natural. Cuando la tarde empezó a ceder, Valentina se levantó con una sonrisa decidida.

—"Hoy cocino yo" —anunció.

Sabía que el plato favorito de William era la lasaña, y quería agasajarlo con su versión especial, esa que preparaba con paciencia y dedicación. La cocina se llenó pronto de aromas irresistibles: el sofrito de la carne con especias, el toque de la albahaca fresca y el aroma del queso gratinándose en el horno. William no perdió detalle. Se apoyó en la pared, cruzando los brazos con una expresión de absoluta fascinación, observándola con una mezcla de admiración y deseo. Ver a Valentina moverse con tanta destreza y seguridad en su hogar, rodeada del vapor de la cocina, lo hacía sentir que estaba viviendo un sueño que no sabía que tenía.

—"Podría verte hacer esto toda la tarde" —le soltó él con voz baja, sin moverse de la pared, logrando que ella le lanzara una mirada juguetona y un poco sonrojada.

Finalmente, la cena estuvo servida. Las capas de la lasaña estaban perfectamente doradas y el humo subía en espirales sobre la mesa. Valentina sirvió dos porciones generosas, donde las capas de pasta y salsa se fundían a la perfección. Se sentaron frente a frente en la pequeña mesa, iluminados apenas por una luz cálida que hacía que la escena pareciera sacada de una revista. William no tardó en dar el primer bocado. Su reacción fue inmediata: soltó un suspiro de satisfacción y dejó el cubierto un segundo, procesando el sabor.

—"Vale... esto es de otro mundo" —dijo él, con una honestidad que le brillaba en los ojos—. "Dicen que el amor entra por el estómago, y creo que acabo de caer rendido. Es la mejor lasaña que he probado en mi vida".

Valentina soltó una pequeña risa, sintiendo un calorcito especial en el pecho. Mientras cenaban, el ambiente se volvió magnético. Las miradas que se cruzaban sobre la mesa eran intensas y cargadas de significado; ya no eran las de dos viejos amigos, sino las de dos adultos que se deseaban y se admiraban. En cada silencio, mientras degustaban la cena, sus ojos se encontraban y se sostenían por segundos que parecían eternos, comunicando una atracción que el lenguaje no alcanzaba a explicar. En medio de la cena, William dejó el tenedor a un lado y la miró fijamente, con una ternura que desarmó a Valentina. No era solo por la comida; era por ella, por el momento y por la paz que reinaba en esa casa mientras afuera el mundo se congelaba. En ese comedor en las Carolinas, entre bocados de lasaña y silencios elocuentes, ambos supieron que esa noche no era el final de una visita, sino el cimiento de algo mucho más profundo. Al terminar la cena, un silencio cómodo y expectante se instaló en el comedor. William ayudó a Valentina a llevar los platos hacia el fregadero, moviéndose en ese espacio reducido con una sincronía que parecía ensayada. El calor residual del horno y el aroma del vino creaban una atmósfera envolvente mientras la nieve seguía golpeando suavemente los cristales de las ventanas. Mientras ella enjuagaba las copas, William se acercó para dejar los cubiertos. En ese movimiento mínimo, sus manos se rozaron. A diferencia de la noche anterior en el porche, esta vez Valentina no dio un paso atrás. Sintió de nuevo esa descarga eléctrica recorriéndole el brazo, pero en lugar de huir, dejó que sus dedos permanecieran allí, sintiendo la piel cálida de William contra la suya. El tiempo se detuvo. Ella levantó la mirada y lo encontró ya observándola, a escasos centímetros de distancia. Él dejó los cubiertos a un lado, sin romper el contacto, y giró su mano para entrelazar sus dedos con los de ella.

—"Vale… no tienes idea de cuánto tiempo he esperado este momento" —susurró William con una voz cargada de una honestidad cruda.

Sus miradas se anclaron. Valentina vio en los ojos de él no solo el deseo, sino el respeto y la admiración que tanto había anhelado encontrar en alguien. Él llevó su mano libre hacia el rostro de ella, apartando con infinita ternura un mechón de cabello que caía sobre sus ojos. Sus dedos rozaron su mejilla con la misma suavidad con la que la nieve caía afuera. William se inclinó lentamente, dándole todo el espacio para decidir. Valentina cerró los ojos, acortando ella misma la distancia final. Y, finalmente, sucedió. Fue un beso que supo a espera terminada y a promesas nuevas. Empezó de forma lenta, casi tímida, como si ambos temieran romper la magia del momento, pero pronto se volvió profundo y seguro. Valentina sintió que el peso de los últimos años se desvanecía en ese contacto; ya no era la niña que él conoció ni la mujer herida por su pasado. Era ella, plena y libre, encontrándose de nuevo con el hombre que el destino le había guardado para el momento justo. Cuando se separaron apenas unos milímetros, todavía con las frentes unidas y las respiraciones entrecortadas, William sonrió y le dio un pequeño beso en la punta de la nariz.

—"Definitivamente" —dijo él en un susurro—, "esta es la mejor visita de mi vida".

Después de aquel beso que pareció detener el tiempo en la cocina, el silencio que quedó en la casa no era incómodo, sino vibrante, lleno de una energía que todavía les erizaba la piel. Valentina, con las mejillas encendidas, lo acompañó hasta la entrada. Afuera, la noche estaba fría y el cielo se había despejado, dejando ver una luna brillante que hacía resplandecer la nieve acumulada. William se puso su abrigo, pero sus ojos no se apartaban de los de ella. Antes de abrir la puerta, la tomó suavemente por la cintura y le dio un último beso, corto pero posesivo, como queriendo llevarse el sabor de ella para el camino.

—"Realmente no me quiero ir" —confesó él en un susurro, con una sonrisa ladeada que delataba cuánto le costaba dar el paso hacia afuera.

—"Lo sé… yo tampoco quiero que te vayas" —respondió Valentina con sinceridad—, "pero necesitas descansar. Mañana tienes un viaje largo y hay que rezar para que el hielo no retrase más los vuelos".

William asintió, resignado. Se despidieron con una última mirada cargada de promesas y él bajó los escalones del porche con cuidado de no resbalar. Valentina se quedó apoyada en la puerta, viendo cómo las luces del auto alquilado se encendían y cómo él se alejaba lentamente por la calle desierta de su vecindario. Al llegar al hotel, William se sintió extraño. La habitación, aunque elegante, se sentía fría y vacía en comparación con el calor del hogar de Valentina y el aroma de pasta recién hecha. Se quitó la chaqueta y se desplomó en la cama, mirando al techo con una sonrisa de incredulidad. No podía dejar de pensar en cómo ella se dejaba guiar al bailar, en su inteligencia al hablar de su negocio y en la suavidad de su piel. Sacó su teléfono y, antes de cerrar los ojos, le envió un último mensaje:

"Ya estoy en el hotel. La habitación se siente demasiado silenciosa sin tu risa. Espero que mañana el clima me deje salir, pero una parte de mí desea que el avión se retrase solo para tener una excusa y volver a tu puerta. Descansa, Vale".

Valentina, que ya estaba bajo las cobijas esperando noticias suyas, leyó el mensaje y sintió un vuelco en el corazón. Le contestó con una sonrisa dibujada en el rostro:

"Descansa tú también, William. Mañana será otro día. Avísame apenas sepas algo del vuelo. Que sueñes conmigo".

Esa noche, a pesar de estar en lugares diferentes, ambos durmieron con la misma sensación de plenitud. William, revisando constantemente la aplicación de la aerolínea, esperaba que su vuelo de regreso a Florida saliera a tiempo, no porque tuviera prisa por irse, sino porque sabía que, una vez que aterrizara en Florida, empezaría a contar los días exactos para su próximo regreso a las Carolinas. La mañana siguiente, el sol se reflejaba con una intensidad cegadora sobre la nieve que empezaba a ceder. William llegó al aeropuerto temprano, sorteando los charcos del deshielo y sintiendo esa mezcla agridulce de quien debe volver a sus responsabilidades, pero deja el corazón en otro código postal. Mientras hacía la fila para el control de seguridad, William no dejaba de revisar las pantallas de salidas. Finalmente, el letrero de su vuelo hacia Florida cambió a un verde brillante con la palabra:
CONFIRMADO.
Inmediatamente, sacó su teléfono y le escribió a Valentina:

"El clima nos dio tregua. Vuelo confirmado. Ya estoy en la puerta de embarque, pero te juro que una parte de mí se quedó contigo. Gracias por estos días, Vale. El avión despega en una hora".

Valentina recibió el mensaje mientras abría su cafetería. El aroma del café recién molido inundaba el local, pero su mente estaba en la terminal aérea. Sonrió al leerlo y se tomó un segundo para responder, apoyada en la barra de mármol que tanto esfuerzo le había costado conseguir:

"Me alegra que todo esté en orden. Avísame cuando aterrices en Florida. Aquí se siente un poco más de frío ahora que no estás, pero me quedo con el calor de estos días. ¡Buen viaje!".

Ese intercambio de mensajes marcó el inicio de una nueva etapa: su relación a distancia. Durante las semanas siguientes, las videollamadas se convirtieron en su momento sagrado. William le mostraba sus proyectos en Florida y ella le compartía los avances de su negocio y sus rutinas de gimnasio. William aterrizó en Florida unas horas después y, tal como prometió, la llamó de inmediato.

—"Ya estoy en casa, Vale" —le dijo por teléfono mientras caminaba por el calor húmedo de su ciudad—. "Pero te aviso desde ya: estoy contando los minutos para que el próximo vuelo sea el tuyo viniendo hacia acá".

Valentina se rió, sintiendo que el corazón palpitaba al ritmo de una nueva canción. Sabía que su vida en Carolina del Sur estaba llena de trabajo y metas, pero ahora había un hilo invisible que la conectaba a otro estado, con un hombre que no solo la quería, sino que la admiraba profundamente. A pesar de las millas, la conexión no hizo más que fortalecerse.

Valentina se sentía más motivada que nunca; saber que tenía a un hombre como William apoyándola desde lejos, admirando su crecimiento y contando los días para volver a verla, le daba una energía renovada.

Capítulo 14:

Un febrero que cambió todo

Durante las semanas previas a febrero, la distancia se convirtió en un motor para ambos. William, en Florida, se encontraba sumergido en un ritmo de trabajo frenético; su mente ingeniera no descansaba, pero entre reparaciones de electrodomésticos y reuniones, el pensamiento de Valentina era su único respiro. Sentía una mezcla de orgullo por ella y una impaciencia creciente por volver a tenerla cerca. Por su parte, Valentina no se quedaba atrás. Su cafetería estaba en su mejor momento, y ella dividía sus horas entre la administración del negocio, sus intensas rutinas en el gimnasio y esas llamadas nocturnas que eran su refugio. Sin embargo, el calendario les puso un reto: el 14 de febrero. William deseaba con todas sus fuerzas estar con ella, pero la realidad era dura. Tenía una reunión crucial a primera hora del lunes en Florida que no podía posponer. Para cualquier otro, las nueve horas de manejo de ida y las nueve de vuelta para un solo día habrían sido una locura, pero para William, Valentina valía cada kilómetro. El sábado por la noche, tras terminar su jornada, William no buscó su cama. Se subió a su auto, preparó un café cargado y emprendió el viaje hacia el norte. Mientras manejaba por las autopistas oscuras, su mente solo proyectaba la imagen de la sonrisa de Valentina. No sentía cansancio; sentía determinación. A las 8:00 de la mañana del domingo, el sol apenas empezaba a calentar las calles de Carolina del Sur cuando William estacionó su carro frente a la casa de Valentina. Ella, que esperaba un simple mensaje de "Feliz San Valentín" por WhatsApp, casi deja caer su taza al verlo por la ventana.

Ese día fue un sueño hecho realidad. Desayunaron juntos, caminaron por el parque mientras el aire fresco les recordaba su paseo en la nieve y luego se perdieron en la oscuridad del cine, tomados de la mano como dos adolescentes. Pero William tenía un as bajo la manga. Semanas atrás, había investigado minuciosamente cuál era el lugar más especial de la ciudad, decidido a que esa noche fuera inolvidable. El restaurante era una joya arquitectónica: una antigua casona convertida en un santuario de alta cocina, iluminada exteriormente por luces de hadas que envolvían los árboles centenarios. Al entrar, el ambiente era la definición misma del romance. El aire estaba impregnado de un perfume sutil a flores frescas y cera de vela. William había reservado una mesa en un rincón íntimo, cerca de una chimenea que creaba un resplandor ámbar sobre ellos. Valentina estaba radiante; el brillo de sus ojos superaba cualquier joya. William la observó en silencio por unos segundos, simplemente agradecido de estar ahí.

—"Nueve horas de camino se sienten como un minuto si el destino eres tú" —le dijo él, rompiendo el hielo mientras el mesero servía un vino tinto de reserva.

La cena fue una danza de sabores: platillos de autor que Valentina degustaba con curiosidad profesional, mientras William le explicaba, con esa inteligencia que tanto la cautivaba, cómo había planeado cada detalle del viaje. Las miradas que intercambiaban a la luz de las velas eran profundas, cargadas de una gratitud inmensa. William admiraba la fuerza de la mujer que tenía enfrente, y Valentina se sentía, por fin, valorada. El hecho de que él hubiera manejado toda la noche solo para verla un par de horas le demostraba que no estaba con alguien que daba excusas, sino con un hombre que creaba oportunidades. Al salir del restaurante, bajo el cielo estrellado de las Carolinas, el mundo parecía detenerse. William sabía que en pocas horas tendría que subir de nuevo al auto para manejar otras nueve horas de regreso y llegar a su reunión, pero mientras caminaban hacia el carro abrazados, sintió que esa cena había sido el mejor combustible para su vida.

La noche de San Valentín llegaba a su fin y el peso de la realidad comenzaba a asomarse: en pocas horas, William tendría que enfrentar nuevamente la carretera para estar en su reunión del lunes por la mañana en Florida. Al llegar a la puerta de casa de Valentina, el motor del auto se apagó y el silencio de la madrugada los envolvió. Valentina, con el corazón apretado por la preocupación y la ternura, le tomó la mano con fuerza mientras lo miraba a los ojos bajo la luz tenue del tablero del coche.

—"William, me da miedo que manejes así… has estado despierto casi 24 horas" —le susurró ella, con un tono que mezclaba ruego y admiración—. "Quédate un par de horas más, duerme en el sofá, descansa aunque sea un poco antes de salir".

William se giró hacia ella, soltó un suspiro suave y, con una lentitud llena de afecto, llevó su mano al rostro de Valentina, acariciando su mejilla con el pulgar. Sus ojos, aunque cansados físicamente, brillaban con una vitalidad que no venía del café, sino de ella.

—"Mírame, amor" —dijo él con voz firme pero dulce—. "Nueve horas de ida fueron para encontrarte, y las nueve de regreso serán pensando en lo que vivimos hoy. Te juro que ver tu sonrisa y tenerte así, de frente, me dio más energía de la que cualquier descanso podría darme. Me voy con el tanque lleno de ti".

Se bajaron del auto y caminaron hacia el porche. El aire frío de la madrugada contrastaba con el calor de su cercanía. Frente a la puerta, Valentina lo abrazó con todas sus fuerzas, escondiendo el rostro en su pecho y aspirando por última vez su perfume antes de la nueva espera. Él la rodeó con sus brazos, protegiéndola del frío, y le depositó un beso largo y profundo en la frente, quedándose ahí un momento, como queriendo memorizar ese instante.

—"Eres mi prioridad, Valentina. Nunca lo dudes" —le susurró al oído.

Finalmente, se separaron. William bajó los escalones, se subió al auto y, antes de arrancar, bajó la ventanilla para lanzarle un beso con la mano. Valentina se quedó en el porche, abrazándose a sí misma, viendo las luces traseras del carro alejarse hasta convertirse en dos puntos rojos que se perdían en la carretera. Entró a su casa sintiéndose la mujer más afortunada del mundo. Sabía que esa noche, mientras ella dormía, un hombre increíble estaría cruzando estados enteros solo para cumplir con su trabajo, pero con el corazón encadenado a esa pequeña ciudad de Carolina del Sur. Conmovida por el sacrificio que William había hecho en San Valentín, Valentina decidió que ya era hora de que ella diera el paso. No podía permitir que solo él cargara con los kilómetros. Con una determinación silenciosa, comenzó a organizar su propio "Operativo Florida". Valentina pasó las siguientes tres semanas moviendo piezas en secreto. Como dueña de su cafetería, tuvo que delegar responsabilidades, entrenando a su empleada de confianza para que el negocio no decayera en su ausencia. Mientras tanto, entre series de gimnasio y cierres de caja, investigaba vuelos y coordinaba con una aliada inesperada: la madre de William, con quien ya había empezado a forjar un vínculo telefónico. Quería que la sorpresa fuera total. Compró un boleto para un jueves por la mañana, planeando quedarse hasta el domingo. La emoción la desbordaba; cada vez que hablaba con William por videollamada y él le decía cuánto la extrañaba, ella mordía su labio para no soltar la noticia. El miércoles por la noche, solo doce horas antes de despegar, William la llamó como siempre, viéndose un poco agotado por el trabajo. Valentina ya no pudo más.

—"William, mañana no me llames a la cafetería" —dijo ella con una sonrisa misteriosa.

—"¿Por qué? ¿Vas a estar muy ocupada?" —preguntó él, confundido.

—"No… es que no voy a estar ahí. Mañana desayuno en las Carolinas, pero almuerzo en Florida. Voy a verte, Will".

El silencio del otro lado de la línea fue absoluto por tres segundos, seguido de un grito de alegría que hizo que Valentina riera a carcajadas. William no podía creerlo; la sorpresa había surtido efecto. Cuando Valentina aterrizó en Florida, el aire tropical y las palmeras la recibieron con una energía vibrante, muy distinta a la sobriedad de su ciudad. William la esperaba en la salida, y el abrazo que se dieron fue el de dos personas que finalmente sentían que el rompecabezas estaba completo. Ese fin de semana fue el de las presentaciones oficiales. William quería que Valentina conociera su mundo entero, y eso incluía a sus hermanos mayores, quienes eran los pilares de su vida en Florida. Roberto, el hermano mayor, los invitó a su casa. Era un hombre de carácter protector y alegre, muy parecido a William. Valentina quedó encantada con su esposa, Saraí. Desde el primer segundo, ella la recibió con un abrazo genuino, de esos que eliminan cualquier rastro de nerviosismo. Saraí, que ya conocía la historia de los cinco años de espera a través de los relatos de William, miró a Valentina con una complicidad inmediata. Roberto observó a su hermano menor y le dio una palmada en la espalda, aprobando en silencio: sabía que William por fin había encontrado a la mujer indicada. Al día siguiente visitaron a Karla, la hermana de William. Ella recibió a Valentina con una sonrisa radiante y un entusiasmo contagioso. No hubo rastro de evaluaciones o juicios; al contrario, Karla la trató como si ya la conociera de toda la vida, facilitando que Valentina se sintiera relajada desde el primer minuto. Ver a William en su entorno familiar fue una revelación para Valentina. Observó cómo él jugaba con sus sobrinos, la forma respetuosa en que hablaba con sus hermanos y el amor profundo que sentía por sus raíces. William, por su parte, sentía un orgullo inmenso al ver a Valentina desenvolverse con tanta gracia y seguridad ante su familia. En un momento a solas en el patio trasero, Karla volteó la mirada hacia Valentina y le confesó algo que la dejó sin aliento:

—"Sabes, William siempre ha sido un hombre de metas claras, y desde que estás tú, lo veo con una paz que no tenía. Gracias por traer esa luz a su vida".

Valentina sintió que se le hacía un nudo en la garganta ante la profundidad de sus palabras.

Al final del día, Valentina se dio cuenta de que la familia de William era un reflejo de él mismo. La dulzura de Karla y la complicidad de Saraí le demostraron que estaba entrando a un círculo donde las mujeres se apoyaban y se celebraban entre sí. Ya no se sentía como "la novia que viene de visita", sino como un miembro más de la familia que la había acogido con los brazos abiertos. Él la observaba de reojo, apoyado en la rama gruesa de un árbol. Su mente no estaba en los proyectos del trabajo ni en la reunión del lunes. Estaba en la forma en que Valentina había brillado esa tarde. Se sentía inmensamente orgulloso. Pensaba en las nueve horas de manejo de aquel San Valentín y sonreía para sí mismo; lo haría cien veces más solo por este momento de quietud a su lado. William caminó hacia Valentina, estiró la mano y la puso sobre la de ella. El contacto ya no era solamente eléctrico como en el baile; ahora era algo más profundo: era seguridad. Valentina entrelazó sus dedos con los de él y apoyó la cabeza en su hombro, dejando que el calor nocturno los envolviera. En ese silencio compartido, bajo el cielo estrellado de Florida, la palabra "visita" se quedó pequeña. Ambos confirmaron, sin necesidad de hablar, que aunque sus hogares estuvieran en estados diferentes y las millas los separaran físicamente, sus corazones ya habían mudado sus pertenencias al mismo lugar. Para cerrar con broche de oro ese viaje transformador, la última noche William reservó una mesa en un exclusivo restaurante cuya terraza se extendía prácticamente sobre la arena, permitiendo que el susurro del Atlántico fuera la música de fondo de su última noche en Florida. El ambiente era de un romanticismo absoluto. Velas protegidas por cristales titilaban sobre el mantel de lino blanco, y el cielo se había teñido de un azul profundo salpicado de estrellas. Valentina lucía espectacular; el clima tropical le había dado un brillo especial a su piel y su sonrisa reflejaba la paz de quien se sabe amada y aceptada. La conversación fluyó con la misma naturalidad que las olas. Él no podía dejar de mirarla. Mientras brindaban con una copa de vino blanco helado, William confesó lo que sentía al verla interactuar con su mundo:

—"Verte con Karla y Roberto, ver cómo Saraí te miraba como a una hermana… me hizo darme cuenta de que no solo encajas en mi vida, sino que la completas".

Le dijo esto buscando su mano sobre la mesa. Su pensamiento era claro: no quería que la distancia fuera el tema principal; solo quería disfrutar de la magia del enamoramiento. Ella, conmovida por la calidez de su familia, le explicó que nunca se había sentido tan "en casa" estando lejos de su propia ciudad.

—"William, este viaje me cambió. Vine a conocer a tu familia, pero terminé conociéndote a ti a través de los ojos de la gente que te ama".

Valentina se sentía en una burbuja de felicidad, disfrutando de cada bocado de la cena y de la atención constante que él le brindaba. Inevitablemente, el hecho de que ella regresara a las Carolinas al día siguiente surgió en la charla. Sin embargo, en lugar de verlo como un problema pesado, lo abordaron con la ligereza de quien está profundamente enamorado.

—"Son solo unas horas de vuelo o unas cuantas millas" —comentó William con una sonrisa optimista—. "La distancia es solo un espacio físico, porque hoy siento que estamos más cerca que nunca".

Valentina asintió, apretando su mano.

—"No quiero pensar en los aeropuertos hoy. Solo quiero recordar este olor a sal, este vino y la forma en que me miras".

Decidieron dejar las conversaciones profundas y los planes logísticos para después; esa noche era para el romance, para los besos robados entre plato y plato y para la promesa silenciosa de que este sentimiento solo estaba empezando a crecer. Al terminar la cena, caminaron descalzos por la orilla del mar durante unos minutos. El agua fresca mojaba sus pies mientras la luna llena iluminaba su camino. Fue una despedida perfecta del viaje, sin dramas, llena de la esperanza de quien sabe que ha encontrado un tesoro y que, sin importar el mapa, siempre encontrará el camino de regreso al otro. Las semanas siguientes se convirtieron en un testimonio de la determinación de William. La dinámica era casi heroica: cada vez que su agenda le permitía un respiro, no lo dudaba. Agarraba la carretera por la noche, devorando kilómetros con la sola idea de ver amanecer en las Carolinas. Pasaban un día juntos, a veces solo unas horas, desayunando en la cafetería de Valentina o simplemente caminando de la mano, para luego verlo partir de nuevo. Fueron un par de meses viviendo en esa burbuja de enamoramiento y adrenalina, donde el cansancio de William parecía no existir y el entusiasmo de Valentina se mantenía intacto. Pero toda burbuja tiene un momento en el que la realidad decide tocar a la puerta. Sucedió un domingo por la noche, frente a la puerta de la casa de Valentina. El aire era fresco y el vecindario estaba sumido en un silencio cómplice. William ya tenía las llaves del auto en la mano, listo para las nueve horas de regreso a Florida. Se acercó a ella para la despedida habitual, la tomó por la cintura y le plantó un beso en la boca, uno que se sintió distinto a los demás: más largo, más definitivo, más cargado de verdad. Al separarse apenas unos milímetros, él la miró a los ojos con una vulnerabilidad que Valentina nunca le había visto y soltó las palabras:

—"Te amo, mi amor".

En ese instante, el mundo de Valentina se paralizó. Fue como si el sonido del viento y el zumbido de los grillos se apagaran de golpe. El corazón le dio un pálpito violento, pero no fue solo alegría lo que sintió; fue el impacto de la realidad. Como un balde de agua fría, en segundos se cuestionó hacia dónde iba todo aquello. Se amaban, sí, pero vivían en estados distintos. ¿Cómo funcionaría? ¿Quién dejaría su vida? ¿Era este el preludio de un dolor futuro o el inicio de algo más grande? La magnitud de sus sentimientos la golpeó con tal fuerza que se quedó en shock. William la observaba, esperando una respuesta, pero las cuerdas vocales de

Valentina se sintieron de piedra. Ella no le dijo un "te amo" de regreso. No porque no lo sintiera, sino porque el miedo y la sorpresa le ganaron la partida.

Incómoda y abrumada por la intensidad del momento, bajó la mirada, fijándola en sus propios pies. Pasaron unos segundos que parecieron eternos. Finalmente, levantó el rostro y lo volvió a ver, forzando una sonrisa tímida, una de esas que dicen todo lo que la boca calla. Le habló con los ojos, intentando transmitirle que su silencio no era rechazo, sino un alma tratando de procesar que su vida podría cambiar para siempre. Se acercó a él y lo envolvió en un abrazo protector, hundiendo el rostro en su cuello.

—"Ve con cuidado" —susurró ella, aferrándose a él unos segundos más de lo normal.

William, que conocía bien los silencios de Valentina, no la presionó. Le dio un beso suave en la sien y subió a su auto. Mientras él se alejaba, Valentina se quedó apoyada frente a la ventana, viendo las luces desaparecer, sintiendo por primera vez que el "te amo" que no dijo le quemaba en la garganta, mientras la pregunta sobre el futuro de su relación empezaba a dar vueltas en su cabeza sin descanso. Esa noche, el silencio de la casa se sintió más pesado que de costumbre. Valentina no encendió la televisión ni buscó distracciones; se limitó a quedarse sentada en la cama, con la mirada perdida en la pared. Las palabras de William rebotaban en su mente como un eco incesante. Sentía una calidez inmensa, pero también un nudo de ansiedad que se le instalaba en el estómago. Repasó la escena una y otra vez: la luz del porche, la mirada vulnerable de él, su propio silencio. Se durmió casi por agotamiento mental, con el eco de esa confesión grabado en su mente. A las 2:17 de la madrugada, Valentina abrió los ojos de golpe. No había tenido una pesadilla, pero su cuerpo reaccionaba como si la hubiera tenido. El pecho le latía rápido y una sensación familiar —esa mezcla entre ilusión y miedo— le apretaba las costillas.

Te amo...

No era la primera vez que escuchaba esas palabras en su vida. Pero era la primera vez que no venían acompañadas de control, exigencias o manipulación. Esta vez habían sido limpias. Vulnerables. Sin condiciones. Y eso, paradójicamente, la asustaba más. Se sentó en la cama y apoyó la espalda en la cabecera. La habitación estaba en penumbra, iluminada apenas por la luz azulada que entraba por la ventana. Respiró profundo. ¿Lo amaba? La respuesta le llegó antes de terminar la pregunta. Sí. Lo amaba en la forma en que la miraba cuando hablaba de sus proyectos. En la manera en que manejaba nueve horas solo para verla un rato. En cómo no la presionó cuando guardó silencio. En cómo siempre la hizo sentir elegida, nunca perseguida. Lo amaba. Pero amar significaba riesgo. Y ella había aprendido que el riesgo podía costar demasiado caro. Tomó su teléfono. Eran las 2:23 a.m. Dudó unos segundos. Sabía que él estaría manejando todavía o tal vez habría hecho una parada para descansar unos minutos. Escribió. Borró. Volvió a escribir. Finalmente envió:

Valentina:
"¿Ya vas a mitad de camino?"

La respuesta tardó unos minutos.

William:
"Acabo de parar por gasolina. ¿Todo bien?"

Valentina miró la pantalla. Su corazón volvió a latir fuerte.

Valentina:
"Todo bien."

Qué frase tan pequeña para todo lo que estaba sintiendo. Escribió de nuevo:

"Sí. Solo quería saber cómo ibas."

Los tres puntos aparecieron en la pantalla…dudó…desaparecieron…y volvieron a aparecer.

William:
"Vale… ¿te asusté?"

La honestidad de la pregunta la atravesó. Él lo había notado. Valentina cerró los ojos un segundo y escribió.

Valentina:
"Me moviste el piso."
La respuesta llegó casi de inmediato.

William:
"No era mi intención asustarte. Solo… fue lo que sentí."

Valentina sostuvo el teléfono entre las manos. Ya no había presión en sus palabras, solo verdad.

Valentina:
"Lo sé. Fue… darme cuenta de que esto es real."

Del otro lado de la carretera, dentro del auto detenido bajo las luces blancas de la gasolinera, William sonrió en silencio.

William:
"Yo puedo esperar lo que necesites. No tienes que decir nada que no estés lista para decir."

Valentina sintió cómo algo dentro de ella se acomodaba.

Valentina:
"Gracias por entenderme."

Luego añadió:

"Termina de manejar con cuidado. Voy a intentar volver a dormir un poco."

Hizo una pausa antes de escribir lo último.

"Que Dios te acompañe en el camino. Buenas noches, Will."

La respuesta fue breve, pero cargada de ternura.

William:
"Amén. Descansa, amor."

El mensaje terminaba con un emoji de corazón rojo.

Capítulo 15:

Apostándole al amor

Al día siguiente, la jornada en la cafetería fue una prueba de fuego. Valentina atendía clientes y servía pedidos mecánicamente, pero su mente estaba a cientos de kilómetros. Por fin, cuando el sol se ocultó y ambos terminaron sus labores, el teléfono vibró. Era la videollamada habitual, pero esta vez la energía era distinta. Valentina se sentó sobre su cama y contestó la llamada. Al aparecer la imagen de William en la pantalla, él se veía algo cansado, con esa incertidumbre marcada en los ojos por el silencio de la noche anterior. Valentina tomó aire, buscando las palabras exactas.

—William, anoche me dejaste sin palabras —comenzó, apretando el teléfono con ambas manos. Su voz sonaba firme, pero cargada de una fragilidad evidente—. Me quedé toda la noche despierta, meditando, repasando cada letra de lo que me dijiste. Y aunque fue hermoso, me trajo una realidad que no pude ignorar. Me pasé las horas cuestionando hacia dónde va esto realmente, William. Vivimos en estados diferentes, tenemos vidas construidas en lugares distintos… ¿cuál es el plan?

William la escuchaba en silencio, viendo cómo la vulnerabilidad se apoderaba de ella.

—Lo que estoy sintiendo por ti es demasiado fuerte. Es tan real que me asusta.

Hizo una pausa, tragando saliva antes de soltar lo que más le dolía reconocer.

—Estar a distancia me está dando mucho miedo, William. Tengo miedo de terminar lastimada. Tú sabes lo que pasé antes… yo no quiero volver a sufrir. Mi relación anterior me dejó marcas que me tardaron muchos años en sanar, y pensar que estamos construyendo algo tan profundo en estados diferentes me hace sentir que estoy caminando hacia un abismo.

William se quedó helado. La revelación lo dejó en el aire, como si el suelo se hubiera desvanecido bajo sus pies. No se esperaba que el miedo fuera tan palpable ni que su confesión hubiera desatado semejante tormenta de inseguridades en ella. Por primera vez, no supo cómo aliviar la situación con una broma o una visita sorpresa. No dijo mucho. Sus pensamientos eran un caos de protección y desconcierto. No quiso profundizar en ese momento porque entendió que cualquier promesa de "todo estará bien" sonaría vacía ante el peso de la distancia.

—Te entiendo, mi amor —respondió tras un largo suspiro, con un tono cargado de respeto y una pizca de tristeza—. De verdad lo hago. Lo que menos quiero en esta vida es que sufras, y menos por algo que tenga que ver conmigo. Si necesitas claridad, te la voy a dar.

El ambiente se volvió denso, cargado de incertidumbre.

—Creo que es mejor que nos tomemos un pequeño espacio —sugirió Valentina, con el corazón en un hilo—. Necesitamos pensar en lo que hablamos hoy, en hacia dónde vamos realmente.

William asintió lentamente, respetando el límite que ella acababa de trazar.

—Está bien. Tómate el tiempo que necesites. Aquí estaré.

Al colgar, Valentina dejó caer el teléfono sobre las sábanas. Se sentía vacía, pero al mismo tiempo aliviada de haber soltado la carga. Sin embargo, el silencio de la casa, que antes era paz, ahora se sentía como una fría advertencia de lo que sería su vida si ese "espacio" se volvía permanente.

Los días de silencio fueron un tormento para William. En Florida, el sol parecía brillar menos y su habitación se sentía como un cascarón vacío. No podía sacarse de la cabeza la imagen de Valentina en la videollamada, con el miedo reflejado en sus ojos y esa barrera que el pasado y la distancia habían levantado entre los dos. Él lo sabía en lo más profundo de su ser: ella era la mujer de su vida, y no estaba dispuesto a dejarla ir por una cuestión de geografía. Esa noche, después de un largo día de trabajo, antes de acostarse, William hizo algo que no solía hacer con frecuencia. Se sentó en la orilla de su cama, juntó sus manos y lanzó una oración al cielo. No pidió dinero ni éxito profesional; pidió claridad.

—Dame una señal —susurró en la oscuridad—. Dime si debo dejar mi vida aquí, mis hermanos, mi comodidad, para iniciar de cero en su ciudad. Dime si este riesgo vale la pena para trazar un camino juntos.

Se acostó con el corazón latiendo con fuerza, entregándole a Dios su incertidumbre y esperando, con fe, que la respuesta llegara pronto. A la mañana siguiente, el sonido de una notificación en su teléfono lo despertó. Era un aviso de su página web de venta de repuestos de electrodomésticos. William se levantó, se sirvió un café y se sentó frente a su computadora para procesar la orden, como lo hacía cada día. Sin embargo, al abrir los detalles del envío para imprimir la etiqueta, sus ojos se abrieron de par en par. La dirección de entrega le resultaba extremadamente familiar. Miró el número una, dos, tres veces. El código postal era el mismo de

Valentina. William se quedó inmóvil, con la respiración contenida. En un país con más de 40,000 códigos postales, la única orden que había caído esa mañana, justo después de su oración, pertenecía exactamente a la misma ciudad y al mismo sector donde vivía la mujer que amaba. Ahí estaba. No era una coincidencia; era la revelación que había implorado.

—Es aquí —se dijo a sí mismo con una sonrisa de absoluta certeza—. Esta es la respuesta.

En ese instante, cualquier rastro de duda se disipó. El miedo al riesgo fue reemplazado por una determinación inquebrantable.

—Me voy a mudar. Voy a apostarlo todo por nosotros —decretó en voz alta.

Sin perder un segundo, tomó su celular con las manos todavía temblorosas por la emoción y le escribió a Valentina:

"¿Podemos hablar esta noche cuando ya estés en casa?
¿Te llamo a las 9 p. m.?"

En las Carolinas, el teléfono de Valentina vibró sobre la barra de la cafetería. Al ver el nombre de William en la pantalla, sintió que se le oprimía el pecho. Llevaban días en ese "espacio" que se sentía como un desierto, y leer ese mensaje le provocó una oleada de nerviosismo. ¿Sería para despedirse? ¿Para decirle que el espacio sería permanente?

La ansiedad de tener que esperar todo el día era insoportable, así que le contestó de inmediato:

"Sí, está bien. Estaré esperando tu llamada".

Valentina pasó el resto de la jornada como en un trance. Cada cliente que entraba, cada café que servía era solo una distracción del tic-tac del reloj. Por su parte, William pasó el día organizando mentalmente su mudanza, con el alma encendida. Sabía que la conversación de esa noche no sería una más; sería el momento en que la distancia dejaría de ser una amenaza para convertirse en un recuerdo del pasado. La noche cayó sobre las Carolinas con una quietud expectante. Valentina cerró la cafetería y condujo a casa con las manos apretadas al volante, tratando de calmar los latidos de su corazón.

William, en Florida, caminaba de un lado a otro en su sala, con la certeza de quien ha tomado la decisión que cambiará su vida para siempre. Cuando el reloj marcó la hora acordada, el teléfono de Valentina vibró. Ella contestó al primer tono.

—Hola, William —susurró, con la voz cargada de una mezcla de alivio y temor.

—Hola, Vale —respondió él. Su voz no sonaba dubitativa ni triste; sonaba con una claridad y una fuerza que ella no esperaba—. He pensado mucho en lo que dijiste. En tus miedos, en lo difícil que es la distancia y en que no quieres volver a sufrir. Y tienes razón. Esta distancia no nos deja ser quienes podemos ser juntos.

Valentina cerró los ojos, preparándose para lo peor, pensando que él diría que lo mejor era terminar. Pero William continuó:

—No voy a dejar que nos perdamos por vivir en estados diferentes. No voy a permitir que el miedo gane. Así que he tomado una decisión: me mudo para allá, mi amor.

El silencio del otro lado de la línea fue absoluto. Valentina se sentó lentamente en el sofá, procesando las palabras.

—¿Qué dijiste? —logró articular.

—Me voy a mudar a tu ciudad —repitió él con una sonrisa que se adivinaba a través del auricular—. Ya lo decidí. No quiero una relación de visitas cada quince días. Quiero una vida contigo. Quiero estar ahí para desayunar juntos, para apoyarte en tu negocio y para que no tengamos que despedirnos frente a tu casa a las dos de la mañana.

Valentina sintió que las lágrimas empezaban a asomarse, pero esta vez eran de una felicidad abrumadora. La seguridad de William la envolvía como un escudo contra todos sus traumas pasados.

—¿Hablas en serio? —preguntó ella, con la voz entrecortada—. ¿Dejarías todo en Florida por… por nosotros?

—Lo apuesto todo por nosotros —respondió él sin dudar—. Me he puesto una fecha: ¡agosto! Me mudo en agosto. Eso me da exactamente dos meses para organizar mi negocio allá, vender algunas cosas, encontrar un apartamento cerca de ti y cerrar mi ciclo en Florida. En agosto, Valentina, la distancia se acaba.

Valentina soltó un suspiro largo, sintiendo cómo el peso que llevaba en los hombros desde la llamada anterior desaparecía por completo. Los dos meses de espera ya no se sentían como un castigo, sino como una cuenta regresiva emocionante.

—William… no sé qué decir. Estoy en shock, pero esta vez es de pura felicidad —confesó ella, limpiándose una lágrima—. Gracias por elegirnos. Gracias por ser el hombre que no huye ante los problemas.

Esa noche hablaron durante horas. Ya no había miedos, solo planes. Hablaron de las áreas donde él podría buscar un apartamento, de cómo sería su rutina diaria y de la libertad que sentirían al no tener que mirar el reloj para irse al aeropuerto. William guardó para sí el secreto de la "señal divina" del código postal; sabía que llegaría el momento perfecto para contárselo, pero por ahora, el milagro era saber que en agosto sus mundos finalmente serían uno solo.

Capítulo 16:

El inicio de una nueva etapa

Los siguientes sesenta días fueron una coreografía perfecta de ilusión y logística. La incertidumbre que antes los separaba se transformó en un proyecto compartido. Ya no hablaban de "si esto funcionaría", sino de dónde pondrían la cafetera y en qué parque saldrían a caminar por las tardes. William, con su mente de ingeniero técnico, creó una lista de tareas para cerrar su vida en Florida, pero su parte favorita del día era cuando, tras horas de trabajo, se conectaba con Valentina para mostrarle sus avances. En sus ratos libres, escudriñaba aplicaciones de bienes raíces. Cada vez que encontraba algo prometedor, le enviaba el enlace a Valentina de inmediato. El teléfono de Valentina no dejaba de vibrar con fotos de salas iluminadas, cocinas modernas y balcones. "Mira este, mi amor, tiene una ventana enorme donde podrías poner tus plantas" o "Este está a solo diez minutos de tu cafetería; llegaría en un abrir y cerrar de ojos". Ella se convirtió en sus ojos en la ciudad. Valentina, conociendo cada calle y cada rincón, descartaba opciones basándose en el tráfico o la seguridad. "Esa área es muy ruidosa, amor, mejor este otro que está cerca del parque donde nos gusta caminar". Fue una dinámica hermosa donde él ponía los recursos y ella aportaba el conocimiento del "hogar". A pesar de que la familia de William adoraba a Valentina, la magnitud de la decisión empezó a generar tensiones naturales. Mientras él sellaba las cajas de su vida en Florida, la realidad de lo que estaba dejando atrás se volvió palpable para todos, especialmente para su hermano mayor. Roberto, con su instinto protector y su mentalidad pragmática de hermano mayor, no podía evitar ver el riesgo financiero y emocional que esto implicaba. Un día, mientras ayudaba a William a cargar uno de los muebles más pesados, se detuvo, se limpió el sudor de la frente y lo miró con seriedad.

—William, detente un segundo —le dijo, bajando la voz—. Sabemos que Valentina es una mujer increíble, de esas que no se encuentran dos veces. Pero... ¿estás seguro de esto? Estás dejando tu red de apoyo, tu familia, tu comodidad. ¿Realmente vas a dejar todo por una mujer?

William siguió cerrando la caja en la que estaba trabajando, pero sus movimientos eran tranquilos. Roberto continuó, sembrando la duda que cualquier persona racional tendría:

—Es un riesgo enorme, hermano. Te mudas a un estado donde no tienes a nadie más que a ella. ¿Y si no funciona? ¿Y si después de seis meses se dan cuenta de que la convivencia o la cercanía no eran lo que esperaban? Te vas a quedar en el aire.

William dejó la cinta adhesiva a un lado y se puso de pie para enfrentar a su hermano. No había enojo en su rostro, solo una determinación que Roberto no le había visto nunca.

—Entiendo que te preocupe, Roberto, y te lo agradezco porque sé que me quieres —respondió William con voz firme—. Pero no estoy escuchando esos miedos. Lo que siento aquí adentro no es impulso, es certeza. Por primera vez en mi vida, tengo una paz absoluta sobre el camino que estoy tomando. Sé que es un riesgo, pero me da más miedo el riesgo de perderla a ella por no ser lo suficientemente valiente.

William le puso una mano en el hombro a su hermano y añadió:

—Tengo seguridad en lo que somos. Prefiero irme y apostarlo todo que quedarme aquí preguntándome qué habría pasado. Si no funciona, al menos sabré que lo intenté con el alma. Pero mi instinto me dice que esto es solo el principio.

Roberto suspiró, viendo que no había marcha atrás. Aunque en su mente seguía cuestionando la lógica de dejarlo todo, la mirada de William lo convenció de que no había forma de detenerlo.

—Está bien —dijo Roberto, dándole un abrazo—. Aún no estoy convencido de que sea la decisión más inteligente, pero te apoyo porque eres mi hermano y porque veo que ella te ha convertido en un hombre más decidido. Vamos, terminemos de cargar esto.

Hubo noches en las que el cansancio de organizar una mudanza interestatal pesaba, pero bastaba una videollamada para que William recuperara las fuerzas.

—Faltan cuatro semanas, Vale —le decía, sentado entre cajas de cartón—. Ya vendí el último mueble que no me llevaré. Mi vida cabe en este camión ahora, y no puedo esperar para descargarla cerca de ti.

Valentina le enviaba fotos de las cosas que ella estaba comprando para "su bienvenida": una planta nueva, una taza especial o simplemente el calendario donde tachaba los días con una cruz roja. El miedo de Valentina a ser lastimada se había disuelto ante la evidencia de los hechos; William no solo le estaba diciendo que la amaba, se lo estaba demostrando con cada caja sellada y cada contrato firmado. Finalmente, encontraron el lugar perfecto: un apartamento acogedor, con suelos de madera y mucha luz natural, ubicado en un punto estratégico que les permitía estar cerca, pero manteniendo cada uno su independencia inicial. Cuando William firmó el contrato digitalmente y le envió la captura de pantalla a Valentina, ella saltó de alegría en medio de su cocina. Agosto ya no era una fecha en el calendario; era el inicio de su nueva realidad. El día de la partida llegó con un sol radiante sobre Florida, pero el ambiente en el estacionamiento era una mezcla de nostalgia y determinación. William no había contratado un gran camión de mudanza; su vida entera, sus sueños y su futuro cabían en la misma camioneta que utilizaba para su trabajo de reparaciones y venta de repuestos, a la que llamaban "La Bestia". Ese vehículo, que era su herramienta de sustento, se convirtió en el arca que transportaba su nueva existencia.

William acomodó con precisión cada una de sus pertenencias: sus herramientas, el inventario de partes de electrodomésticos que vendía por su web, un sillón, su televisor y las pocas maletas de ropa y objetos personales que decidió conservar. Al cerrar las puertas traseras de la van, el sonido metálico retumbó como un punto final a su etapa en el sur. Roberto estaba allí, observando "La Bestia" cargada hasta el tope. Ver que su hermano se iba con todas sus herramientas de trabajo le hizo entender que William no iba a "probar suerte", sino a plantar su bandera.

—Ahí llevas todo, ¿verdad? —preguntó Roberto, mirando la gran camioneta—. Tu vida, tu taller y tu corazón en un solo carro.

—Es todo lo que necesito —respondió William con una sonrisa tranquila mientras subía al asiento del conductor—. Llevo mi trabajo conmigo, así que mi oficina será la ciudad de Valentina.

La despedida de Karla fue, quizás, la que más le apretó el corazón a William antes de girar la llave del motor. Mientras

Roberto representaba la duda racional, Karla era el refugio emocional. Ella se acercó a la ventanilla de la van, con los ojos un poco cristalinos pero una sonrisa llena de orgullo.

—Vas a estar bien, hermanito—le dijo Karla, tomando su mano a través de la ventana—. No dejes que los miedos de los demás te pesen. Valentina es especial, y el amor de verdad siempre requiere un poco de locura. Cuídala mucho y prométeme que no te olvidarás de nosotros.

William la abrazó desde el asiento del conductor, sintiendo esa dulzura que siempre la caracterizaba.

—Jamás, Karla. Gracias por creer en nosotros desde el primer día.

Desde ese momento, para él, Florida ya era parte de su pasado; su presente y su futuro estaban en una camioneta rumbo al norte, esperándolo con el aroma a café y la sonrisa de la mujer que le había devuelto la fe en el amor. Con ese último adiós, la van arrancó. A medida que avanzaba por la autopista, William veía por el retrovisor cómo la silueta de sus hermanos se hacía pequeña, pero en su pecho la sensación de libertad crecía. Llevaba su taller, sus repuestos y su vida entera en ese vehículo. Mientras tanto, en las Carolinas, Valentina no podía quedarse quieta. Había limpiado el nuevo apartamento de William dos veces, aunque ya estaba impecable. Tenía las llaves en su bolsillo, tocándolas a cada momento para asegurarse de que eran reales. Sabía que él venía en esa camioneta, manejando solo, cargando no solo objetos, sino la apuesta más grande que un hombre podía hacer por una mujer. Nueve horas después, el paisaje cambió del verde tropical de Florida a los árboles frondosos y el aire más fresco de las Carolinas. Cuando el GPS le indicó a William que estaba a solo diez minutos de su destino, sintió una descarga de adrenalina. Entró a la ciudad de Valentina no como un turista o un visitante de fin de semana, sino como un residente. Cuando finalmente dobló la esquina de la calle de su nuevo apartamento, vio a Valentina. Ella estaba de pie en la acera, con los brazos cruzados para protegerse de la brisa, mirando ansiosamente cada carro que pasaba. Al ver la camioneta blanca de William, soltó un grito ahogado de emoción y corrió hacia el borde de la calle. William estacionó el vehículo, apagó el motor y, por un segundo, se quedó sentado inhalando el silencio. Lo había logrado. En ese instante supo que Roberto se equivocaba. El riesgo no era mudarse; el riesgo habría sido quedarse en Florida y perderse la oportunidad de ver esa mirada todos los días de su vida. Se bajó de "La Bestia" y, antes de que pudiera decir una palabra, Valentina se lanzó a sus brazos, rodeándole el cuello con fuerza. Él la levantó del suelo, girando con ella mientras el sonido de sus risas llenaba la calle vacía.

—Ya estoy aquí, mi amor —susurró él contra su oído—. No más maletas, no más aeropuertos. Esta vez me quedo.

Valentina se separó un poco, con las mejillas bañadas en lágrimas de alegría, y sacó del bolsillo un juego de llaves con un llavero nuevo.

—Bienvenido a casa, mi vida.

Entraron juntos al apartamento vacío, que aún olía a pintura fresca y madera, pero para ambos ese espacio se sentía más lleno que cualquier palacio. William regresó a la camioneta, bajó la primera caja —con algunas de sus herramientas de trabajo— y se la entregó.

—Tú decides dónde va la primera pieza de nuestra nueva vida —le dijo él con una mirada cargada de devoción.

Tras las primeras risas y el alivio del encuentro, comenzó la verdadera labor. La noche cayó sobre la ciudad mientras ellos, con una energía que solo el entusiasmo puede dar, se dedicaron a descargar la camioneta. William subía las cajas con sus pertenencias, mientras Valentina lo ayudaba a organizar lo básico para que el apartamento empezara a tener alma. Pasaron las horas entre el sonido de la cinta adhesiva rasgándose y el eco de sus voces en las paredes vacías. El cansancio físico empezó a ganarles terreno cerca de la medianoche. William terminó de inflar el colchón que sería su cama provisional en medio de la sala, rodeado de cajas a medio abrir. Valentina, con los ojos pesados por el esfuerzo de un día cargado de emociones, se sentó en el borde del colchón "solo por un momento". Pero el cansancio era absoluto; se recostó de lado, apoyando la mejilla sobre su brazo y, sin darse cuenta, se quedó profundamente dormida. William, que estaba en la cocina terminando de acomodar unas piezas, se acercó para decirle que ya era hora de que ella fuera a su casa a descansar. Al verla, se detuvo en seco. Valentina dormía con una expresión de paz absoluta, con el cabello algo desordenado y la respiración tranquila. Le causó tanta ternura verla allí, en medio de su nuevo hogar, que no tuvo corazón para despertarla. Con movimientos lentos para no hacer ruido, apagó la luz del pasillo, dejando que solo la claridad de la luna entrara por el ventanal sin cortinas. Se quitó los zapatos, se recostó a su lado con cuidado y la abrazó por la espalda, protegiéndola. En ese momento, con el aroma de Valentina llenándole los sentidos, cerró los ojos y se sumergió en un sueño reparador.

Cuando volvió a abrirlos, la luz suave de la mañana ya inundaba el apartamento. El sol de las Carolinas entraba con fuerza, iluminando las cajas y el espacio que ahora le pertenecía. Se giró lentamente y vio a Valentina, que aún seguía profundamente dormida, ajena al inicio del nuevo día. Se quedó hipnotizado mirándola. Con la punta de los dedos, le acarició el rostro con una delicadeza infinita, apartándole un mechón de pelo de la frente. Se inclinó y le dio un beso suave en la mejilla, sintiendo la calidez de su piel. Mientras la observaba en silencio, un pensamiento se instaló en su mente con la fuerza de un decreto: así era como quería despertar el resto de su vida, a su lado. Ya no había dudas, ni kilómetros, ni miedos ajenos. En esa habitación semivacía, William supo que cada sacrificio y cada hora de manejo habían valido la pena. El despertar de Valentina fue lento, envuelto en una confusión dulce. Al abrir los ojos y encontrarse en el apartamento de William, le tomó un segundo recordar que ya no era un sueño: él estaba allí. Se estiró sobre el colchón inflable y se encontró con la mirada de William, que la observaba con una adoración que la hizo sonreír de inmediato.

—Buenos días, residente oficial —susurró ella, aún con la voz ronca por el sueño.

—Los mejores días de mi vida, Vale —respondió él, dándole un abrazo que selló el inicio de su primera mañana juntos.

Valentina se quedó ahí, refugiada en su pecho, escuchando el latido rítmico del corazón de William. En ese instante, todo el ruido del pasado —el miedo a ser lastimada que la había paralizado meses atrás y las dudas sobre la distancia— se desvaneció por completo. La seguridad que él le brindaba al haberlo dejado todo por ella la llenó de una valentía nueva. Se separó apenas unos centímetros para mirarlo a los ojos. Ya no había shock, ni confusión, ni necesidad de bajar la mirada. Con una claridad absoluta y una ternura que le desbordaba el alma, soltó las palabras que su corazón venía gritando en silencio:

—Te amo, William.

El tiempo pareció detenerse de nuevo, pero esta vez fue diferente a aquella noche en el porche. William sintió que el aire se le escapaba de los pulmones; había esperado tanto por escuchar esas palabras, y recibirlas precisamente en su primera mañana como habitantes de la misma ciudad fue el regalo más grande que pudo imaginar.

—Te amo tanto —repitió ella, reafirmando cada letra mientras le acariciaba la mejilla.

William la estrechó contra él con más fuerza, hundiendo el rostro en su cabello. Aquel "te amo" no era solo un sentimiento; era el sello de un pacto. Era la respuesta a su mudanza, a sus nueve horas de manejo y a su apuesta total por ella. En esa habitación vacía, rodeados de cajas y sobre un colchón de aire, Valentina le entregó finalmente la llave de su corazón, sabiendo que, por fin, estaba en casa. Esa mañana, como aún no tenían mesa, el ingenio de William entró en acción. Usó una de las cajas más grandes y resistentes, la colocó en medio de lo que sería el comedor y puso un mantel individual que Valentina había traído de su casa. El "banquete" fue sencillo pero inolvidable: café caliente que ella había traído en un termo y unos cruasanes frescos de su propia cafetería. Sentados en el suelo, uno frente al otro, con la caja de cartón como testigo, empezaron a trazar el mapa de su nueva cotidianidad. Él le explicó que, aunque seguiría gestionando su página web de repuestos, ahora que estaba allí planeaba ofrecer sus servicios de reparación técnica a domicilio en la ciudad.

—Mañana mismo empiezo a repartir tarjetas y a actualizar mi ubicación en línea —dijo con entusiasmo.

Ella, emocionada, le propuso poner publicidad de sus servicios en la cafetería.

—Todos mis clientes siempre necesitan a alguien de confianza que repare algo, amor. ¡Vas a tener trabajo de sobra!

Decidieron que esa mañana él la acompañaría a la cafetería, no para despedirse antes de un vuelo o un viaje largo, sino para conocer el camino que, a partir de ahora, recorrería constantemente. Mientras compartían el café, la conversación fluyó hacia los pequeños detalles: qué supermercado estaba cerca, a qué hora cerraba el gimnasio y qué ruta era la mejor para evitar el tráfico. Eran cosas mundanas, pero para ellos, después de meses de distancia, hablar de estas nimiedades era un lujo absoluto. William la miró por encima de su taza de café, viendo cómo Valentina anotaba algunas cosas en una servilleta. Se dio cuenta de que lo que Roberto llamaba "un gran riesgo", para él era la inversión más segura de su vida.

—¿Sabes qué es lo mejor de este desayuno? —preguntó William.

—¿Qué? —respondió ella, curiosa.

—Que cuando termine el día y cierres la cafetería, no tengo que llamarte por video. Puedo verte en cualquier momento.

Valentina sintió que se le iluminaba el rostro. Ese desayuno sobre una caja de cartón sabía mejor que cualquier cena de lujo, porque tenía el ingrediente que les había faltado siempre: la permanencia. Esa mañana, William acompañó a Valentina a su cafetería. Mientras caminaban hacia la entrada, ella sentía que el suelo era más firme y el aire más ligero. William, con su mano entrelazada en la de ella, observaba las fachadas de los negocios vecinos con la curiosidad de quien sabe que ahora ese es su vecindario. Al llegar a la puerta del negocio, Valentina se detuvo un segundo. Miró el rótulo de su cafetería y luego miró a William. Siempre había entrado ahí como la mujer independiente y fuerte que sacaba adelante su sueño sola; hoy, lo hacía como una mujer que había encontrado a su compañero de vida. En cuanto pusieron un pie dentro, el aroma a grano tostado los envolvió. Sus empleados, que habían vivido de cerca los suspiros de Valentina frente a la pantalla del celular y sus viajes relámpago, se quedaron congelados al ver a William entrar cargando unas cajas de suministros que él mismo se había ofrecido a llevar.

Valentina caminó detrás de la barra con una sonrisa que iluminaba todo el local.

—¡Buenos días a todos! —exclamó, llamando la atención incluso de los clientes que ya leían el periódico en las mesas—. Muchos de ustedes conocen a William por mis historias y por sus visitas cortas... pero hoy quiero presentarles oficialmente al nuevo residente de nuestra ciudad.

Puso una mano sobre el brazo de William y, con un brillo de orgullo en los ojos, continuó:

—Él es el emprendedor que finalmente dejó las palmeras de Florida para mudarse aquí. Es el hombre que decidió que la distancia no iba a ganarnos.

Hubo un pequeño aplauso espontáneo de los clientes más fieles, aquellos que ya se sentían parte de la familia de la cafetería. Los empleados se acercaron a darle la bienvenida con apretones de mano y bromas. William, con su humildad característica, agradeció a todos, sintiéndose aceptado de inmediato en el pequeño reino que Valentina había construido. William no perdió tiempo. Aprovechó ese primer día para instalar en un rincón estratégico de la cafetería un pequeño porta-tarjetas de madera que él mismo había preparado. En las tarjetas se leía: "William: Reparación de Electrodomésticos y Venta de Repuestos".

—Así, cada vez que alguien venga por un café y comente que se le arruinó la lavadora o el refrigerador, sabrán a quién llamar —dijo, guiñándole un ojo a Valentina.

Al mediodía, durante un breve descanso, se sentaron en una de las mesas del rincón. William tomó la mano de Valentina sobre la madera y le susurró:

—Tenías razón, Vale. Este lugar tiene una energía increíble. Gracias por dejarme ser parte de él.

Ese primer día en la misma ciudad fue la prueba de fuego que ambos superaron con creces. Ya no eran dos personas distantes que se enviaban fotos para acortar los kilómetros; eran dos emprendedores apoyándose bajo el mismo techo, construyendo no solo una relación, sino un futuro sólido donde cada café servido y cada máquina reparada era un ladrillo más en el hogar que soñaban formar. Valentina sentía una satisfacción inmensa al verlo desenvolverse en su cafetería. No se sentía invadida; al contrario, sentía que su presencia le quitaba un peso de los hombros. Por su parte, William disfrutaba de la energía del lugar, dándose cuenta de que el negocio de Valentina era un reflejo de su propia fuerza y calidez. Al caer la tarde, cuando el último cliente se retiró y el aroma a café empezaba a mezclarse con la frescura del anochecer, compartieron un momento de calma absoluta en el local.

—¡Lo logramos, amor! —dijo ella, apoyando la cabeza en su hombro mientras él la rodeaba con el brazo—. Es el primer día de nuestra vida en la misma ciudad.

—¡Y fue perfecto! —respondió él—. Verte trabajar, ver cómo la gente te quiere… solo me confirma que tomé la decisión correcta al venir aquí.

A pesar de la intensidad de sus sentimientos y de haber pasado la noche anterior juntos debido al agotamiento de la mudanza, mantenían la decisión de vivir en casas separadas por el momento. Valentina quería que William tuviera su propio espacio para establecer su taller y su independencia en esta nueva ciudad, y él respetaba profundamente ese proceso. Sabían que, para que lo de ellos fuera sano y duradero, debían ir paso a paso. Cuando llegó el momento de cerrar el local, William la acompañó hasta su auto. Esta vez, la despedida no tenía ese sabor amargo a aeropuerto o a carretera interestatal.

—¿Te veo mañana para desayunar? —preguntó él con una sonrisa traviesa.

—Mañana y todos los días, mi amor —contestó Valentina, dándole un beso corto pero lleno de promesas.

Mientras ella se alejaba en su coche y William caminaba de regreso a su nuevo apartamento, ambos sentían una libertad que nunca habían experimentado. Estaban cerca, estaban presentes y, lo más importante, sabían que al día siguiente no habría una pantalla de por medio, sino la realidad compartida de una vida que apenas comenzaba a florecer.

Capítulo 17:

La disciplina de un toro

Los meses siguientes fueron una demostración absoluta de carácter y sacrificio. William no se había mudado solo para estar cerca de Valentina; se había mudado para construir el cimiento sólido sobre el cual ella pudiera caminar segura. Entendía que, para pedirle que fuera su esposa, primero debía demostrarse a sí mismo —y al mundo— que era capaz de prosperar desde cero en una tierra nueva. William se convirtió en un reloj de precisión. Cada mañana, el despertador sonaba puntualmente a las 6:00 a. m. Mientras la ciudad aún dormía y la luz del alba apenas teñía las ventanas de su apartamento, él ya estaba sentado frente a su computadora con una taza de café humeante. Dedicaba la primera hora del día a organizar su ruta. Con la eficiencia de un ingeniero, trazaba los puntos en el mapa para gastar la menor cantidad de combustible y tiempo posible.

Enviaba mensajes de confirmación a cada cliente:

> *"Buenos días, soy William.*
> *Confirmando su reparación para las 8:00 a.m.*
> *Escribe una C para confirmar o X para cancelar".*

Quería que su reputación fuera impecable: puntualidad, honestidad y excelencia. Bajaba a su camioneta, que ahora estaba perfectamente etiquetada con su logo, y revisaba su inventario de repuestos. Nada podía faltar. A las 7:30 a. m. ya estaba en la carretera. Manejaba de un extremo a otro de la ciudad, enfrentándose al tráfico y al clima, subiendo y bajando herramientas pesadas, reparando refrigeradores en cocinas calurosas o instalando piezas en lavanderías estrechas.

Había días en los que el cansancio físico era extenuante. Sus manos tenían los callos del trabajo duro y el rastro del aceite y el metal. Pero cada vez que recibía un pago, no veía simplemente dinero; veía un fondo sagrado. Ahorraba cada dólar con una disciplina de hierro, separando lo necesario para sus gastos y destinando el resto a una cuenta específica: el fondo para el anillo de compromiso. A veces, su jornada laboral se extendía más allá de lo previsto. Entre emergencias de clientes y pedidos de última hora, terminaba su día a las 9:00 de la noche. Llegaba a su apartamento agotado, con la espalda adolorida, pero con el corazón encendido. Valentina, desde su cafetería, observaba este despliegue de voluntad con una admiración silenciosa. Ella sabía que él estaba trabajando duro, pero no sospechaba la magnitud del plan que William guardaba en secreto. A veces, le llevaba un almuerzo rápido a algún punto de su ruta o lo esperaba con una cena caliente cuando él finalmente terminaba.

—Estás trabajando demasiado, Will —le decía ella a veces, acariciándole el rostro cansado.

—Vale la pena, amor. Todo esto tiene un propósito —respondía él con una sonrisa cansada pero llena de luz.

Para William, esas quince horas diarias de trabajo no eran un peso; eran el precio de su libertad y de su futuro. Cada reparación exitosa era un paso más cerca de esa joyería donde ya había visto el diamante que imaginaba en la mano de Valentina. Estaba demostrando que era un hombre de provecho, un protector, y que el riesgo que tomó al dejar Florida estaba rindiendo los frutos más dulces de su vida. Esa mañana, el sol entró por la ventana del apartamento de William con una intensidad distinta, como si el mismo cielo supiera que ese sería un día muy especial. Antes siquiera de prepararse su café, se sentó en su pequeño escritorio y abrió su caja de ahorros y sus estados de cuenta. Con el corazón latiendo a mil, hizo el conteo final. Ahí estaba: cada dólar ahorrado tras jornadas de quince horas, cada sacrificio de esos meses de "sol a sol", se había materializado en la cifra exacta. Ya estaba listo.

Antes de ir a la joyería, William sabía que debía dar un paso fundamental por el profundo respeto que le tenía a Valentina y a su historia. Se acomodó frente a su teléfono y marcó la videollamada a los padres de ella. Cuando los rostros de sus futuros suegros aparecieron en pantalla, William respiró hondo. No hubo rodeos; su voz sonaba firme pero cargada de emoción.

—Los llamo porque quiero que sepan lo mucho que amo a su hija —comenzó diciendo—. He trabajado muy duro para construir un futuro para ella aquí. Hoy voy a comprar su anillo y quería pedirles formalmente su mano y su bendición. La reacción fue inmediata. El entusiasmo y la calidez inundaron la pantalla. Los padres de Valentina, que habían visto cómo ese hombre dejó su estado y su comodidad por amor, no dudaron ni un segundo.

—William, no tienes que pedirlo, ya eres parte de nosotros —le dijeron conmovidos—. Nada nos hace más felices que saber que ella estará al lado de un hombre como tú. Bienvenido a la familia.

Con el corazón ensanchado por la bendición de los padres, William se tomó un café rápido, sintiendo que la cafeína era innecesaria con la adrenalina que recorría su cuerpo. Se vistió con esmero y manejó hacia la joyería más prestigiosa de la zona. Al cruzar la entrada del establecimiento, el brillo de las vitrinas lo recibió con una elegancia silenciosa. Una vendedora se acercó con amabilidad y William, sin titubear, le dijo las palabras que habían estado grabadas en su mente durante meses:

—Busco un anillo de compromiso. Pero no cualquiera. Quiero el mejor que pueda conseguir para el amor de mi vida.

La vendedora, conmovida por la determinación en sus ojos, empezó a mostrarle diferentes cortes y monturas. William observó diamantes redondos, cortes princesa y esmeralda, pero su mente buscaba algo que gritara "Valentina": algo elegante, eterno y brillante como su sonrisa.

Finalmente, tras ver varias opciones, sus ojos se detuvieron en uno. Era una pieza exquisita, un diamante con una pureza que capturaba la luz de manera mágica, montado en una banda de oro que simbolizaba la fortaleza de su unión. Era ese.

William sacó su tarjeta, sintiendo un orgullo inmenso al pagar. No le dolió ni un centavo; al contrario, sentía que estaba intercambiando meses de sudor por un símbolo de eternidad. Cuando la vendedora le entregó la pequeña caja de terciopelo, la sostuvo entre sus manos un momento, sintiendo el peso de su promesa.

Salió de la joyería con el anillo en el bolsillo, caminando con la seguridad de quien ya no solo tiene un plan, sino que tiene el destino entre las manos. Solo faltaba el momento perfecto para ver esa joya brillar en el dedo de la mujer que lo había cambiado todo.

Capítulo 18:

Un 'sí' bajo cielo nuevo

Octubre llegó con su aire fresco y sus tonos dorados, trayendo consigo el aroma de las hojas secas y una luz especial que bañaba la ciudad. Para William, este mes no era solo el inicio del otoño; era el marco perfecto para el plan que había tejido con tanta paciencia y esfuerzo. Era el cumpleaños de Valentina, y él sabía que no habría mejor regalo que una promesa de eternidad. La mañana del cumpleaños comenzó con el sonido del teléfono de Valentina. Al contestar, la voz de William la envolvió con la calidez de siempre, cantándole "Las Mañanitas" con una devoción que la hizo despertar con una sonrisa de oreja a oreja.

—Feliz cumpleaños, mi reina. Hoy el día es todo tuyo —le dijo él con entusiasmo—. Ponte más bella de lo que ya eres, porque esta tarde voy a pasarte a buscar para consentirte como te mereces. Tenemos una cita.

Valentina pasó el día sumergida en ese ritual de amor propio que toda mujer disfruta en su fecha especial. Se arregló las uñas, dedicó tiempo a su cabello y respondió, entre risas y alguna lágrima de alegría, la lluvia de mensajes y llamadas de su familia en la distancia. El ambiente en su casa era de pura celebración, pero en el fondo de su pecho sentía una cosquilla de anticipación; presentía que esa noche sería diferente. A las 5:00 p. m., puntual como siempre, William llegó por ella. Al verla, se quedó sin aliento; Valentina irradiaba una luz que ninguna joya podría igualar. Se dirigieron a un restaurante que William había elegido cuidadosamente: un lugar con luz tenue, paredes de ladrillo visto y una terraza que ofrecía una vista privilegiada de la ciudad.

Al sentarse, el mesero les sirvió dos copas de champán. Las burbujas subían mientras brindaban por la vida de Valentina y por el camino que habían recorrido juntos. Conversaron por horas, recordando anécdotas de sus meses de distancia y riendo por lo lejos que habían llegado. Tras el brindis, disfrutaron de un plato fuerte exquisito y cerraron con un postre de chocolate que compartieron entre miradas cómplices. El ambiente era perfecto: el sonido de un piano de fondo, el murmullo suave de otras parejas y la sensación de que el tiempo se había detenido solo para ellos. Al terminar, William pidió la cuenta con una calma que ocultaba los nervios que empezaban a apretarle el pecho.

—Caminemos un poco por el centro, Vale. La noche está hermosa —sugirió él.

Sin que ella lo notara, William fue guiando sus pasos con precisión hacia un punto específico. Los sonidos de la ciudad empezaron a ser reemplazados por el rugido constante y relajante del agua. Llegaron justo frente a las cataratas, el lugar exacto donde meses atrás, en su primera visita desde Florida, se habían sentado a platicar por horas, redescubriendo quiénes eran. El sonido del agua cayendo creaba una cortina de privacidad absoluta. William se detuvo, tomó las manos de Valentina entre las suyas y la miró con una intensidad que le erizó la piel.

—Valentina, mira este lugar —comenzó él con la voz cargada de emoción—. Fue justo aquí donde nuestra magia comenzó a brillar de nuevo después de tantos años desde que nos conocimos en nuestro país. Quizás en aquel entonces el destino decidió que no era nuestro momento, pero hoy, después de todo lo que hemos luchado, estoy seguro de que este lo es.

Valentina sintió que el aliento se le escapaba. Sus ojos se humedecieron al instante y un escalofrío de felicidad recorrió todo su cuerpo. William no se detuvo; metió la mano en su bolsillo y extrajo la pequeña caja de terciopelo que contenía el fruto de todos sus meses de trabajo duro.

—Te amo con cada fibra de mi ser, y después de despertar a tu lado aquella primera mañana, supe que no quería pasar un solo día de mi vida lejos de ti. Vale, mi amor… ¿te quieres casar conmigo?

Al abrir la caja, el diamante capturó el reflejo de las luces de la ciudad y el brillo de la luna, resplandeciendo con una pureza asombrosa. Valentina estaba en shock, llena de una dicha que no le cabía en el pecho. Las lágrimas finalmente rodaron por sus mejillas, pero eran lágrimas de triunfo, de amor y de paz. Sin pensarlo dos veces, con el corazón gritando de alegría, se lanzó a sus brazos y exclamó:

—¡Sí! ¡Mil veces sí, mi amor!

Bajo el estruendo de las cataratas y la mirada cómplice de la noche de octubre, se fundieron en un beso que sellaba no solo un compromiso, sino el inicio formal de la familia que siempre soñaron ser. Con las manos aún temblorosas por la emoción, William tomó la mano izquierda de Valentina. Con una delicadeza infinita, deslizó el anillo en su dedo; la joya encajó perfectamente, brillando con una intensidad que parecía sellar el destino que ambos habían estado construyendo. Fue en ese momento, con el sonido de las cataratas como fondo y el peso del compromiso ya en su mano, cuando William sintió que era el momento de revelarle el secreto que había guardado durante meses.

—Vale, hay algo que nunca te conté —dijo él, rodeándola con sus brazos para protegerla del fresco de la noche—. Aquella noche en que decidimos darnos un espacio, yo estaba destrozado. Sentía que te perdía y no sabía qué hacer. Así que me aferré a mi fe y le pedí a Dios una señal. Le pedí que me dejara saber si debía dejar mi vida en Florida para venir por ti.

Valentina lo escuchaba con los ojos muy abiertos, conteniendo el aliento.

—A la mañana siguiente —continuó William— recibí una sola orden en mi página web. Una sola entre miles de posibilidades en todo el país. Cuando vi la dirección de envío, era tú mismo código postal. Exactamente el lugar donde tú vivías. En ese segundo supe que no era una coincidencia, era la respuesta que había pedido.

Valentina rompió a llorar de nuevo, pero esta vez era una mezcla de asombro y gratitud. Entendió que su amor no solo era una decisión de dos personas, sino algo que el cielo había guiado.

La adrenalina del "sí" aún corría por sus venas cuando decidieron compartir la noticia. Sentados todavía frente a las cataratas, William activó una videollamada grupal. Aparecieron los rostros de los padres de Valentina y, casi al mismo tiempo, los de Roberto y Karla.

—¡Miren! —exclamó Valentina, levantando su mano izquierda frente a la cámara con una sonrisa radiante.

El grito de alegría inundó el auricular. Karla saltaba de emoción; Roberto, por primera vez, sonreía sin reservas.

—William, ese código postal fue el mejor negocio de tu vida —bromeó Roberto—. Y me alegra haberme equivocado.

Más tarde, mientras caminaban de regreso al auto, surgió la pregunta inevitable: ¿Cuándo?

Valentina abrió el calendario en su teléfono.

—Tiene que ser una fecha que signifique algo para nosotros —dijo William.

Sus miradas se cruzaron.

—El 2 de enero —susurraron casi al unísono.

Era la fecha perfecta: el día de su reencuentro había sido esa misma fecha después de cinco años. Ahora sería el día de su unión ante Dios y los hombres.

—Será un reto organizar todo en tres meses —calculó William—, pero es el momento ideal.

—Es un mensaje para nosotros mismos —respondió Valentina—: no vamos a perder ni un segundo más.

Esa noche se despidieron sabiendo que ya no soñaban con un futuro incierto; ahora caminaban hacia un altar concreto.

Las fiestas navideñas y el fin de año fueron un torbellino de abrazos, maletas y reencuentros. Por primera vez en mucho tiempo, el apartamento de William y la casa de Valentina estaban llenos de voces familiares. Todos estaban allí por una sola razón: ser testigos del triunfo de un amor que desafió la lógica, el tiempo y la distancia.

Capítulo 19:

El destino nunca llega tarde

El 2 de enero amaneció con un cielo despejado y un aire fresco que parecía renovar las promesas del invierno. Valentina despertó antes de que saliera el sol, sintiendo que el corazón le latía con un ritmo acelerado, una mezcla de paz absoluta y una adrenalina eléctrica. Lo primero que hizo fue tomar su teléfono y marcar el número de William.

—Hoy es el gran día, amor —susurró ella, con la voz cargada de emoción—. Hoy iniciaremos una nueva etapa en nuestras vidas. Finalmente, el 2 de enero será nuestro para siempre.

Al otro lado de la línea, William, quien ya estaba despierto y mirando por la ventana su nueva ciudad, respondió con una ilusión que se sentía en cada palabra.

—No puedo esperar para verte caminar hacia mí. Estoy listo para este gran paso.

Tras colgar, Valentina intentó desayunar. Se preparó un café y un croissant con huevo, un guiño a sus mañanas en la cafetería, pero la comida apenas le pasaba por la garganta. La emoción y los nervios eran tan grandes que sentía el estómago cerrado, pero cada sorbo de café le recordaba que este era el combustible para el día más importante de su vida. Pocas horas después, el ambiente en su habitación se transformó en un santuario de belleza. Llegó la encargada de peinarla, quien empezó a trabajar en un recogido elegante pero natural. Mientras tanto, Valentina decidió maquillarse ella misma.

Quería reconocerse en el espejo; quería que cada trazo de sombra y cada capa de rímel fueran puestos con sus propias manos, con la calma de quien sabe exactamente quién es y cómo quería lucir ese gran día. Su madre no se separó de su lado. Con una ternura infinita, la ayudaba a organizar las joyas, el perfume y el velo, compartiendo consejos en voz baja y conteniendo las lágrimas de orgullo al ver a su hija convertida en una novia radiante. Mientras tanto, la actividad en el apartamento de William era incesante. Los hermanos de Valentina se encargaban de los últimos viajes, llevando cajas con detalles finales, libros y objetos personales que ella aún tenía en su casa. Durante los últimos meses, William y Valentina habían dedicado cada fin de semana libre a amueblar ese apartamento juntos. Ya no era solo el lugar donde William trabajaba con sus repuestos; ahora había una mesa de comedor donde cabían todos, un sofá acogedor elegido por ambos y cuadros que contaban su historia. Los hermanos de Valentina acomodaban las últimas piezas, sintiendo que estaban ayudando a darle forma al santuario donde nacería esta nueva familia. Ya solo faltaba que ella entrara por esa puerta con su vestido blanco para que el lugar dejara de ser un apartamento y se convirtiera, oficialmente, en un hogar. William, mientras tanto, se vestía con su traje, sintiendo el peso del anillo en el bolsillo y la bendición de tener a toda su gente cerca. La espera de cinco años y el sacrificio de los últimos meses se resumían en este día: el 2 de enero ya no era una fecha de reencuentro, era el primer día del resto de su historia. El ambiente dentro de la iglesia era una extensión del alma de ambos: un refugio de paz y elegancia rústica. La estructura, con sus altos techos de madera tallada, crujía suavemente, otorgando una solemnidad que parecía venir de siglos atrás. El aire estaba impregnado de una mezcla exquisita de aroma a pino fresco y cera de abeja, proveniente de las decenas de velas que flanqueaban el pasillo, cuyas llamas bailaban creando sombras cálidas en las paredes. La decoración de invierno se completaba con arreglos de flores blancas y detalles en azul turquesa, un contraste vibrante que recordaba la pureza del compromiso y la profundidad del cielo que los había guiado. William estaba de pie frente al altar, con la espalda más recta que nunca. A pesar de su formación técnica y su mente lógica, en ese momento se sentía desbordado. Sus manos, ocultas tras su espalda, temblaban levemente. Sentía el peso de la mirada de su familia y la de Roberto, quien desde la primera fila lo miraba con un respeto profundo. Para William, cada segundo de silencio era un repaso de su vida: comenzando por cuando la conoció en la universidad, su mudanza a Estados Unidos, su reencuentro en un país ajeno, su cambio a una ciudad nueva y el anillo comprado con el sudor de su frente. Todo lo había traído a este preciso momento. De repente, los primeros acordes de la canción de entrada rompieron el murmullo. Las puertas del fondo se abrieron de par en par y una luz blanca inundó el pasillo. Allí estaba ella. Valentina caminaba lentamente, sujeta con firmeza del brazo de su padre. Se veía etérea, casi celestial, con su vestido de encaje blanco que se ceñía a su silueta antes de fundirse en una cola larga y majestuosa que barría el suelo con elegancia. El velo flotaba detrás de ella como una bruma ligera. Cuando William la vio, el mundo exterior desapareció. Ese hombre de mente fuerte se desarmó por completo. No pudo contener las lágrimas; la emoción, acumulada durante meses de lucha y años de espera, le ganó la partida. Las lágrimas rodaron por sus mejillas sin control, borrando cualquier rastro de la rigidez que intentaba mantener. Verla caminar hacia él no era solo ver a una novia; era ver la respuesta a todas sus oraciones. Al llegar al altar, el padre de Valentina se detuvo. Sus ojos también brillaban de emoción. Tomó la mano de su hija, la depositó sobre la de William y, en un gesto de entrega absoluta, rodeó a su futuro yerno en un abrazo protector. Se acercó al oído de William y, con una voz cargada de la autoridad que solo un padre posee, le susurró:

—Te entrego mi tesoro más valioso, cuídala.

William, con la voz quebrada por el llanto, pero con una firmeza que venía desde lo más profundo de su ser, le respondió en un susurro cargado de honor:

—Con mi vida entera.

El padre de Valentina asintió, le dio un beso en la frente a su hija y dio un paso atrás. En ese momento, William tomó la mano de Valentina. Sus dedos se entrelazaron. Estaban allí, frente a Dios, sus amistades más íntimas y su familia, listos para que el "te amo" que se dijeron en un colchón inflable se transformara en un "hasta que la muerte nos separe".

William habló desde el alma:

—Valentina, durante mucho tiempo pensé que mi vida se definía en mis sueños profesionales, mi familia y mis proyectos. Pero el día que recibí aquella señal del código postal, entendí que el destino no me estaba enviando a una ciudad, me estaba enviando a ti. Hoy entiendo que mi hogar no es una dirección en el mapa. Mi hogar es cualquier lugar donde tú estés. Prometo ser tu refugio, el hombre que trabaje día y noche para que nunca te falte nada y hacerte feliz el resto de tu vida. Valentina, con la voz entrecortada por la felicidad, juró amarlo en la salud y en la enfermedad, en la abundancia y en aquellos días de esfuerzo donde apenas comenzaban a construir su mundo. Un suspiro colectivo pareció recorrer el lugar, y en medio de esa emoción contenida, el sacerdote pronunció:

—Lo que Dios ha unido, que no lo separe el hombre.

William rodeó la cintura de Valentina y la besó con una pasión que contenía más de cinco años de historia. Al darse la vuelta para caminar hacia la salida, ya no como dos novios, sino como señor y señora Villatoro, la marcha nupcial estalló con júbilo. Las pesadas puertas de madera se abrieron y el aire frío de enero los recibió. Una lluvia de pétalos blancos cayó sobre ellos, lanzada por sus hermanos, padres y amigos que gritaban de alegría. Roberto, con una sonrisa de oreja a oreja, fue el primero en abrazarlos fuera, reconociendo que aquel "gran riesgo" se había convertido en la mayor bendición de la familia. La recepción fue una explosión de alegría y calidez que contrastaba con el frío invierno exterior.

El salón estaba bañado en una luz ámbar, con velas flotando en centros de mesa de cristal y el murmullo emocionado de dos familias que finalmente se unían. Cuando el maestro de ceremonias anunció la entrada de los recién casados, el salón estalló en aplausos. Valentina y William caminaron hacia el centro de la pista, envueltos en una atmósfera mágica. Al llegar al centro, la música comenzó a sonar; era esa canción romántica y especial cuya letra parecía haber sido escrita para ellos, narrando cada kilómetro recorrido, cada encuentro y cada promesa hecha en la distancia. William la tomó de la cintura y ella apoyó sus manos en sus hombros, entrelazando los dedos detrás de su nuca. Se miraron a los ojos y el mundo alrededor desapareció. Mientras bailaban lentamente, Valentina veía en los ojos de William no solo al hombre que amaba, sino al compañero que había cruzado fronteras por ella. William, por su parte, sentía el roce del encaje de su vestido y el aroma de su perfume, sabiendo que ya no habría más despedidas. Los invitados los rodeaban en un círculo de amor, viendo cómo la pareja se susurraba palabras al oído al ritmo de la melodía. El ambiente estaba cargado de una paz absoluta; era el baile de la victoria. Al terminar la canción, el salón se llenó de un silencio respetuoso para el brindis. Los meseros pasaron rápidamente distribuyendo las copas de champán, cuyas burbujas brillaban bajo las lámparas de cristal.

El papá de Valentina se puso en pie, levantando su copa con mano firme, pero ojos vidriosos. Con voz profunda, expresó su gratitud:

—Como padre, uno siempre teme quién cuidará el corazón de su hija. Hoy, mi corazón está tranquilo. William, eres un hombre trabajador, respetuoso y, sobre todo, un hombre que le da a Valentina el lugar que merece. Gracias por ser ese hombre que ella necesitaba.

Luego fue el turno de Roberto. Tomó el micrófono, soltó una pequeña risa nerviosa y miró a su hermano.

—Muchos saben que yo soy el de los números y la lógica. Cuando William me dijo que lo dejaría todo en Florida para mudarse por amor, le dije que estaba loco. Creí que se estaba arriesgando demasiado, que estaba dejando su estabilidad por una incertidumbre. Pero estar aquí esta noche, viendo cómo se miran y lo que han construido en estos meses, me confirma que su locura era la mayor de las sabidurías. Fue tu mejor decisión, hermano, y estoy inmensamente feliz por ustedes.

El ambiente pasó de la emoción profunda a una complicidad vibrante cuando William, con una chispa de picardía en los ojos, tomó el micrófono. Se acercó a Valentina, le tomó la mano y miró a los invitados, soltando una carcajada antes de empezar.

—Antes de brindar, tengo que confesarles algo que muy pocos saben. Nosotros nos conocimos en la universidad, cuando apenas teníamos 18 y 19 años. En aquel entonces, Valentina decidió terminar conmigo porque decía que yo "no era un hombre serio".

Las risas estallaron en el salón mientras Valentina se cubría el rostro con una mano, riendo también por el recuerdo.

—Pero no era que yo no fuera serio —continuó William, mirándola fijamente—. Lo que pasó fue que un día le dije, muy convencido, que yo me veía casándome exactamente a los veinticinco años. Ella pensó que yo estaba bromeando o que era demasiado tiempo… ¡y por eso me terminó! Pero miren dónde estamos hoy: celebrando nuestra boda, y efectivamente tengo veinticinco años. Cumplí mi palabra.

Los aplausos llenaron el salón. Valentina sintió un pinchazo en el corazón. Mientras los invitados reían por la increíble coincidencia del destino, ella hizo un recorrido veloz por el tiempo. Recordó a aquellos jóvenes universitarios, las discusiones de pasillo y la madurez que ambos habían tenido que adquirir por separado. Entendió que William siempre fue su destino, pero que el universo había sido sabio.

Aquel momento no era su tiempo; ambos necesitaban crecer para reencontrarse en el instante exacto en que sus almas estuvieran listas para el "siempre".

Con elegancia, levantó su copa de champán. Sus ojos se encontraron con los de William y, sin necesidad de micrófono, moviendo apenas los labios, le dijo:

—Te amo.

Le guiñó el ojo con esa complicidad que nació años atrás en un pasillo universitario y que ahora se había consagrado en el altar. El brindis fue estruendoso, las copas chocaron y la fiesta cobró una energía nueva, celebrando no solo un matrimonio, sino la precisión perfecta del destino. Al terminar la boda, llegaron al apartamento, su nuevo hogar, aún envueltos en la magia de la celebración. William la alzó en sus brazos como en las películas, y entre risas suaves y miradas cómplices, entraron a esa nueva vida que comenzaban juntos. Esa noche, en la quietud del instante, se encontraron el uno en el otro con una conexión profunda, como si dos almas que siempre se buscaron finalmente se reconocieran y se hicieran una sola. El amanecer del 3 de enero llegó con una paz que ninguno de los dos había experimentado antes. No había el ruido de un aeropuerto, ni la prisa de una maleta que cerrar, ni la ansiedad de una despedida. La luz suave del invierno se filtraba por las cortinas de su habitación, iluminando los muebles que con tanto esmero habían elegido juntos. Valentina fue la primera en abrir los ojos. Permaneció en silencio, disfrutando del calor de las sábanas y del peso reconfortante del brazo de William sobre su cintura. En la mesa de noche, las dos alianzas de oro descansaban juntas, brillando tenuemente bajo el sol matutino. Ya no eran promesas guardadas en una caja de terciopelo; eran la realidad de su nueva vida. William despertó poco después y, al verla observándolo, le dedicó esa sonrisa que ella tanto amaba.

—Buenos días, señora Villatoro —dijo él, con voz profunda y serena.

—Buenos días, esposo mío —respondió ella, acomodándose en su pecho.

Se quedaron así un largo rato, sin prisas. Eventualmente se levantaron para preparar su primer desayuno como esposos. Esta vez no hubo cajas de cartón; se sentaron a su mesa de comedor, rodeados de la decoración que ya reflejaba la esencia de ambos. Valentina preparó el café mientras William organizaba la cocina, moviéndose con una sincronía natural. Mientras desayunaban, miraron por la ventana hacia la ciudad que ahora les pertenecía a los dos.

—Tuvimos que perdernos para encontrarnos de verdad, ¿no crees? —dijo Valentina, tomando su mano.

—Tuvimos que crecer para saber qué era lo que realmente queríamos proteger —respondió él—. Y lo que quiero proteger es esto, todos los días de mi vida.

Ese 3 de enero marcó el cierre del prólogo de su historia y el inicio de un nuevo capítulo. Ya no había kilómetros que contar, solo años por vivir. El destino había jugado sus cartas con precisión quirúrgica, demostrando que cuando dos almas están destinadas a estar juntas, ni el tiempo, ni la distancia, ni la lógica pueden detener el plan perfecto de Dios.

Capítulo 20:

La cosecha da fruto

Los primeros diez meses de casados fueron un testimonio de lo que dos personas pueden lograr cuando reman en la misma dirección. No hubo una "luna de miel" eterna en el sentido del descanso; su celebración fue el trabajo duro. William consolidó su empresa de servicios técnicos, convirtiéndose en el nombre más confiado de la ciudad, mientras Valentina expandió su cafetería, convirtiéndola en un referente local. Trabajaban de sol a sol, pero al final del día, el cansancio se disolvía al cruzar la puerta de su hogar y encontrarse el uno al otro. Eran un equipo imparable, un engranaje perfecto donde el éxito de uno era el orgullo del otro. Una mañana de ese primer año, el aire en la habitación se sintió diferente. Valentina despertó con una sensación extraña, un presentimiento que no nacía de la mente, sino de lo más profundo de su ser. Había tenido un sueño revelador, uno de esos que te dejan el corazón latiendo a un ritmo distinto. Sin decir nada, mientras William ya estaba en la habitación contigua sumergido entre facturas y ordenes de partes en su escritorio, ella se dirigió al baño. Con manos temblorosas, realizó una prueba de embarazo. El silencio del baño era absoluto, roto solo por el sonido de su propia respiración. Y entonces, ocurrió. Dos rayitas aparecieron con una claridad asombrosa. Valentina se quedó petrificada frente al espejo. Sus manos volaron instintivamente a su vientre, aún plano, mientras sus ojos se inundaban de lágrimas. Se miraba a sí misma y no podía creer que la vida estuviera floreciendo allí mismo, fruto del amor de su vida. La ilusión la desbordó y, sin poder esperar ni un segundo más, llamó a William desde la habitación.

—"¡William! ¡Ven un momento, por favor!" —gritó con la voz quebrada por el llanto.

William, al escuchar el tono de la voz de su esposa, dejó la pluma sobre el escritorio y se levantó de inmediato. Entró al cuarto con curiosidad y una pizca de preocupación, encontrando a Valentina sentada en el borde de la cama, con el rostro bañado en lágrimas, pero con una luz en los ojos que él nunca había visto.

—"Ven, siéntate aquí conmigo" —le pidió ella, palmeando el colchón a su lado.

William se sentó, tomándole la mano. Valentina lo miró con una ternura infinita y, con el corazón en la mano, comenzó a hablar:

—"Tú eres el hombre que siempre pedí, el que siempre soñé. Te amo como nunca pensé que se podía amar... y hoy, ese amor ha dado su fruto. Sé que serás un excelente papá".

En ese momento, ella extendió su otra mano y le mostró la prueba de confirmación. William se quedó sin palabras. Sus ojos, siempre analíticos y enfocados, se pusieron de cristal al instante. Las lágrimas rodaron por sus mejillas mientras la magnitud de la noticia lo golpeaba: iba a ser padre. William envolvió a Valentina en un abrazo protector, hundiendo el rostro en su cuello mientras ambos sollozaban de pura dicha. Luego, se separó apenas para verla a los ojos y la besó con una ternura tan profunda que parecía un susurro del alma.

—"Tú me aceptaste en tu vida cuando lo único que yo tenía para ofrecerte era mi amor y mi esfuerzo por salir adelante" —dijo William con la voz entrecortada, sosteniendo el rostro de Valentina entre sus manos—. "Hoy te prometo que lucharé todos los días para que nunca les falte nada. Todo lo que yo haga, cada gota de sudor y cada paso que dé será para ustedes".

Valentina lo miró con un orgullo que le ensanchaba el pecho. Le apretó la mano con fuerza, sintiendo que aquel reencuentro no solo había salvado su amor, sino que había dado origen a una nueva vida. Ya no eran solo dos personas en un apartamento; ahora eran una familia en crecimiento, y el futuro, que antes era una incertidumbre, ahora brillaba más que cualquier diamante.

Capítulo 21:

Legado de amor y prosperidad

Nueve años habían pasado desde aquel invierno del 2 de enero en que se juraron amor eterno. El tiempo, lejos de desgastar su vínculo, lo había fortalecido hasta volverlo indestructible. Su hogar ya no era aquel apartamento de recién casados; habían comprado una casa donde ahora vivían en una residencia amplia y luminosa, llena de risas y juguetes, donde Victoria y Valeria, sus dos hijas, corrían por los pasillos, personificando el sueño que un día nació de una "solicitud de amistad". Valentina, con la paz de quien ha conquistado sus metas, había vendido su cafetería. Ahora dedicaba su tiempo a lo que más amaba: la crianza de sus pequeñas, disfrutando de una libertad económica que solo el éxito arrollador de William podía brindar. Su empresa no solo había crecido; se había convertido en un imperio. Aquel técnico que empezó con una caja de herramientas era ahora el director ejecutivo de la compañía de servicios más profesional de todo Estados Unidos. Había superado a más de 200 competidores a nivel nacional y había sido galardonado con un prestigioso premio. Pero el mayor triunfo no fue el dinero, sino la unión. Gracias a la solidez de su empresa, habían logrado lo que antes parecía imposible: traer a los padres y hermanos de Valentina. Ahora, toda la familia residía en la misma ciudad, compartiendo domingos de asados y cumpleaños, cumpliendo la promesa de que nadie volvería a estar lejos. Ese año, el 14 de febrero, bajo un cielo estrellado y un ambiente cargado de romance, William y Valentina se sentaron a cenar en un restaurante exclusivo para celebrar su noveno aniversario. El lugar estaba decorado con rosas rojas profundas, velas blancas que emitían una luz suave y el eco lejano de un violín. Chocaron sus copas de un vino exquisito, y el sonido del cristal fue el eco de mil batallas ganadas.

—A veces miro hacia atrás y no puedo creer que todo esto nació de aquellos jovencitos en la universidad —dijo Valentina, acariciando la mano de su esposo.

William sonrió con una nostalgia dulce en la mirada.

—Nació de dos jóvenes que no estaban listos, pero que siempre estuvieron destinados —respondió él—. Y lo que viene es aún mejor.

Hizo una pausa antes de añadir, con esa seguridad que siempre la enamoraba:

—Pronto pondremos la primera piedra en el terreno nuevo que acabamos de adquirir. Nuestra casa soñada, con el jardín que querías para las niñas… un castillo para mi reina.

Conversaron por horas sobre los sueños que aún les quedaban por cumplir, sobre los viajes pendientes y sobre la felicidad de ver a sus padres envejecer cerca de ellos. Eran, en toda la extensión de la palabra, un equipo invencible. Al terminar la cena, William, movido por un recuerdo cargado de significado, le pidió que caminaran hacia su lugar favorito: las cataratas donde diez años atrás él se arrodilló por primera vez. El sonido del agua cayendo seguía siendo el mismo, pero ellos eran personas nuevas, más fuertes y sabias. Justo frente al rugido del agua, la escena se repitió como un regalo de la vida. William se detuvo y, con una emoción que los años no habían podido apagar, se arrodilló. De su bolsillo extrajo una pequeña cajita color turquesa. Al abrirla, un anillo deslumbrante capturó cada destello de luz: un diamante central tres veces más grande que el primero, rodeado de una elegancia absoluta. Era William cumpliendo su palabra de prosperidad; era el hombre que ahora, con más madurez, le entregaba a su mujer lo que siempre supo que merecía.

—"Valentina" —dijo él con la voz vibrante—, "hace años te prometí que lucharía por ustedes. Hoy, con nuestra familia completa y nuestros sueños realizados, quiero preguntarte: ¿Te quieres volver a casar conmigo y renovar nuestros votos en nuestro próximo aniversario?"

Valentina, con la piel erizada y los ojos empañados por lágrimas de gratitud absoluta, se abalanzó hacia él. Lo abrazó con la misma fuerza que aquel día de hace tantos años, sintiendo que el tiempo era solo un testigo de su victoria.

—"¡Sí! Te elijo a ti todos y cada uno de mis días, una y otra vez, por el resto de mi vida" —exclamó ella.

Bajo la luna de febrero, mientras el agua de las cataratas seguía su curso eterno, William y Valentina sellaron su pacto una vez más. Ya no eran dos jóvenes buscando un camino; eran dos pilares que habían construido un imperio sobre la roca más sólida que existe: el amor incondicional. El gran día de la renovación llegó con la misma magia que aquel primer 2 de enero, pero esta vez con una luz más madura y profunda. La iglesia estaba nuevamente decorada con flores blancas, pero ahora el pasillo no solo lo recorría Valentina; a sus costados, sujetando con fuerza sus manos, caminaban Victoria y Valeria. Las niñas, vestidas como pequeñas versiones de su madre, avanzaban con pasos ilusionados, convirtiéndose en el testimonio vivo de que el amor de sus padres había dado los frutos más hermosos. William las esperaba en el frente, y al ver aparecer a las tres mujeres de su vida, su corazón se ensanchó de una manera que no creía posible. Ya no era el joven que luchaba por estabilidad; era el hombre que lo había logrado todo. Cuando estuvieron frente a frente, se tomaron de las manos. Valentina miró a William a los ojos y, con la voz firme y cargada de una gratitud que le desbordaba el alma, pronunció sus votos:

—William, amor de mi vida, hoy, después de estos diez años de matrimonio, miro a nuestras hijas y al hogar que hemos construido, y solo puedo decirte una cosa: si tuviera que repetir cada lágrima, cada duda y cada sacrificio con tal de llegar de nuevo a ti y tener a Victoria y a Valeria a nuestro lado, no cambiaría ni una sola de mis decisiones. Todo lo que viví valió la pena, porque me trajo a tus brazos.

William la miró con una adoración infinita y tomó sus manos con firmeza.

—Valentina, hace diez años prometí amarte cuando apenas sabíamos lo que era la vida. Hoy te prometo algo más grande: ser el hombre que sostenga este hogar con honor, proteger a nuestras hijas con mi vida y recordarte, incluso en los días difíciles, que volvería a elegirte una y mil veces. No solo te amo por lo que hemos construido, sino por la mujer que eres cuando nadie está mirando. Y mientras respire, este será mi lugar: a tu lado.

El sacerdote, con una sonrisa, los invitó a sellar su promesa.

—"Sí, acepto hoy, mañana y siempre" —dijeron al unísono.

Se fundieron en un beso profundo y eterno bajo la cúpula de la iglesia, mientras sus hijas se abrazaban a sus piernas, sellando así un pacto que ya no solo era de dos, sino de una familia entera unida por un hilo invisible de amor.

Esa noche, cuando la fiesta terminó y el silencio volvió a reinar en su hermosa casa, Valentina se quedó sola en la penumbra de su habitación. Se sentó en la orilla de su cama, sintiendo la suavidad de las sábanas y la paz de su hogar. En sus manos sostenía una retratera de plata que pesaba con la gravedad de los tesoros verdaderos. Había impreso una de las fotos de la renovación de votos para guardarla allí, tangible y eterna. En ella, la imagen brillaba bajo la luz tenue de la lámpara. Sus dedos recorrieron el cristal, deteniéndose en los rostros de sus dos hijas —su mayor legado— y luego en la mirada de William, que la observaba en la foto con la misma intensidad azul con la que la miró a la salida del laboratorio de cómputo hace más de quince años, pero ahora con la profundidad de un amor que había resistido el tiempo. Con un suspiro cargado de gratitud, colocó la retratera en su mesa de noche, en el lugar de honor, sellando su presente.

En ese momento, Valentina se quedó perdida en sus pensamientos, mientras su mente se transformaba en un proyector de sombras y luces. De repente, ya no estaba en su hermosa casa de Estados Unidos: se vio a sí misma como aquella joven llena de dudas en su país natal, con el corazón encogido por la incertidumbre. Se dio cuenta de que conocer a William en la universidad había sido una preparación para su futuro juntos. Que, aunque en aquel entonces no lo sabía —y ese aún no era su tiempo—, su momento llegaría una vez ambos estuvieran preparados el uno para el otro. Recordó a Federico y, esta vez, el recuerdo no trajo miedo, sino una punzada de alivio clarificador. Entendió que aquel camino oscuro, aquella arma de metal frente a su rostro y la manipulación constante habían sido la oscuridad necesaria para que aprendiera a reconocer la luz. Sin la necesidad de protegerse, nunca habría diseñado aquel plan de negocios que fue su boleto de salida; sin el terror que la obligó a huir, nunca habría tenido el coraje de cruzar el océano para emprender su propio negocio y jamás se habría reencontrado con el amor de su vida. Rememoró el shock de la mudanza, el frío cortante de los primeros inviernos que le calaba los huesos y el cansancio de las jornadas de sol a sol en un país ajeno que, contra todo pronóstico, se había convertido en su hogar definitivo. Se dio cuenta de que su vida no había sido una serie de coincidencias, sino una guerra ganada por la valentía de no rendirse, batalla por batalla. Cada error, cada lágrima derramada y cada desafío que tuvo que enfrentar habían sido piezas de un rompecabezas perfecto. Comprendió que vender su cafetería no fue un final, sino la semilla. Esa primera empresa fue el puente que trajo a sus hermanos y a sus padres, dándoles un nuevo horizonte. Aunque aquel primer negocio ya no le pertenecía, su apertura fue la llave que liberó el futuro de toda su familia. Todo lo que vivió —absolutamente todo— la había llevado hacia William, hacia el hogar que él fundó y hacia la mujer inquebrantable que era ahora.

En ese momento todo cobró sentido.

«Mi historia merece ser contada», se dijo a sí misma en un susurro que sonó como un decreto absoluto. «

Impulsada por una fuerza interna que reclamaba ser escuchada, Valentina se levantó. Caminó hacia su escritorio y abrió su computadora. El brillo azulado del monitor iluminó su rostro decidido, revelando la certeza que la habitaba.

Sus dedos se posicionaron sobre el teclado con una seguridad absoluta. Valentina comenzó a teclear, convencida de que su historia pertenecía a todo aquel que decide enfrentar sus miedos para salir adelante; demostrando que, aunque el camino sea difícil, la determinación es la herramienta que permite transformar la adversidad en valentía para alzar el vuelo, cruzar fronteras y alcanzar, finalmente, el sueño que uno desea construir.

Con una sonrisa de quien finalmente ha hecho las paces con su historia y encontró su propósito, comenzó a escribir. En la parte superior de la página, con letras negritas y firmes, tituló su verdad:

"Valentina: Un sueño sin fronteras"

ACERCA DEL AUTOR

Soy de origen árabe, nacida y criada en Honduras, y actualmente radico en los Estados Unidos. Soy diseñadora gráfica, empresaria, esposa y madre, pero más allá de los títulos, soy una mujer que encontró en el arte su forma de entender y reconstruir el mundo.

Desde mi infancia, la creatividad ha sido mi lenguaje y mi refugio: desde la danza y el canto hasta la literatura, cada forma de expresión me permitió darle sentido a mis emociones y a mi historia.

Mi vida dio un giro determinante cuando enfrenté una crisis personal en mi país natal que puso en riesgo mi seguridad. En medio de ese momento de vulnerabilidad, tomé la decisión de emprender el vuelo: transformar el miedo en disciplina, dejarlo todo atrás y comenzar de cero en una cultura distinta.

Con la visión estratégica de mi formación en diseño, la pasión por el arte culinario, y la determinación que forma parte de mi esencia, fundé y consolidé mi propia empresa: una cafetería artesanal que se convirtió en símbolo de resiliencia y en el pilar que me permitió reunir nuevamente a mi familia.

Con mi primera obra literaria, *Valentina: Un sueño sin fronteras*, busco unir mi sensibilidad artística con mi experiencia de vida para ofrecer un mensaje de esperanza y empoderamiento.

Mi propósito es demostrar que, sin importar cuán oscuro sea el pasado o cuán altas parezcan las fronteras, siempre existe dentro de nosotros la capacidad de reinventarnos y rediseñar nuestro propio destino.

www.ingramcontent.com/pod-product-compliance
Lightning Source LLC
Chambersburg PA
CBHW051825150726
47998CB00001B/295